Feminist Reflections

on Childhood

Feminist Reflections on Childhood

A History and Call to Action

PENNY A. WEISS

TEMPLE UNIVERSITY PRESS
Philadelphia • *Rome* • *Tokyo*

TEMPLE UNIVERSITY PRESS
Philadelphia, Pennsylvania 19122
tupress.temple.edu

Library of Congress Cataloging-in-Publication Data

Names: Weiss, Penny A. author.
Title: Feminist reflections on childhood : a history and call to action / Penny A. Weiss.
Description: Philadelphia : Temple University Press, 2021. | Includes bibliographical
  references and index. | Summary: "This book recovers a history of feminist thought
  and activism that demands greater voice and respect for young people, and urges
  contemporary social theorists, too, to do greater justice to children"—Provided by
  publisher.
Identifiers: LCCN 2020038642 (print) | LCCN 2020038643 (ebook) |
  ISBN 9781439918685 (cloth) | ISBN 9781439918692 (paperback) |
  ISBN 9781439918708 (pdf)
Subjects: LCSH: Children—History. | Children—Social conditions. | Children's
  rights—History. | Feminist theory—History.
Classification: LCC HQ767.87 .W34 2021 (print) | LCC HQ767.87 (ebook) |
  DDC 305.2309—dc23
LC record available at https://lccn.loc.gov/2020038642
LC ebook record available at https://lccn.loc.gov/2020038643

9 8 7 6 5 4 3 2 1

In beloved memory of

Isaiah Matthew Mejia

2000–2018

The aim of each thing which we do is to make our lives and the lives of our children richer and more possible.

—**AUDRE LORDE**, "Uses of the Erotic: The Erotic as Power"

Women's past is at least as rich as men's; that we do not know about it, that we encounter only interruptions and silence when we seek it, is part of our oppression. Unless and until we can reconstruct our past, draw on it, and transmit it to the next generation, our oppression persists.

—**DALE SPENDER**, *Women of Ideas*

Equating a fetus with a child . . . reduces a child to a biological abstraction, ignoring the child's own subjectivity, personal history, and embeddedness in a concrete community.

—**JOEY SPRAGUE AND MARGARET GREER**,
"Standpoints and the Discourse on Abortion"

That is what our children can offer us, and what we can offer them: a chance to learn from them, even as we try to teach them.

—**ROBERT COLES**, *The Moral Intelligence of Children*

A child is a child of everyone.

—**SUDANESE PROVERB**

Contents

PART IV: CONTEMPORARY THREADS

Preface

The ideas in this book come from a lifetime of interacting with and thinking about children. These experiences inform and inspire me as I think about how we can better conceive of children as fully human and as abundantly deserving of voice and respect.

My adult life centered on children as much as anything else. As a young adult, I found myself the de facto "child person" at a shelter for battered women. I grew up the youngest child—the "baby"—in an apolitical, divided, and isolated family. Before the shelter, I didn't know much about the variety of adult-child relations within families, between families, and with "outsiders" to families. Then I discovered I was good with those younger than me and comfortable and comfortably curious about relating with them. The young people at the shelter taught me about damage to and resilience of the soul and the myriad consequences of domestic violence and love. My commitment to young people was born at that shelter in South Bend, Indiana.

Still in my twenties, I worked next at an infant care center (ages six weeks to two years old) that catered to indigent and professional families. I got an education there not only about what the very youngest among us are capable of but also about children and class, mostly through various adults' responses to the diversity of children and families. I became especially interested in and drawn to the "difficult" kids there, determined to understand why they were considered so troublesome and what was needed (especially) for adults to see and treat them with more respect and tolerance. I continued to observe diverse relationships between children and adults and to find my own ways of being an "adult" with different young people.

In the shelter and the daycare center, I felt more outrage over than admiration for the ways young people were talked with, to, and about and for how they were treated and mistreated, rewarded and punished, neglected and "managed." The injustices I witnessed never ceased to rankle. Since I also saw how much work and care parents and teachers put into their relationships with children, I became convinced that the problems had their roots beyond the individual—social, ideological, and political aspects of adult-child relations were compromising and even poisoning the relationships. I have wanted to explore those aspects since my days working in childcare.

And then, in my thirties, I had three children of my own—three differently amazing and deeply loved children from whom I have learned the most important of life's lessons and whose perspectives I continue to draw from and cherish. Trying to develop and apply feminist models and practices of childrearing has been the most challenging and rewarding of my feminist (and life) experiences. It has been a long and ongoing experiment, as perhaps all childrearing is, in which my children became increasingly active participants as they grew, and in which my partner became more and more invested as well. I am so indebted to them for conversations over the years, first in the sandbox and now on Facetime; for the privilege of getting to watch these three babies come into their own as young adults (and for getting to *kvell* a little); and for the immeasurable love between us that has, truly, meant everything to me and has kept me as firmly grounded as I can be in this world.

These formative experiences—combined with my already somewhat-anarchist feminist soul—led me to help found an alternative preschool and elementary school that my kids (and, later, three of my foster children) attended. I taught there for two years and then participated in many other ways during the long years I had a child there, including cleaning (since all families rotated in on this chore) and teaching special classes on carpentry (about which I knew next to nothing beforehand) and on social justice (about which I initially thought I knew a good deal but learned more by talking with the kids about it). Because of the nature of the school and the closeness of those families who were part of it, I had substantial, long-term relationships with a good number of children there; in fact, many of them are my Facebook friends today, some twenty years later (and I recently met up with several of them, most joyfully). Families who joined the school participated for a range of pedagogical and political reasons and were both professional and working class. The New Community School in Lafayette, Indiana, is where I learned the most about educational theories and practices.[1]

In my forties, I was also privileged to work with, love, and be challenged by eight foster children of various races and ethnicities, ages six months to ten years, who lived with us for as few as three months and as long as a year. From them, I learned more about the range of childhood experiences, the resources of the young, and the challenges of developing a voice in sometimes heart-wrenching, always trying, circumstances. I remain grateful for their willingness to take the risk of engaging in relationships with me after all that they had already been through. Most of their parents were also willing to work with me, which is not at all what I was led to expect by child protection workers. During this period, I learned too much about the costs of social policies that punished their families more than they supported them and about the inanities of child "welfare" systems. I also learned a great deal about how to love a variety of children, especially children who have experienced trauma.

I coached coed and then girls' soccer for about ten years during much of this time and learned more there about the relationships among young people from ages six to sixteen: about how they do and do not learn and how they can be heartened or discouraged, included or made an outsider. Watching them explore their physical strengths and what it means to work together was a new and special treat.

These experiences—these children—are what ground me in this book, and some reappear in the stories that introduce certain sections. There is no question in my mind that it is these young people to whom I am accountable. Because of them, I feel a delicate and layered responsibility to make the world a safer, better, more nurturing, more inspiring place for children. This book is but one means toward such ends. I have tried to represent well the strengths and abilities that children possess as well as the injustices that they endure and the hurdles that they face. Even when the contents of this book seem removed from these kids, they are present to me, checking and inspiring me.

NOTE

1. Several of us wrote an article on the founding of the school. It is called "Building (the) New Community (School)." Published in *Educational Forum*, you can read it on my website: https://pennyweiss.files.wordpress.com/2017/08/weiss_building-the-new-community-school.pdf.

Acknowledgments

In coming to the ideas in this book, I owe the most to my children, not only their past childhoods, on which I draw, but also their present young adult lives. Linden commented on one chapter and talks with me regularly about parenting as he and Hannah begin their own exciting adventures with Zev and Alma. Their thoughtfulness about and enjoyment of children are contagious. Avian, who works with children every day as a clinical social worker, read even more parts of an early draft. She inspired me to organize it differently and helped give the book its current shape. As someone who encourages her clients to speak and listen, she especially encouraged me to make my own voice more prominent. Brennin, in her distinctive, writerly way, edited many chapters, improving their flow and clarity. Her talent with the written word humbles me, and I cherish the conversations we had over the book. Thank you, thank you, to each of you. I love you all so.

Finally, Robert, with whom I shared many of my adventures with children—raising our own, building the New Community School, and fostering—also commented on a draft version of the book. His gentle and philosophical spirit came through in his remarks on the text, as they did in our co-parenting. I am, indeed, indebted.

I dedicate this book to Isaiah, once my foster child, who only made it to age seventeen. I deeply mourn his loss. Some of his stories are in this book. I thank his mom, Becky, for having such a generous heart that she was able to appreciate the time Isaiah spent with my family and to allow our families to become intertwined. We all loved him.

Earlier drafts of two chapters were previously published. Chapter 3 was previously published as "The Everyday Silencing of Children" in *Learning for Democracy: An International Journal of Thought and Practice* 6, no. 2 (2016): 23–38, and Chapter 4 was previously published as "Reflections on Childhood in the History of Feminist Thought" in *Signs: Journal of Women in Culture and Society* 43, no. 4 (2018): 979–1004, © 2018 by Penny A. Weiss.

I am grateful to Temple University Press and especially appreciative of the expert copy editing done by Heather Wilcox.

Feminist Reflections

on Childhood

I

Introducing the Child and Feminist Perspectives

1

Who/What Is a Child?

Children are in the news every day. They are buried deep in complex statistics and highlighted as the main subjects of legislation. They come into view as victims and as perpetrators. They emerge as influencers and among the too-easily influenced. They show up as refugees, as users of technology, as consumers, as prisoners, and as students. Occasionally, they emerge as people with opinions. The understanding of childhood that frames all these stories is fuzzy at best and inconsistent at worst. Many assumptions about childhood go unspoken, and many myths about our care for the young go unchallenged. We're even unclear on what defines a child—is it a developmental stage? A legal category? Is there something universal called "childhood," or does it vary by place and circumstance? As we report on their lives, we portray them in vastly contradictory ways, often incompletely, and sometimes with surprise about what they know or what they can do. All of this confusion has consequences.

From Children in the News to Ideologies About the Child

In March 2018, thousands of students across the United States walked out of schools to protest gun violence and the policies that contribute to the stunning proliferation of school shootings.[1] These protests were student-led, and even elementary-age youth participated, with or without the approval of school authorities. "The emergence of people not even old enough to drive as a political force has been particularly arresting, unsettling a gun control debate that had seemed impervious to other factors," reporters noted.[2] Some youngsters saw important, exciting "parallels in a video they watched about youth marches for civil rights in 1963."[3] Hundreds of thousands turned out for the March For Our Lives, "in the most ambitious show of force yet from a student-driven movement."[4]

In May 2019, more than a million students around the world walked out of school to demand that their governments do more to combat climate change; they had done this one Friday each month since February, initially moved by the posts of Swedish teenager Greta Thunberg (later recognized as *TIME* magazine's 2019 "Person of the Year"). In this case, too, most of those on the streets were nonvoters, but they still felt called to urge their governments to act, and they demanded a response. Young people were experiencing themselves as meaningful political actors.

Children are in the news in less promising ways too. At the U.S.-Mexico border, reports are not of children calling for governments to be more responsible but of young people being without the protection of any government. In unprecedented numbers, alone and with families, youth come "looking to escape dead-end poverty, violence and a lack of opportunities to study or work," and along the way they "face a staggering array of threats, from thieves and rapists to hunger, loneliness and death."[5] At least six children have died in U.S. custody.[6] It is not even known how many children have been separated from their parents at the border or how many are in custody. Even after "the [Donald] Trump administration announced it would end its practice of separating undocumented families," the practice appeared to persist.[7] Save the Children expressed "grave[] concern about the treatment and well-being of children from Latin American nations who are in the custody of the United States government after crossing the U.S.-Mexico border," emphasizing the due-process rights that children possess and the trauma of separation for the children and their subsequent vulnerability to abuse.[8] They urged focus on the best interests of the children and worried about "the loss of childhood" entailed in family separation and family detention.

In January 2019, a law was proposed in the Philippine Congress that would make people as young as nine criminally responsible, a change from the age of fifteen. As part of "President Rodrigo Duterte's deadly antidrug campaign," he wanted to go after "underage offenders working for drug gangs."[9] Even acknowledging gangs' strategic use of children, child advocates contested how widespread such practice is (perhaps two percent of crimes, they claim, are committed by children) and pointed to the dire economic conditions of these children's lives that make such work attractive.

They expressed concern about everything from the dangers to youth of being detained in crowded adult detention centers to the trauma that such youngsters would endure in facing criminal trials.

How are we to think about these diverse stories? Our images of childhood do not easily accommodate the idea of young people as political actors. We think that they are too young to understand the complexities of politics, too inarticulate and inexperienced to be leaders in a movement, too immature to follow through on difficult, demanding tasks. And yet it may be adults' perceptions of childhood that are the stumbling block rather than childhood itself, for those views flatten, exclude, distort, and constrain at least as much as they capture and celebrate.

We wrestle uncomfortably with how responsible youth of various ages are, especially (but not only) legally. At the border and in prisons, we are often "placing the burden on a child for failures of institutions meant to protect them."[10] When they engage in illegal acts, from "consensual" sex to prostitution to drug running to soldiering in rebel armies, we are unsure whether to treat them as criminals or victims. We seem to know that the circumstances of their young lives need to be understood, but we often want there to be limits to "extenuating circumstances," such as extreme poverty and a history of abuse. Are children in need of protection, or are they (also) dangerous? Such issues reappear in the news regularly around the world.

In all these cases in the news, our treatment of children interacts with ideologies about them, reflecting and perpetuating inconsistent and often harmful views and allowing myths to persist—mollifying myths that resist needed change. Without question,

> the predominant image we hold of the young child is one of innocence and weakness, needing protection, although this has not always been the case and is not a universal image. As children enter adolescence in our culture, their image often shifts to one of "barely rational, unsocialized, and unlawful" . . . needing to be controlled and punished. (Callaghan, Long-Wincza, and Velenosi 2017, 18)

There are multiple images of youth to appeal to, from innocent to dangerous, and adults can choose from among them in their treatment of children, sometimes inconsistently, and sometimes for their own ends. Importantly, these images, even in their variety, are too often used to justify the silencing and the subordination of young people, which is not in their interest or the interest of the communities of which they are a part.

The characterization of children as innocent, and of childrearing as rightly geared toward protecting that innocence, has always proved problematic. These ideals have never been universally applied. Children from lower classes have been put to work, for example, and those from racial minorities have not escaped the demonizing characterizations commonly applied to their adult social groups. Further, such glib depiction of youth as untouched and unknowing fails to reckon with the complexities of young peoples' lives, including the various traumas, challenges, and thrills they experience or the complicated sexual, intellectual, social, and political lives they lead. The association of youth with innocence persists, nonetheless, and it not only blinds us to important aspects of children's lives but legitimizes our ignorance of their very real needs, desires, and contributions.

Too, the idea that we "protect" children is a myth that flies in the face of all kinds of statistics. According to Children International, one child in every seven will be born into poverty in the United States. Globally, more than three million children each year die from malnutrition.[11] The United Nations Children's Fund (UNICEF) estimates that 150 million children worldwide are engaged as child laborers, meaning that "they are either too young to work or are involved in hazardous activities that may compromise their physical, mental, social or educational development." It adds, "In the least developed countries, nearly one in four children (ages five to fourteen) are engaged in labour that is considered detrimental to their health and development."[12] The International Labour Organization estimates that a million children "are in a forced labour situation as a result of trafficking."[13] The National Children's Alliance reports that "nearly 700,000 children are abused in the U.S. annually," primarily suffering from neglect, with the youngest being the most vulnerable.[14] Armed conflicts around the globe bring special harms to millions of children and young people, many of which have lasting, even lifetime effects. They may witness the deaths of loved ones or be forced to bear arms themselves; some are raped, and others are forced into prostitution for subsistence; their educational opportunities are deeply compromised; and their very moral foundations may be shaken. "In the past ten years, as a result of armed conflict, over 2 million children have been killed, 6 million have been disabled, 20 million are homeless, and more than 1 million have become separated from their caregivers."[15]

Girls face additional gender-specific traumas and challenges. According to the United Nations Educational, Scientific and Cultural Organization (UNESCO), "Traditionally, all societies have given preference to males over females when it comes to educational opportunity," and still today, "virtually all countries face gender disparities of some sort."[16] Early marriage to older men is another problem, one that ends girls' educations and increases their chances of at-risk pregnancies, domestic violence, social isolation, and economic dependence. While around one in twenty-five boys will be sexually abused before the age of eighteen in the United States, perhaps one in seven girls will be victimized, 20 percent before the age of eight. Globally, around 7.4 million children ages five to eleven are domestic workers, as are 3.8 million ages twelve to fourteen. Among the dangers these child domestic workers face—and some two-thirds of them are girls—are physical and sexual violence.

Minority children in most cultures also face specific challenges based on their identities. In the United States, for example, Black children are hyperdisciplined, suspended, and expelled from school at higher rates than White children; are already targeted by law enforcement;[17] are more likely to be removed from their homes by the child welfare system; and often live in "fragile urban neighborhoods" made more vulnerable by cuts to safety-net programs.[18] Similarly, across Europe, Roma children are segregated in educational settings, often in decrepit buildings; are "as much as 27 times more likely to be diagnosed with mental disability than their non-Roma peers;"[19] and "face bullying and harassment" in school and marginalization everywhere else.[20]

Other kinds of wrongs against the young are less easily quantifiable. Citizenship is generally an all-or-nothing proposition, with little effort made to give the young as much voice in as many contexts as possible. Most educational environments are teacher-centered rather than student-centered, usually meaning that passivity and obedience are required of students and that "force-feeding" of material is the norm. In everyday conversations, children are interrupted and discounted at rates that surpass those of many other marginalized groups.

Simple slogans about how "children are our future" wrongly imply that we normally make their welfare and their voices our personal and social priorities. We do not. We seem more often to begrudge them the resources they need to be healthy, safe, and well educated. We do not build communities that value them and provide them with opportunities to develop their potential and to give back. Child-friendly societies are by far the minority. And our fuzziness about childhood, the inconsistencies we tolerate, only grows.

The issues shaping the lives of children testify to the vulnerability and exploitation of a group of people—diverse themselves by age as well as by sex, race, class, ability, ethnicity, nationality, and religion—that every emancipatory movement should recognize and address as systemic violations of fundamental rights. We don't often think of children as a political group that needs better treatment, and yet by the usual criteria, they do constitute such a group. We legislate differently for them as a class. Formally and informally, we regulate them in ways that we would never find acceptable for adults. We believe that adults and the state have responsibilities toward them, but we waver about how much we will really hold those actors responsible when they fail to fulfill those duties. As political scientist Elizabeth Cohen has so well documented, children's status as citizens is complicated—they "inhabit an uncertain space between alienage and full citizenship" (2005, 221).

Being a young person can be challenging when one wants to make one's voice heard, to be treated decently, to love and to be loved—in other words, to be seen as a fully human being actively engaging with the world. This situation has existed in many eras, even as childhood has meant different things in different time periods:

> It seems to be a particular condition of post-modernity that there are so many concerns around the need to preserve children's innocence and so much legislation to protect children, while at the same time children have never been more exposed to realms that were previously the preserve of adults. It is critical that feminists engage in debate around these issues. (Spongberg 2008, 287)

It is indeed critical that feminists engage in debates about the conditions of children's lives. In fact, one argument of this book is that feminists have long done so and that we need to remember and build on that rich history. Another argument in this book is that feminists are quite well poised to engage further in such work. In the instance just discussed, for example, we can easily see that long-standing feminist critiques of women's supposed innocence, an innocence that was prescribed for and even demanded of them and that then was used to justify their exclusion from various jobs and civic duties, would be quite useful in raising questions about the supposed innocence of children—its truth and limits, its psychology and politics.[21] Feminist analysis is also necessary because "age always intersects with other socially constructed categories such as gender, race, and sexuality" (Field and Syrett 2015, 2), and intersectionality is among feminists' principal methods used for understanding the dynamics of oppression.

Taking children seriously, whether as conversationalists, thinkers, or citizens, does not require that we erase every distinction between those younger and older. It does mean thinking about children as members of various communities, including families, schools, friendship circles, and civic groups. Young people come to understand themselves individually and socially in such contexts, contexts that I, as a feminist political theorist, tend to characterize as political—as involving collective, goal-based associations influenced by various other social formations and ideas, influencing members' senses of self, and requiring and developing resources for joint action.

Children as Social and Political Actors

Feminist analysis, I believe, encourages us to be wary of what Australian women's studies scholar Barbara Baird calls "child fundamentalism"—focus on the "pure and innocent child, conceived outside of history and outside of politics" (2008, 293). Baird writes:

> Child fundamentalism is challenged when we refuse the child as a nostalgic object from a perfect past and as a symbol of a utopian future. Refusing child fundamentalism means allowing all that it disallows: the historical and political contingency of childhood and its variability; its gendered, classed and racialised nature; childhood desires and actions; and childhood excesses. (296)

Children are never really outside politics or beyond discussing in political terms. Nonetheless, one trait minimized in most conceptions of children is their existence as social and political actors, people who are affected by and trying to affect their circumstances for themselves and others, often in resistance to structures and practices that want them or others to be subservient, obedient, or invisible. However, I believe that such a portrayal is (and has been) crucial to feminist understandings of childhood.

Bolivian feminist and labor activist Domitila Barrios de Chungara (1937–2012) writes about how she and her father negotiated for her to be able to take her younger sisters with her to class, since otherwise she would have to have stayed home to care for them (her mother had died). Two years later, the school ended the practice, and Chungara left her siblings alone to go to school, against her father's wishes, and leading to the death of one of them. At one point, having been thrown out of school, she watched the class through a window. Active in trying to obtain her own education, she concludes that there is a role that children do and should play in political action:

> I think it's so important for us revolutionaries to win that first battle in the home. And the first battle to be won is to let the woman, the man, the children participate in the struggle of the working class, so that the home can become a stronghold that the enemy can't overcome.

Because if you have the enemy inside your own house, then it's just one more weapon that our common enemy can use toward a dangerous end. (Chungara 1978, 36)

Egyptian feminist activist and memoirist Huda Shaarawi (1879–1947) also made autonomous decisions in her young life. Raised in the harem of an aristocrat who died when she was young, she formed relationships with older women with broader outlooks than her mother's, including her father's widow. She writes:

I loved *Umm Kabira* [literally Big Mother] immensely, and she returned that love and showed compassion toward me. She, alone, talked frankly with me on a number of matters. . . . She knew how I felt when people favoured my brother over me because he was a boy. . . . I withdrew into myself and resented those around me. I began to spend the afternoons in the garden amid the fruit and flower trees, and the birds, fish, and pet animals. I preferred the companionship of these creatures to the company of humans who injured my self-esteem. (Shaarawi 1986, 34, 37)

She made decisions about with whom to interact about what and got the support she needed.

Finally, Mary Harris Jones—better known as Mother Jones (1837–1930), the famed American labor activist—led children in at least two actions against child labor. "These little children were striking for some of the freedom that childhood ought to have," she writes in her autobiography (1972, 73). Like Chungara and Shaarawi, Mother Jones understood how social institutions and practices can exclude, harm, or marginalize children (due to their gender, race, and class as well as their age) and how children often take self-affirming actions in response, sometimes in alliance with adults.

Other Ways of Characterizing Childhood

An oft-repeated idea is that prior to the Middle Ages, children were thought of and treated as "miniature adults," a view that has to be somewhat overstated, since one cannot easily mistake a crawling, nonverbal, needing-to-be-fed, growing, one-year-old for an adult. Another view, probably sounder, is that they were property, belonging to their parents, whose authority over them was largely unchallenged and unchecked. Wikipedia defines a child as "a human being between the stages of birth and puberty."[22] Teenagers, then, are something other than children. The United Nations (UN) Convention on the Rights of the Child defines a child as "a human being below the age of 18 years unless under the law applicable to the child, majority is attained earlier." The UN thus concedes that the definition is political and acceptably variable.

Childhood has often been divided into developmental stages. According to the Child Development Institute, there are infants/babies (birth to age two years), toddlers/preschoolers (ages two to five years), school-age children (ages six to twelve years), and adolescents/teenagers (ages thirteen to eighteen years),[23] although others break those large chunks into additional categories. Famed Swiss psychologist Jean Piaget (1896–1980) distinguished the phases intellectually: sensorimotor (birth through ages eighteen to twenty-four months), preoperational (toddlerhood through early childhood [ages two to seven years]), concrete operational (ages seven to twelve years), and formal operational (adolescence through adulthood).[24] German developmental psychologist Erik Erikson (1902–94) divided the stages psychosocially, by psychosocial crisis and basic virtue: trust versus mistrust, and hope (infancy to age eighteen months); autonomy versus shame, and will (to age three years); initiative versus guilt, and purpose (ages three to five years); industry versus inferiority, and competency (ages five to twelve years); and ego identity versus role confusion, and fidelity (ages twelve to eighteen years).[25] Thus, biological distinctions exist between adulthood and the stages that precede it, as do political, moral, and cognitive ones.[26] All experts seem to agree that children are, in fact, "humans," although it is not clear that we really treat them fully as such.[27]

The definition of childhood that we choose matters, because on such bases we ascribe rights and responsibilities. Based on their ages, we punish people differently (inside and outside formal criminal justice systems), mandate attendance in schools (or forbid it in the paid workforce), and give people more or less decision-making power over their bodies (to pierce or tattoo or to have sex), to cite just a few examples. My goal is not a single, universal definition. There are so many criteria on which we can make distinctions, so many cultural considerations, and the fact that age matters more in some contexts than in others. But that complexity need not stop us from coming up with feminist perspectives on childhood: looking at feminist views on widespread practices involving the young and imagining and working toward more just relationships and environments. In fact, the muddle of views should invite us to be more open to feminist thinking about the young, because the mostly-female authors have usually been in different relationships with children than have the male authorities, and because their focus on issues of power and justice often brings different, neglected issues to the forefront. Their ideas and practices are truly provocative and, dare I say it, original, a term that historian Berenice Carroll (1990) shows has rarely been applied to women thinkers.

Luckily, in this project, my goal is to start with what feminists have said about children and childhood rather than with an abstract definition, although those cited here provide useful points of comparison. Given feminism's commitments to equality and freedom from oppression, this approach allows me to explore whether certain understandings of childhood are, in fact, more conducive to liberatory ends, and how women's often distinctive experiences as girls and mothers inform their thinking about childhood. How inclusive is feminism, actually and potentially, when it comes to the wrongs against young people, and what understandings of children and childhood are most and least conducive to giving the young voice and getting them respect?

The Form of the Book

I began my other books with a clear "table of contents" in mind—a picture of what I wanted the whole to do and look like. With this book, however, I struggled. How could I incorporate such dissimilar voices, disparate issues, and works from different time periods into a coherent whole? Could I make sense of what seemed to me exceedingly complex issues and avoid the temptation to turn away slyly from difficulties? I *knew* all the source that I had to draw from: current events; texts from the history of political thought, mostly by feminist social and political thinkers; autobiographies of historical feminist theorists; historical and contemporary feminist manifestos, where we can see how children appear on feminist agendas; academic and popular writing on particular issues of parenting and teaching; feminist science-fiction literature that envisions dystopian worlds where children are silenced and violated, and more utopian alternatives where young people thrive; and my analytic sharpness, my political fight, and my tenderness.

In drawing on such diverse sources as well as my observations of and interactions with children of all ages, races, and classes, in all the locations discussed above and more, I follow my feminist foremothers, for they too read educational treatises, discussed childhood with friends and family, studied their own experiences through autobiography, and explored better alternatives in their nonfiction, their fiction, and their lives. Their lessons are linked to what we today might call critical pedagogy: in no necessary order, observe diverse practices; study a range of books; consider and converse about them; and experiment. Be sensitive *and* critical, generous *and* demanding. Employ feminist skepticism and methods, including giving attachment and experience the central place they deserve. Repeat. The origin of this work, and the passion behind it, is particular stories and certain episodes engraved in my heart. I use feminist sources that I trust to wrestle with them. That is my "organizing principle"—my conversational method, about which I have written a bit elsewhere (Weiss 1998).

I have long struggled and experimented with form in my writing. While I mastered the academic journal article and book early in my career, by the time I wrote my second book, I was already straying and experimenting. My motives for departing from the norms and traditions of academic writing are probably common: readers and writers can find academic arguments to be tiresome, formulaic, elitist, and even deadening. In school, I was directed to edit the passion out to make my work appropriately scholarly, even though that passion motivated me to do the work well and made it interesting to read. Too, much of the historical work I was reading varied in form. So, just as young artists often begin by imitating the "masters," I tried writing via lists, dialogue, and letters, as did my feminist predecessors, explaining the origin of each piece I wrote and making the process of thinking through things more visible (instead of just presenting and defending my conclusions). Due to my working-class origins and my politics, writing fairly plainly comes easily to me, though no doubt over the years my vocabulary and references have become more those of an insider to the academy. You definitely hear my voice in these pages.

I include examples and stories in the book (my own and those of the authors I use) to support a point and to begin an inquiry. As my friend Amber Knight pointed out to me, it seems especially appropriate in a book on childhood that stories be present, given the role of stories in children's lives. We create story-time hours at the public library, emphasize reading in many classrooms, and encourage reading stories aloud to the young at home. Further, children love to tell stories: ghost stories around the campfire, tales of adventures among their toy animals, and reviews of what happened at school. The forms their tales take—less linear and more meandering, sometimes mixing the "real" and the "imagined"—tend to lead to their dismissal; however, adults lose out on knowledge and show disregard for the ways of young people by discounting or ignoring them. I counter this trend by centering my encounters, my stories, with various young people. I use them to introduce two main sections of the book. I also include stories from adults in the final section.

The Contents of the Book

In addition to these introductory thoughts about who/what is a child, I add to Part I a second chapter that asks why *feminist* reflections on children are particularly important or useful. What does that lens have to offer? And aren't feminists, after all, sort of opposed to the family structure and to child-rearing? While the whole book is, in essence, an argument for the relevance and importance of feminist reflections, these early comments help open the door to such a perspective.

Part II, on voice and silence, starts with a set of stories that should ground the book, emphasizing themes of voice and recognition. Then, in Chapter 3, "The Everyday Silencing of Children and the Feminist Politics of Voice," I follow up on these stories and lay out some of the problems to be addressed in this book by centering the silencing of children, a problem in itself and related to the invisibility of children's concerns in many contexts. I have three goals in this chapter: make clear the place that silencing has in the everyday lives of the young, touch on some representative practices that reinforce that silence, and explore whether recent feminist consideration of voice and silence is broad enough to capture the silencing of the young.

Part III, which I call "Historical Threads," contains three chapters that explore various contributions of historical feminists to the topic of childhood, a history that I argue has largely been lost to us but that we will benefit mightily from reclaiming and expanding. I begin, though, with another set of stories that sets the stage for the inquiries that follow, focusing on such political themes as freedom, participation, and community. Chapter 4 then examines how political concepts, such as tyranny and resistance, that have been used to understand and critique sexual inequality and to argue for women's freedom are also used with surprising consistency and efficacy in early feminist discussions on the status and treatment of youth. This application is not the result simply of "adding and stirring"—of taking concepts used in one arena (sexual equality) and employing them in another (the status of youth)—but a case of the concepts being developed through study of the inequality of women and children, among others. It is my great pleasure to work in this chapter with the writings of Mary Wollstonecraft, Frances Wright, Elizabeth Cady Stanton, Ellen Key, and Simone de Beauvoir to showcase this long tradition.

In Chapter 5, I take a deeper look at two other historical thinkers—Charlotte Perkins Gilman and Emma Goldman—to emphasize some of the diversity of feminist critiques and visions of childhood rather than common threads and traditions. This chapter makes visible two different frames that feminists have used to understand and revision childhood: an anarchist feminist perspective and a socialist feminist one. We get to see how one's political commitments make visible different wrongs to children, and especially how they lead to different priorities in rethinking and restructuring children's lives.

To finish out the historical section but also begin the transition into contemporary work, in Chapter 6, I draw on my recently published collection of collectively authored feminist declarations and manifestos from around the world, documents that emerged from feminist gatherings, organizations, and conferences. I was struck as I amassed those documents by where and how, for centuries, children kept showing up on feminist agendas; again, the centrality of these issues to feminism was not very familiar to me in my own decades of feminist thinking and activism. Yet in these manifestos, which lay out the wrongs of patriarchy (and racism, classism, and colonialism) and offer visions of a more feminist world, children's issues are definitely visible. I try to capture something of the evolving sense of what issues surrounding childhood were deemed important to the authors as feminist activists and thinkers.

Altogether, my major contributions in Part III are the rediscovery of a thrilling and radically feminist tradition advocating for the liberatory treatment of youth and a demonstration of how women we know primarily as feminist thinkers and women we know primarily as feminist activists have, in fact, important and distinctively feminist takes on childhood.

Part IV moves from historical to contemporary analysis. I look at the contributions that recent feminist-friendly theorizing might make to more liberatory childhoods. Chapter 7, titled "Learning from Feminist Epistemology," argues that the silencing of children, the theme so central to this book, constitutes an injustice that we should be prepared to address. I use a book very important to contemporary feminist epistemology—Miranda Fricker's *Epistemic Injustice: Power and the Ethics of Knowing*—to convey the seriousness of the wrong—the injustice—of the everyday silencing of young people. I consider why Fricker virtually ignores conversational norms between children and adults in this path-breaking book and look to see whether the idea of being wronged as knowers can nonetheless help us rethink where, when, with whom, and about what children should be invited to participate in conversation.

Chapter 8, "Learning from Feminist Disability Theory," looks at the contributions that feminist disability theory might make to recognizing the voices of children. Disability theory pays a great deal of attention to relations between unequals (especially patients with impairments and doctors) and argues for the importance of all perspectives, even in unequal relations.

Because the relationship between adults and children is also in some ways a relation between unequals, I tap disability theory for what it might teach us about more respectful interactions between adults and youth.

Chapter 9, "Learning from Queer Theory," rounds out considerations of contemporary feminist-friendly theorizing. Queer theory has especially been interested in youth who are, for some reason, "different." It includes studies of the effeminate boy and the tomboy, for example, as well as gay youth. It is also very thoughtful about what it means to talk about "the child" in destructive or mindless ways and how we might do better. Overall, these three chapters take the conversation from historical feminist contributions to childhood studies to contemporary trends that do or might offer us visions and strategies for more constructive adult-child relations.

I close out this section by again bringing together historical and contemporary sources, this time in a united tradition of speculative fictional stories that offer quite a bit of information on what feminists think makes childhood (un)livable. In all the secondary literature on these books, childhood is not a theme that gets much attention. I remedy that. And I leave readers with visions of what kinds of social arrangements we might want to avoid in the name of that respect for young people that I argue is intrinsic to feminism, and where we might want to direct our energies in restructuring homes, schools, and communities. I end that with a short afterword.

Politically, respectful treatment of young people is near the top of my own agenda, as my book shows that it has been for innumerable other feminists. Combining that concern here with my love of historical feminist theory and activism, presenting a feminist history of reflections on childhood, has been a journey of intellectual and political discovery, excitement, and commitment. May my readers experience even part of my fascination and joy at this recovery!

NOTES

1. For a list of school shootings that is sure to astound, see https://en.wikipedia.org/wiki/List_of_school_shootings_in_the_United_States. Accessed on April 20, 2018.

2. Vivian Yee and Alan Blinder, "National School Walkout: Thousands Protest against Gun Violence across the U.S.," *New York Times*, March 14, 2018.

3. Christopher Carbone, "National School Walkout: Students Protest Gun Violence, Call for Action One Month after Parkland Shooting," *Fox News*, March 14, 2018.

4. "March For Our Lives Highlights: Students Protesting Guns Say 'Enough Is Enough,'" *New York Times*, March 24, 2018.

5. "Detentions of Child Migrants at the U.S. Border Surges to Record Levels," *New York Times*, October 29, 2019.

6. "Six Children Died in Border Patrol Care. Democrats in Congress Want to Know Why," *ProPublica*, January 13, 2020.

7. Geneva Sands, "81 Children Separated at Border since Trump's Executive Order on Dividing Families," *CNN*, December 6, 2018.

8. "U.S. Border Crisis," Save the Children, 2019, available at www.savethechildren .org/us/what-we-do/emergency-response/us-border-crisis.

9. Jason Gutierrez, "Philippine Law Would Make 9-Year-Olds Criminally Liable," *New York Times*, January 22, 2019.

10. Ibid.

11. "Global Poverty," Children International, available at https://www.children.org /global-poverty.

12. "UNICEF Data: Monitoring the Situation of Children and Women," UNI-CEF, available at https://data.unicef.org/topic/child-protection/child-labour/.

13. "Trafficking in Children," International Labour Organization, available at http://www.ilo.org/ipec/areas/Traffickingofchildren/lang--en/index.htm.

14. "National Statistics on Child Abuse," National Children's Alliance, available at https://www.nationalchildrensalliance.org/media-room/national-statistics-on-child -abuse/.

15. Robert T. Muller, "The Invisible Trauma of War-Affected Children," *Psychology Today*, April 27, 2013, available at https://www.psychologytoday.com/blog/talking -about-trauma/201304/the-invisible-trauma-war-affected-children.

16. "World Atlas of Gender Equality in Education," 2012, available at https://www .macfound.org/media/files/UNESCO-world-atlas-gender-education.pdf.

17. Crystal Webster, "Black Children Have Always Known State Violence," *Washington Post*, June 15, 2020.

18. "Families for Kids of Color: A Special Report on Challenges and Opportunities," available at https://www.issuelab.org/resources/9261/9261.pdf.

19. Gwendolyn Albert et al., "Segregation of Roma Children in Education—Successes and Challenges," 2015, available at https://library.parenthelp.eu/wp-content /uploads/2018/02/segregation_of_roma_children_in_education_-_successes_and _challenges_-_final-1.pdf.

20. "Segregation, Bullying and Fear: The Stunted Education of Romani Children in Europe," Amnesty International, April 8, 2015, available at https://www.amnesty .org/en/latest/news/2015/04/the-stunted-education-of-romani-children-in-europe/.

21. The overlap of issues between children's and females' "invisible" domestic work has largely, ruefully, been missed in Peru's movement of working children, a movement of some ten thousand working youth, where there has not been "a sustained discussion of feminism in the movement," and "there is a loss here," complicated by the question of whether children have a right to work (Villarin and Taft 2018, 258–260).

22. "Child," *Wikipedia*, available at https://en.wikipedia.org/wiki/Child.

23. "The Ages and Stages of Child Development," Child Development Institute, available at https://childdevelopmentinfo.com/ages-stages/#.WO-ePlPyuV4.

24. "Piaget Stages of Development," WebMD, available at https://www.webmd .com/children/piaget-stages-of-development#1.

25. Saul McLeod, "Erik Erikson's Stages of Psychosocial Development," Simply Psychology, 2017, available at https://www.simplypsychology.org/Erik-Erikson.html.

26. It is interesting that we do not as readily divide adulthood into developmental stages.

27. An interesting philosophical podcast, *What Is a Child?*, can be found at https://soundcloud.com/philosophytalk/what-is-a-child.

REFERENCES

Baird, Barbara. 2008. "Child Politics, Feminist Analyses." *Australian Feminist Studies* 23 (57): 291–305.

Callaghan, Karyn, Victoria Long-Wincza, and Cheryl Velenosi. 2017. "'Of, Not For . . .': The Evolving Recognition of Children's Rights in a Community." *Journal of Childhood Studies* 42, no. 4 (Winter): 17–36.

Carroll, Berenice. 1990. "The Politics of 'Originality': Women and the Class System of the Intellect." *Journal of Women's History* 2, no. 2 (Fall): 136–163.

Chungara, Domitila Barrios de. 1978. *Let Me Speak! Testimony of Domitila, a Woman of the Bolivian Mines.* New York: Monthly Review Press.

Cohen, Elizabeth. 2005. "Neither Seen nor Heard: Children's Citizenship in Contemporary Democracies." *Citizenship Studies* 9 (2): 221–240.

Field, Corinne, and Nicholas Syrett. 2015. *Age in America: The Colonial Era to the Present.* New York: New York University Press.

Jones, Mary. 1972. *The Autobiography of Mother Jones.* Chicago: Charles S. Kerr and Company.

Shaarawi, Huda. 1986. *Harem Years: The Memoirs of an Egyptian Feminist.* Old Westbury, NY: The Feminist Press.

Spongberg, Mary. 2008. "The Child." *Australian Feminist Studies* 23, no. 57 (September): 287.

Villaran, Alejandro Cussianovich, and Jessica Taft. 2018. "Feminist Intuitions in Peru's Movement of Working Children." In *Feminism and the Politics of Childhood: Friends or Foes?*, edited by Rachel Rosen and Katherine Twamley. London: UCL Press.

Weiss, Penny. 1998. "Conversation as Method." *Conversations with Feminism: Political Theory and Practice.* Lanham, MD: Rowman and Littlefield.

2

Why *Feminist* Reflections
on Childhood?

The very concept of distinctly feminist reflections on childhood is surprising to many; the subject of this book can appear confusing, or even absurd. Feminist perspectives on the early years of life are not widely enough known to be easily available to us and are rarely seen as essential to an enlightened analysis of the issues surrounding either feminism or childhood. Troublingly, in fact, there is even an assumed tension between what gender equality requires and what children need. Women's subordinate status—including their primary orientation toward and unequal obligations in the domestic sphere—has often been justified by the responsibilities women have to the young; their liberation, then, would seem to be at the expense of children, rather than in children's interest in deep, complex, and provocative ways. Feminism thus has a bad reputation when it comes to "the family" that leads many to think that feminism is uninterested in—or, indeed, is hostile to—children. I want to explore that association (or, rather, dissociation), starting with the many well-known myths about feminism behind it.

Myths, not unlike metaphors, proverbs, and legends, serve particular social functions. The task of myths is not exactly to convey fact but to lend credibility to and "represent the fundamental beliefs of a particular group" (Sharma and Sharma 1997, 144). Social myths are tied to the experiences and interests of that group and strive to establish cultural values that can guide future generations in a way that is seen as consistent with social stability (and even social control). Myths can be responses to specific, sometimes dramatic, and often imminent social changes. Once parsed, the myths about feminism, in relation to family and children, reveal aspects—or "truths"—of feminism and anti-feminism: what each prioritizes socially, what each fears, and so forth. Innumerable websites "debunk" the myths about feminism; my task is to give them their space and then to look at the values they embody.

Feminism has much more to say about childhood, family, and parenting than is captured by the all-too-familiar negative caricatures. For centuries, the day-to-day practices of feminist families have been lived and understood to be challenging, caring, difficult, critical, imaginative arenas where the rubber meets the road. They have been attempts to practice in adult-child relations what we preach about everything from democracy and happiness to justice and equality. Ultimately, we want to grasp the contributions that a distinctly feminist frame makes to liberatory thinking about young people. But first, we have to confront certain obstacles in the popular social imaginary—widely shared understandings about feminism that prevent us from looking to it as a resource and an inspiration, particularly in relation to children and families.

Myths and Realities: Attacks and Counterattacks

The accusations leveled against feminists in the popular imaginary include hating men, being lesbians, and equating heterosexual sex with rape.[1] It has been said that feminists are anti-marriage, sometimes even likening the institution to legalized prostitution.[2] One way in which feminists are said to have contributed to the destruction of marriage, seemingly by intention, is by recognizing every variety of family as equally legitimate, including lesbian and gay families, polyamorous relationships, and single-parent families. They supposedly advocate making divorce as easy and "faultless" as possible.[3] It's not difficult to see how these views can be portrayed as being harmful to children, who are assumed to need such things as marital stability and positive male *and* female parental role models.

Further, the feminist personality, when not described as pathological,[4] is portrayed as too self-interested and independent to be part of the give and take of family life. Thus, feminists have been accused of being too "selfish" to sacrifice for children. They are associated with a pro–day care stance, preferably government-subsidized sites where they can "dump" their youngsters and leave caring up to strangers and the state, injuring all parties, and especially damaging fragile parent-child attachments.[5] By inviting the state into family matters, whether through funded preschools or legislation on domestic violence, they are also said to wrongly politicize what should be personal. Thus, feminists not only fail to reproduce and to meet the needs of children; they threaten our very freedom.

Their anti-children stance is said to be further visible in their extreme support for birth control (going so far as to distribute condoms for free in high schools) and their supposed support for abortion on demand, including government-subsidized abortions for poor women.[6] Evidence of feminists' anti-family posture is found in their appeal to "feminist buzzwords like 'agency' and 'choice'" to justify "selfishly" controlling their reproduction.[7] "Many people, women included, think that feminists hate children because they 'enslave' you."[8]

Prominent among the myths in the social imaginary is the idea that feminists deny the special and unique role that mothers play in the lives of their children. In the name of equality, they supposedly want fathers to assume roles that men cannot and should not try to fill (lest they be inadequate or become feminized, threatening everything from their self-esteem to national security). While claiming to respect the choices of the individual, feminism, it is said, equates being "only" a wife and mother with oppression and unhappiness. Careers are thought to be feminists' top priority, particularly ones so demanding as to be incompatible with a family orientation.

It's a pretty bleak picture. There are, in fact, not many wrongs in the world for which feminism has not been blamed; it has been called a threat to the (gendered) social order, and even to civilization as we know it. Most of the ills for which it is supposedly responsible are traced back to feminism's having corrupted women's relationships with home, husband, and children. Feminism is blamed for declining marriage rates among heterosexuals and rising marriage rates among homosexuals; for the sad and dangerous emasculation of men, professions, and nation and for the unattractive and unnatural masculinization of women; and for the commercialization and professionalization of care work, which anti-feminists prefer be done by women, for free, out of love.

Inequality means that women are forced to try to walk a narrow, imaginary line where they will not, for example, be held responsible for either neglecting children *or* "overprotecting" them, for putting too much into them *or* not enough. Usually, they cannot win or must walk on eggshells, as oppression allows or even demands. Feminism finds this unacceptable. So too, though, according to the right, are feminists supposedly able to walk a "moderate" and "acceptable" path and only condemned for stepping off of it. This line, too, is mythical and hamstrings the movement. For feminism to be "acceptable," it is asked to "accept" precisely what feminism questions. And, it must be asked, "acceptable to whom?"

The vitriol regarding feminism is not a relic of the past. Looking at a multiplicity of recent online essays and blogs, feminists today are still accused of "spook[ing] a generation of women into not having children,"[9] hating cooking,[10] and "look[ing] down on the science and art of creating a nurturing home life where children are raised well and husbands are kept happy."[11] The tune has not changed much. At "best," one might say, "there is tremendous dissent and vehement disagreement today among people around the world about the status and importance of equality."[12]

Despite this barrage, others continue to argue for the compatibility of feminism and care for and about children; they even see in each practice the potential to hold the other more accountable, to hold it to high standards. As writer Ellen Keim notes, "The majority of women who start out as feminists end up being mothers," and, perhaps more surprisingly, motherhood turns even more women into feminists:

> Another ironic thing is that many women don't become feminists *until* they have children. They suddenly see all the pitfalls that befall a woman who is trying to raise children in a disinterested world. They begin to think for the first time what kind of people they want their children to become. Do they want them to be restricted by the roles society assigns to them? Do they want them to be victims of discrimination either on the receiving end or the giving end? Don't they want their children to be strong *and* sensitive regardless of their gender? And what if they have gay or transgendered children? Or a teen who gets pregnant—or gets a girl pregnant? What if they themselves get divorced or were always single mothers?[13]

Being a good parent can, in fact, mean being a feminist parent: one who is attentive to how unfriendly to children many social practices are, one who is motivated for the sake of children to create a more equitable world, and one who rears children to be just to all genders.

Feminism is not merely an individual choice; instead, it is a political movement advocating changes in social practices, priorities, and policies. With regard to families in particular, Keim sums up some required changes related to children, schools, and families that demand more than an individual's attention and action—they would be social accomplishments:[14]

- Quality and affordable childcare, including after-school care
- Equal sharing of household and child-raising duties
- Fair compensation for women's work, both in and out of the home

- Parent-friendly policies in the workplace and in society
- Sexual equality (including equal access to sex education, birth control, and sexual fulfillment)

As we will see in a later chapter, the place of children on feminist agendas throughout history and around the globe is even broader than what is portrayed on this list, including, for example, concern with the social environments in which children are raised, the amount of social resources spent on children, and the particular effects of war on young people. Critically, this sort of inspiring feminist attention to children is missing in anti-feminist portrayals of a nightmarish and selfish movement. And, unfortunately, people are more familiar with conservative portrayals of feminism than with feminist portrayals of feminism. My aim is to begin the project of reclaiming the history of visionary feminist thinking about and working with children—to focus on feminism's long historical determination to bring children and families into discussions of equality and social justice. "The only thing #WomenAgainstFeminism has taught me is that there are lots of women who have no idea what feminism is."[15]

It is tempting to assert that myths about feminism are merely and entirely anti-feminist fabrications or propaganda; however, like most social myths, these characterizations and charges contain truth and fiction.

Feminism *is* "anti-family" if, by "the family," one means a male-headed household in which the father is *the* authority, the sole wage earner, and the "protector" of weaker, dependent women and children who do not exercise independence of will or judgment. Feminists see male authority in the household as unnecessary and undesirable. Is the feminist desire for egalitarian families problematic, or is the problem the inequality and violence of the patriarchal family? Feminists oppose the patriarchal family as being incompatible with equality, justice, voice, and opportunity for *all* family members and as being all-too-compatible with multiple (and historically prevalent) forms of abuse of women and children. In the end, it could be said that it is *feminists* who promote families, and even family values. It is *feminists* who demand respect for multiple forms of the family, who strive to give families the resources they need to thrive (from safe neighborhoods and good schools to birth control and parental leave), and who emphasize the welfare of children who are disadvantaged or marginalized by systems of oppression.

If "femininity," or being a "real" woman, means repeated, unlimited sacrifice of the self for husband and children, then feminists *are*, in fact, too "selfish" to be "good" wives and mothers. But does rejecting unrestrained self-sacrifice (of time, career aspirations, one's own range of interests) mean unconcern for anyone but the self, or is it a demand that self-sacrifice have its limits and that the "burden" of compromise be borne by more than one member of the family and also be shared by society, lest that one become an object rather than a subject? Feminists urge that if caring for home and family is essential and valuable work, then *all* adults (and communities) should participate in this important and often enriching labor. Further, they demand that caregivers have the resources for self-care and opportunities for civic engagement and participation in the paid labor force. Such practices do not destroy families; they actually more fully support them. Thus, like all charges hurled against feminism, especially with regard to children, this one is both "correct" and "wrong."

I have been exploring the myths not to determine whether they are true or false; instead, I am interested in how they present us with the opportunity to confront our social assumptions and priorities. The myths make clear the need to reconsider the conditions under which we think that children can thrive and to rethink the ways in which we organize care work and affective labor.

Feminism should be seen as *decidedly pro-families*, as it calls for more democratic families (in decision making, in having one's voice respected, etc.), an end to family violence (including incest, child abuse, marital rape, and battery), equal opportunities (at work, in the community, and for leisure activities), the sharing of responsibilities among the adults in the family (including childcare, meal preparation, and housework), greater respect and care for children (including adequate food, safe environments, opportunities for self-development, and good schooling), and recognition of the diversity of families (from foster families and multiple-family households to respect for those who choose and who choose not to marry). This agenda cannot be characterized as either anti-male or anti-children. Instead, it gives voice to inspired and inspiring values. And this assessment is true despite conservatives' seeming monopoly on concern with "values" and "morality."

Families can even serve as stronger foundations of the state (a conservative concern) when they are all respected by it and thus more likely to support it, in turn; they are more stable and enduring (a conservative concern) if they are set up to succeed through inclusive and effective policies and with support from various social authorities, including religions and public opinion. Regardless of whether private households should or must serve as "refuges" in a dog-eat-dog world (another conservative concern), they must also be subject themselves to the demands of justice for all members.

I want to say a little more about the difference a feminist lens makes. I show more of what is distinctive about a feminist perspective on childhood by looking at a story about babies that lacked such a lens and then making clear the questions and concerns that feminism can (and must) add to it.

Non-Feminist versus Feminist Approaches to the Study of Youth: An Example

> The babies we studied have a general appreciation of good and bad behavior, one that spans a range of actions.
>
> —PAUL BLOOM, "The Moral Life of Babies"

> The sense of justice develops very early, and may be used as a basis for a large range of conduct.
>
> —CHARLOTTE PERKINS GILMAN, *Concerning Children*

A newsworthy story about the moral orientation of the very young delighted me. There is cause to be hopeful any time the cognitive and moral abilities of groups of people are taken seriously and celebrated when those capacities are usually underestimated or dismissed. But I was surprised that the author thought these were "new" discoveries about babies, since women have been saying much of this for a very long time (as the nearly identical quotes above show). And I was deeply disappointed at the total absence of feminist sensibilities—in the authors cited, the moral framework appealed to, and the questions asked about childrearing practices.

While working at Yale's Infant Cognition Center, Paul Bloom and his colleagues explored the moral life of babies in a variety of experiments. Based on measuring things like eye movements, they were able to show that even infants demonstrate a preference for actors and puppets that treat others nicely (sharing toys or helping with a task, for example) and a distaste or even repulsion for those who are mean or selfish. The babies looked longer at and rewarded the "moral" behavior they witnessed and frowned at or even punished those who misbehaved or were naughty. "Humans do have a rudimentary moral sense from the very start of life," Bloom concludes.[16] "Some sense of good and evil seems to be bred in the bone."

Bloom suggests that his work "on baby morality might seem like a perverse and misguided" endeavor. Initially seeming to treat the possibility of infant morality as preposterous (or assuming that readers would), he asks, "Why would anyone even entertain the thought of babies as moral beings?" He cites a lengthy roster of highly respected historical figures whose writings about children argue against such a possibility: "From Sigmund Freud to Jean Piaget to Lawrence Kohlberg, psychologists have long argued that we begin life as amoral animals," he says, later adding that figures from the social theorist Jean-Jacques Rousseau to the psychologist and philosopher William James also found childhood to be morally unpromising territory. These widely held views about infants' amorality have played a central role in defining the most basic tasks of parenting and socialization, historically and today, for they establish the nature of the "material" with which adults are working and set out the goals of childrearing. But, Bloom says, there has been a "great discovery in modern psychology" revealing that all these esteemed authors might be very wrong. This revelation sounds like ground-breaking stuff for those of us interested in the nature and rearing of children.

I note that every one of the numerous authorities Bloom cites, from Confucius to Charles Darwin to John Rawls, is male. Had he read more widely, he would have come across quite different viewpoints on the moral life of the very young that would make his "discovery" quite a bit less earth-shaking. As the quotes at the opening of this section suggest, Bloom has rediscovered what Charlotte Perkins Gilman knew a century earlier.

Female and/or feminist authors like Gilman are not generally granted much credibility. They rarely show up on classroom reading lists, scholars write but few books about them, and, as in this news article, psychologists do not cite them in their essays on infant morality. We too-often read women theorists (when we read them at all) assuming that they have less to teach us, even on those few topics about which they are supposed to be, as with children, more intimately involved and "naturally" expert. "We continually fail to listen to and respect what women themselves have to say about how they bring up their children. Indeed, this almost amounts to a failure to acknowledge that mothers do indeed have views that can be expressed and listened to at all" (Ribbens 1994, 1).

Bloom is basically right about the moral lives of babies. Very young humans demonstrate, in ways that adults can recognize, a sense of fairness to self and others. How is it that feminists reached similar conclusions a century or more *before* what Bloom calls "one of the great discoveries in modern psychology"? Only he, as opposed to women authors like Gilman, had "the help of well-designed experiments" (and a university position, a laboratory, assistants, etc.) that allowed him to "see glimmers of moral thought, moral judgment and moral feeling even in the first year of life." But we did not have to wait for the advances of cognitive scientists capable of measuring the eye movements of babies to reveal this, and such scientists will, in the end, take us only so far. Standardized measurements can be useful, but they cannot replace judgments about what to measure, the significance of the findings, or realizations about what cannot be so measured (Muller 2018).

The problem is not only that Bloom did not cite women who already knew what he is now "discovering," like colonists arrogantly "discovering" an already-inhabited land. The even larger problem is that in the social agenda that Bloom lays out based on his "discovery," there is no feminist sensibility. Feminists *must* be part of the conversation about the implications of infant morality, as parents, teachers, and citizens.

Bloom claims, for example, that "one important task of society, particularly of parents, is to turn babies into civilized beings—social creatures who can experience empathy, guilt and shame; who can override selfish impulses in the name of higher principles; and who will respond with outrage to unfairness and injustice." This sounds very familiar. But just in this one sentence, look at what he leaves out! There are important, feminist questions to be raised and wrestled with. What do we mean by "civilized," at home and abroad, and who determines this standard? After all, horrors have been committed in the name of "civilizing," in childrearing and in establishing empires. Do we "*turn* babies into . . . social creatures," or do forms of sociality come naturally and get easily nurtured? What opportunities for a full social life will we provide for the socially inclined young? *Toward whom* will we encourage children to be empathetic? Where will empathy be discouraged or seen as inappropriate? After all, we currently allocate empathy and social resources according to who we think "deserves" them and who supposedly does not warrant our care. Similarly, in whom do we usually foster "guilt and shame," over what matters, and with what consequences? Should we make people feel guilty and shameful over different things (say, for contributing to sexual inequality rather than for having sex) or strive to eliminate such feelings (what else motivates good behavior?)? What counts as the "selfishness" we should strive to override? Who usually gets charged with being selfish, and against what good, "selfless" deeds done by whom are they compared? Are women expected to be the most "selfless," despite the fact that men are more rewarded for acts of fellow feeling? What are "our" higher principles, whose voices have been left out in determining them, and how do communities come together to embody them? Finally, who determines what injustices deserve our "outrage," and who, by contrast, is charged with overreacting and oversensitivity to other (gendered, racialized) forms of "unfairness"?

Given the privileged tradition in which Bloom places his own work, I worry about who will and will not be invited into the next level of conversation about these questions. If women are missing as historical authorities, will they have a role as contemporary authorities? After all, Bloom talks about baby morality as if the very concept of moral development has not been subject to contemporary feminist critique. Carol Gilligan's famous critique of Lawrence Kohlberg's stages of moral development, for example, raises the question of whether Bloom is talking about a "male" definition of abstract morality based on law and justice or a "different," relational voice based on compassion and care. What even counts as baby morality?

Bloom not only definitively places himself in a tradition that excludes historical feminist contributions; he *continues* to ignore them in the present. This approach impedes *his* science as well as more inclusive feminist approaches to knowledge.[17]

If we opened our minds and our canons to a wider range of thinkers and granted women the epistemic authority that their views so clearly deserve, we wouldn't call Bloom's truth about babies "new." "Scientists" at Yale University are revisiting events and ideas in the laboratory that have already been carefully considered and written about by infant caregivers and observers. Somehow (some knowable how), those earlier knowers did not count as experts, their methods did not count as social studies, and their subjects were deemed uninteresting. In addition, Bloom says little about the sorts of large and delicate questions that concerned and still occupy feminists: what, for example, might it mean to treat the young with civility rather than only wonder about how to civilize them? We need not wait for another scientific "finding" before we begin to redesign our homes and schools and rethink our relationships and practices—we already know enough, I show in the next chapters, about injustices and injuries in young people's lives.

We need to accept that what gets called "our tradition" is incomplete and biased. How, after all, could Aristotle so unqualifiedly have claimed that children never resent the authority of the father? Did the nineteenth-century philosopher John Stuart Mill, who said that children could not engage in deliberation, ever talk with a child? How much thought did the seventeenth-century political thinker Thomas Hobbes put into the parent-child relationship, when he said, in the same book, that the relation between parent and child was like all other contractual human relationships, and also that it could not be possibly be contractual? We need to seek other voices and perspectives. We need to learn from more people and ask bigger questions.

Concluding Thoughts

Bloom, like the anti-feminists considered, leaves me with more questions than answers about childrearing practices and adult-child relations. In the rest of this book, I turn to a range of sources for answers—historical and contemporary figures writing in a variety of genres and traditions across time. Bloom is not alone in failing to build on historical feminist knowledge or failing to bring feminists' perspectives into contemporary conversations about childhood. And social psychology is not the only field dealing with children that needs expansion. In my own field of political theory, theorists have more often than not left children out of their theorizing, operating as if humans are not politically interesting until adulthood (and even as adults, only interesting in tasks not usually involving children). Political scientist Gal Gerson characterizes the situation that feminist theorists then confront:

> Hatched from the parental capsule, the complete persona is the subject of political theory. The rationality that characterises this persona is analogous to teeth: invisible at birth, its later emergence is foretold. . . . Such theories give little further thought to the relationship between politics and the maturation process. Being intra-familial, nurture and socialization are beyond politics. (2002, 795)

Feminists refuse to accept that "nurture and socialization are beyond politics." That claim is a fabrication, and one with dire consequences for children and their caregivers. Political theorist Eileen Hunt Botting has also worked to incorporate childhood into political thought. In her treatment of Mary Shelley's *Frankenstein*, she "puts the question of children's rights at the very heart of the text," seeing "the Creature as a child who has been subjected to political injustice through his abandonment, abuse, and neglect" (2018, 3) and attributing to Shelley the desire "to engage philosophical questions concerning children's rights to the means for their healthy development and well-being—fundamentally, rights to warmth, food, water, clothing, shelter, care, education, family, community, and, most crucially, love" (3). In contrast to the canon of political theory that Gerson, Botting, and I critique, a tradition that professors still determinedly teach to the rising generation, the feminists we encounter in this book, historical and contemporary, pay a great deal of attention to childhood. They tend to write more and differently about the first stages of life. They do not just lecture to children, as it were, telling them what to become; instead, they respectfully converse with them. They display a willingness—even an eagerness—to learn more about children, to think about them as openly (and politically) as they do any other subject they investigate (and they would hardly be satisfied by counting infants' eye movements). They are not just trying to make children fit into a predetermined scheme—a scheme usually determined without children particularly in mind—but trying to build one based in part on their well-being. Feminists learn from children themselves, from their recollected childhoods, from their parenting, and from other systems of inequality. Their experiences, as shaped by gendered, racialized, and other systems of domination, inform their inquiry, which makes their work distinctive. They ask big political questions about children and childhood that nonfeminists and anti-feminists avoid or redirect.

Let us now turn to them.

NOTES

1. Most of the claims about feminism in this section are so commonplace as to require no particular source—indeed, our familiarity with them, not their origin, is my point. However, I do cite a few interesting cases in these footnotes. The view that heterosexual sex is rape is often attributed to Andrea Dworkin, especially her book *Intercourse* (1987), despite her claims to the contrary.

2. One early explorer of this idea is Emma Goldman, especially in "Marriage and Love" and "The Traffic in Women," both in *Anarchism and Other Essays* (1911).

3. In the United States, California was the first state to enact "no fault" divorces, in 1969. This law meant that one party did not have to prove a state-recognized "wrong" on the part of the other to be granted a legally recognized separation. In "Five Myths about No-Fault Divorce," Stephen Baskerville, author of *Taken into Custody: The War against Fathers, Marriage, and the Family* (2007), writes, in opposition, that "the no-fault revolution was engineered largely by feminist lawyers, with the cooperation of the bar associations, as part of the sexual revolution." Available at https://winteryknight .com/2013/12/23/stephen-baskerville-five-myths-about-no-fault-divorce-2/.

4. The earliest feminist I found who is described as neurotic for being a feminist is Mary Wollstonecraft. See Ferdinand Lundberg and Marynia Farnham, *Modern Woman: The Lost Sex* (1947).

5. They are a bit dated, but congressional opponents of the 1971 Comprehensive Childcare Act, which Congress passed but President Richard Nixon vetoed, took these arguments to new lows in their portrayals of "warehouses" of disaffected youngsters.

6. The Hyde Amendment, passed in 1976, excludes abortion from the health-care services provided to low-income people through Medicaid, with few exceptions.

7. Amanda Prestigiacomo, "Feminists Are Anti-Motherhood. Here's Proof," Daily Wire, April 5, 2016, available at https://www.dailywire.com/news/4671/feminists-are -anti-motherhood-heres-proof-amanda-prestigiacomo.

8. Ellen Keim, "Why More Mothers Aren't Feminists," Femagination, June 10, 2009, available at http://www.femagination.com/1026/why-more-mothers-arent -feminists/.

9. "Has Feminism Really 'Spooked' Women Out of Having Children?" May 29, 2013, available at https://glosswatch.com/2013/05/29/has-feminism-really-spooked -women-out-of-having-children/.

10. "Why Do Feminists Hate Cooking?" Prick with a Fork, April 3, 2013, available at https://prickwithafork.com/2013/04/03/why-do-feminists-hate-cooking/. Also see Natalie Jovanovski, "'I'm Not a Feminist . . . I Love Cooking!' Why Food Is a Feminist Issue," Feminist Current, January 4, 2015, available at https://www.feministcurrent .com/2015/01/04/im-not-a-feminist-i-love-cooking-why-food-is-a-feminist-issue/.

11. Mollie Hemingway, "Why Do Feminists Denigrate Domestic Work?" Hot Air, April 3, 2013, available at http://hotair.com/headlines/archives/2013/04/03/why-do-feminists-denigrate-domestic-work/.

12. Kathy Caprino, "What Is Feminism, and Why Do So Many Women and Men Hate It?" *Forbes*, March 8, 2017, available at https://www.forbes.com/sites/kathy caprino/2017/03/08/what-is-feminism-and-why-do-so-many-women-and-men-hate-it /#60f8e1647e8e.

13. Ellen Keim, "Why More Mothers Aren't Feminists," Femagination, June 10, 2009, available at http://www.femagination.com/1026/why-more-mothers-arent -feminists/.

14. Ellen Keim, "Having It All." Femagination, July 19, 2009, available at http:// www.femagination.com/1207/having-it-all/.

15. Celina Durgin, "Anti-Feminists Baffle Feminists," *National Review*, July 28, 2014, available at https://www.nationalreview.com/article/383683/anti-feminists -baffle-feminists-celina-durgin.

16. Paul Bloom, "The Moral Life of Babies," *New York Times Magazine*, May 9, 2010, p. MM44. A shorter version is available at https://www.nytimes.com/2010/05 /09/magazine/09babies-t.html.

17. His unquestioned affinity for evolutionary biology and its explanations of human behavior also poses problems from a feminist perspective.

REFERENCES

Botting, Eileen Hunt. 2018. *Mary Shelley and the Rights of the Child: Political Philosophy in Frankenstein*. Philadelphia: University of Pennsylvania Press.

Gerson, Gal. 2002. "Liberal Feminism: Individuality and Oppositions in Wollstone-craft and Mill." *Political Studies* 50 (4): 794–810.

Muller, Jerry. 2018. *The Tyranny of Metrics*. Princeton, NJ: Princeton University Press.

Ribbens, Jane. 1994. *Mothers and Their Children: A Feminist Sociology of Childrearing*. Thousand Oaks, CA: Sage Publications.

Sharma, Rajendra, and Rachana Sharma. 1997. *Social Psychology*. London: Atlantic Publishers.

II

On Voice and Silence

Interlude: The Stories
(Voice and Silence)

An Unexpected Moral to the Story

It was story time in "The Middles" classroom, where I was volunteering. "Z,"[1] a self-possessed five-year-old, plopped himself on my lap. Without much thought, I ran my fingers through his longish hair as we settled down to listen. "Z" pulled his head forward and asked me to stop.

Grateful that he felt comfortable enough to assert himself with me—especially since I'm not his parent—I said, "Sure. Thanks for telling me." I think I was thanking him for being genuine with me—telling me what he wanted, maybe valuing our emerging friendship. I was pleased that I was not the only one enjoying the experience of sitting together.

He did a double take, turning to face me fully. "Really?"

He was so surprised by my acquiescence that I realized this experience must not be a familiar one for him. If he hadn't asked me to stop—which couldn't have been easy—the other alternatives were for him to get up without explanation or to endure something he clearly did not enjoy. He did the perfect thing.

As we listened to the teacher's animated storytelling, I wondered how unusual it is for a youngster to speak up and be heard, how rare for a child to try to put some limits on adults and have it end well. If such things are so uncommon, kids must think of adults as often unresponsive, even intimidating, and see their own place in the world as a subordinated one, where just asking for what you want can be fruitless and unwelcome. How dare we demand that *they* always adapt or abandon their own desires and tolerate whatever we are doing! What is so frightening to us adults as to preclude our listening, no less adapting ourselves, to youngsters?

I kept his story with me as the class moved on to the next activity, held it as I left the classroom, and now I'm grateful that I have carried it with me for twenty-five years, waiting until I had a place to write it down and start story time all over again.

Roll Call

I saw something similar when I brought "R," a foster child, to the first day of summer school. The teacher said hello but mispronounced "R's" name. I saw her cringe. I realized that she was not going to correct the teacher she had just met. As she walked to her seat, head down, shoulders slumped, I corrected the teacher's pronunciation of her name.

Again, something I thought of as such an ordinary exchange caused a child to do a double take.

"R's" prior experience with adults and conflict of any kind was so negative, and shaped her understanding of social interaction so much, that the role she learned to play was a silent, background part. It was safer for her to be called by someone else's name than to speak up. It may also have been unusual for her to see that adults could speak to each other peacefully when there was some "disagreement" between them. Maybe it was even surprising that an adult had spoken up on her behalf.

We need to model civil discourse more often and better—among adults and between adults and children! Even though I had been running late bringing "R" to class, it would have been so simple—indeed, it should be automatic for all teachers!—to take the time to ask me, or the child directly, if they were saying her name correctly. From the moment of introduction, caring enough to ask and listening to a child's answer could be standard operating procedure.

I think "R" would have sat there all summer, cringing every time she had to respond to the name that wasn't hers.

"My Friend Died!"

We have a great deal of trouble with language with most of our foster children, who often have quite impoverished vocabularies and limited experience with conversation. One day, "N" came home from school and blurted out, "My friend died!" We assumed we would have been informed by the school if someone in her class had died. After a great deal of questioning ("Someone in your room?" "A friend from the playground?" "'Died' meaning got very sick?"), we finally figured out that her principal had announced over the public-address system that the ex-governor of the state had died. (He announced this death to elementary school kids?) "N" had no idea what an "ex-governor" was, and "friend" was a word that to her meant "any nice person." If the principal sounded sad, she likely concluded that the "ex-governor" must have been a nice person, a friend.

I could have assumed that "N" didn't know what she was talking about when she first announced the death of a "friend," but instead I made the better choice to assume that she meant *something*—something important to her or something that she maybe wanted help to understand and process. It isn't always easy to do the work of interpretation, and surely I don't always have the patience and even imagination to carry it off. But how rewarding for both of us to understand that "the cow was green" meant that "N" was excited to see a cow in a lush green pasture. I keep trying to figure out what it even means to tell someone that they don't know what they're talking about and the terrible impact on children of so often hearing from adults that their words, their thoughts, are nonsensical.

A Very Important Hug

We had two siblings as foster children, an eight-year-old girl and her six-year-old brother, the latter more troubled than his older sister. One day, as we were watching television together, I looked down where they were on the floor and caught some movement I could swear looked like him moving away from lying on top of her. I was immediately made more suspicious by her nervous reaction to my seeing. Days later, in the pool, he grabbed my breast; his face was almost without affect, and I questioned to myself whether it was purposeful. But a third incident sealed the deal—there was clearly problematic sexual behavior on his part. I called their social worker. Because they were young enough, the social worker had initially told me that they could share a bedroom, but we immediately moved the girl into one of my daughters' bedrooms. The social worker kept encouraging me to keep both kids. But I was so anxious that something would happen between them when our eyes were turned that I finally told the social worker either to remove one of them or to remove both of them. Many days later, they found another placement for the boy.

At that point, they had been with us for about three months. During this time, the older child had not touched me—no hand holding, hugging, or even casual touching. When we read stories, she made sure to sit about a foot away, so there would not even be any "accidental" contact. I had never encountered a child so physically withdrawn and isolated and determined to stay that way.

The day they removed her brother, however, everything changed. Even as he was being driven down the driveway, she ran over in the yard and hugged me. (She didn't really know how to hug, it turned out. Her hugs were more like body slams. I was determined to stay put during them, however, because I was so pleased to see the barrier between us come down, and so she would get the message that I emphatically welcomed her embrace.) That night, she sat right by my side as we read, our legs touching. She started talking more, to everyone.

I told her counselor about the amazing change in "S's" behavior. I said it must be that due to the sexual abuse, she was relieved beyond belief that her brother was gone. The counselor disagreed, saying that the difference in her was due to the fact that she was heard—her feelings (previously expressed through body language more than words) mattered and led to action on her behalf. I saw the sexual contact, saw her discomfort, and did something about it.

That the effects of being heard can be this immediate and dramatic absolutely bowled me over. During the entire year I had contact with "S," in our home and after she returned to her mother, her behavior stayed the same— she joyfully enjoyed hugs, piggyback rides, and wrestling.

We later learned that the siblings were reunited in an adoptive family. I was heartbroken. I could not stop wondering what happened to her voice.

Crying for Attention

"L" was a resident in the shelter I worked at in graduate school. She had a four-year-old and an infant. She had the usual assortment of problems battered women usually have and additional health and transportation issues stemming from being in a wheelchair. Because of the friendship we developed, and my concern for the state her children were in, I volunteered to watch her baby at my home for a few days so that she could more easily take care of the numerous tasks facing her.

This baby had spent much of her life in a crib, a bottle propped on a pillow for feedings. The third morning she was with us, we heard her crying upstairs. We realized then that until that moment, she had basically been silent. Had she already learned, at just six months old, that it did not pay to cry for help? And here she was, just days later, crying for us to come and get her!

Humans, including infants, are very tuned in. This baby had previously figured out that crying was a waste of energy. Just be passive and, at some point, you will likely get some food or a clean diaper. Crying doesn't make them appear any faster; in fact, it may make the bringer of food and diapers gruffer and less likely to linger pleasantly. Crying also takes energy. But then she figured out—is it possible, after just three days?—that things had changed, that people were responding to her more. She could safely ask for what she needed with reasonable expectation of having her needs met.

Voice came first, easily, naturally, to the newborn. Silence was learned as a better survival strategy, rather quickly, in response to external stimuli (or the lack thereof). But her voice did not simply disappear. Luckily, the sense that she should make some noise had not been dormant for long. I imagine that the longer silence is the best choice, the harder it is to know what you want and to know how to ask for it, with any confidence. I also wonder at how we underestimate how extensively babies interact with their worlds.

Building The New Community School

I had heard that a small group was going to meet to discuss the possibility of starting an alternative elementary school. I was immediately interested, even enthralled by the possibility. Putting my kids in day care and elementary school had been a generally difficult, sometimes even harrowing experience.

One issue that drew me revolves around voice and silence. When "L" was six, I sat in on his kindergarten class. I watched the teacher repeatedly chastise the "bad" kids for behavior that went unnoticed or unmentioned when the "good" kids did it. I saw that "L" stayed a bit outside the circle. He was a "good" kid, even getting the "good behavior" award (I know, I know) his very first week in after-care. I started to worry that his desire to please, or at least to stay out of certain kinds of trouble, would silence him. I wanted him in a setting where, instead, his voice would be welcome and encouraged, where he would see his behavior as less subject to constant surveillance and external judgment, and where, when there *were* issues, we would have more creative responses than red checkmarks on a public chart.

"B," on the other hand, was a ridiculously vocal four-year-old. Unlike "L," whose early skills leaned heavily in the areas his school paid less attention to—analytic, perceptual, and so forth—"B's" were in reading and writing, which every teacher sees and applauds. Yet I worried about her fate, given her speed and enthusiasm—the probability that teachers would want her to sit down and shut up, that her competence and drive would inconvenience them. She desperately needed a school with an individualized curriculum that celebrated energy rather than seeing it as a threat to order.

"A" was only two and combined the strongest suspicion of strangers with the keenest interest in other people. She did not easily fit into boxes. I wanted people in her life who would give her the room she needed and would respect her wishes (including for bodily autonomy).

I understood then that what encourages voice and what silences it are not the same for every child. The demand that families and schools understand such individual differences is not small or easy, yet it could be our most important goal. We've learned about the importance of adapting to children's different learning styles but have had much less focus on what enables and encourages voice and active participation in different kids. I think there are at least two huge hurdles to that goal: the stubborn obsession with children's "obedience" (passivity, quiet) and the predominating concern with some feeble concept of "order" that constantly directs and restricts kids. Very little in our schools and families is built around children's self-direction and initiative, things that require them using their voice and being heard.

My Shadows

At nearly six, our foster child "M" followed me everywhere. Both he and my dog Diego would wait to see where I would go next. While Diego was being a loyal dog, more comfortable by my side than anywhere else, "M" just seemed lost. Often, he found something to do alongside me. But if I shifted, so did he, so he clearly was not just looking to be set up with some activity.

It started to become clear that what he wanted was conversation, and if I did not keep one going, he tried. But he usually asked the most obvious questions: "We're outside, aren't we?" "We're in the sandbox now, right?" How was this chatter useful? Was he trying to stay connected or to keep himself visible? Or, given how unstable the state of his world was, was he checking out his understanding of things and situations?

Had anyone talked to him? Read to him? Sung or turned on the radio? "M's" vocabulary was more that of a three-year-old than a five-and-a-half-year-old about to enter kindergarten, where he was clearly going to "fail."

We did a workbook together, getting "M" ready for the type of kindergarten work we knew would be coming. On top of the significant challenges of rhyming, finding opposites, and figuring out which letters have what sounds, we were faced with hurdles erected by a limited vocabulary. How could he pick what rhymes with "hat" when he could not identify the flying bat? He couldn't "correctly" say what sound "bell" begins with because he called it a "ding dong," couldn't rhyme "clown" with "crown" because he had never heard the word "crown," and couldn't find the "p" picture because he had no idea what a "puppet" even was.

So often we got stuck when we were trying to explain something to him, because we needed words and ideas that he didn't know.

"What's that you're looking at?"

"This is a map."

"A mat?"

"No, a map. It helps you find how to get places, like what street to go on."

"A street?"

We feel like we are trying to build an edifice without bricks. "Bricks?" "Like blocks, but made of concrete." "Concrete?"

Feminist literature talks about what is left out of patriarchal languages, but what of a child to whom language itself is almost out of reach or who must use it in unusual ways? I loved that the first time "M" saw the beach, he ingeniously called it a giant pool, and there's something "right" about calling a bell by its sound. Still, he had been silenced by neglect and abuse. It would be hard for him to understand, and to be understood. His confidence was so shaky.

We worked hard together. I made sure that he had a lot of successes. But he was frustrated at school, seeing maybe for the first time how "behind" he was. Using my hand to show distance, I talked with him about just how far back he had started out, how incredible his progress had been, and how much the gap between him and his classmates was narrowing. Truly, he was so bright in every possible sense. He got the distance thing immediately and smiled with pride.

In her autobiography, Charlotte Perkins Gilman writes that as a young teenager, she watched adults "sit around . . . interminably talking on matters of religion and ethics," which gave her the advantage "of hearing ideas discussed as the important things of life, instead of gossip and personalities." Sweet "M" had missed that so far: hearing the words, working with the concepts, seeing the topics, communicating about them.

In her 1923 essay "Loss of Speech through Isolation," Anna Julia Cooper reports telling the older brother of a young sibling in his care that "it isn't right for you to deal in dumb signs in conveying what you mean. You owe that child the English language. You are grown and have travelled. You can express yourself and interest her in the wonderful world outside that you have had glimpses of. She will never be anything but a dumb, shut-in creature unless you make opportunities for her to cultivate human speech!" Cooper then visits the girls' mother, who is isolated and equally reluctant to speak. It is not until she learns some of the family's history that she comes to understand. "Her husband, an innocent man, had been torn from her arms by an infuriated mob and brutally murdered—lynched. The town realized its mistake afterwards when the true culprit confessed but it was too late to bind up that broken family."

I thought of the violence in "M's" family, which was now multigenerational. They struggled with many children, and there was so much resentment and injury in the household. I tried to see his family with the same sympathetic eye that Cooper brings to the family she portrays, "worthy an Epic for its heroic grandeur and unconquerable grit!" Truly, the mother was fighting back for all she was worth. Would that inheritance also be of some advantage? Would it ever help "M" come to voice?

Surprise!

In 1999's *A Voice for the Child*, Janusz Korczak (the pen name of Henryk Goldszmit) writes, "The child is honest. When he does not answer, he answers. He doesn't want to lie, and he is too frightened to tell the truth. To my surprise I have stumbled upon a new thought. Silence is sometimes the highest expression of honesty."

I wonder at Korczak's surprise (a common theme here), given his vast experience with children in orphanages, where he even assembled a children's republic with a court, a newspaper, and a parliament. His "Declaration of Children's Rights" contains such lovely items as "The child has the right to make mistakes," "The child has the right to have secrets," and "The child has the right to be taken seriously." These resolutions are so respectful of young people.

But did Korczak really not know that when we frighten children, silence can become their best option? In such situations, silence is a refuge for them, a safe space (and an indictment of us). We are wrong to violate it, especially without first ensuring safety. Is his surprise about the fact that all-too-common practices induce such fear in kids as to silence them, about the fact that children come up with coping strategies in an attempt to stay safe, or about the fact that children prefer to avoid lying? Surprise is better than being lackadaisical about fear-inducing practices, but I wonder about the common, erroneous assumptions that possibly gave rise to surprise—that children are not tuned in to their environment, that children are not competent enough to devise survival strategies, that children lie as often as not. I prefer the Korczak who writes, "You will never understand children if you belittle their qualities."

NOTE

1. Names and details have been changed for privacy reasons. When possible, I asked the subjects of the stories for their permission before publishing.

3

The Everyday Silencing of Children and
the Feminist Politics of Voice

We regularly write children off as individuals with voices worth hearing, questions worth addressing, and wills worth recognizing. It happens in classrooms, households, the press, and scholarly literature. A "core dynamic of oppression of all kinds is the silencing of the subjugated" (D. Crenshaw and Seymour 2009, 12). "Silencing" is a term used to describe situations in which words do not exist to capture the experiences of marginalized groups, where education is denied that would enable the oppressed to use the words that do exist, or where the context in which certain people act is so unresponsive, distorting, threatening, or punitive that they might as well or dare not speak. Virtually every liberatory political movement opposes silencing as an indignity and a disenfranchisement, an erasure of some essential part of the self and a loss to society of potentially vital contributions, conversations, and commitment. Yet outside of extreme cases—war zones, child abuse, and orphanages, for example—precious little discussion of the silencing of children exists in either popular or academic literature.

The question that informs this chapter concerns the extent to which the profoundly important feminist work on voice and silence is sufficient for thinking about the silencing of children or whether the addition of children to the conversation presents us with an opportunity—or even a demand—to strengthen our theorizing and activism regarding the voices of young people. As with other social movements, some have suggested that at its very heart, "feminism is concerned with finding a voice" (Gordon 1990, 127). "Voice" represents more than simply "speech." As Barrie Thorne describes it, "The theme of 'voice'—voicing experiences, claiming the right not only to speak but also to be listened to—has become a metaphor for political recognition, self-determination and full presence in knowledge" (2002, 1).

My starting point is that we clearly understand that "women speak in ways that are limited and shaped by men's greater social power and control, exercised both individually and institutionally" (Devault 2004, 229). Using common sense, we might expect that children's speech is also shaped by their even more profound personal and institutional powerlessness and by the usually unquestioned, often unchecked control that adults exercise over them. We need to understand how this general status quo, and variations on it, affects children, adults, and various communities.[1]

In most contexts, feminists understand that silencing and voice involve issues ranging from epistemological authority to democratic politics. We understand that the impact of silencing touches psychological well-being and the fabric of civic community. But the silencing of children most definitely is not similarly framed, and the reason seems obvious: children are not seen as participants in the life of politics or of reason. Further, childhood is frequently associated with freedom from burdensome obligations, and preferred images of childhood are ill fits for talk of politics, inequality, and oppression. Such factors make it quite difficult to hear and believe and rectify the silencing or to take seriously the claim I am arguing for here: that injustice is part of the very structure, the *normal* experience of childhood.

Since this chapter is about the "everyday silencing of children," in what follows, I first briefly discuss feminist interest in a focus on the everyday and how that lens provides a distinctive and invaluable approach to feminist work on children, just as it does on other topics. Then, I explore several social practices and pronouncements that are dismissive of young people, variously ignoring, excluding, or condemning them, usually without explanation, without defense, or without evil intent. Because I argue that what we are confronted with is a *political* problem, with a broad range of material manifestations, the examples I select come from varied sources—the popular press, social science research, the history of philosophy, and online resources. After this lengthy but necessary setup, I turn to an example of a common, everyday practice: interruption. I am fascinated by the attention paid to children interrupting adults and the contrast with how adults interrupt children and other adults and the variance in how we talk about interruption based on the age of the interrupter.

When norms of interruption invisibly and forcefully get incorporated into the everyday, they can have broad, deep, and even lasting effects that feminists would never choose to endorse. Thus, I close with thoughts about what is at stake when we silence the young and why, despite the personal labor and institutional change involved, adults should commit ourselves to doing the necessary work to invite in, listen to, and incorporate the disparate voices of children of all ages, sexes, races, classes, and abilities.

"Children Should Be Seen and Not Heard"

Classroom rules (and no, I am not exaggerating or making any of these up!):

- "No talking in the hallways."
- "Use polite speech."
- "No talking in the bathrooms."
- "Follow all directions without argument."
- "Do not talk to other students . . . during independent work time."
- "Obtain permission before speaking."
- "Do not 'call out' in class or make comments not related to the lesson."
- "Do not smack your lips [or] tsk."
- "Complaining is not allowed!"[2]

Rules like these are not only found on classroom bulletin boards; all the above were posted online, intended as models to be helpful to other teachers. They demonstrate that—to a degree that is often truly astonishing—adults regulate what children can say, to whom, about what, when, where, and in what tone. There are consequences to abiding by such classroom rules and for breaking them. Upholders of these regulations claim legitimacy based on other authorities, including religious texts, parenting books, teaching manuals, and social norms of etiquette and civility itself. The enforcers—enthusiastic or merely reflexive—include friends and strangers.

The saying that "children should be seen and not heard" is but a succinct capturing of questionable everyday practices. We should add to that proverb "until and unless adults request and control their speech." This frighteningly familiar saw seems historically to have been applied especially to young females (Martin, n.d.). It equates being "good" with being quiet, adaptive, undemanding, and, perhaps especially for girls, silently attractive (they *can*, in this sense, be seen). This horrid saying makes clear that adult-adult conversations take priority, presumably based on some assumption of the greater superiority of (the topics of? the depth of?) adult-only conversations (and their utter irrelevance or inappropriateness for even older young people), and reveals adults' social privilege (children cannot tell adults to "shut up," "mind your own business," "ask permission before speaking," or regulate their speech in other ways). This fifteenth-century proverb, which we might assume is but a charmingly obsolete remnant of a less enlightened era, continues to evolve. Today, for example, we turn to technology when we do not want to engage with children or deal with their "noise" (ladybren 2013). We distract them with TVs in our cars for short drives, and we give them iPads to play and occupy themselves with, even when we could join in their games or conversations instead. (As children age, however, their parents frequently worry about—and are even mystified by—the way teenagers close themselves off, staying online or in their rooms, disdainful, finally, of adult interruption. Again, the matter seems to be a "problem" mostly because of adult desire for control.)

The sheer number of situations and places in which rules for children of all ages—and in all grade-levels, to some extent[3]—forbid or significantly limit speech fails to teach them (or adults) the social and intellectual value of civil conversation. The rules also make quite clear that in the hierarchy of values, voice does not rate very highly. These are mighty formidable messages to send anyone, especially, I ultimately argue, to young people.

In *Concerning Children* (1900), social theorist Charlotte Perkins Gilman explains that individuals and societies must address much more than severe cases of child abuse, neglect, and impoverishment. While horrible in their own right, we at least *understand* such incidents and situations as devastating, wrong, and preventable—and make some attempts to intervene for the sake of the child. She asks that we confront the way most of us deal with children most of the time: the small, common, everyday acts that, in fact, deeply influence who children are and can become. In thinking about the ways we fail to listen to children—interrupting their speech and quiet, alternately forbidding and discounting their words—I hold onto the concerns of this inspiring philosophical foremother. I try, however, to bring them into the contemporary era, where we have access to an additional century of feminist theory and practice to bring to bear on the problems that occupied her and still bedevil us. Gilman says that these everyday practices are not only wrong but also connected to more easily identifiable, obviously abusive practices. In a great example of circularity, the unquestioned, common-place presence of these everyday injustices creates the problems we use to justify those original, everyday acts of silencing. Yet all of us (I hesitate only a little in saying) participate in these ordinary practices of disrespect. We need to reassess widely accepted practices: make visible their short- and long-term harms; consider what changes are required for children to be seen *and* heard, for their voices to be believed *and* valued; and weigh our responsibility and our power to help enact these changes.

Everyday experiences sustain and reinforce inequality, which the enormously influential Gilman was not the first or last feminist theorist to recognize. Going back at least to the work of Mary Astell (1668–1731) and Mary Wollstonecraft (1759–97), we find detailed analyses and critiques of everyday gendered practices, such as flattery, courtship, and dress. They "get" how daily rituals and customs almost invisibly, but nonetheless effectively, create and reinforce women's vulnerability and subordination.[4] Feminists continue to address the politics of ordinary gendered practices today: from opening doors (Frye 1983) to closing topics of conversation (Tannen 1990), from surgically "improving" bodies (Davis 1995) to accepting others' verdicts that one cannot be improved (Belenky et al. 1997), and from suppressing one's story for the sake of outsiders' (assumed) perceptions of intracommunity well-being (K. Crenshaw 1989) to limiting one's physical movements for the sake of "safety" and propriety (Griffin 1982). Each author cited above concludes that these unevenly performed and differently read acts reinforce inequality and contribute to various forms of silencing. It is, then, in these everyday acts that we can see "habits" that shape minds and bodies, "routines" that enforce notions of in/ability and ir/relevance, and "norms" that demand or expect self-sacrifice, even of one's voice, which others come to see as "normal" and even preferable.

One of the most important and earliest contemporary feminist sociological theorists of the "everyday," Dorothy Smith, understands that the complex, wide-ranging, already-existing environment into which we all enter nonetheless affects people differently:

> The actualities of our everyday world are already socially organized. Settings, equipment, "environment," schedules, occasions, etc., as well as the enterprises and routines of actors are socially produced and concretely and symbolically organized prior to our practice. By beginning from . . . original and immediate knowledge of [the] world, sociology offers a way of making its socially organized properties first observable and then problematic. (1974, 11)

A feminist look at the "everyday" involves a study of comprehensible social organization that is so "normal" as to be almost invisible. It involves not only relatively "neutral" practices but also unjust practices that can and must be made visible and addressed.[5] A focus on everyday norms, then, points us to the too-readily unquestioned and taken-for-granted and, eventually, to the emancipatory struggles that resist them (Andrews 2012; Bargetz 2009). Such resistance usually bears the burden of being deemed dangerous, misguided, or insignificant. This negative response shows that something is clearly at stake in "the little things."[6]

Feminists today and throughout history have understood the overwhelming power of the everyday to legitimize and enforce inequality; they have also found cracks in it in which resistance can take root. Most often, they see how people participate in these everyday practices without questioning or analyzing them—they can seem so trivial!—even though these norms and rituals are so consequential. My hope is to more fully apply these hard-won feminist lessons about silencing and the everyday to childhood, where, along similar lines, we prize obedience in the young and call quiet children "good," where "talking back" is a punishable offense (hooks 1989), and where being told "No!" is a source of children's daily frustration (Stanton [1898] 1993, 10). As Gilman says, "The child who 'minds' promptly and unquestioningly is the ideal" ([1900] 2003, 30). This book is, in part, a response to feminism encouraging us—in the words of Cynthia Enloe and in the spirit of authors from Astell and Wollstonecraft to Gilman and Smith—to "expand[] our investigatory agenda, . . . exert more intellectual energy . . . [and] engage[] with those who take any power structure as unproblematic" (2004, 2–3).

The Dismissals

> Men might be free, but women must still obey. Women are beginning to be free, but still the child remains,—the under-dog always; and he, at least, must obey. On this we are still practically at one,—Catholic and Protestant, soldier and farmer, subject and citizen.
>
> —CHARLOTTE PERKINS GILMAN, *Concerning Children*

A troubling near-universality of opinion appears on the topic of children's proper place, even among groups who agree on little else, as the Gilman quote above illustrates. The following examples of children being underestimated or dismissed are purposely drawn from very different arenas to help illustrate the breadth of the problem—not just its pervasiveness but also its intrinsically political character. The authoritativeness and the thoughtlessness with which these dismissals are issued *precisely* mirror the way many "everyday" ideas and practices are expressed and enforced.

The first arena is philosophy. Philosophers of the highest repute—in this case, the great liberal thinker John Stuart Mill (1808–73)—often toss aside all their most cherished principles when it comes to children, and they do so irresponsibly and with minimal reflection. Mill famously asserts

one very simple principle, as entitled to govern absolutely the dealing of society with the individual. . . . That principle is, that the sole
end for which mankind are warranted, individually or collectively, in
interfering with the liberty of action of any of their number, is self-
protection. That the only purpose for which power can be rightfully
exercised over any member of a civilized community, against his will,
is to prevent harm to others. ([1859] 1978, 9)

In Mill's freest society, individuals decide for themselves matters great and
small, from what kind of lives they want to lead to whom they will choose
as friends to what kind of food they will eat. Interfering with someone else's
freedom is justified *only* if someone's actions will cause harm to another (conversation, even if intended to persuade, is not interference to Mill). In that
case, individuals and the state may interfere to maintain the freedom of others and of the society. But before delving into the meaning of, justifications
for, and consequences of his core principle in his major political treatise *On
Liberty*, Mill stops and makes clear that children—not only the very young
but anyone below a society's age of majority (which, we have seen, can vary
dramatically)—are explicitly excluded from its application:

> It is, perhaps, hardly necessary to say that this doctrine is meant to
> apply only to human beings in the maturity of their faculties. We are
> not speaking of children, or of young persons below the age which the
> law may fix as that of manhood or womanhood. Those who are still
> in a state to require being taken care of by others, must be protected
> against their own actions as well as against external injury. (9)

In contrast with adults, then, interfering with the decisions and actions of
children is acceptable in more situations for more reasons: not only to prevent
them from harming others or the social order but also to prevent them from
harming themselves or from being injured by another. (It is adults who are
expected to determine the potential harm and assess the risk.) The grounds for
the exclusion of children from this principle are terribly important here: beside
the fact that they are "still in a state to require being taken care of by others,"
Mill adds that they are not "capable of being improved by free and equal discussion. Until . . . [they are], there is nothing for them but implicit obedience
to an Akbar or a Charlemagne, if they are so fortunate as to find one" (10).

The possible objections here are numerous and damning. The first set
of issues revolves around "care." Mill never inquires into what principles *do*
apply to those who "require being taken care of by others." Caught up in the

dynamics of liberal (if utilitarian) individualism, he does not speak of the extent to which we *all* require some care. Too, care relationships themselves require an analysis of their justice—such as whether the cared-for have as much say in their treatment as they reasonably can and whether the caregivers are protected as workers and citizens (Moskop 2015). Mill treats all of these issues as politically irrelevant. Second, all that Mill *does* recommend for children is obedience—a dangerous and undemocratic "virtue" (in fact, the one most opposed by Gilman, which we see later). The recommendation overlaps mightily with silencing, which Mill usually opposes. Next, he leaves children's fate to luck (if, indeed, the situations he describes are "lucky!"). What if they are *not* so "fortunate" as to find an Akbar (who combined warmongering with religious tolerance and cultural interests) or a Charlemagne (another militaristic emperor, with decidedly less religious tolerance—but who at least supported cultural and intellectual pursuits in the papacy)? Declaring despotism a legitimate mode of government for children, Mill, like others before and after him, justifies forms of dominion over the young that he deems illegitimate and dangerous for others.[7] How are children to be prepared for robust democratic citizenship if they have not participated in civil discourse and have experienced only despotic rule? This question raises the last and most fundamental issue: Mill's claim that minors are not "capable of being improved by free and equal discussion." Children *learn* to discuss, more and more proficiently with practice—the sort of practice that Mill denies them and that classroom rules today still fail to appreciate or encourage. I wonder (again): did the adult Mill ever really converse with a child, whether of five or fifteen? The *development* and *nurturing* of democratic virtues in young people appear uninteresting to Mill (as to so many canonical political thinkers). Yet "discussion" can (and perhaps usually does) take place among "unequals," including adults and children, in ways that push all parties to greater clarity of argument and insight.[8]

My second example of the everyday silencing, dismissal, or invisibility of young people is from the popular press—specifically, a "throwaway" line in which the author thoughtlessly, even if entirely unintentionally, follows in Mill's footsteps. Since this piece does not involve a developed argument about children, I treat it more quickly than Mill's.

In a *New York Times Magazine* cover story on her experience with marital therapy, journalist Elizabeth Weil begins by "wondering why I wasn't applying myself to the project of being a spouse. . . . [I]n no other important aspect of my life was I so laissez-faire." She compares her relative inattention to her marital relationship (which she thinks is fairly common among "her peers," whoever they are) to things she sees people more often applying themselves to: work, for example, and, obviously important here, raising children. But then comes this statement:

> Perhaps we'd been striving in raising children and not in marriage because child-rearing is a dictatorship and marriage is a democracy. The children do not get to vote on the direction of the relationship, on which sleep-training or discipline philosophy they like best. But with a spouse, particularly a contemporary American spouse, equality is foundational, assumed. (2009)

My first problem is Weil's assumption that contemporary American marriages are generally democracies, a claim that seems undercut even by her account of her own marriage, no less by statistics on everything from domestic violence to unequal hours spent on housework. But what seems reminiscent of Mill is Weil's uncritical reference to and acceptance of "dictatorial" childrearing practices (she says her children were four and seven at the time of the writing). The acceptance of this dictatorial arrangement seems automatic, reflexive, thoughtless—everyday. But dictatorship is, by definition, an unjust form of government where the will of the ruler is unrestricted, and accountability to the ruled or outsiders is minimal.

I wonder, in reading Mill and Weil, how it is that everything we know about power, leadership, and authority is tossed aside when it comes to children. What evidence is there that the possession of despotic power by *anyone* actually encourages them to be *more* attentive and thoughtful or prompts them to work harder to do things right, as Weil claims? In general, we know that such devices and practices as external input, limited and checked power, open-minded conversation, and accountability lead to better use of authority. In addition, children *do*, in fact, "vote" (Weil's claim notwithstanding), giving tacit consent by complying, for example, or resisting by not sleeping or abiding.[9] Not seeing or counting such things, such "feedback," is part of the silencing of young people. But perhaps the myth must simply be preserved that children do not, cannot, and should not possess power of "presence" (Thorne 2002, 1) in their families or communities and that it is thus implausible and undesirable for adults to negotiate with them, as they (supposedly) do with one another. "Throwaway" sentences like Weil's justify not listening to children about such issues as discipline and such rituals as sleep-time— even while she was learning that there was at least some value in talking with and being heard by her partner about everyday household issues, such as who cooks, who has leisure time, and so forth.

Moving from popular literature, we can also see the write-off of the young in social science research. One scholar admits that "there has been remarkably little research into how children make sense of contemporary patterns of family life, and children's perspectives on their everyday lives has been largely ignored" (Morrow 2002, 166). Another concedes that children's voices have been "unheard and their experiences largely concealed in the knowledge created by sociologists, anthropologists and historians" (Thorne 2002, 1). Even in the field of early childhood studies, where children are at the very center of the discipline, "the most critical voices that are silent in our constructions of early childhood education are the children with whom we work. Our constructions of research have not fostered methods that facilitate hearing their voices" (Cannella 1998, 10).[10]

We could—and should—approach the "knowledge" resulting from such scholarship with the same skepticism that we bring to accounts of harems written by men with no possible access to women's quarters (L. Ahmed 1982) or to philosophical accounts of women's nature, needs, or knowledge, where they are spoken for and about but rarely speak in their own voices. This repeated absence is a giant red flag—a parade of red flags. Being silenced means being "left out of . . . accounts of one's own life . . . or included in demeaning and disfiguring ways" (Lugones and Spelman 1983, as quoted in Pearsall 1998, 20). Just as feminists "distrust . . . the male monopoly over accounts of women's lives" (20), so should we distrust those accounts of the young in which children are only spoken for and about, where we operate on the assumption that they *cannot* converse and must only be dictated to—we should, in fact, *expect* "demeaning and disfiguring" content. Although they have not been applied with much consistency, feminist lessons do apply perfectly here to the young.

Sometimes it even seems that people go out of their way to insult children, as though it bestows some sort of legitimacy on the rest of what they have to say. For example, in a short online piece on curiosity, blogger Cindy Dove praises and encourages more inquisitiveness in daily life—and then expresses frustration at the curiosity of the young:

> In the spirit of full disclosure, when my kids were little and in the "why" phase there were moments when I wanted to throw my hands in the air and say "because," with no room for further discussion. However, most of the time I find curiosity appealing. (2012)

Again, what is noteworthy is the way in which children are exempted from ideas about desirable and laudatory behavior, *even when* they are particularly associated with that quality or action, as they are with curiosity. They just can't win! Curiosity is good, except when children are inquisitive. Children are somehow *too* inquisitive, so their curiosity becomes bothersome to adults, including their parents.

Dove's essay ignores the important fact that adult curiosity is often bothersome to other adults who prefer that certain matters remain closed, not to mention the burden on children of prying, overly inquisitive adults. Dove seems to feel no need to defend adult intolerance of curiosity when the curious are pesky young people; she ignores the experiences and perspectives of the young, and, as in so many examples already noted, she portrays youth as a homogenous group with little in common with adults.

The number and range of locations where the young are dismissed or ignored indicate that we are in the presence of a political problem. In the case of gender oppression, "the real and symbolic silencing of women has a long history and is inscribed across philosophical, literary, legal, popular cultural, natural and social science discourses" (Luke 1994, 211). The silencing of children needs to be understood as involving similarly widespread patterns of disempowerment and disrespect. Such patterns vary according to factors that include location, gender, age, class, and race, so that the voices of the more marginalized are considerably more objectionable than those of more privileged youth, younger children are more discounted than older ones, and so forth. But even while behaviors that "challenge authority" are more tolerated among, for example, "gifted" children than "at-risk" young people, silencing is present in the lives of all of them.

If you search the Internet for "marginalization of children," you will learn about how some children marginalize other children, how certain socially marginalized children are more at risk for such illnesses as HIV and depression, and how social programs might successfully target marginalized kids, such as illiterate children or children from hard-to-reach geographical areas. No matter how many pages of search results you scan, you simply will not find a literature about the marginalization of childhood itself, about how *adults* marginalize young people, or about how institutions and everyday practices exclude and demean them. Googling the "silencing of children" leads us back to extreme cases: children in war zones, child abuse, or children in orphanages. There is no discussion of such ordinary, pervasive, and outrageous rules, published online and visible on classroom walls, as "Follow all directions without argument" and "Obtain permission before speaking." Anthropologist Allison James is unusual in acknowledging that children "continue to find their voices silenced, suppressed, or ignored in their everyday lives. Children may not be asked their views and opinions, and even if they are consulted, their ideas may be dismissed" (2008, 261).[11]

These examples and practices provide ample proof that when it comes to children's voices and silencing, we're not even looking at the problems, much less asking how we can solve them. What counts as problematical is defined or presented in a way that tends to maintain the injurious status quo in families, schools, and communities. Everyday practices are mostly left unexamined, just as questions that pose more radical challenges to the existing state of affairs are generally thought to be unreasonable or unnecessary, if not hopelessly utopian, inquiries. With few exceptions, any serious talk about including children, respecting children, and accommodating children has the taint of fanciful dream weaving or destructive delusion.

Voice and Silence

Feminist theorizing on silence and voice, if and when applied to the silencing of the young, helps make visible the particular and problematic politics of talk that surrounds and even defines childhood. Feminism teaches us to ask important questions about what is at stake, and for whom, in established social practices; makes visible the mutually reinforcing strategies of silencing; ties the practices to larger social structures and systems; and demands reconsideration of what has been deemed neutral, necessary, and nice in conversation.

Despite its seemingly obvious utility for grappling with the silencing of youth, feminist theory is built on stories and examples that come almost exclusively from practices among adults and rarely uses stories of children in building theory. As a consequence, feminist theories of voice and silence are constructed *without* the experiences of children to inform them in any central way—sometimes, as we have seen, young people are actively excluded from the investigation; sometimes, it "just happens," as everyday practices do. Clearly, additions, reframing, and modifications—in light of common childhood experiences—will make our theorizing about silencing broader, subtler, and more inclusive.

First, such theorizing establishes at the outset that we cannot simply say that voice equals power and that silence equals oppression. Silence can be a refuge as well as an act of resistance, and, unfortunately, not all speech is genuine, voluntary, or respectful. Second, rather than speaking of speech and silence only as polar opposites, the real possibilities are significantly more complex. Feminists emphasize that a "focus on silence . . . does not intend to convey a monolithic, oppressive force which renders women speechless" (Fletcher 1995, 45). We may speak to some people, but not others, and under certain conditions, but not all. We may tell part of our story, but not the whole of it, due to anticipated responses, effects on ourselves and others, or our own ambivalences. The practices known to affect one's ability to speak and to be heard are numerous and diverse, including one's identity, family history, education, and conversational style as well as the gendering and racialization of language, credibility, and authority. Not only is silence not total; the forms it takes, and the degree to which it exists, vary even in one's life and for members of one's social group.

Interruption of Speech and of Quietude

There are two incredibly important aspects of the practice of "interruption" that affect children. The ones I focus on here may at first seem disparate, yet they are, in fact, surprisingly similar: interference with children's silence, and with their speech. When children are regularly interrupted, corrected, or forced only to listen, they lose their rightful role in coming to grips with their own experiences. Dictated to, instead of conversed with, they do not get to negotiate over memories or interpretations. Yet "having the opportunity to talk about one's life, to give an account of it, to interpret it, is integral to leading that life rather than being led through it" (Lugones and Spelman 1983, as quoted in Pearsall 1998, 20).

I began thinking about children and quietude when I considered that while I more often overhear adults yelling, "Listen to me!" to children, I also frequently hear, "Answer me!," "Tell me!," and "Do you hear me?!" In the ordinary speech practices that contribute to women's oppression, commands to attend to the speaker and to speak in response are not as explicitly or overtly present. Their frequency in ordinary adult-child relations reveals facets of power and privilege: the demand for response is the lack of a right to remain silent, often entails self-incrimination (sometimes followed by immediate punishment), and is a denial of privacy and personal space with daunting repercussions. The command to *listen* is a demand for *attention*, regardless of whatever else the child might be doing or considering. It also often involves the imposition of the adult's "correct" understanding of events, usually without fully hearing the child first. Reckoning with the meaning and consequences of these demands led me to think more deeply about both children's quiet and other forms of interruption and intrusion.

Writer Tillie Olsen explains that there are "natural silences, that necessary time for renewal, lying fallow, gestation, in the natural cycle of creation" (Olsen 1978, n.p.). I worry that too often we deny children this space. Yet such natural silence is easy to see in a child playing alone. They turn a toy or an empty tin can over and over in their hands; outside, dirt drifts through their fingers, repeatedly and idly; sitting at water's edge, they enjoy the feel of the push and pull of waves; they make piles of sticks or line up their cars without obvious (to adults) purpose and without haste. Despite the prevailing stereotype, kids are *not* actually loudly and frantically in motion all the time. Notably and unfortunately, however, that stereotype is frequently used to justify controlling their behavior. They can be very present in quiet acts that require and reinforce internal calm. These scenarios necessitate being left alone, where their actions can be self-directed. Even in settings where there is no particular need for interruption, simple observation in classrooms, living rooms, and playgrounds make clear that—for a variety of reasons—many adults do not like to leave children alone or undirected and prefer roles that involve interference. At best, that interference is correction and enhancement; at worst, it is surveillance and control (Garber 2010).[12] This situation has been of concern to feminists for centuries:

> Throughout the animal kingdom . . . every young creature requires almost continual exercise, and the infancy of children . . . should be passed in harmless gambols . . . without requiring very minute direction from the head, or the constant attention of a nurse. In fact, the care necessary for self-preservation is the first natural exercise of the understanding, as little inventions to amuse the present moment unfold the imagination. But . . . the child is not left a moment to its own direction, particularly a girl, and thus rendered dependent— [then] dependence is called natural. (Wollstonecraft [1792] 1988, 41)

Wollstonecraft is not alone in expressing these thoughts, as numerous feminist thinkers have long "observed and problematized" (D. Smith 1974, 11) the everyday interruptions in general and the different forms and degrees of it determined by such factors as a child's sex. Gilman, too, notes, "To the boy we say, 'Do'; to the girls, 'Don't'" ([1898] 1966, 55). Both are interruptions.

As a result of interruption, children are often denied natural silences, times of renewal or gestation, or even times of unbroken concentration. A child may resist and find these times when they are not "supposed to": among my favorites as a coach were the butterfly watchers on the soccer field. These young players—some towns start organizing and instructing teams with children as young as three!—needed time to observe and follow the butterfly. What assumptions about childhood make us blind to their need for quiet, solitude, and self-direction? What does it mean to be denied such refuge and uninterrupted activity?

Politically, slave narratives offer much to learn from here: "the denial [to slaves] of a private realm," of a "private life," was critical in keeping them "at the constant beck and call of the master" and in removing the conditions necessary for "expressing any independent will" (Ackelsberg and Shanley 1996, 221). There are potentially profound implications for *anyone* who has very limited privacy; still, for children, these effects seem *especially* dire, for two reasons: first, their "independent will" and fundamental sense of self and others are still emergent and thus might need more protection; second, their claims against others, and attempts to set limits upon what others can demand of them, have extremely limited legitimacy, meaning that they will generally have to yield to the interrupter. Yet feminist theorizing on silence and voice has, to my knowledge, not attended much to these dangerous dynamics in the lives of the young. Our theorizing needs to be expanded, refined, and made attentive to more populations.

Children's words, not just their silence, are interrupted. On this subject, sometimes called one of the "communication practices of the powerful" (Weiss and Fisher 1998, 37), there seems to be a reasonably tidy application of gender theory to adult-child interactions. But I also think it is an area where including children in the conversation changes what we can see and learn about the practice. Feminists have studied the rates at which men and women interrupt both men and women as well as the range of purposes of interruption, from domination to cooperation. Children's words are ridden roughshod over even more than women's speech is, but the reasons for and effects of this are similar. Three points, however, merit further thought. First, adults *regularly* and generally thoughtlessly interrupt children—despite the fact that they often make quite a huge deal about teaching children how rude the practice is when children engage in it. Adults sometimes establish elaborate hoops that children must jump through, or rules they must abide by, to speak to them. This quite visible double standard, perhaps as much as the interruptions themselves, reinforces for both parties the lesser importance of the child's voice. And children know of and feel this diminishment! In Gilman's words, on a slightly different topic, "We talk glibly about 'the best good of the child,' but there are few children who are not clearly aware that they are 'minding' for the convenience of the 'the grown-ups' the greater part of the time" ([1900] 2003, 43). Kids get the message.

Second, the interruptions often express a really strong impatience with and disrespect for the ways in which children speak and the processes by which they reach decisions. Children are hardly blind to messages that they are "slow," or even "stupid," their language inferior or wrong. There seems to be little burden on adults to listen harder, to translate, to wait attentively, to become fluent, or to leave open the possibility that they may learn. The assumption seems to be that "children are somehow disabled or prevented from speaking out, and that, therefore, they need a helping hand" (James 2008, 262). Again, this dynamic does not seem to characterize male-female conversation and so needs more attention from feminists thinking about voice and silence.

Finally, the popular literature on interruption varies dramatically depending upon whether it is about adults or about children. The literature on adults asks important questions about the variety of forms and intentions of interruption, muses about its usefulness and its limits, and explores how general norms of conversation actually allow for overlapping voices rather than only turn taking. The literature on children interrupting, however, is quite a bit less scholarly and tends to demean the youthful interrupter. It attributes to children a narrower and mostly negative range of motives, especially impulsiveness and self-centeredness (Rock 2015; Spicer 2010). It fails to recognize the mutuality of interruption, instead considering it to be a one-way and constant irritant inflicted on well-behaved parents with perfect speech etiquette, a difficult and persistent challenge to teachers' need for classroom order, and even a challenge to civil, democratic norms of politeness. The distinctive tone of talk about children's interruptions shows that we have not fully dealt with them in the literature on voice and silence. Based, then, on differences between male-female and adult-child interruption, more attention should be paid to the latter.

Another aspect of interruption speaks to its content more than its frequency: "From early childhood on, over the course of our cultural education, we learn to take experience as bearing on knowledge in many different ways" (Creary 2001, 375). It is through our conversations about our experiences that we gain increased understanding about what happened and why and learn how to think about our experiences. Interruption can be a limit on children's speech that enforces their subordination, not only to adults, but also to adult versions of children's worlds.

Reckoning with the silencing of children will enrich our understanding of the politics of silence and voice, for these distinctive practices speak to important issues: from the need to build social trust between adults and children, to recognizing the variety of forms of voice and silence takes, to making visible the institutionalization of submission.

What's at Stake

> Dare to criticise a system of training based on obedience, and
> you are instantly assumed to be advocating no system at all, no
> training, merely letting the child run wild and 'have his own
> way.' . . . Now this will, no doubt, call up to the minds of many

> a picture of a selfish, domineering youngster, stormily ploughing
> through a number of experimental adventures, with a group of
> sacrificial parents and teachers prostrate before him. . . . How
> little grasp we have of the real processes of education.
>
> —Charlotte Perkins Gilman, *Concerning Children*

How like the weaponized, nightmarish images of women's equality Gilman's imagined scenario is! The image of "free" children terrorizing adults is reminiscent of the historical cartoons portraying bespectacled, serious-looking women in masculine garb going out to vote, leaving behind clueless men in aprons holding screaming children in a house strewn with toys and dirty dishes (Franzen and Ethiel 1988). How impoverished are such imaginations! And how do the fears behind these images compare with what we should really be fearful of? What is actually at stake?

The first thing we stand to gain, if we listen virtuously and sympathetically to children, is good policy in classrooms, families, and states. It turns out, not all that surprisingly, that "when they do not listen to young people, adults' assumptions about children's needs are frequently off the mark" (UNICEF 2002). Adults have been shown to be wrong in their estimations of what children think about or prefer on topics from playgrounds, bullying, and education to sex, violence, and divorce. We should object to any policy based on incorrect assumptions, incomplete information, or flawed reasoning, which therefore results in ineffective or unjust practices. We should also, therefore, object to the silencing that contributes to the errors. "Listening to what children say about their everyday lives and experiences can allow us to both theorize and act on their understandings in relation to larger issues of social and political change" (James 2008, 267).

As clear as the mandate to object to silencing sounds, learning to listen to children requires retraining on the part of adults. Adults have to become skillful at hearing the young, rather than hearing what they want to hear (something they accuse young people of doing—listening selectively). We need the political understanding to see that "children's voices are easily distorted by cultural and other factors. . . . We need to put the processes that give rise to potential delusion and mis-communication under the spotlight" (Mannion 2007, 407). Related, grown-ups have to give up the "adultist" idea that they always know better than those who are younger, in terms of such matters as what those who are younger need and how those needs should be met. This practice of listening to the young also applies to their input concerning topics less immediately related to them. Children are sponges, it is often said; they are observers, used to having to figure out how things work and what people want. Why would we think that their musings are limited only to what affects them rather than also what they see around them and what they hear; what they see makes people happy and sad, angry and conversational; and how adults justify certain things, and why they often see things differently? From infancy, the young are observing, feeling, and trying to make sense of things. But we have to watch and listen to them, consult and negotiate with them, to find out any of this.

Secondly, failing to listen to children puts them at risk. "Silencing children contributes to a world where they are victims of inequality, abuse, exploitation, poverty and fear" (UNICEF 2002). Children who speak and participate are safer, healthier, and more active. Currently, we endorse what puts them at risk, all the while uttering platitudes about how what we do is for their own good. Silencing and repeated exercise of "power over"—like the more obviously abusive practices we condemn—have well-documented negative effects on the young: from self-loathing, to resentment of the silencer, and from retreat, to rebellion. Instead, as Gilman suggests, we should nurture the gradual increase of children's empowerment. Otherwise, as social reformer Frances Wright discussed nearly two centuries ago, we will "see the youth launching into life without compass or quadrant. We should not see him doubting at each emergency how to act, shifting his course with the shifting wind" ([1829] 1973, 112).

A *New York Times* op-ed piece on some celebrity cases of child sexual, psychological, and physical abuse caught my attention a few years ago. Titled "No More Suffering in Silence," it moved from the incidents among the famous to general statistics that its author called "sobering" and phenomena he called "epidemic." The author, editorialist Charles Blow, made clear that all kinds of people are perpetrators, that children of all ages are vulnerable, and that silence damages. But to have as the culmination of the essay the following paragraph reveals a general ignorance about the silencing of children:

> We need a public education campaign that speaks directly to children—on Nickelodeon and Cartoon Network, at the beginning of G-rated movies, on classroom bulletin boards, everywhere. Nothing graphic, just something simple: "If it feels wrong, it's wrong. Say something. It's your body." (2009)

Kids know it's wrong—often the perpetrators even tell them so, as do their own anger and hurt. I am not saying that it would not help to have that message spoken more loudly from more places, as Blow suggests, especially more places where children of every culture and class, as well as their adults, can see it. But Blow assumes (contrary to everyday silencing and to all the statistics regarding child abuse) that when children speak, adults listen. In fact, adults are "not prepared to listen" to children, which "effectively render[s them] . . . inaudible." They *are* speaking—but are not heard. And, most unfortunately, we have many ways to justify such our incredulity when they do speak, especially given common "attacks on the credibility of children" that characterize them as liars, fantasizers (Goddard and Mudaly 2006), poor observers, and thinkers who are "suggestible and acquiescent" (Lewis 2010, 14). As Gilman so rightly says, everyday silencing (including not listening) perpetuates more extreme forms of abuse.

Even the idea that we usually treat children as if their bodies *are* theirs is similarly questionable. More often, we tell them who to go kiss or hug, what they may or absolutely cannot wear, and what parts of themselves they may or must not touch. We tell them to stay put or to go over there, as if they have no control over their physical selves.[13] If someone is treated as if they have nothing interesting to say, no credibility, no judgment, and no say over their physical selves, how will they be able to talk with authority to a skeptical adult about frightening and difficult things? And how many adults are then prepared to listen? If we deceive ourselves about how easy it could be to fix things, we become complicit in keeping the young at risk.

A third consequence of the silencing of children is made visible in an essay on "family discussions." It asserts that children's suggestions in such meetings often involve more fairness and more creativity than do the ideas of parents (Andrus 2003). Other writers defend the contributions of children by noting that older youth "bring a different perspective and life experience that only they are capable of, one that is born of their own unique experiences and politics. We're arguing that teenagers have something to offer morally and politically—and we don't get far by ignoring them or their perspective" (Baumgardner and Richards 2005, 51). As a rule, we should begin our interactions with children, as with adults, by assuming that they might well enrich the conversation and our actions, not as though we are doing them a great favor by listening.

Unfortunately, rather than serving as the basis for the argument that children's perspectives need to be represented, their "distinctiveness" has been used to disqualify them from participation, to mark them as unfit. Feminists are familiar with the strategy of marking members of a sex, a caste, a race, or a religion, or people with certain bodies or particular sexual preferences as different and therefore not appropriate or equipped to participate in certain activities or arenas: the priesthood, marriage, certain jobs, legal status, and so forth. The argument that children, by virtue of their youth, are distinct from those with a recognized right to participate *must* not stop us from joining them in conversation. Instead, any difference should lead us to ask more questions, questions that we should raise in all the situations noted above. Is there adequate evidence to support the asserted difference between adults and children, its universality, and its relation to specific social consequences? Do similarities receive as much attention? Do we overgeneralize about "youth," or also take into account differences among the young, from age and race to class and religion? Are there ways to bring in marginalized voices—either on the same or different terms? How much is participation being valued? How imaginatively have we studied the many paths to and forms of participation?

The basic point is this: we have learned little if we still accept the claim of the powerful that those who are excluded are only excluded because their limitations make their participation impossible or impractical. We cannot still be convinced by this overused line! We cannot still assume that those with greater power positively itch with desire to include greater numbers or kinds but are stumped by the inherent, inevitable, defining, disqualifying defects of those on the outside. Instead, we should recall what was expressed in 1926 by philosopher Suzanne LaFollette: "Most people, no doubt, when they espouse human rights, make their own mental reservations about the proper application of the word 'human'" ([1926] 1973, 545).

The fact that certain processes cannot accommodate certain people should lead us to questions about the processes and environment rather than about those who fail to thrive in them. Children have been silenced by the very conceptualizations of children and childhood. We know from feminism, from efforts to empower the poor, the rural, the aboriginal, people with mental and physical disabilities, and people of color, that those on the top do not easily recognize the intellectual gifts or the perspectives of those who to them are outsiders, unfamiliar, different. In academic disciplines, politics, and organizations, it has long been understood that issues of who gets to speak and about what, and who gets heard, involve fundamental questions of status, representation, respect, participation, exclusion, and authority. We know that processes and procedures are not neutral but established by certain groups for certain ends, in discussions that exclude many people and perspectives. Let us not be stopped from seeing these dynamics when it comes to those younger.

Finally, let's look at the issue on the level of democratic community. Studies suggest, predictably, that when they themselves are shown respect, "children learn the value of respect in sustaining democratic ideals" (S. Smith 2014). When children are given opportunities to practice dialogue and to use democratic strategies, they learn to respect themselves and one another (Andrus 2003). Sociologist Dorothy Smith insists that feminists in particular should pay more attention to dynamics in schools, because they "reproduce circles of exclusion from agency" and thus present "a profound impairment of the democratic process in our societies" (2000, 1150). Democracy presupposes the existence of citizens who can reason well independently *and* in civil conversation. Democratic societies must nurture such skills in individuals, families, classrooms, and communities. But the silencing of youth is deeply counter to this democratic demand. No one becomes suddenly, magically capable of democratic citizenship the day they celebrate reaching the age of majority. And being left out can "contribute to distrust in the system" (Ho 2011, 116) that we supposedly later want them to join.

If listening to children furthers knowledge, leads to better policies for children, keeps children safer and healthier, enhances democratic politics, and is consistent with feminist principles, we need to learn how to listen better.

> The case for involving children in decision-making at school and at home is clear and compelling. . . . "Joint decision-making," which includes more child participation, is a predictor of higher achievement and lower misconduct across all ethnic groups. . . . Opportunities to practice making decisions give one more confidence and proficiency. (Rubin and Schoenfeld 2009)

Research just as "unequivocally identifies the serious detrimental effects that accrue from a lack of such involvement" (ibid.). Period.

Concluding Thoughts

> The problems that feminism seeks to address—violence, discrimination, lack of agency, and fear—can be best conquered by raising the next generation to believe deeply in respect for all people. When you have admiration for differences, you will be less likely to act violently toward another person, fear them, and thus discriminate against them, or create or sustain a system that robs a portion of the population of agency. . . . Teaching and modeling self-respect and respect for others set in all aspects of a child's upbringing is the best foundation for compassion and respect.
>
> —Paige Lucas-Stannard,
> "Want to Be a Feminist Parent?: 4 Goals to Consider"

Feminist theorizing about silencing helps us see that the everyday silencing of children involves ordinary practices that disempower the young, establishing models of goodness for children that incorporate destructive ideals of submissiveness, obedience, silence, and yielding to another's will. Or, from the opposite angle: having a strong will and ideas of one's own, expressing them, and expecting to negotiate with others are inconsistent with being a good child, as they are with femininity. Obviously, these lessons from childhood continue to influence us as we age, in ways that we have not even identified.

Interruption of children—of their speech, their activity, even their quietude—comes down to questions of power and access:

> Differences of power are always manifested in asymmetrical access. . . . The parent has unconditional access to the child's room; the child does not have similar access to the parent's room. . . . The child is required not to lie; the parent is free to close out the child with lies at her discretion. The slave is unconditionally accessible to the master. Total power is unconditional access; total powerlessness is being unconditionally accessible. (Frye 1983, 103)

At its best, feminist theory extends to and learns from the experiences of the young. We need to dig more deeply, do so more consistently, and allow our findings to influence our theories and our practices.

It should go without saying that "children and young people do welcome opportunities to 'have a say'" (Lewis 2010, 15). Given our stubborn refusal to recognize and make room for this desire and ability in children, most institutions and individuals are inexpert at listening to children, making them feel heard, and giving them the greatest chance to speak and exert some influence.

We absolutely need to attend to a range of behaviors if we mean to tackle the everyday silencing of children: the ways we wrongly characterize adult-child relations as properly and acceptably tyrannical, enact classroom rules that problematize and overregulate children's speech, and accept and normalize adult interruptions of young people's speech and quietude. Further, we must understand the connection between respecting children and issues ranging from mental health to the possibilities of an inclusive, democratic, and feminist future. We simply must develop better ways of including and incorporating the young into our everyday processes, even if that requires revising those processes.

Here is what I think we can see and know when feminist political thought meets work on the silencing of children: the silencing effect of the patriarchal family trickles down to children; norms of inequality are taught to them, but also masked; unnecessary restrictions on children's freedom and voice negatively affect democracy and community; practices that silence children reinforce other kinds of marginalization; a variety of tactics are used to discount what young people say; degradations in schools, families, and organizations reinforce each other; conversation and relations between children are discounted; there are lifelong effects of experiencing inequality and injustice as children; and children try a lot of strategies to resist silencing.

We need our models of participation, inclusion, voice, and respect to cover not simply the areas where everyone is able, adult, confident, literate, and experienced—but also those where age and other factors change those dynamics. We have more options than hoping that a benevolent dictator appears.

I believe that adults being willing to share power with children "is, in its truest sense, a very radical agenda" (Lewis 2010, 17). It is time to tackle that agenda. "Policy and practice and research on children's participation is better framed as being about child-adult *relations*" (Mannion 2007, 405) rather than about children alone. If feminism really is to be "for everyone," all forms of silencing must be contested, and change in all parties is required. "What, then, has the parent to do[?] . . . [They are] to encourage in [their] child a spirit of enquiry, and equally to encourage it in [themselves]" (Wright [1829] 1973, 112). A model of mutual change and open-mindedness by all parties is consistent with the goals of voice and genuine dialogue. It is less children who need to change than adults and adult-child relations; it is not only children who will benefit but also adults, adult-child relationships, and communities.

As I have more than hinted at in this chapter, historical feminist theorists have often spoken to problematic aspects of everyday adult-child relations. The argument that children deserve to be listened to is not new; it is, in fact, part of a long and rich feminist tradition. That history deserves a fuller presentation, for it is only rarely evoked, used, or even remembered.

NOTES

1. My focus is on adult-child relationships and the settings in which they mostly take place: schools and homes. While I do not tackle relationships among children here, the literature shows that they can indeed have different characteristics and serve other purposes than do adult-child relationships; however, the latter affects the former and often takes place in the same dominant institutional frames.

2. Most of these rules range from common to ubiquitous, from preschool through high school. Examples of hallway rules are available at http://nolachuckey.greenek12 .org/ and https://www.orange.k12.nj.us/Page/5939; regarding bathrooms at https://

learningward.wordpress.com/culture/; on independent work at https://www.scribd
.com/doc/64681989/8th-Grade-Honors-ELA-Into-Letter-andSyllabus; on calling out
at http://loies.weebly.com/classroom.html; and regarding complaining at https://kb065
.k12.sd.us/classroom_rules_and_expectations.htm and https://sites.google.com/site
/misskarleighstewart99/classroom-rules-and-expectations. But truly, the sources are
endless.

3. There are related rules even through "adult education" classes, though from high
school on, there is often mention of students being more "adult" now, generally meaning that they are expected to self-enforce the old rules.

4. Many historical feminist theorists who discuss the everyday (some of whom I
cover in the next chapters) also make visible girls and women who resist such norms
and practices in various ways, including the "tomboy" or "romp" (Mary Wollstonecraft), the "spinster" (Mary Astell), the determined intellectual (Sor Juana Inés de la
Cruz), and female wage earners (Jane Addams).

5. In *Living a Feminist Life* (2017), Sara Ahmed offers a brilliant treatment of why
this feminist questioning of the everyday is so critical and what it entails for feminists
and nonfeminists.

6. Unfortunately, even the turn to the everyday first looked at the lives of men.
Interestingly, women and children are rarely the "first" priority; even the saying
"women and children first" was originally meant to apply to unusual life-threatening
situations (the drowning of a ship)—in other words, the opposite of the everyday.

7. John Stuart Mill himself was raised by a father whom one could call "tyrannical" in his determination to produce a genius. Mill began training in Greek at the age
of three, and his intense study in the natural sciences, history, and literature did not
end until he was twenty, when Mill had a nervous breakdown; in his autobiography,
he attributes that breakdown to this course of study and consequent lack of "normal"
childhood feelings. In other words, one might have expected him to be more thoughtful about the tyranny of adults over children.

8. Mill's philosophical practice of drawing simple and uncrossed boundaries
between adults and children finds its way into some contemporary feminist theory
as well. For example, Nancy Fraser writes, "Justice requires social arrangements that
permit all (adult) members of society to interact with one another as peers" (2001,
29). Sadly, what justice requires among non-adults, or in adult-child relations, is never
discussed, the exclusion of youth getting only parenthetical attention. We need only
remember the "classroom rules" discussed earlier to see the skirting of these issues as
worrisome.

9. Political scientist James Scott, author of *Weapons of the Weak* (1985), sees important practices such as noncooperation as subtle, everyday forms of resistance found in
a wide variety of subordinated groups (although young people are not his focus).

10. Perhaps the neglect of children's voices in this discipline is related to Heather
Anne De Lair and Eric Erwin's claim that overall, "feminist ideas have been neglected
in the field . . . of early childhood education" (2000, 153).

11. The primary emphasis of Allison James's piece is on the contributions that the
discipline of anthropology can make to the discipline of childhood studies. While
important, her essay does not draw out the implications to include classrooms and
households.

12. Devastating research has revealed that poorer, less-educated parents talk significantly less to their children than those of higher socioeconomic status, and all talk less to boys than to girls. "Disparities in word usage correlate[] so closely with academic success that kids on welfare do worse than professional-class children entirely because their parents talk to them less" (Rosenberg 2013). I am not criticizing interaction, especially conversation.

13. Respect for the bodily integrity of children is not often discussed outside the realm of sexual abuse. Two people who do attend to the everyday disrespect for such bodily integrity are Charlotte Perkins Gilman (2003 [1900]) and Paige Lucas-Stannard (2013).

REFERENCES

Ackelsberg, Martha A., and Mary Lyndon Shanley. 1996. "Privacy, Publicity, and Power: A Feminist Rethinking of the Public-Private Distinction." In *Revisioning the Political: Feminist Reconstructions of Traditional Concepts in Western Political Theory*, edited by Nancy Hirschmann and Christine Di Stefano, 213–233. Boulder, CO: Westview.

Ahmed, Leila. 1982. "Western Ethnocentrism and Perceptions of the Harem." *Feminist Studies* 8, no. 3 (Autumn): 521–534.

Ahmed, Sara. 2017. *Living a Feminist Life*. Durham, NC: Duke University Press.

Andrews, Tom. 2012. "What Is Social Constructionism?" *Grounded Theory Review: An International Journal* 11 (1): 39–46.

Andrus, Susan M. 2003. *Beyond Mars and Venus: Lessons of Dialogue and Peace*. Norfolk, VA: Wordminder Press.

Bargetz, Brigitte. 2009. "The Politics of the Everyday: A Feminist Revision of the Public/Private Frame." In *Reconciling the Irreconcilable*, edited by I. Papkova, Vienna: IWM Junior Visiting Fellows' Conferences, Vol. 24. http://www.iwm.at/publications/5-junior-visiting-fellows-conferences/vol-xxiv/the-politics-of-the-everyday/.

Baumgardner, Jennifer, and Amy Richards. 2005. *Grassroots: A Field Guide for Feminist Activism*. New York: Farrar, Straus and Giroux.

Belenky, Mary Field, Blythe Mcvicker Clinchy, Nancy Rule Goldberger, and Jill Mattuck Tarule. 1997. *Women's Ways of Knowing: The Development of Self, Voice, and Mind*. New York: Basic Books.

Blow, Charles M. 2009. "No More Suffering in Silence." *New York Times*, October 9, 2009.

Cannella, G. S. 1998. *Deconstructing Early Childhood Education: Social Justice and Revolution*. New York: Peter Lang.

Creary, Alice. 2001. "A Question of Silence: Feminist Theory and Women's Voices." *Philosophy* 76: 371–395.

Crenshaw, D. A., and J. Seymour. 2009. "The Resounding Sounds of Silence in Play Therapy." *Play Therapy* 4 (1): 10–12.

Crenshaw, Kimberle. 1989. "Demarginalizing the Intersection of Race and Sex: A Black Feminist Critique of Antidiscrimination Doctrine, Feminist Theory, and Antiracist Politics." *University of Chicago Legal Forum* 1989, no. 1 (Article 8): 139–167.

Davis, Kathy. 1995. *Reshaping the Female Body: The Dilemma of Cosmetic Surgery.* New York: Routledge.

De Lair, Heather Anne, and Eric Erwin. 2000. "Working Perspectives within Feminism and Early Childhood Education." *Contemporary Issues in Early Childhood* 1 (2): 153–170.

Devault, Marjorie L. 2004. "Talking and Listening from Women's Standpoint: Feminist Strategies for Interviewing and Analysis." In *Feminist Perspectives on Social Research*, edited by Sharlene Nagy Hesse-Biber and Michelle L. Yaiser, 227–250. Oxford: Oxford University Press.

Dove, Cindy. 2012. "Curious—Inquisitive." Purposed Lives, June 27, 2012. http://www.purposedlives.com/2012/06/27/curious-inquisitive.

Enloe, Cynthia. 2004. *The Curious Feminist: Searching for Women in a New Age of Empire.* Berkeley: University of California Press.

Fletcher, Ruth. 1995. "Silences: Irish Women and Abortion." *Feminist Review* 50 (Summer): 44–66.

Franzen, Monika, and Nancy Ethiel. 1988. *Make Way! 200 Years of American Women in Cartoons.* Chicago: Chicago Review Press.

Fraser, Nancy. 2001. "Recognition without Ethics?" *Theory, Culture and Society* 18:21–42.

Frye, Marilyn. 1983. *The Politics of Reality: Essays in Feminist Theory.* Trumansburg, NY: Crossing Press.

Garber, Benjamin. 2010. "Play Can Help Kids Digest Life." *Nashua Telegraph*, May 16, 2010.

Gilman, Charlotte Perkins. (1898) 1966. *Women and Economics.* New York: Harper and Row.

———. (1900) 2003. *Concerning Children.* Walnut Creek, CA: AltaMira Press.

Goddard, Chris, and Neerosh Mudaly. 2006. "Silencing the Children." *The Age*, May 20, 2006. http://www.theage.com.au/news/in-depth/silencing-the-children/2006/05/19/1147545518389.html.

Gordon, Tuula. 1990. *Feminist Mothers.* New York: New York University Press.

Griffin, Susan. 1982. *Pornography and Silence.* New York: HarperCollins.

Ho, Anita. 2011. "Trusting Experts and Epistemic Humility in Disability." *International Journal of Feminist Approaches to Bioethics* 4, no. 2 (Fall): 102–123.

hooks, bell. 1989. *Talking Back: Thinking Feminist, Thinking Black.* Cambridge, MA: South End Press.

James, Allison. 2008. "Giving Voice to Children's Voices." *American Anthropologist* 109, no. 2 (June): 261–272.

ladybren@yahoo.com. 2013. "New Meaning to Children Should Be Seen but Not Heard." *BlogHer.* https://ladybrensworld.blogspot.com/2013/04/new-meaning-to-children-should-be-seen.html.

LaFollette, Suzanne. (1926) 1973. "Concerning Women." In *The Feminist Papers: From Adams to DeBeauvoir*, edited by Alice Rossi, 541–565. New York: Bantam Books.

Lewis, Ann. 2010. "Silence in the Context of 'Child Voice.'" *Children and Society* 24:14–23.

Lucas-Stannard, Paige. 2013. "Want to Be a Feminist Parent?: 4 Goals to Consider." *Everyday Feminism.* http://everydayfeminism.com/2013/04/feminist-parenting/.

Lugones, Maria C., and Elizabeth V. Spelman. 1983. "Have We Got a Theory for You! Feminist Theory, Cultural Imperialism and the Demand for 'the Woman's Voice.'" *Women's Studies International Forum* 6 (6): 573–581. Reprinted in *Women and Values: Readings in Recent Feminist Philosophy*, edited by Marilyn Pearsall, 19–32. Belmont, CA: Wadsworth, 1998.

Luke, Carmen. 1994. "Women in the Academy: The Politics of Speech and Silence." *British Journal of Sociology and Education* 15 (2): 211–230.

Mannion, Greg. 2007. "Going Spatial, Going Relational: Why 'Listening to Children' and Children's Participation Needs Reframing." *Discourse: Studies in the Cultural Politics of Education* 28, no. 3 (September): 405–420.

Martin, Gary. n.d. "The Meaning and Origin of the Expression: Children Should Be Seen and Not Heard." *The Phrase Finder.* http://www.phrases.org.uk/meanings /children-should-be-seen-and-not-heard.html.

Miklikowska, Marta, and Helena Hurme. 2008. "Family Influence on the Democratic Orientation of Adolescents." Poster presented at the International Society of Political Psychology 31st Annual Meeting, Paris, France.

Mill, John Stuart. (1859) 1978. *On Liberty.* Indianapolis, IN: Hackett Publishing.

Morrow, Virginia. Untitled review of *The Changing Experience of Childhood, Families and Divorce. Acta Sociologica* 45 (2002): 166–168.

Moskop, Wynne. 2015. "The Problem of Unjust Care: Feminist Care Theory and Global Justice." Paper presented at Western Political Science Association, April 2015.

Olsen, Tillie. 1978. *Silences.* New York: Delacorte.

Rock, Amanda. 2015. "Teaching a Child to Stop Interrupting Conversations." https:// www.verywellfamily.com/how-to-stop-an-interrupting-child-2764632.

Rosenberg, Tina. 2013. "The Power of Talking to Your Baby." *New York Times Opinionator*, April 10, 2013. http://opinionator.blogs.nytimes.com/2013/04/10/the -power-of-talking-to-your-baby/

Rubin, Ron, and Jonas Schoenfeld. 2009. "Becoming Our Own Leaders: Decision-Making at School and Home." *Reclaiming Children and Youth* 18 (3): 7–11.

Scott, James C. 2013. *Weapons of the Weak: Everyday Forms of Peasant Resistance.* New Haven, CT: Yale University Press.

Smith, Dorothy E. 1974. "Women's Perspective as a Radical Critique of Sociology." *Sociological Inquiry* 4, no. 1 (January): 1–13.

———. 2000. "Schooling for Inequality." *Signs* 25, no. 4 (Summer): 1147–1151.

Smith, Sarah A. 2014. "Teaching Children Democratic Citizenship." *Forever Families.* https://foreverfamilies.byu.edu/teaching-children-democratic-citizenship.

Spicer, Susan. 2010. "Teach Your Kids to Stop Interrupting." Today's Parent, June 7, 2010. http://www.todaysparent.com/kids/preschool/teach-your-kids-to-stop -interrupting/

Stanton, Elizabeth Cady. (1898) 1993. *Eighty Years and More: Reminiscences, 1815– 1897.* Boston: Northeastern University Press.

Tannen, Deborah. 1990. *You Just Don't Understand: Women and Men in Conversation.* New York: HarperCollins.

Thorne, Barrie. 2002. "From Silence to Voice: Bringing Children More Fully into Knowledge." *Childhood* 9, no. 3 (August): 251–254.

UNICEF. 2002. "The State of the World's Children." http://www.unicef.org/sowc02/.

Weil, Elizabeth. 2009. "Married (Happily) with Issues." *New York Times Magazine*, December 1, 2009. http://www.nytimes.com/2009/12/06/magazine/06marriage-t.html?.

Weiss, Edmond H., and Bronwyn Fisher. 1998. "Should We Teach Women to Interrupt? Cultural Variables in Management Communication Courses." *Women in Management Review* 13 (1): 37–44.

Wollstonecraft, Mary. (1792) 1988. *A Vindication of the Rights of Woman*. New York: W. W. Norton.

Wright, Frances. (1829) 1973. "Of Free Inquiry." In *The Feminist Papers: From Adams to de Beauvoir*, edited by Alice Rossi, 108–117. New York: Bantam Books.

III

Historical Threads

Interlude: The Stories
(Participation, Justice, and Community)

Bouncing Ideas

I am standing guard at a game at an elementary school fair, somewhat reluctantly being a good citizen. My job involves standing outside one of those blow-up bouncy cages, big enough for several children to jump around in, sort of like a trampoline with soft mesh walls and a ceiling. My assigned task: ensure that only four children enter at a time and let them know when their turn is over. *Keep 'em moving.*

I survey the front of the line and notice that the next four people include two small children and two much older ones. It doesn't seem to me like the best combination for boisterous communal bouncing. I turn to the older two and say: "Your turn is next. But if you want to go in with two older kids, you can wait one more turn. What do you want to do?"

They seem utterly surprised to have someone ask for their input. Yet it was such an easy matter on which to ask for their preference. In response, the two of them talked quietly and then told me they wanted to wait and go in with other bigger kids.

Not only did they get the apparently radical message that their individual preferences actually carry weight, that their participation matters; they also had the opportunity to talk and decide together, which seems to be a skill and practice that we should value and encourage more. If kids do not even get to decide the easy stuff, how are they to learn to make bigger decisions? What will be the impact on their later relationships and communities of a failure to learn to negotiate and reach a consensus? Democratic citizenship can start with asking for input.

Mostly, I still remember, with sadness, their surprise at being consulted. I did, however, also remember the pride in their voices when they announced their decision to me.

Bedeviling Stanton

In her 1897 autobiography, Elizabeth Cady Stanton recalls her young distaste for the color red, born of having to wear "red cloaks, red hoods, red mittens, and red stockings . . . six months of the year." This memory inclines her to indulge her niece's distaste for "everything pea green," although the reasons for her niece's preference were not the same. "Although we cannot always understand the ground for children's preferences, it is often well to heed them," she asserts.

Stanton was eventually able to figure out that her niece's aversion was linked to her having "heard the saying, 'neat but not gaudy, as the devil said when he painted his tail pea green.'" Apparently, the niece did not want to be associated with the devil.

What if Stanton had not been able to track the source of her niece's aversion? What if she had thought the association of a color with the devil unreasonable—silly, even? Is an adult's failure to understand, or their judgment that a preference is somehow invalid, a sufficient reason simply to ignore or overrule a child's inclination? On what grounds can adults claim such power; hold a veto on everything or anything? Do their judgments come to seem to children to be as arbitrary and groundless as the children's positions appear to adults? Who is left, then, to model just relationships?

Hitting a Wall

We are strolling through a park. "B" is about six. She eagerly asks whether she can walk up on top of the wall. I look over the wall to see how far down it is on the other side. I tell her, "Okay. It looks like if you fall, you won't get too hurt." She seems surprised by my response (the consistency of young people's surprise reveals the consistency of certain messages that even very young people learn about themselves, adults, and adult-child relations), so I try to figure out why. It seems that what I have done is to demystify the process by which adults make decisions. I notice later that "B" uses this process of evaluating risks to decide for herself whether to embark on certain ventures. Why, then, do we issue orders more often than we share our thinking about something? We are not only making more work for ourselves but also rein-forcing children's artificial dependence, leaving youngsters unable to make sound, thoughtful decisions on their own. Writing in 1784, Judith Sargent Murray recommends the following: "I would from the early dawn of reason, address her as a rational being. . . . Was she, I say, habituated thus to reflect, she would be taught to aspire; she would learn to estimate every accomplish-ment, according to its proper value."

("B" did walk on the wall and did not fall.)

Preparing for Freedom

You'd think that maybe the neglected child would be the most prepared for freedom. I've met a six-year-old taking care of younger siblings, seen a four-year-old changing a baby's diaper, and heard a seven-year-old talk about making dinner and important phone calls. Often without supervision, they are daily forced to make complicated choices, whether that be what to say to a "nosy" neighbor, or what to do after school when parents are not available to care for them. They are responsible, and they daily fulfill obligations that we often do not associate with childhood. From necessity, they often have developed practical living skills far beyond their years and peers.

But, in fact, these children are terribly prepared for liberty. Their knowl-edge has huge gaps, and their information is often just plain wrong, putting them in situations where they are set up to fail. They make decisions *know-ing* that they do not know what they are doing, because they know that they have to do *something*. When I work with them, they get impatient, having to think things through and taking time. They have not been taught how to solve problems well or to think about how things work. Here, demystifying the process by which adults make decisions becomes burdensome. But so is not knowing.

I see "M" at age five staring at a hose and then crying for help when the water stops, not even thinking to look for a kink in the line. With toys, too, he asks for help, lacking confidence in how to play, especially with more imaginative materials, such as a set of blocks or toy animals. These kids often "fake it," in play as in decision making. They have often made choices based on avoiding abuse or saving someone else from harm, and when cir-cumstances change so that harm is not threatened, their lack of internal radar comes through. Seeing how abused and neglected kids are so ill-prepared for freedom and democracy, I wonder: what do they teach us about how to do better for everyone? However, I also wonder how we can build on what diverse children *have* accomplished and what they *do* know.

It's Decided

"B" is twelve and trying to decide whether she wants to take classes at the middle school or continue to home school. The five of us are in the car, talking about it. "A," who is nine, hasn't joined in, so I ask what she thinks. Her comment is so thoughtful that it is clearly decisive, and we all realize that we are done with the conversation. With regret, I note my own surprise at her input.

It is not so easy to erase the old tapes, the low expectations that we have about children participating in important decision making.

Troubling the Troublesome Child

Alice Dunbar-Nelson, associated with the Harlem Renaissance, wrote a beautiful story in 1895 titled "Titee." The main character is a schoolboy with a reputation for trouble: "A practical joke he relished more than a practical problem, and a good game at pinsticking was far more entertaining than a language lesson." But Dunbar-Nelson reclaims this "troublesome boy," who seems above all "to make his teacher's life a burden." First, she lists all the things he knows rather than those he does not, even while these things do him no good in school. Mostly, they are lessons learned from walking, observing, and conversing. The reader perhaps is made to wonder about all that children might know that we fail to see or to acknowledge and thus fail to build upon.

The story becomes a mystery as Titee's habits suddenly change. He eats less and disappears more. Searching for him one night, his family members find him "upon the side of the track . . . with a broken leg." Why was he out there in the first place? "The secret of Titee's jaunts was out. In one of his trips around the swamp-land, he had discovered the old man dying from cold and hunger in the fields. Together they had found this cave, and Titee had gathered the straw and brush that scattered itself over the ground and made the bed. . . . And thither Titee had trudged twice a day, carrying his luncheon in the morning, and his dinner in the evening, the sole support of a half-dead cripple."

We generally exclude children from our definitions of community—at best, marking them only as "dependents"—and in doing so, we are much less likely to see their contributions or our own dependencies on them. We miss their connections to all kinds of things and people rather than learning from and celebrating such relations and recognizing children's compassionate humanity. At some level, I simply do not know why we identify the "trouble-maker" in the child so much more readily than we do the peacemaker and community builder. We should be more thoughtful about what even counts as "making trouble" and the positive role that troublesome acts like Titee's can play in settings from daycare centers to rural communities.

"Just Like Marfin Luffer!"

"A" is three years old. She is playing on the indoor climber in her room at school, which everyone loves. The teacher looks up and reminds the kids of the rule that only three of them can be on the top level at a time. "A," who loves to hear and tell her own stories about Martin Luther King Jr., says, in her little lisp, "We can change the rules just like Marfin Luffer did!"

Her teacher eagerly tells me this story when I pick "A" up. She marvels at how a three-year-old can recall an important historical event she had heard about and then apply its lesson to a totally different setting. "A's" enthusiasm for rethinking a rule is contagious and made more reasonable by having a "respectable" troublemaker like King as a positive model. A thoughtful three-year-old asks an adult to think about more possibilities or at least to explain a rule that didn't, in the end, seem all that necessary to the group of four kids on the climber, and everyone lives.

"Put It All on the Syllabus"

I am at a well-funded workshop for university faculty and staff on the subject of "civility" that we have been "strongly encouraged" to attend. Following the guest speaker's talk, I listen to members of the audience talk about how disrespectful students are, from the too-familiarly addressed emails they send faculty to their distracting use of technology in class. The solution that keeps being brought up at the workshop is to "put it all on the syllabus." Lay down the rules. Return to them as needed. Little classroom dialogue is required, which, of course, is quite convenient for instructors (who, as many syllabi claim, still retain the right to make changes to those documents as needed). The workshop conversation reminds me of all those horrible books for K–12 teachers on how to "manage" the classroom which I encountered when teaching elementary school.

I think about how, in teaching as in parenting, adults have so many opportunities to model, experiment, and send messages. How can it be that all we advocate at this workshop is an inflexible set of rules that is supposed to cover all these "annoying" situations? What alternative rules could create respectful relations? When I taught elementary school, I came up with one classroom rule (actually, the rule was a question): "Is what you're doing stopping you or anyone else from learning?" With gentle prompting, the children were able to figure out the answer on their own and even sometimes to adapt their "troublesome" behavior so that it could continue in a different way that was more compatible with learning.

I realize that no one came to this workshop to talk about how *they* could be more respectful, especially of students (or, for faculty, of staff). Does the creation of an ever-more-detailed set of policies—I've seen fifteen-page syllabi—show our respect? Or could it be that simply by being older and/or more educated, we're making respect a one-way street—something owed to us? It seems to me that civility, the topic of the day, requires action on everyone's part.

Incivility

I heard a professor at a conference tell a story about a student who was very behind in his class and who came to his office at the end of the semester. The student asked him what she could do. The professor, laughing as he recalled the episode, said to the student, "Pray."

Now, I have had my share of stuck students at the ends of semesters, trying to do in forty-eight hours what they once had six or ten weeks to accomplish, and I know the frustration behind this professor's comment. But I also imagine that the student was in distress—either earlier in the semester, when she got behind, or at present, trying to catch up—and having a joke made about it was not recognizing that distress. Maybe it just didn't make for a good punch line at a conference, but did that professor ask the student what had happened or what she imagined that she could still do? Did he share with her what the institutional options were, beyond what she might have known, or make referrals that dealt with either the causes of the absences or the consequences? Did the professor step in earlier himself by keeping track of absences and checking in with students who were getting behind?

Is the same disrespect that we show to very young people in K–12 classrooms also showing up in college classrooms? Do older adults replicate the patterns they experienced as children, now that they themselves have become parents, teachers, and friends of young people? In *Pornography and Silence: Culture's Revenge against Nature*, Susan Griffin writes, "The silence we have inherited has become part of us."

Imagine if we respected young adults, if we thought that part of our job as professors was to help them find, develop, and express their voices in civil conversation and in democratic communities. What would our college classrooms look like then?

Off Leash

I am at a dog park. One woman there has a nearly full grown and lovely black Labrador, one of my favorite breeds, given my memories of my beloved Diego. The woman is the dominant figure at the park today, more so even than the many and varied canines joyfully gamboling, free from their leashes. I think she must love attention the way I detest it—that is, attention is her goal, while the reasons for it are not so relevant.

What brings all eyes and ears to her is not only her volume, which is impressive, but the nearly nonstop character of her patter. Most of it is directed to her dog, although it is clearly for the benefit of the humans. She talks while surely knowing that her words mean nothing to the dog: she tells him not to go in the little mud puddle by the communal water bowls because she hates mud and does not want to have to put him in a bath when they get home. If he is not by her side, she calls him constantly—"Where are you?," "Where did you get to?," "What are you doing now?"—although the park is not large enough to get lost in and is fenced. If he *is* by her feet, on the other hand, she tells him repeatedly to go off and play.

I hear echoes of other playgrounds (which also reminds me of how similarly people talk to babies and dogs). Once, I watched a parent giving a child more directions on some play equipment than I thought possible to devise. It was a little merry-go-round that children run around pushing and then jump on for a ride. This parent repeatedly offered instructions to her child: to sit and not stand, to hold on with both hands instead of one, to sit in the center rather than on the outside (where it is much more fun), to not go too fast, and to watch the puddles. The directions were uninterrupted and interminable. Another day, at the ballpark, I watched a parent tell her child to move away from her feet, and then, when the child was just a few yards away, to come back right now. Despite being in a very safe environment with plenty of familiar faces and many children afoot, this parent constantly verbally monitored, questioned, and corrected her son's location and actions.

None of this noise seems either necessary or constructive: quite the contrary, in fact, as it must either annoy or befuddle the child and challenge their self-confidence—and maybe even their confidence in their parents.

As I watch the black Lab, I wonder whether these other playground scenarios I recall really might have something in common with the dog park. I feel the unfortunate answer like a punch in the gut. What connects these incidents is the mindlessness of the speech: the constant attempt to control, despite the absence of any real need for control or coherence to the directions; the utter lack of respect for the desires of the animals and the children; and the legitimacy that the senseless directives still claim because, in the end, the adults are being "good" child minders and pet owners by keeping a constant eye on things . . . right?

4

Reflections on Childhood in
the History of Feminist Thought

Tyranny and Resistance

In 1970, Shulamith Firestone presented the following challenge: "We must include the oppression of children in any program for feminist revolution or we will be subject to the same failing of which we have so often accused men: of not having gone deep enough in our analysis, of having missed an important substratum of oppression merely because it didn't directly concern us" (104). Firestone's call for feminism to pay attention to childhood keeps resurfacing. In 1987, Barrie Thorne asked, "How can we . . . bring children more fully into sociological and feminist thought, including our conceptions of human agency and social change" (95), and she stated that a "broadened understanding of children" would "enhance feminist visions of and strategies for change" (86). Another decade later, Jane Helleiner mourned "the marginality of childhood within feminist scholarship" (1999, 28). She asked for "a more consistently feminist analysis that would examine the articulations of both generation and gender" and treat children "as active participants in family (or other) social relations" (29).

Despite these repeated, uniform calls for feminist analysis of childhood, confusion exists about how much and what sort of philosophical and political attention, feminist and otherwise, has been paid to children. Rosalind Ladd claims that while "a long philosophical tradition addresses the role of children in society and the duties of parents and society to them," it is nonetheless the case that "a connection . . . between feminism and increased interest in children . . . [is] more recent[]" (1995, 2), by which she means post-1960s. Erica Burman and Jackie Stacey agree that "until recently there has been little explicit discussion of how the child and childhood have been, and more importantly, should be understood within feminist theory and politics" (2010, 227), but their examples of progress are only post-1990. Susan Turner and Gareth Matthews, on the other hand, even contest Ladd's assumption that there is *any* "long philosophical tradition address[ing] the role of children." They write, "It is no overgeneralization . . . that philosophers in the western tradition have not written about children in any systematic way. Locke's *Thoughts on Education* and Rousseau's *Emile* are notable exceptions. . . . But one would be hard-pressed to think of anyone else" (1998, 1). Like many other overly broad claims about what unnamed feminists in general supposedly have or have not said and done, repeated assertions about feminist inattention to "gender and generation," as Helleiner puts it, are not backed up with much evidence of silence where consideration might have been expected. Where are these commentators looking? What counts as feminist perspectives on childhood?

I am actually not "hard-pressed" to think of a long roster of people beside John Locke and Jean-Jacques Rousseau who write "in any systematic way" about children; in fact, the others I have in mind have broader agendas and more innovative, inclusive ideas than do Locke and Rousseau, as I document in a moment. Unfortunately, as they search for works about children, the commentators quoted above seem unaware of the history of female social and political philosophers.

In this chapter, I contest the assumption that feminism has failed to address either the oppression or the agency of children. I argue, instead, that it has *long* been understood by a great many feminists that the subordination of women is much like and complexly interwoven with problematic ideas about childhood and oppressive social patterns of childrearing. Historically, the subjugation of children is quite regularly treated as part and parcel of feminism's challenge to a multiplicity of forms of domination and of its commitment to alternative visions of individuality and community.

To name but a few examples of thinkers who contradict these skeptics, consider Mary Wollstonecraft (1759–97), a British feminist theorist who worked within and between liberalism, romanticism, and socialism. Gender issues are central to her major treatises, *A Vindication of the Rights of Men* (1790) and *A Vindication of the Rights of Woman* (1792), and her novel, *Maria* (1798), but she also wrote to and about children in *Thoughts on the Education of Girls* (1787) and *Original Stories from Real Life* (1788). Her anthology, *The Female Reader*, contains literary excerpts chosen "for the improvement of young women," and she translated two children's books. Jane Addams (1860–1935) is usually associated with American pragmatism and democratic theory and with the phenomenal achievements of the Chicago settlement-house complex Hull-House. The author of such feminist works as *Democracy and Social Ethics* (1902) and *The Long Road of Woman's Memory* (1916), she also penned *Child Labor* (1905) and *The Spirit of Youth and the City Streets* (1907). Egyptian writer Nawal El Saadawi (1931–), a feminist and socialist, is the author of such feminist works as *Women and Sex* (1972) and *Woman at Point Zero* (1975). Saadawi treats childhood as central in *A Daughter of Isis* (1999), makes links between her life in prison and her experiences as a child in *Memoirs from the Women's Prison* (1983), and published her younger self's *Diary of a Child Called Souad* ([1944] 1990) for other children who might want to write.

On the subject of sexual equality, Swedish thinker Ellen Key (1849–1926), who wove her way through a radical liberalism and socialism, authored *The Morality of Woman* (1911), *Love and Marriage* (1911), and *The Woman Movement* (1912); she also wrote, regarding children, *The Century of the Child* (1909) and *The Younger Generation* (1914). In addition to works on Native Americans and the enslaved, American Lydia Maria Child (1802–80), often linked with transcendentalism, wrote *Brief History of the Condition of Women, in Various Ages and Nations* (1845); on children, she edited *Juvenile Miscellany* (1826–34), penned the three-volume *Flowers for Children* (1844–46), and authored *The Mother's Book* (1831) on childrearing and *The Girl's Own Book* (1833). In 1837, British social theorist Harriet Martineau (1802–76) wrote *Society in America*, criticizing the undemocratic nature of slavery and the impoverished education of females. Regarding the young, she wrote *Household Education* (1848), a handbook on childrearing; a book of stories for children called *The Playfellow* (1841); and the children's novel *Crofton Boys* (1844).[1]

The list of historical feminists addressing gender and youth is quite lengthy. While they draw little notice for such work today (although they often did during their lifetimes), I argue that they paid solemn, often central, attention to the lives of children and connected the problems of young people to the conditions of women's lives and to multiple systems of inequality. Judging by the comments above regarding the absence of feminist attention to children, it is clear that this history is now almost unknown to us. I consider this loss consequential and unjustified, because of the inspiring content of the work and the general poverty of our treatment of children. A primary goal of this chapter is to begin to remember and reclaim this history, so that we can learn from and build upon it.

Feminists have often defended women's freedom and equality by distinguishing woman's nature, status, and fate from that of children. The demand that women not be treated as if they were minors was behind historical campaigns for women's rights to own property and make binding contracts, for example, and still informs calls for women to have a voice in the community and be taken seriously as knowers and doers. This tactic of differentiating women's situations from those of children responds to many practices that infantilize and trivialize women but, most unfortunately, leaves the second-ary status of children unopposed or even reinforced.

The historical feminists I present in this chapter do better than that. They show that the political concepts that feminists have used throughout history to describe and challenge sexual inequality were also used with sur-prising consistency and effect to challenge the inferior status and poor treat-ment of youth. I find this lost history truly stunning.

To show that the status and treatment of children are central concerns of historical feminist writers, I explore how several thinkers, spanning about a cen-tury and a half and working in different political traditions, use the same under-standings of tyranny and resistance in their critiques of the authority of men over women and of adults over children. First, I explore tyranny, by using the works of Mary Wollstonecraft, Frances Wright (1795–1852), Elizabeth Cady Stanton (1815–1902), and Ellen Key. Then, I compare how three theorists—Mary Woll-stonecraft, Elizabeth Cady Stanton, and Simone de Beauvoir (1908–86)—talk about women's resistance and children's resistance. Together, the two sections show the depth and breadth of a distinctly feminist analysis of an oppressed group not based on gender alone, although age intersects with gender. Overall, my hope is that we reclaim these radical insights and the broadened understand-ing of feminism's agenda of which they are an integral part.

Tyranny

In various typologies of political regimes, tyranny has long been classified as a corrupt, destructive, and illegitimate form of government. Tyrannies grant some too much (even unlimited) or an unwarranted kind of authority over others. Despots put their self-interest above the interests of the populace and can rule arbitrarily and without effective checks. Tyrannies vary according to what parties hold how much power over which others in what areas of their lives, how that power is exercised, and the bases on which it is justified. Despots mask their abuses of power in a multitude of ways.

Historically, feminists turned to notions of illegitimate, despotic governance and applied them to the supposedly most unpolitical of all relationships—those between the sexes. Feminists used the language of tyranny to showcase the disharmonious gendered social relations caused by legitimizing the virtually unchecked power of men over women and then used these now more accurately described and problematized relationships as an argument for more gender equality, greater autonomy for women, and expanded social democracy, as was increasingly recommended for colonized states and citizens subject to oppressive rulers. Feminist thinkers used the same term—tyranny—in their analyses of childhood, and for the same ends—that is, they politicized usually depoliticized relationships and critiqued the virtually unchecked power of adults over children.

Overall, feminist arguments about the tyranny experienced by children testify to the existence of a genuine tradition—a consistent thread linking thinkers despite the different political theories they are often linked with as well as their varying eras and countries of origin. All four authors discussed below claim that just as men systematically oppress women, adults, including women, often act tyrannically toward the young—that is, they exercise illegitimate and arbitrary authority over them almost with impunity. The young have few defenses against adults, despite serious consequences to their rights, their liberty, and often their bodies.

Mary Wollstonecraft on Tyranny

To begin, Wollstonecraft defines the project of her famous *A Vindication of the Rights of Woman* as being about "the rights of women *and* national education" ([1972] 1988, 3; my emphasis); the book, that is to say, is about issues pertaining to youth and to women. An understanding of the potential abuses of power is woven throughout her text. Her general understanding of tyranny is as an always-present danger, since "power, in fact, is ever true to its vital principle, for in every shape it would reign without controul and inquiry" (150). Tyranny is rule by unreason (68), most commonly "built on prejudices" (101), always "degrading [to] the master and the abject dependent" alike, and subversive of morality (5).

In criticizing relationships between the sexes, Wollstonecraft does not hesitate to use such words as "oppression" (5, 35, 37), "enslavement" (22, 33, 37), and "subjugation" (5, 37) or to call men "tyrants" (101). She accuses them of acting as tyrants when they "*force* all women, by denying them civil and political rights, to remain immured in their families groping the dark" (5). Other aspects of men's tyrannizing include the following: "Women are not allowed to have sufficient strength of mind to acquire what really deserves the name of virtue" (19); they are restricted from most "employments and pursuits" (44, 75, 148–149); they are not "allowed to judge for themselves respecting their own happiness" (5); their education is neglected, especially as "strength and usefulness are sacrificed to beauty" (7, 41); disrespected, "they are treated as a kind of subordinate being, and not as a part of the human species" (8); and often they are expected, docilely, to obey (19, 25, 72, 83), since they are, after all, "created for his convenience or pleasure" (26–28, 73). When men act as tyrants, they deny women's full humanity, which leads to contempt for them, and they put obstacles on women's path to self-development and citizenship, which tragically narrows women's worlds, their options, and their abilities. As part of the tyranny of patriarchy, women, like other subordinated groups, are encouraged (even forced) to be weak and dependent, and then they are blamed and ridiculed for being so (117, 120). They are made vulnerable to a variety of outrages and deceptions (126). They are not given equal, direct voice in their communities or even interpersonal relationships. Requiring their obedience to men is the ultimate denigration to being less than fully human and rational and sensitive.

Moving from her analysis of patriarchy to that of childhood, fully a third of the references to tyranny in *Vindication* come in chapters on education. Wollstonecraft recognizes that "parental affection, indeed, in many minds, is but a pretext to tyrannize where it can be done with impunity" (150–151) and that "parents often love their children in the most brutal manner" (150). Such tyranny is exercised largely without consequences to the abuser of power.

One element of the tyranny experienced by children concerns the extent of parental power—the constant oversight and its consequent dependence: "The child is not left a moment to its own direction, particularly a girl, and thus rendered dependent—dependence is called natural" (41) and, especially for girls, "limbs and faculties are cramped" in the name of "personal beauty" (41). The tyranny of parents and teachers over children also consists in the demand for obedience (150, 154) and concomitant neglect of their reason. Adults do not advocate "the respect that will bear discussion" (151) but "subjugate a rational being to the mere will of another" (153, 155) to a greater extent and for longer than necessary. "It is easier, I grant, to command than reason; but it does not follow from hence that children cannot comprehend the reason why they are made to do certain things habitually" (156).

Wollstonecraft takes a developmental approach, arguing that education should "slowly sharpen the senses, form the temper, regulate the passions as they begin to ferment, and set the understanding to work before the body arrives at maturity; so that the man may only have to proceed, not to begin, the important task of learning to think and reason" (21). She encourages day schools, so that children will have intense relations with other children as well as with their families. Children "should be excited to think for themselves; and this can only be done by mixing a number of children together" (157). One must not be always under the direction of another and unable to "dare to speak what they think" (158). The consequences of tyrannical power are always undesirable and often broader than suspected: "the absurd duty, too often inculcated, of obeying a parent only on account of his being a parent, shackles the mind, and prepares it for a slavish submission to any power but reason" (153). Since humans will resist, "what, indeed, can tend to deprave the character more than outward submission and inward contempt?" (168). Yet this is the consequence of tyranny over children.

Wollstonecraft writes, "Obedience, unconditional obedience, is the catch-word of tyrants of every description" (150), and she strenuously critiques both systems of domination for equating the goodness of youth and of women with submission. In neither case is the group on the bottom treated as equal citizens, despite the fact, for example, that schoolchildren are capable of establishing systems of justice for misbehavior (170) and that women have the mental and moral capacities to be full political equals. Like women, children are too often put on display (163), like objects, and have their rational faculties and their physical health neglected, corrupting social relations in general. Power exercised by adults over children and men over women is often misrepresented as a good, unchecked and virtually unlimited. The effects are not just on individuals but on social classes. As Eileen Botting (2016) has argued, Wollstonecraft can be read as an early defender of children's rights—positively, to parental care, and negatively, to not be abused. Her opposition to tyranny extends to all of its manifestations.

Frances Wright on Tyranny

Wright offers a second example of a historical theorist exploring the concept and practice of tyranny by studying multiple groups, including the working class and the enslaved as well as women and children. "Time and again, writers stressed the interrelation of Wright's sins: her irreligion; her contempt for the clergy; her attacks against inequality in education, employment, property, and, above all, marriage" (Ginzberg 1994, 203). She was, among other things, a founder of the Nashoba community, a failed experiment to educate and ultimately free enslaved Black people. She is linked with diverse movements and thinkers, including pragmatism and freethinking, Robert Owen and Jeremy Bentham. Her most famous works include *Views on Society and Manners in America* (1821) and *Course of Popular Lectures* (1829), and she lectured to thousands assembled in "mixed audiences."

Wright endorses a general principle to argue for limits on all forms of legitimate authority: "Do we exert our own liberties without injury to others—we exert them justly; do we exert them at the expense of others—unjustly . . . step[ping] from the sure platform of liberty upon the uncertain threshold of tyranny" ([1834] 2004, 82–83). Men, she argues, have crossed that line vis-à-vis women.

Wright speaks of women as ignorant and enslaved, bound in "mental chains" (88), and of men as establishing their "pretentions upon the sacrificed rights of others," ultimately reducing everyone's liberty (82–83). Women's inadequate education—"the neglected state of the female mind" (32)—leaves them in a state of vulnerability, she argues, and is incompatible with human improvement, republicanism, and liberty. Wright objects to the tyranny of "traditional marriages as not only ensuring female dependency on men but turning women into the legal property of their husbands while denying them the right to their own property" (Kissel 1993, 6), again making them objects. Her agenda is broad: "She advocate[s] such specific reforms as equal education for women, liberalization of divorce laws, more sexual freedom, teaching methods of birth control, and legal protection of a married woman's property" (Kendall and Fisher 1974, 59). Women were seen and treated as lesser beings. She concludes, "Until power is annihilated on one side, fear and obedience on the other, and both [sexes] restored to their birthright—equality. Let none think that affection can reign without it; or friendship, or esteem. Jealousies, envyings, suspicions, reserves, deceptions—these are the fruits of inequality" (Wright [1834] 2004, 89). Sexual tyranny is socially disastrous.

Unlike the more famous John Stuart Mill, who agrees with Wright about the definition and centrality of liberty as non-interference with one's freedom but excludes children from its application, Wright includes children as equally deserving of liberty. She writes (and I must quote this amazing passage at length):

> Who among us but has had occasion to remark the ill-judged, however well-intentioned government of children by their teachers; and, yet more especially, by their parents? In what does this mismanagement originate? In a misconception of the parent from the principle of liberty, in his assumption of rights destructive of those of the child; in his exercise of authority, as by right divine, over the judgment, actions, and person of the child; in his forgetfulness of the character of the child, as a human being, born "free and equal" among his compeers; that is, having equal claims to the exercise and development of all his senses, faculties, and powers, with those who brought him into existence, and with all sentient beings who tread the earth. (83–84)

Wright analyzes numerous devastating infringements on children's liberty and individuality, practices that automatically signal an abuse of power. She notes the broad, ill effects on children, effects characteristic of illegitimate rule. She criticizes the despotic extent of adult authority, reaching to children's "judgment, actions, and person." As she does with women, Wright speaks of children as "by turns, made a plaything and a slave" (33). They are "commanded to believe," "trembling under the rod," and "launching into life without compass or quadrant" (84). Wright criticizes those who simply dictate to children what to believe and even "command his feelings" (84) as well as those who educate only boys.

Wright's critiques of the tyrannies of men over women and of adults over children show a consistent application of principles, deeply rooted in ideals of democratic equality and free enquiry, to all groups of citizens subject to domination. Tyranny is the enemy of democracy, reason, and respect. She concludes that "in proportion as your children are enlightened, will they prove blessings to society" (87). Similarly, she says, "until women assume the place in society which good sense and good feeling alike, assign to them, human improvement must advance but feebly." Her overall stance is that tyranny is individually and socially destructive, leaving the tyrannized—including women and children—vulnerable and fearful, condemned to obey, with unequal rights and power and a lesser voice in the community.

Elizabeth Cady Stanton on Tyranny

Stanton, who was "attracted to various forms of political radicalism" (Wiki 2016), also believed, like Wollstonecraft, that no one "ever saw a human being that would not abuse unlimited power" (1854). In the "Declaration of Sentiments" ratified at the 1848 women's rights convention at Seneca Falls, New York, that she helped convene, she famously writes, "The history of mankind is a history of repeated injuries and usurpations on the part of man toward woman, having in direct object the establishment of an absolute tyranny over her" (1848b). The evidence of tyranny, provided in a long list of specific grievances and a complex series of resolutions, includes the lack of political and property rights, double moral standards of behavior, and the lack of educational and employment opportunities. The social, legal, and religious status quo left women dependent upon men socially and economically (even if they earned their own money) and without the respect of men or even self-respect. Laws, customs, and social mores celebrated and justified rather than regulating or reining in men's power over women, which was seen as operating in multiple arenas (the household, the workplace, the church, etc.). Such diffusion and reinforcement of male authority was held to be in opposition to the interests and the happiness of women, consistent with defining tyranny as a form of rule relatively unconcerned with the well-being of the governed.

Stanton critiques several justifications of man's "authority over woman," questions the range of its legitimacy, and makes clear its central destructive effects—female "degradation and ignorance" (1848c). The essence of illegitimate rule is captured in many ways, including "his prerogative to command, ours to obey—his duty to preach, ours to keep silence"; and "her wishes should she have any must be in subjection to those of her tyrant—her will must be in perfect subordination, the comfort of the wife, children, servants one and all must be given up wholly disregarded until the great head of the house be first attended to." She argues that male domination is incompatible with "principles of universal justice," with "harmony in the domestic circle," and with women's "duty to resist oppression wherever she many find it at home or abroad, by every moral power within her reach" (ibid.).

Stanton describes the situation of children in the terms she also chooses to capture the oppression of women. She writes, "I see so much tyranny exercised over children, even by well-disposed parents, and in so many varied forms,—a tyranny to which these parents are themselves insensible,—that I . . . hope that I may do something to defend the weak from the strong" ([1898] 1987, 2). As she discusses "that everlasting no! no! no!" (10–11) so often endured by the young, Stanton writes, "I well remember the despair I felt in those years, . . . over the constant cribbing and crippling of a child's life" (11).[2] In "Our Girls," she defines a particular unhappiness that hits young girls:

> They have awakened to the fact that they belong to a subject, degraded, ostracised class: that to fulfill their man appointed sphere, they can have no individual character, no life purpose, personal freedom, aim or ambition. They are simply to revolve round some man, to live only for him, in him, with him, to be fed, clothed, housed, guided and controlled by him, to-day by Father or Brother, tomorrow by Husband or Son, no matter how wise or mature, they are never to know the freedom and dignity that one secures in self-dependence and self support. *Girls feel all this*, though they may never utter it, far more keenly than kind Fathers imagine. (1880; my emphasis)

This is the language of oppression: "constant cribbing and crippling," control, want of freedom, lack of dignity, dependence, always mattering less or coming second. The same piece also speaks about degradation, humiliation, being pleasing, and slavery. Stanton claims that supposedly free girls share a fate with the enslaved: "There is a Procrustean bedstead ever ready for them [both], body and soul, and all mankind stand on the alert to restrain their impulses, check their aspirations, fetter their limbs, lest, in their freedom and strength, in their full development, they should take an even platform with proud man himself" (1860).

Ellen Key on Tyranny

Key, another influential intellectual who defies easy ideological description, wrote diverse works, from biographical studies of Elizabeth Barrett Browning and George Eliot to essays on socialism, education, and pacifism. She, too, was a believer in progress and a strong democrat. She has been called a "difference feminist" because of the depth of her commitment to and appreciation of women's work as mothers, a reconsideration of affective labor as socially important, creative, and potentially socially transformative (Hirdman 1991, 242). Key imagines "a Society, in which the welfare of the new generation is the centre to which all social-political plans, at heart, are aiming" (1912, 90). Because of how central children are to her socialist vision, she also imagines "fathers with time and leisure to share with the mothers the task of education and to share with them and the children the joys of the home life, as well as of the remainder of existence" (90). Parenting allows for individual expression while countering individualism.

In Key's feminism, "the fundamental condition for social equilibrium is the same as for human happiness and lies in the law of equal freedom. And this means that every one, without regard to difference between sex and sex, man and man, must have the right and the opportunity to develop and exercise his own capacities" (1912, 50–51). She endorses legal equality and, beyond that, equal development of individuality. Key advocates for the right to divorce, disdaining the marriage that "is continued under the compulsion, the distaste or the resignation of one of the two" (1911, 9). Only love, "legally sanctioned or not, is moral" (17), she contends. She sees in the status quo of her time "enmity between the sexes" rather than "mutual understanding" (27) and disapproves that what is demanded of women is to live down to "certain prejudices which are still called virtues" (42). She particularly criticizes the "archaic ideal" by which "renunciation" and "self-denial" are considered "the highest attribute of woman" (61, 53) and endorses in its stead self-assertion and self-development. Self-denial as a virtue means coming last, not placing demands or limits on others, being less than, and having fewer opportunities for voice and expression; such a virtue, like submission, is a set-up for and expression of tyranny.

Key's attention to tyranny in adult-child relations has at least three foci: the use of violence, the extent of power, and disrespect for children. On the last, she recommends that adults "respect the joys of the child, his tastes, work, and time, just as you would those of an adult" (1888, 31). Disrespect for those considered one's unequal combines inequality with disdain for the subordinated in a wholly demoralizing manner for children. Key, like the other thinkers, sees children as being quite perceptive of how they are being treated and what is thought about them, regardless of what is said by adults (2). The alternative she suggests is "to show him the same consideration, the same kind confidence one shows to an adult" (2). She asks that we look upon the child as "an entirely new soul, a real self whose first and chief right is to think over the things with which he comes in contact" (5). Full consideration and confidence are tantamount to respect.

Regarding the extent of power, Key repeatedly returns to the idea that children are constantly interfered with and rarely left in peace (2), despite the fact "that during the whole life the need of peace is never greater than in the years of childhood" (3). As she powerfully conveys, "Obstacles, interference, corrections, the whole livelong day. The child is always required to leave something alone, or to do something different, to find something different, or want something different from what he does, or finds, or wants" (3). This loss of individual liberty and of privacy is tied to tyrannical practices. "Children are treated as if their personality had no purpose of its own, as if they were made only for the pleasure, pride, and comfort of their parents" (6). This treatment as "lesser than" or "secondary to," as a means rather than an end, is again characteristic of illegitimate authority.

The third element of Key's critique of adult-child relations is her detailed criticism of corporal punishment. She provides a direct analogy with her critique of patriarchy, arguing that in moving away from violence, "parenthood must go through the same transformation as marriage" (15), which has at least progressed "from the time when man wooed with a club and when woman was regarded as the soulless property of man, only to be kept in order by blows" (15). She links physical punishment of children with torture, imprisonment, and mistreatment of animals (13). She claims it equally affects soul and body (14), even "injur[ing] her instinctive feeling of the sanctity of her body, an instinct which even in the case of a small child can be passionately profound" (19). Use of physical force is rule by fear, again, a familiar element of tyranny (19). She claims that "violent interference in the physical and psychical life of the child may have lifelong effects" (18). It negatively affects the educator/parent too: "Administering corporal punishment demoralizes and stupefies the educator, for it increases his thoughtlessness, not his patience, his brutality, not his intelligence" (16). Our use of punishment reflects a failure to see the world from the child's point of view (16), a self-centeredness more associated with illegitimate than legitimate forms of government as well as with marginalization.

Key understands that in male-female and adult-child relationships, tyranny can be exercised in an "inconsiderate and brutal manner" or by milder means (1911, 62). She defends the freedom of all from tyranny, in the name of soul freedom. "Every child," she proclaims, "is a new world" (65).

Ranking Tyranny?

While historical feminist theorists effectively use "tyranny" to describe similar and intertwined practices and structures that contribute to the subordination of women and of children, two differences also appear. One difference concerns surveillance. All four authors suggest that adult interference with and control over children's activities, especially those of girls, is more constant and extreme, in general, than is male surveillance over women's activities, appearance, and so forth, which is extreme enough. When added to the fact that children may have little independence of movement or freedom of choice regarding with whom to associate, the everyday subordination of the young may be even more dangerous and harder to sidestep than that of adult women. Perhaps by adulthood women are "trained" enough to require less constant control, or perhaps the surveillance of women's lives by public opinion makes up the difference; the matter is worth more thought.

Second, Wollstonecraft mentions that men "subjugate women, even though [they] firmly believe that [they] are acting in the manner best calculated to promote their happiness" ([1792] 1988, 5), while none of the others ascribe such positive if ultimately unhelpful motives to men. All the authors, though, make references to parental "insensibility" and good intentions. Parent tyrants are perhaps not so self-centered as are male tyrants, possibly because considerations of "care" of some sort are more built into adult-child relationships; nonetheless, parents are embedded in a hierarchical and coercive system in which the ordinary is often abusive (and Key notes that she, like the others, is talking not just about "cruelties committed by monsters [or] sex perverts" but "of conscientious, amiable parents and teachers who, with pain to themselves, fulfill what they regard as their duty to the child" [1888, 17]). The "insensible" parent tyrant shows that caring relationships can be unjust and that the goodwill of an adult provides inadequate protection for the youngster.

Resistance

Certain ideas and practices can render it difficult to perceive the conditions of women's and children's lives as oppressive and to name the behavior of their oppressors as tyrannical. There are also barriers to seeing women and children as actors resisting that tyranny.

Resistance presupposes agency—a capacity to act independently, freely make choices, or act according to one's will, alone or collectively. One obstacle to seeing children's resistance is that everything from philosophy to law to parental authority denies that minors can or should possess the requisite agency for resistance. Quite the reverse is the case, in fact, as being without such agency—being vulnerable, manipulable, dependent, and less than fully rational—is the quality often used to describe the very state of being a child. All too similarly, submissiveness, something less than full rationality, and vulnerability are culturally coded as feminine, marking women's agency, too, as undesirable if not simply impossible. In a patriarchy, to be female, or to be feminine, is to be submissive rather than noncompliant, as is being a "good" child.

Seeing women and children acting against oppression and injustice invites and requires rethinking the "nature" of "the woman" or "the child" and positively reinterpreting many acts that have been read as evidence for women's and children's lack of competence and agency. Sarah Hoagland has insightfully shown how "the concept [of] 'femininity' is used to bury and obscure female resistance, as well as female autonomy and female bonding" (1982, 85). Even descriptions of the effects of gender-based violence have been constructed to normalize "passivity" among the victimized and to obscure everyday resistance (Calgary Women's Emergency Shelter 2007). Hoagland, it turns out, has numerous historical predecessors. Resistance, then, is a second concept that can be used to show how feminist foremothers often use similar political framings in their analyses of women and of children.

Like the authors I study, I use the word "resistance" expansively to include the incalculable variety of actions across time, place, and circumstance that might rightly be captured by it. The sorts of things that must be understood as resistance include acts that make visible the veiled harms of an unequal status quo; express respect for women and/or children and whatever is associated with them, which systems of oppression devalue; attempt to disrupt sexist and/or adultist practices; deny the privileged the benefits of inequality; reject or express contempt for the submissiveness and obedience demanded of the dominated; imagine and/or create alternatives to dehumanizing policies and practices; embody a refusal to believe in or abide by mandated inferiority or exist outside dictated norms of "inferior" behavior; distance oneself from or minimize complicity with practices of domination; demand or create space and voice for alternative viewpoints and stigmatized groups; and eschew physical, verbal, and sexual violence against the subjugated, replacing it with respect.

It is essential that we reckon with the limits and effects on resistance imposed by systems of inequality and with the distinct impact of local and individual circumstances and possibilities; to do otherwise is to participate in the erasure of crucial actions and actors and to distort our understanding of the political. In discussing the resistance to tyranny embodied and employed by women and children, I again use the works of Wollstonecraft and Stanton but also add Beauvoir to the mix.

Mary Wollstonecraft on Resistance

Wollstonecraft has been charged with failing to see women as actors for their own liberation (Poovey 1984, 79)—a claim that is overstated, at best. She focuses on and criticizes women's submissiveness, for sure, but her targets are the authors (Jean-Jacques Rousseau and Edmund Burke, most prominently) who suggest that weakness and passivity in women are natural traits that lead to mutually satisfying relationships with men and contribute to the welfare of society. Her preferred woman, in contrast, is lively, rational, and critical rather than conformist, pleasing to others, and obedient. Wollstonecraft clearly recommends resistance to prejudice and inequality and provides a number of examples of how one can challenge, criticize, and create.

By Wollstonecraft's standards, women resist patriarchy when they act as autonomous moral agents and "exercise control of both the external—financial, educational, and political—circumstances of their lives and the direction of their own affections" (MacKenzie 1993, 36). Revolt for women might take the form of an independent source of income, authorship, or political participation. Wollstonecraft had no dearth of real-life female action figures. She knew, and knew the works of, many intellectually and socially active women, including Mary Hays and Catharine Macaulay. Wollstonecraft's women distance themselves from oppression on a daily basis by acting and treating one another as active, self-respecting, sensible human beings instead of as fragile, feminine male fantasies.

Wollstonecraft knew that actual women, in addition to her fictional and aspirational figures, resist within the unequal, patriarchal world they inhabit. First, Wollstonecraft observes and writes about the French Revolution, in which women were central actors. Readers of *An Historical and Moral View of the Origin and Progress of the French Revolution and the Effect It Has Produced in Europe* confront women in a variety of roles exhibiting nonsubmissive traits. Women are shown "resist[ing] oppression," being among "the rational few," and exhibiting "public spirit" and "independence of spirit" ([1975] 2016). Second, although simply refusing to be subordinate or to exercise arbitrary authority is a more thorough and promising form of resistance, and although tyranny is always problematic, some private cunning and tyrannical acts by women are, according to Wollstonecraft, examples of rebellion. In opposition to the demand that women serve and submit, and when legitimate roads to direct action are mostly closed, these acts are attempts to grab *some* voice, *some* power. They are rejections of blind subordination to the authority of men. Third, in her response to anti-feminist fear of "masculine women," Wollstonecraft suggests that what these people are wrongly negatively reacting to is rational women exercising human virtues that are mistakenly defined as masculine. She sees such women frequently, then, and encourages her readers to join this revisioning.

Turning to her numerous works about or for children, Wollstonecraft similarly targets authors and practices that endow girls with natural inclinations and talents that suit them for indoor, sedate, domestic play and chores and that eschew educating them for much else. She tracks girls' lives from infancy and insists to parents and educators that "knowledge should be gradually imparted, and flow more from example than teaching" ([1791] 1972, xviii). Such a process equips children physically, emotionally, and mentally to act autonomously and resist when resistance is appropriate. Wollstonecraft overtly participates in the training she endorses. In *The Female Reader*, for example, she familiarizes young readers with a selection of reading passages that make visible the conflicts and controversies that arise from women's prescribed roles, rather than celebrating those roles or calling them "natural" (Hanley 2013), preparing them to counter their oppression. In *Original Stories*, Wollstonecraft's tutor Mrs. Mason instructs her female charges, "It is always a proof of superior sense to bear with slight inconveniences, and even trifling injuries, without complaining or contesting about them. The soul reserves its firmness for great occasions, and then it acts a decided part" ([1791] 1972, 15). Even children can experience great occasions when the soul firmly rejects injury and oppression. Mrs. Mason teaches kindness and consideration above all. She reminds children of their dependence and teaches that, in fact, "we are all dependent on each other" (71).

Wollstonecraft does not imagine that every girl eventually simply succumbs to the wealth of forces at work in her subordination. Most notably, she portrays "a girl, whose spirits have not been damped by inactivity, or innocence tainted by false shame, [who] will always be a romp" ([1792] 1988,

43). In fact, she realizes "that most of the women, in the circle of my observation, who have acted like rational creatures, or shewn any vigour of intellect, have accidentally been allowed to run wild—as some of the elegant formers of the fair sex would insinuate" (43). Apparently less "well-behaved" girls *do* sometimes make history.

Resistance benefits from experience and education but does not require them, according to Wollstonecraft. It only requires disgust or frustration with being tyrannized and some small space in which to give voice to that disapproval or to create and nurture something/someone else. Opportunities arise daily, if one looks beyond social revolutions for understandings of resistance. Opposition is challenging, however, because of the presence of tyrants and internalized oppression, which chafes at first at becoming exactly that dangerous and undesired person about whom one has been warned. Too, women and children are encouraged to seek the seductive "rewards" that a fragile femininity and charming childlike presence bestows. However, it turns out that training in obedience and submission is never entirely effective, and a variety of relationships often unexpectedly provide means, motive, and opportunity for opposition. Though resistance is difficult and sometimes dangerous, Wollstonecraft portrays youthful and adult female resisters as being happier and freer than are those who conform and submit.

Elizabeth Cady Stanton on Resistance

Women enduring patriarchal oppression have the right to resist it. As Stanton writes, "We did assemble to protest against a form of government existing without the consent of the governed, to declare our right to be free as man is free" (1848c). More could not be at stake. After naming certain power relationships and structures as being tyrannical toward women, Stanton recommends taking action to bring about change. Two ideas about resistance emerge in the "Declaration of Sentiments" (1848b).

First, "Sentiments" (like the "Declaration of Independence," which provided a format and some content) asserts that preceding revolutionary action may be a stage during which the oppressed should "suffer, while evils are sufferable," a time when "patience" is a political virtue. But if matters may become intolerable, the oppressed have the right—and even duty—to resist. Resistance then becomes a political virtue. This stage is defined by the presence of tyranny, as previously described; at least some "women do feel themselves aggrieved, oppressed, and fraudulently deprived of their most sacred rights" (ibid.).

Second, "Sentiments" reveals that those who resist are wise to "anticipate no small amount of misconception, misrepresentation, and ridicule" (ibid.), despite the fact that the wrongs against women may involve the trampling of precisely those rights professed and celebrated by those doing the trampling. On this point, "Sentiments" is unfortunately prescient, as the negative public reactions to it attest (although even Stanton expressed some surprise "that what seemed to us so timely, so rational, and so sacred, should be a subject for sarcasm and ridicule" [(1898) 1987, 149]). Knowing that "every allusion to the degraded and inferior position occupied by woman all over the world, has ever been met by scorn and abuse" (1848a), she recommends that women "buckle on the armor that can best resist the keenest weapons of the enemy—contempt and ridicule" (1848c).

Stanton continued throughout her life to resist and to expand the opportunities for others to do so. "Woman herself must do this work," she writes, "for woman alone can understand the height and the depth, the length and the breadth of her own degradation and woe. Man cannot speak for us" (1848a). She urges persistence in the effort—"our struggle shall be hard and long," she again prophetically warns—and advocates using a variety of tactics: "the pens, the tongues, the fortunes, the indomitable wills of many women" must be brought to bear (ibid.).

One form of opposition Stanton advocates is withdrawing support for inequality. For example, she critiques "education societies" that provide for the education of young men but not of young women:

> [Men] can easily secure an education. Whilst woman poor and friendless robbed of all her rights, oppressed on all sides, civilly, religiously, and socially, must needs go ignorant herself—the idea of such a being working day and night with her needle stitch, stitch, stitch . . . to educate a great strong lug of man. . . . The last time an appeal of this kind was made to me I told the young lady I would send her to school a year if she would go, but I would never again give one red cent to the education society, and I do hope every christian woman who has the least regard for her sex will make the same resolve. (ibid.)[3]

Stanton counsels activism on issues from parenting, dress, slavery, temperance, suffrage, and education to religion, domestic violence, employment, property rights, and divorce. She advises women to read, write, ask questions, demystify, reinterpret, give speeches, collaborate, organize, petition, engage in civil disobedience, "educate women into rebellion," go to conventions, work with other progressive movements, subject "superstition" to "reason and free thought" (1860), and rear children with more freedom and less violence. A regular attendee of meetings and conventions for the abolition of slavery and for women's rights, she *saw* resistance regularly.

Stanton also claims space for children's legitimate resistance to the tyranny to which they are daily subjected. She opens the radical possibility that some things strongly and negatively associated with children, such as having tantrums, "[a]re really justifiable acts of rebellion against the tyranny of those in authority" ([1898] 1987, 12). She sees young children, like women, justifiably resisting illegitimate authority, even in the acts usually used as evidence of their inferiority and irrationality and used to justify power over them.

Girls in "rebellion against the tyranny of those in authority" repeatedly appear in Stanton's writing, even though it focuses on their relentless and debasing training in a limiting femininity. In "Our Girls," for example, we meet "young girls [who] pine . . . for the stimulus of work and wages, something to widen their ambitions and love of distinction" (1880). There is an eighteen-year-old "full of genius, force and fire," who wants "to be educated for the stage," who gives "marvelous" private theatrical performances (ibid.); and a "proud girl [who] repudiates these invidious [sex] distinctions, laughs at the supercilious airs these boys affect and braces up her mind to resist their tyranny of sex. She feels she is the peer of any boy she knows" (ibid.). Another girl graduating high school "has outstripped the foremost in sciences and languages" and is still ambitious, still "has a will of her own and desires the dignity of independence and self-support" (ibid.). Despite the general despair over the perishing, miserable girls that informs the piece, the rebel never disappears from its pages. In fact, she continues on as an adult, perhaps becoming, as the essay ends, "the girl who earns her bread or makes for herself a name[, who] has all the boy has to surmount and these artificial barriers of law and custom in addition" (143), or the one who "wak[es] up to the degradation of these [wedding] ceremonies" (157), or who becomes another Anna Dickinson, Maria Mitchell, Harriet Martineau, Elizabeth Barret Browning, George Sand, or Harriet Beecher Stowe (the list is lengthy), "in spite" of everything (ibid.).

Stanton brings an even greater everyday quality to our understanding of resistance and introduces a vast range of issues on which to act as well as a diversity of strategies that can be employed. She insists that those who are subject to domination have the right, power, and knowledge required to oppose the status quo. Stanton makes visible not only how resistance is used as evidence for continued authority over the discontented but also how to prepare for backlash. Like Wollstonecraft, she sees how tyranny inevitably leaves some room for the acts of resistance by women and children that speak from and to the better parts of ourselves as individuals and members of communities.

Simone de Beauvoir on Resistance

Considering resistance in the thought of Beauvoir allows us to see how yet another strain of feminist political philosophy in another time period joins in treating the resistance of women and of children seriously. Beauvoir was yet one more wildly prolific author, writing on a multitude of subjects (including aging, violence, inequality, and freedom) in a variety of forms. Her own history of activism includes "opposition to France's war in Algeria, participation on the 1966 Russell Tribunal to bring war crimes charges against the United States' actions in Vietnam, work with young French Maoists in the 1970s, and penning and signing the Manifesto of the 343 for abortion rights in France in 1971" (Marso 2016, 21).

Beauvoir writes about women and men who are "aggressive . . . adversaries" of feminists as well as those who "champion their cause," and in *The Second Sex* ([1949] 2009), she studies both groups in different historical periods, within and across various political traditions and divisions. Thus, while Wollstonecraft's and Stanton's accounts preserve memories of their female contemporaries who resist, Beauvoir gives such figures more of a history.

Beauvoir shows that one can find examples of feminist activism as well as examples of accomplished women in virtually every time and place. Different issues are more pressing and have greater legitimacy in various locales and eras. Progress is often uneven according to issue and across classes of women, as recognized in historical and contemporary calls for a truly inclusive feminist agenda. Feminist victories often "arouse[] new attacks" against women ([1949] 2009, 99), as Stanton, too, documents, because the norms are so entrenched and the interests involved are so invested. The constructed tension between women's productive and reproductive roles is especially enduring, as is that between women of different classes. As Wollstonecraft and Stanton also note, women's training in pleasing femininity does not readily create feminist rebels, but women's experiences of subordination do. As Beauvoir summarizes, "The woman problem has always been a man's problem" (118–119). A "transformation in masculine ethics" is required to complement the work of women activists, and feminism needs to be an ambitious, bold, autonomous movement (119).

In *Memoirs of a Dutiful Daughter* ([1958] 2005), Beauvoir says of her youth, "I refused to submit to that intangible force: words. What I resented was that some casual phrase beginning 'You must . . .' or 'You mustn't . . .' could ruin all my plans and poison all my happiness. . . . I seemed to be confronted everywhere by force, never by necessity" (12). She finds that her own "refus[al] to submit" is not, in fact, uncommon, as she turns to study childhood. As with Stanton and Wollstonecraft, most children's resistance that Beauvoir documents is among girls. In each case, the reason given is the greater freedom allowed boys than girls, in play, education, dress, and duties, meaning that boys have less oppression against which to react. Further, rebellion by boys is "boys being boys"—often acceptable or tolerated rather than seen as troubling and needing urgently to be squelched. Again like Stanton, Beauvoir often reinterprets acts used to demean childhood and justify authority over the young as acts of resistance, from "scenes and rages" to giggling, which she calls "one of the most common forms of adolescent contestation" ([1949] 2005, 421).[4] "It is clear," she explains, "that all the faults for which the adolescent girl is reproached merely express her situation" (429).

The sheer number of times that resisting girls appear in *The Second Sex* is astonishing. So is the variety of ways in which they express their distaste for the limits imposed upon them because they are young and female.[5] The earliest examples that Beauvoir mentions are of very young girls drawn to stories of "fairies, mermaids, and nymphs who escape male domination" (348). As girls come to see their mothers' inferior stations, rebellion increases: "She dedicates a cult to women who have escaped feminine servitude: actresses, writers, and professors; she gives herself enthusiastically to sports and to studies, she climbs trees, tears her clothes, tries to compete with boys" (357). Later, we see a girl "annoyed at being oppressed by rules of decency, bothered by her clothes, enslaved to cleaning tasks, held back in all her enthusiasms" (357).

Perhaps because Beauvoir views the consequences of training for submissiveness as cumulative, and the pressure to conform and girls' powerlessness increasing as she grows, forms of rebellion include some that are self-destructive, and her work does not so much end with a recalling of famous women resisters as with some degree of consent to femininity. Yet girls' rebellion against, or at least ambivalence toward, femininity never completely disappears: "At times she does her hair, she uses makeup, dresses in organdy, she takes pleasure in appearing attractive and seductive; she also wants to exist for herself and not only for others, at other times, she throws on old formless dresses, unbecoming trousers; there is a whole part of her that criticizes seduction and considers it as giving in" (421). Also omnipresent are acts "affirming one's autonomy arrogantly . . . [and] rejecting the established order as well as defying its guardians" (424). Women do not so easily lose touch entirely with their younger rebellious selves.

Beauvoir, like the others, sees children's (especially girls') resistance as a reaction to both the conditions of their childhood and their "future enslavement." As long as inequality is the dominant condition of the status quo, resistance will nearly always be accompanied by some degree of going along with the stream. Resistance, however, like conformity, has positive cumulative effects.

Common Ground

Wollstonecraft, Stanton, and Beauvoir all develop and apply their philosophical and political insights to the lives of women and children. Children do not trigger the sort of reaction in feminist thought that they so often do for others who cannot make them "fit" theories made only for (some) adults. All three clearly see the young as agents despite their age and oppressive circumstances.

The three authors also show that the analogy between the two systems of oppression is extremely useful, revealing critical lessons about power and freedom, yet it is not without limits. Children arrive in a world not of their making, and their opportunities to collaborate with each other in opposition are more restricted. Nonetheless, resistance is essential rather than futile, for goods from authenticity to future freedom are at stake. None hesitates a moment to endorse resistance, for children or women. Instead, they focus on where one might resist, how to resist more effectively, and how to prepare for backlash. Given the way that resistance by young people is often treated today as a psychological disorder, or the bane of existence for parents and teachers, the seriousness and thoughtfulness with which our authors consider it are truly remarkable and completely consistent with their analysis of similarly "arrogant" acts by women. In the end, they celebrate the spirit that dares to raise questions about inequality.

From all five thinkers considered in this chapter, we see a history in which gender was not treated in isolation from age (or class or race) and in which questions of inequality were linked to a great many other political and philosophical issues, from war and peace to individual and community. We misrepresent these thinkers when we extract their feminist writings from the body of their work, and we lessen the power of feminism when we ignore their ideas about multiple, intersecting forms of inequality.

Concluding Thoughts

As Corinne Field reads Wollstonecraft, she concludes, "Wollstonecraft placed girls and girlhood at the very center of feminist concerns." Field demands, "It is time for historians of childhood and youth to claim Mary Wollstonecraft's *Vindication of the Rights of Woman* (1792) as a key source for understanding the intersection of age and gender in eighteenth-century Britain and France" (2011, 199). Likewise, Kiersten Nieuwejaar notes that despite the way Jane Addams's "alternative visions for schooling . . . highlight her own understanding of education as a social endeavor" (2015, 12), still, "much of the scholarship has not been written with her educational philosophy solely in mind"; consequently, "Addams'[s] ideas about education remain largely disconnected from each other" in the secondary literature (2). In yet another case, Clémentine Beauvais assert that "Beauvoir's theorization of childhood . . . has more often been mentioned than studied in depth" and that her "thoughts on childhood remain fragmented, and sometimes seemingly disconnected from her existentialist thinking" in the literature about her. Such neglect is misguided, because reflection on childhood "undergirds [her] existentialist ethics" and constitutes a "major contribution to existentialism" (2015, 329). The pattern is compelling. More work, like that which I have attempted in this chapter, is clearly called for.

A cabined view of feminism has contributed to our having limited knowledge of feminist thinking about a great number of subjects; childhood is but one of them. Surely, too, childhood is only one topic where we poorly understand (or even read), or make use of, earlier feminists. Still, it is an especially important subject, for, as the authors studied here argue, the ways in which adults understand, educate, and relate with children have life-long consequences for children and adults. Further, given the intensity and success with which feminism is portrayed by its opponents as anti-family, knowing about more thoughtful, egalitarian, and dignifying feminist reflections on childhood and adult-child relations cannot but be beneficial. And since repeatedly losing our histories means that feminists are often tasked with re-creating the wheel, reclaiming and holding on to historical feminist reflections on childhood allows us to build on and even surpass the work of those who came before us.

There are innumerable reasons for feminism to keep children on its agendas and to recover its history on subjects related to young people (which at least include the silencing of, discrimination against, and exploitation of young people based on their age and such factors as sex, disability, and ethnicity; physical, emotional, and sexual violence against the young; the content, accessibility, and methods of education for democracy; and rights and opportunities to play, to contribute, and to have an adequate standard of living and a safe environment). And feminism has many distinctive tools with which to study and challenge the treatment and status of children. Its experience with the social construction of gender can fully illuminate the understanding of childhood "as a socially and culturally shaped category" (Helleiner, Caputo, and Downe 2001, 135). It has done hard work in other arenas that enable it to show analogies between the lived conditions of women and of children and still treat both groups as heterogeneous. It is all too aware of the tactics and costs behind "glorifying" the innocence of the subordinated and "protecting" them into dependence and vulnerability. It knows how to reveal those who have been treated as unproductive and incapable as, in fact, active and creative contributors to multiple communities. It understands how children, like women, can become tools in battles that are not fundamentally about them, at considerable cost to them. Nonetheless, repeated calls still appear across disciplines, arguing for more feminist attention to the oppression and liberation of these two groups, independently and together. While much work remains undone, there is also much upon which we can build.

The plight of most children around the globe, especially girls, remains of immense concern, in places experiencing conflict, environmental catastrophes, and other crises and in "normal," everyday lives.[6] And children continue to fight and talk back, as individuals and together, too, now often in feminist settings, about their lives, their feminisms, and our world.[7] Listening to and learning from those younger, as we expect them to listen to and learn from those older, have long been part of feminist praxis and require sustained and creative attention.

Neglect or superficial treatment of the young in social and political theory deprives adults of the insights of children, closes children out of epistemic communities, lets citizens avoid truly difficult questions about power and democracy, and allows institutions and practices involved most deeply in children's lives to escape certain kinds of oversight and critique. It leaves relatively untouched unsatisfactory defenses of the silencing of the young in multiple arenas. Historical feminist thinkers provide us with multiple models of how we can do better and show that a liberatory approach to childhood is, indeed, an integral aspect of feminism.

NOTES

1. The pattern continues today; for example, Gloria Anzaldúa wrote of her own childhood in *Borderlands/La Frontera: The New Mestiza* (1987) and authored three children's books.

2. In stark contrast, Audre Lorde discusses the power of "the *yes* within ourselves, our deepest cravings." Do we fear children's desires and "keep[] them suspect" (1978, 57)? At what cost?

3. Elizabeth Cady Stanton also refused to vow obedience at her wedding, and she withdrew from Lane Theological Seminary after "a student-sponsored debate over slavery raised the ire of the institution's board of trustees, and a gag order was issued" (Rogers, n.d.).

4. In *Living a Feminist Life*, Sara Ahmed has a lovely discussion about the resistance that is revealed by giggling "at the wrong moments" or laughing "in a totally

inappropriate manner." She says, "It can be rebellious to be happy when you are not supposed to be" (2017, 63).

5. I find this reminiscent of Frederick Douglass's autobiography, in which the enslaved, including children, resist on virtually every page.

6. According to UNESCO, in 2016, 263 million children, adolescents, and youth—mostly girls—were out of school (http://uis.unesco.org/sites/default/files/documents /fs48-one-five-children-adolescents-youth-out-school-2018-en.pdf); UNICEF says that around three million children die each year from undernutrition (https://www .unicef.org/nutrition/); and CARE adds that 21 percent of girls (40 percent in poor countries) marry before the age of eighteen, while 76 percent of those who are forced to leave their home due to crises, and the majority of the 1.4 billion living in poverty, are women and children (https://care.org/our-work/health/). In 2019, 17 percent of children in the United States lived below the federal poverty level, which is about $25,000 a year for a family of four (https://datacenter.kidscount.org).

7. See, for example, the European Camp of Young Feminists "Manifesto" (2011) and the pan-Canadian young feminist gathering Waves of Resistance "Manifesto" (2008). There have been *encuentros* of young feminists in Latin American since 1998.

REFERENCES

Beauvais, Clémentine. 2015. "Simone de Beauvoir and the Ambiguity of Childhood." *Paragraph: A Journal of Modern Critical Theory* 38 (3): 329–346.

Beauvoir, Simone de. [1949] 2009. *The Second Sex*. Translated by Constance Borde and Sheila Malovany-Chevallier. New York: Vintage.

———. [1958] 2005. *Memoirs of a Dutiful Daughter*. Translated by James Kirkup. New York: Harper Perennial Classics.

Botting, Eileen Hunt. 2016. "Mary Wollstonecraft, Children's Human Rights, and Animal Ethics." *The Social and Political Philosophy of Mary Wollstonecraft*, edited by Sandrine Berges and Alan Coffee, 92–117. Oxford: Oxford University Press.

Burman, Erica, and Jackie Stacey. 2010. "The Child and Childhood in Feminist Theory." *Feminist Theory* 11 (3): 227–240.

Calgary Women's Emergency Shelter. 2007. "Honouring Resistance: How Women Resist Abuse in Intimate Relationships." http://www.faaas.org/assets/cwesresistance bookletfinalweb.pdf.

"Elizabeth Cady Stanton." n.d. *Wikipedia*. https://en.wikipedia.org/wiki/Elizabeth _Cady_Stanton.

Field, Corinne. 2011. "'Made Women of When They Are Mere Children: Mary Wollstonecraft's Critique of Eighteenth-Century Girlhood." *Journal of the History of Childhood and Youth* 4, no. 2 (Spring): 197–222.

Firestone, Shulamith. 1970. *The Dialectic of Sex: The Case for Feminist Revolution*. New York: Bantam Books.

Ginzberg, Lori D. 1994. "'The Hearts of Your Readers Will Shudder': Fanny Wright, Infidelity, and American Freethought." *American Quarterly* 46, no. 2 (June): 195–226.

Hanley, Kirsten. 2013. *Mary Wollstonecraft, Pedagogy, and the Practice of Feminism*. New York: Routledge.

Helleiner, Jane. 1999. "Toward a Feminist Anthropology of Childhood." *Atlantis* 24, no. 1 (Fall/Winter): 27–38.

Helleiner, Jane, Virginia Caputo, and Pamela Downe. 2001. "Anthropology, Feminism and Childhood Studies." *Anthropologica* 43 (2): 135–137, 139–141.

Hirdman, Yvonne. 1991. "The State of Women's History in Sweden: An Overview." In *Writing Women's History: International Perspectives*, edited by Karen M. Offen, Ruth Roach Pierson, and Jane Rendall, 239–258. Houndmills, UK: Macmillan.

Hoagland, Sarah. 1982. "Femininity, Resistance and Sabotage." In *Femininity, Masculinity, and Androgyny*, edited by M. Vettering-Braggin, 85–99. Totowa, NJ: Littlefield, Adams.

Kendall, Kathleen Edgerton, and Jeanne Y. Fisher. 1974. "Frances Wright on Women's Rights: Eloquence versus Ethos." *Quarterly Journal of Speech* 60 (1): 58–68.

Key, Ellen. 1888. *The Education of the Child*. Whitefish, MT: Kessinger Legacy Reprints.

———. 1911. *The Morality of Women*. Chicago: Ralph Fletcher Seymour.

———. 1912. *The Woman Movement*. New York: G. P. Putnam's Sons. http://www.readanybook.com/online/322214.

Kissel, Susan. 1993. *In Common Cause: The "Conservative" Frances Trollope and the "Radical" Frances Wright*. Bowling Green, OH: Bowling Green State University Press.

Ladd, Rosalind Ekman. 1995. *Children's Rights Re-visited: Philosophical Readings*. Boston: Wadsworth Publishing.

Lorde, Audre. 1978. *Sister Outsider*. Freedom, CA: Crossing Press.

MacKenzie, Catriona. 1993. "Reason and Sensibility: The Ideal of Women's Self-Governance in the Writings of Mary Wollstonecraft." *Hypatia* 8, no. 4 (Autumn): 35–55.

Marso, Lori J., ed. 2016. "Simone de Beauvoir." In *Fifty-One Key Feminist Thinkers*, 21–25. New York: Routledge.

Nieuwejaar, Kiersten. 2015. "Learning through Living Together: The Educational Philosophy of Jane Addams." Ph.D. diss., Columbia University.

Poovey, Mary. 1984. *The Proper Lady and the Woman Writer*. Chicago: University of Chicago Press.

Rogers, Dorothy. n.d. "Elizabeth Cady Stanton." *Internet Encyclopedia of Philosophy*. http://www.iep.utm.edu/stanton/.

Stanton, Elizabeth Cady. 1848a. "Address on Woman's Rights." https://susanb.org/wp-content/uploads/2018/12/Elizabeth-Cady-Stanton-Sept.-1848.pdf.

———. 1848b. "The Declaration of Sentiments." https://www.pbs.org/kenburns/not-for-ourselves-alone/declaration-of-sentiments.

———. 1848c. "Seneca Falls Keynote Address." http://www.greatamericandocuments.com/speeches/stanton-seneca-falls.html.

———. 1854. "Address to the Legislature of New York." https://www.nps.gov/wori/learn/historyculture/address-to-the-new-york-legislature-1854.htm.

———. 1860. "Speech to the Anniversary of the American Anti-Slavery Society." https://speakingwhilefemale.co/anti-slavery-stanton1/.

———. 1880. "Our Girls." http://voicesofdemocracy.umd.edu/stanton-our-girls-speech-text/.

———. (1898) 1987. *Eighty Years and More: Reminiscences, 1815–1897.* Boston: Northeastern University Press.

Thorne, Barrie. 1987. "Re-visioning Women and Social Change: Where Are the Children?" *Gender and Society* 1, no. 1 (March): 85–109.

Turner, Susan, and Gareth Matthews. 1998. *The Philosopher's Child: Critical Perspectives in the Western Tradition.* Rochester, NY: University of Rochester Press.

Wollstonecraft, Mary. (1791) 1972. *Original Stories from Real Life; Calculated to Regulate the Affections, and Form the Mind to Truth and Goodness.* Folcroft Library Editions.

———. (1792) 1988. *A Vindication of the Rights of Woman*, 2nd ed. New York: W. W. Norton.

———. (1795) 2016. *An Historical and Moral View of the Origin and Progress of the French Revolution and the Effect It Has Produced in Europe.* London: J. Johnson. http://oll.libertyfund.org/titles/wollstonecraft-an-historical-and-moral-view-of-the -origin-and-progress-of-the-french-revolution.

Wright, Frances. (1834) 2004. *Reason, Religion, and Morals.* Amherst, NY: Humanity Books.

Two Models of Feminist Childhoods

Emma Goldman and Charlotte Perkins Gilman

The previous chapter showed how a diverse cast of historical feminist thinkers all understood certain attitudes and practices of adults toward children as oppressive and tyrannical, and how they all read a range of childhood acts as rightly and matter-of-factly in the tradition of political resistance. Overall, I emphasized that feminists who problematized the unequal relationship between women and men also, for related and intersecting feminist reasons, problematized the unequal relationship between children and adults and analyzed both sets of relations with equal rigor and the same analytic tools. That is a history worth remembering, celebrating, learning from, and building on. Their concerns about and commitments to the young, we saw, cross centuries and political philosophies. And there is even more to this history.

In this chapter, I delve more deeply into two other historical critiques of age-based inequality that give rise to two different models of a feminist childhood and that highlight some different features of adult-child relations. I turn, that is, from a primary focus on common ground among historical feminists to point out some diversity in their thought as well by using the writings of Charlotte Perkins Gilman (1865–1935) and Emma Goldman (1869–1940), who lived at almost the exact same time, the first exclusively and the other primarily in the United States.

In what follows, my goal is to make their visions regarding childhood clear—divergent visions that nonetheless begin with somewhat similar critiques of then-current (and perhaps still-dominant) educational and childrearing practices. To get at these visions, I first ask what each one sees as the nature of the child, especially regarding the child's moral and intellectual life, that most disputed terrain. In the second major section, I look more at the social life and capacities of the young, including ways in which children inter-act with others and with their environments and might be considered political actors and gauges. As I develop both sections, I keep an eye focused on what each author finds most objectionable in contemporary practices and what, for both, constitutes a more ideal (and feminist) childhood. In the end, I hope to be able to present what distinctively anarchist feminist and socialist feminist perspectives have to teach us about respect for children and childhood.

I am drawn to this particular comparison for a couple of reasons. The first necessary feature, as I document in a moment, is that these two figures, like those considered in the last chapter, *talk* about young people. They fit into that tradition that I am recovering of feminist theorists who tackle the relationship between those younger and those older in the same political and philosophical ways in which they tackle the relations between races, classes, and sexes. Unlike most writers in that hallowed patriarchal canon in which I was so well trained, feminist theorists do not treat children or age-based rela-tions as beyond or outside what deserves serious, sustained, political analysis. Even more, these two are deeply troubled by the treatment young people received and the conditions in which they lived—it often seems even to drive their analysis of other topics and so warrants analysis. Again, when I talk about a feminist tradition of analyzing adult-child relations, I do not mean just that these thinkers take the tools and perspectives of feminism and apply them to childhood; they also develop these tools and perspectives in part by analyzing the conditions in which young people live.

I am drawn to the two for yet another reason. Because Gilman is asso-ciated with socialism and Goldman with anarchism, I came to my initial reading of them expecting them to have some starkly different angles and conclusions, just as we today would expect, say, a liberal feminist and a critical race feminist to differ. There are indeed differences, as we will see, but, to my surprise, there is also a great deal of overlap, especially about some of the wrongs done to children. I want to make sense of this similarity. I think in that overlap, we can see some of what is distinctly *feminist* in socialist and anarchist considerations of young people, while in the differences, the socialism and the anarchism come through more strongly. The common ground, then, builds on the last chapter by continuing to explore what historical feminist analysis of childhood is all about, this time in even greater detail. But the differences, especially about what should replace current practices and why, also remind us that feminist consideration of children is informed by and informs the political more generally and that the directions we choose to work in as we strive for more respectful relations between adults and children rely on the solid grounding and inspiring vision that come with political theorizing. In which directions should we coherently and consciously travel, and why? Two possible answers—and there are, of course, others—are laid out here.

The final reason I turn to these two is that both of them draw me in when they write about the young. It is impossible not to feel their passion for the topic of childhood and their utter despair and anger over the mistreatment of youth, which match my own. I see that they get so much right, too, and are so perceptive and often subtle. Yet because they also travel in some different directions, I feel called either to find some way to negotiate between them, perhaps by finding that the choice is context-specific, or to make a decision about which carves the wiser, more compassionate path—the path that will lead to those goals I keep constantly in mind of greater voice and respect for young people. Thus, I take my readers through what they say, using their works extensively, and then compare the two and consider where they lead us. But first, I offer a little background on these two towering authors and activists.

Goldman and Gilman

Gilman, largely self-educated, was a lecturer on various social reforms; author of a vast collection of fiction, nonfiction, essays, and poetry; and perhaps "the preeminent feminist intellectual of the Progressive era" (Rosenberg 2010, 1165). She "had an enormous reputation in her lifetime" and worked "to create a cohesive, integrated body of thought that combined feminism and socialism" (Lane 1990, ix).[1] She wanted to restructure the home and revise social values; revisiting traditional female and male virtues and tasks was part of both, as was reevaluating what was associated with adulthood and childhood. Setting up the interesting contrast with Goldman I pursue here, Gilman notes that "people . . . confuse Socialism with Anarchism," yet the two "are absolute opposites" ([1935] 1963, 320).

Gilman writes at great length about children. In addition to her undeservedly understudied *Concerning Children* (1900), Gilman builds a utopian society in *Herland* (1915) around reformed practices of childrearing and dedicates chapters to the subject of childhood in everything from *The Home: Its Work and Influence* (1903) to her autobiographical *The Living of Charlotte Perkins Gilman* (1935). Like Jane Addams, whose Hull-House she visited a number of times, she "tend[s] to focus on children" (Grimm 1997, 47); as Zona Gale notes, "One of her greatest social contributions is her interpretation of the needs of childhood" (1963, xxv). Despite all of this, amazingly, "Gilman has not" often enough "been viewed within the context of progressive education, early childhood education, or citizenship education" (De Simone 1995), indicating a remarkable gap in the literature about childhood and Gilman.

The similarly self-educated Goldman was also renowned in her day, "one of America's greatest orators," as well as, unfortunately, "one of its most despised anarchist agitators" (Denman 1977, 28). She is rightly reputed to have attempted a deeper integration of women's concerns into anarchism, the movement "which became her lifelong home" (Ferguson 2011, 1). She edited and wrote for the journal *Mother Earth* (which she founded in 1906 and worked on until 1918), as Gilman did for *The Forerunner* (which she edited from 1909 to 1916). Like Gilman, Goldman lectured to untold thousands and mostly eked out a living from writing and lecturing.

The centrality of childhood in the writings of Goldman is less obvious than is its ubiquity in Gilman's work; in fact, my 2009 chapter on Goldman's views about children (which I incorporate and expand a good deal here) is, I believe, among the first to elaborate on and make that topic appear vital to her political thought.[2] I think it possible to shine a light on this aspect of her work without "de-radicalizing her politics" (Ferguson 2011, 9), as some fear would be the case. Goldman does write several (overlapping) essays firmly centered on children: "The Social Importance of the Modern School," "The Child and Its Enemies," "La Ruche," and "Francisco Ferrer and the Modern School." Further, she mentions children in nearly everything she writes. Children are always, it seems, present in her landscape. Whether she is writing about prostitution or patriotism, employment or education, marriage or morality, syndicalism or the state, the relevance of these topics to children, and of children to these topics, comes through repeatedly. "Goldman care[s] deeply for children" and is drawn to the question of "how to avoid the corruption of children in a society whose basic fabric is corrupt" (Denman 1977, 28).

Despite my antipathy to biography, an antipathy rooted in the way that biography dominates the sparse attention given to women thinkers, it is worth noting that Gilman and Goldman both had difficult childhoods. Gilman, reared in various spots in the northeastern United States, had a mostly absent father and a mother who didn't believe in physical affection. Goldman, growing up Jewish in imperial Russia, had a frustrated, violent father and a mother who was "dynamic, intelligent, but embittered . . . [and] generally withdrawn in depression" (Falk 1990, 11), and she, too, longed for more affection (Wexler 1984, 11). Both received a sporadic, patchwork education, primarily due to multiple moves and their families' need for them to start making money when still young, as both, especially Goldman, were reared in economically fragile families (Gilman's extended family had resources that her immediate family lacked). Both were avid readers and self-motivated learners. Each was involved in or aware of educational projects: Goldman, for example, visited a number of schools when she revisited Russia later in life and was a co-creator of the Ferrer Center in New York City, which included "a Modern School, part of an international network of non-authoritarian, joyous learning environments based on the educational philosophy of martyred Spanish educator Francisco Ferrer" (Ferguson 2011, 87). Gilman was familiar with progressive educational reforms, such as those enacted at Chicago's Hull-House, and for a time she supported herself by teaching art. Though it was said of Gilman, it may be equally true of Goldman that her erratic education was connected to her "stark originality and jolting freshness. She sees with an uncontaminated eye and brain, because her ideas were never filtered through a conventional educational process, pounded and bludgeoned into a form acceptable to conventional wisdom" (Lane 1990, 232). Both writers, that is to say, escaped some of the injurious aspects of the educational systems they condemned.

Precisely pinpointing the variety of socialism and of anarchism to which our figures adhered is an impossible task. Each school splinters into many, like a kaleidoscope (for example, "within the anarchism 'family' there are mutualists, collectivists, communists, federalists, individualists, socialists, syndicalists, feminists, as well as many others" [Brown 2003, 106]), and easily available, popular definitions are never based on the ideas of women thinkers. Nonetheless, let me lay out a few essentials of these schools of thought to which each was most attracted and bound.

Goldman embraced anarchism because she was "convinced that the political and economic organization of modern society was fundamentally unjust," and because she was persuaded by anarchism's "vision . . . of liberty, harmony and true social justice."[3] Those three positive goals—liberty, harmony, and social justice—are as foundational as the oppression, violence, and uniformity she opposed. Against authority and "power-over," like all anarchists, Goldman defined anarchism as "the philosophy of a new social order based on liberty unrestricted by man-made law; the theory that all forms of government rest on violence, and are therefore wrong and harmful, as well as unnecessary" (1969, 50). Despite anarchism's facile association with chaos and *disorder*, Goldman saw anarchism, this quote reveals, as a kind of voluntary *social order* that worked without force. In her criticism of the status quo, she speaks out on issues from birth control and conscription to free expression and workers' rights, emphasizing in every case individual access to information and everyone's right to freedom—to design and control their lives. In terms of where she was headed, she writes that "organization as the result of natural blending of common interests, brought about through voluntary adhesion, Anarchists do not only not oppose, but believe in as the only possible basis of social life" (1972, 46). Her anarchism appears here to be of the more communal variety, emphasizing "common interests" and "adhesion," for example. She pays attention to the distinct forms and causes of women's oppression, which male anarchists do not generally do, and which entails critiques of things like love, prostitution, and marriage that are still strongly identified with her and with anarchist feminism. Such analysis and commitment are crucial if women, too, were to be free and fulfilled under anarchism, freed from the authority of church, state, and property as well as the domination of men. Likewise, she looks closely at the institutions in which children spent most of their time and how those institutions—schools and families as well as churches and states—demanded their conformity and obedience rather than nurturing their freedom and individual spirit. If children, too, were to be free, those institutions would have to change, and Goldman is no mild reformer but a revolutionary: anarchism, she writes, "is a conspicuous protest of the most militant type" (35).

Mark Van Wienen uses Gilman's work (along with that of Upton Sinclair and W. E. B. Du Bois) to show the broad influence of socialism in her day, recalling her self-description as a "socialist of the humanitarian kind, based on the first exponents, French and English, with the American enthusiasm for [Edward] Bellamy" (2003, 605). Her feminism and socialism come together in her argument for economic equality—for both sexes—and in her "challenge to laissez-faire capitalism" (Robertson 2018), including what she sees as its masculine competitiveness. Just as Goldman doesn't think anarchism will automatically liberate women, Gilman doesn't think socialism, without a sharper focus, will automatically bring about sexual equality, either; in fact, women's equal contributions (and the "mother instinct") are necessary to realize that end, not a product of it. Her critique of the patriarchal family is different from Goldman's, but it is at least as deep and perhaps even more consistent, as we will see. And just as Gilman envisions an end to economic dependence and isolation in the patriarchal household for women, she looks at unnecessary sources of vulnerability and isolation in children's lives too. Believing that "it is only in social relations that we are human," she wants women to have a greater role in our common life, to develop their social self, and she even speaks at length on the social life of the young. It is then a kind of collectivism, with reformed social relations, ethics, conditions, and institutions, that drives Gilman. She is an ambitious reformist socialist (Van Wienen 2003, 604) who, in the model of Bellamy, "advocate[s] socialism achieved by peaceful, gradual, evolutionary change . . . eliminat[ing] injustices by a further extension of democracy" (Lane 1990, 161).

The Nature of the Child

Children are often defined in comparison with adults, much as women have historically been defined in comparison with men, and the comparisons tend, unsurprisingly, to reflect unfavorably upon children and women in ways that are subsequently used to justify excluding them from aspects of the adult/male world and to legitimize various forms of surveillance over and punishment of them. Children are not rational enough, sufficiently morally developed, or experienced enough, it is variously said, to be given voice, choice, control, or power in families, governments, jobs, or schools. Gilman, however, is less concerned with measuring children against adults to see what the former lack and more interested in (1) establishing common ground between those younger and older, (2) bringing greater justice into children's lives, and (3) cultivating the kind of children capable of leading free, equal, socialist lives as adults. Goldman, also shunning those insidious comparisons so injurious to the young, is most concerned, not too dissimilarly, with (1) knowing what is distinctive about children so that we meet their needs and allow them to flourish, (2) freeing children from systems of oppression, and (3) nurturing the kind of children capable of leading free, equal, anarchist adult lives. Both, this is to say, want to change the environments in which children live, for the sake of their childhoods and to prepare them for particular kinds of adulthoods. It is, perhaps, not completely surprising that thinkers like these two, who offer "thoroughgoing exposés of the surreptitious assimilation of human characteristics to male ones" (Seigfried 2001, 79), would also rebel at the idea that the adult alone contains the essence of what it means to be human; similarly, those who saw men's power over women in such dire forms and with such horrendous consequences would also be uncomfortable with adults having unchecked power over children. It is also unsurprising that two thinkers, living in the same time and place, both wrapped up in their different movements for social change, would overlap in some respects even while differing in others.

Emma Goldman

Given the way that she writes about the young, I use two main strategies for getting at what Goldman thinks is the nature of the child. I look, of course, at her several essays in which children and education receive the most attention.

I also search through her other essays to find the kinds of people and things with which children are grouped, the analogies and metaphors Goldman makes that involve children, and the qualities that she calls "childlike." I move freely among her essays, most of which are developed from speeches.

Morally, Goldman calls savage revenge "child's play" to reveal by comparison the horrors of "civilized" revenge seen in prisons (1969, 119).[4] Goldman's children are relatively harmless. In fact, Goldman's theory depends upon a view of children that says they are not dangerous or destructive. She asserts that belief in the necessity of authority, whether governmental or parental, religious or educational, has "at its base . . . the doctrine that man is evil, vicious, and too incompetent to know what is good for him" (1972, 90). She characterizes children in such ways as to make it "safe" to allow them to develop without force and forceful interference. They have "large, wondering, innocent eyes . . . [that wish] to behold the wonders of the world" (108). They have an "original sense of judgment" (111). Importantly, unlike sometimes less trustworthy adults, who "have so many superstitions to overcome," the child "has no traditions to overcome. Its mind is not burdened with set ideas, its heart has not grown cold with class and caste distinctions" (1969, 148). If we are to allow children to flourish, Goldman summarizes, we need to "destroy the cruel, unjust, and criminal stigma imposed on the innocent young" (1972, 149). As an anarchist who rejects authority and force, and as a feminist aware of the way that women were said to require the guidance of men, Goldman insists that children do not require adult authority because of some defect, deficiency, or danger inherent in them. Even punishment is unnecessary and undesirable, "since the child is thereby led to suppose that punishment is something to be imposed upon him from without, by a person more powerful, instead of being a natural and unavoidable reaction and result of his own acts" (121). Children can learn what they need to know of the material and social world through such natural consequences.

Politically, Goldman makes a reference to "defenceless women and innocent infants" (1969, 104), a pairing that would seem to evoke stereotypical ideas of helpless, endangered dependents. Yet Goldman is employing this tactic to condemn political tyranny. King Umberto of Italy, she recounts, had ordered the shooting of women and children during a bread riot. In the instance she cites, the women and children were acting not helplessly at all but rebelliously and in concert; they were "defenceless" and "innocent" only in comparison to the armed and culpable state. Pairing "children and cotton slaves" (129) as illegitimate sources of wealth, Goldman portrays the child as an economic actor, too, and, like many others, an exploitable one. Again, youth look "harmless" next to the more truly criminal political and economic exploiters Goldman condemns and appear to be more capable and agential than most stereotypes of the young lead us to expect.

In contrast to the relatively positive images that dominate Goldman's view of the potential of the child, those that she uses to show the damage done to children are potent in their negativity and speak to the impact on a child of certain inherently corrupting social forces. Such images, in fact, dominate her work on children. A first set of images contains her criticism of those who do not recognize the humanity of the child, much as the humanity of other social groups, from women to immigrants, is denied. Too often a child, capable of so much more, is "treated as a mere machine or as a mere parrot," which is disrespectful of and abhorred by "every sensitive being" (107). Her feminism is center stage when she compares the fate of a girl being prepared for marriage to that of "the mute beast fattened for slaughter" (230). A child is raised as if it were "inanimate matter for parents and guardians, whose authority alone gives it shape and form." Goldman's children are, most emphatically, fully human; however, they are wrongly silenced and wastefully underestimated by unjust and unnecessary adult authority, bred to meet goals not of their own making, anathema to a feminist anarchist devoted instead to every individual freely developing their potential.

In another set of images, plant analogies abound. We erroneously treat the child as a "delicate human plant [kept] in a hothouse atmosphere, where it can neither breathe nor grow freely" (109), not unlike the ways in which we claim to "protect" some women. She contrasts the "young delicate tree that is being clipped and cut by the gardener in order to give it an artificial form" with the truly well-reared child, who, "allowed to grow in nature and free-dom," can reach "majestic height" and "beauty" (112). We should look at a child as a "budding and sprouting personality" (122). Our practices, however, result in "absolute death and decay to the bud in the making" (113). Like a plant that be "overprotected" to death—overwatered, kept from the sun, and so on—a child's "good" can be wrongly determined to its own detriment, from a wide assortment of political and economic motives as well as from perverted notions of natural beauty and mistaken assessments of children's capacities. Children require freedom to flourish. Goldman would toss out the gardener's shears; Gilman, we will see, would not.

Looking at what Goldman says about the nature of children when they are the main subject of her essays yields results that are consistent with and further develop the ideas touched upon in the analogies and metaphorical asides. Goldman's approach is built upon the notion that children can be driven internally to develop, as the plant analogies hint at. To support "the natural growth of the child," we have to allow it "to grow from within" (1972,

107) rather than stifle it and gradually destroy "its latent qualities and traits" (109). Hence, Goldman characterizes education as properly being "a process of drawing out, not of driving in; it aims at the possibility that the child should be left free to develop spontaneously" (120). These "individual tendencies" of a child are not mysteries, either, but are revealed "in its play, in its questions, in its association with people and things" (108). Goldman's children may be malleable and even exploitable, but they are definitely not blank slates. On the other hand, while they enter the world with unique sets of tendencies and traits, these do not necessarily automatically unfold entirely on their own or in all situations. Still, citing her much-admired Francisco Ferrer, Goldman insists that "All the value of education rests in the respect for the physical, intellectual, and moral will of the child" (1969, 163). She starkly contrasts, then, two approaches: one in which "the child [is] to be considered as an individuality," and the other in which the child is seen "as an object to be moulded according to the whims and fancies of those about it" (1972, 107).

At times, Goldman sounds like Jean-Jacques Rousseau expounding on negative education in the eighteenth century: don't "mold," don't "knead," don't "stifle," don't "cramp," don't "force," don't "cripple," and don't "interfere." She brings the same anarchist perspective to bear on schools, condemning them as she does prisons, institutions attempting to "form" and "reform," and, in fact, finds that against children we routinely use varieties of force that overlap to a frightening degree with those that we employ against prisoners (and in neither case, according to Goldman, does this behavior improve the individuals or benefit their communities, however passionately some might contend otherwise). Her "negative" approach necessarily posits in children a natural desire to learn and develop: "It is reasonable to assume that the child is intensely interested in the things which concern its life" (121).

Goldman's main complaint about most schools is that they have "such little regard for [a child's] personal liberty and originality of thought" (1969, 118), two separate but intertwined things that introduce more ideas on the intellectual life of the young. Like an adult, Goldman's child "is bent on going its own way, since it is composed of the same nerves, muscles and blood, even as those who assume to direct its destiny" (112). Children are more than potentially rational adults, blessed instead with a range of intellectual abilities: they are "ready to receive and assimilate" (1972, 120), can know themselves and their relations to others, can express themselves, can use judgment and initiative, and can work from experience and imagination (121). They even have some advantages over adults. Not only, put negatively, are they "very vivid . . . not yet having been pounded into uniformity"; put positively, "their experience will inevitably contain much more originality, as well as beauty" (121). Goldman characterizes the "young mind" as "fresh to receive and perceive" (64), giving dignity to a youthful stage of life and acknowledging its admirable open-mindedness and perceptiveness. She does note some intellectual limits or problematic tendencies, as she also does for adults, whom she treats as more hoodwinked than they suspect. Youth can be "fickle" (144) and distractible, just like adults who are susceptible to governments' displays of "fireworks, theatre parties, and revelries" (136). They can be "naïve," but so can American adults be, even with regard to "matters of international importance" (64). They can be impulsive and "unsophisticated" (148), but often such simplicity is good in adults as well (225). These are not insurmountable obstacles in providing children freedom.

Goldman does not argue that we should leave children on their own to raise themselves, of course, although she does definitely think that education should be child-directed and that the best teachers only "appeal[] to the child's own energies" (1969, 163). She looks to a model of education that necessarily leaves behind such practices as "imposing, violating, [and] constraining" (163). What we should provide children is a "proper economic and social environment, the breath and freedom of nature, healthy exercise, love and sympathy, and, above all, a deep understanding for the needs of the child" (149). She approvingly cites Sébastian Faure's school, which she says trained the young "in keeping with their individual disposition and abilities" (151) and which was rooted in "affectionate understanding and care of the children." She cites him at length:

> We make a particular effort to awaken the child's interest in his surroundings, to make him realize the importance of observation, investigation, and reflection, so that *when the children reach maturity*, they would not be deaf and blind to the things about them. Our children never accept anything in blind faith, without inquiry as to why and wherefore; nor do they feel satisfied until their questions are thoroughly answered. Thus their minds are free from doubts and fear resultant from incomplete or untruthful replies; it is the latter which warp the growth of the child, and create a lack of confidence in himself and those about him. (152; my emphasis)

She is only quoting Faure, but still, this writing is among the closest in her works on children to words that talk about individual development through education not only in the abstract and for its own sake but in preparation for becoming the kind of critical adult whom Goldman admires. This adult is attuned to social injustices and systems of domination, capable of ameliorating the former and resisting the latter through "observation, investigation, and reflection" (152)—skills learned and practiced in childhood. Goldman's child, much like Mary Wollstonecraft's in *Original Stories*, is exposed to the ugliness of life, "the humiliation, the degradation, the awfulness of poverty," for example (162), to feel and understand it and to opt and work for something better. A child is capable of this kind of understanding.

For Goldman, conformity is the evil in children's lives, achieved through the many arms of adult authority, with individuality and spontaneity its opposites: "It is social uniformity and sameness that harass the individual most" (1972, 93), she asserts. It is nothing short of tragic that from "earliest infancy, every effort is being made to cramp human emotion and originality of thought in the individual into a strait-jacket" (108). We commit "terrible crimes against the young" (1969, 149), she concludes, since we "cripple[] that which is most essential" to the development of their characters (108). The same entities that she condemns for their impact on adults, including religion, the state, capitalism, and patriarchy, she condemns as well for their impact on children. Our eyes are on the future, and the worst of that is turning the child "into a patient work slave, professional automaton, tax-paying citizen, or righteous moralist" (1972, 108). Such work to create this deformed adult employs force, imposes gender roles, and links to a capitalist sense of the child as one's property. Were such efforts to cease and be replaced with individualized attention to the whole child, the child's individual potential could blossom and its latent qualities come to fruition, fulfilling the individual and eventually making them an able, creative member of some future chosen society who can see and resist oppressive social forces. They would not have experienced "power over" as children, and their "power to" would be expansive. Their intellectual, emotional, and ethical capacities would emerge early and be trustworthy guides, better than even the well-intentioned guidance of mature adults. Goldman's wish could almost mirror that which she attributes to Ferrer: "I want my contribution to the cause of liberty to be a young generation ready to meet a new era." It is intriguing that he was charged with such things as "teaching the children . . . to hate God . . . prepar[ing] them to destroy the rich [and]. . . undermining the army by inculcating anti-military ideas" (1969, 162). Such charges could also be laid against Goldman, and would, perhaps, be correct, yet miss the liberation she is seeking.

Charlotte Perkins Gilman

Because Gilman writes at greater length and more directly about childhood, I use different strategies in explicating her thoughts on the nature of the child.

I put her autobiographical and nonfiction work side-by-side, because she so determinedly tries to live out her ideals and to express them in multiple genres. And while her fiction also speaks so centrally to reconceiving childhood, I leave exploration of her utopian works to the chapter on childhood in feminist utopian and dystopian thought, where it is rightly placed in another important tradition.

Gilman's own youthful self is portrayed in her autobiography, *The Living of Charlotte Perkins Gilman*, in ways that make the intellectual life of children appear quite vividly. She remembers the "keen delight to the rational mind" experienced upon learning long division at around age eight ([1935] 1963, 19) and often marks periods of her childhood by what she figures out about life—whether that the answers in books could be wrong and thus that "science, law, was more to be trusted than authority (19) or "that things debarred may sometimes be done—in safety" (19). Always, she draws large lessons from small events. Such mental moments reveal intriguing aspects of herself or the world she inhabits. So intellectually hungry is the young Gilman that a single lecture on hygiene "ma[kes] an indelible impression" and leads to life-long changes in physical culture (28–29). As a young teenager, mental leaps and bounds are normal. She loves physics, for example, and then finds "parallels in psychology" (29) for the laws of friction and inertia. She develops her own religion. She characterizes herself by a distinctive mental attitude: "an incredulity which refuse[s] to accept anybody's say-so, even if it ha[s] been said for a thousand years" (40). Such a trait is not easily tolerated, especially in the young, but Goldman would approve! Before the age of twenty, she "figure[s] it out that the business of mankind [i]s to carry out the evolution of the human race, according to the laws of nature, adding the conscious direction" (42). Such are glimpses into the intellectual life of young people, as seen through Gilman's own life. Her takeaway? "Might not our educators consider if such a soul-expanding experience is not of lasting value to a child; and if, some day, we may not learn how to accustom our children to large feelings instead of keeping them always among little ones" (17).

In her nonfiction treatise on children, Gilman posits that even with regard to "the small acts of infancy," the child "naturally wishes to understand them" ([1900] 2003, 45). Perhaps the worst thing adults can do in response to such desire is to demand an obedient child—worse for the child, who becomes no wiser, and for the future adult, who will not be a capable citizen of a social democracy. She contends, "It is not youth which makes our boys and girls so foolish in their behavior. It is the kind of training we give the little child, keeping back the most valuable faculties of the brain instead of helping them to grow" (21–22). If we redirect the "elaborate efforts" (22) we put into making children obedient, rethink "our absolute desideratum" (30) and "intense reverence for the virtue of obedience" (32), then the "delighted brain" of the child could be "spread and strengthened" (35).

Gilman understands the mental faculties of the child and the adult as identical, a common ground that adults do not always appreciate or make use of. Both, for example, "receive and retain . . . impression; . . . accurately and judiciously collate these impressions; [and] act steadily on these stored and selected impulses" (48). The range of these impressions and abilities in young people is more limited: "That is the condition of childhood. It is for us to gently, delicately, steadily surround the child with such conditions as shall promote this orderly sequence of brain function" (49). But the means we usually use—from preaching to commanding (50)—are all wrong: "We have systematically checked in our children acts which were the natural sequence of their observation and inference; and enforced acts which, to the child's mind, had no reason. Thus we have carefully trained a world of people to the habit of acting without understanding, and also of understanding without acting" (51–52). We prolong weakness and invite tyranny. The ends we seek and the tools we employ are misguided.

In her autobiography, Gilman states, "From [my daughter's] earliest years . . . I always made a steady habit of mentioning a reason for an action with the act" to "accustom[] the young mind automatically to associate cause and effect" (155). This plants in the child the idea that she, too, should have and be able to offer reasons for her own actions. Gilman calls such thoughtful planning ahead in childrearing "pipe-laying" (155–156), although the adult must be aware that "a mental image of what you are told will happen in later years, the predicted loss of something you do not in the least understand of value, has small weight" (158). It is based on an assumption, as well, that "children are naturally reasonable, and most of them, well meaning" (156). Yet her moderate path and reasonable "methods [a]re by no means approved by my friends and neighbors" (158), a constant challenge in most childrearing techniques, perhaps, but especially when using democratic tactics and driven by social justice concerns like feminism (my own childrearing was subjected to similar characterizations and criticisms). Gilman's ideas, like many feminist ideas espoused in this book, can seem to others "not only wrong in principle, but impracticable" (158). Yet the goals for her daughter are merely "understanding and self-control" (159). Why do "discipline and obedience" (158) have the larger fan base? Why is it "scandalous" to "so frankly teach her the simple facts of sex" (160), even when it is in the child's self-interest to know them? Gilman's childrearing is called ruinous and, of all things, neglectful (160–161). She and her daughter "ha[ve] happy years together" (162), until the child goes to live, at the age of nine, with her father and his new wife, who is a friend. More "furious condemnation" follows, despite the fact that the girl "divide[s] her time fairly equally between us" (163). Gilman takes some solace in the fact that in later life, she sees "the most conscientious mamas proudly doing to their children what I was called 'an unnatural mother' for doing to mine" (320).

What Gilman might remind every adult is that "a child learns every day." Even the child who "is not old enough to be taught anything systematically by persons whose business it is to teach" nonetheless are "old enough to be learning the a, b, c of life at the hands of those with whom he chances to be" (77). Everyone, then, potentially has a role in the education of the young. And learning is pleasant activity for children, she insists: "The pleasure of perceiving is keen, the pleasure of his limited but growing reflection is keen, and the pleasure of action is best of all" (78). Children are inherently curious, too, with a "natural and most valuable tendency to investigate and experiment" (240). It is because of such qualities, in fact, that Gilman recommends that even the youngest children be placed for at least part of the day in childcare, in environments made especially for them, where they can be cared for by experts and not by servants (among whom she includes mothers with household duties), and that all parents be well equipped for their important task. After all, "the education of a child consists in every impression received by the growing brain, not merely those received when we are instructing it" (237). Humans need "right education, especially in the very first years," Gilman insists, for the sake of "soul-growth" and ultimately for human progress (252–253), the latter a concept that doesn't much appear in Goldman's writing.

What of the moral life of children? Gilman describes "the code of ethics in use among children" as based on two principles: "that of instant and equal retaliation; or, when that fails, the dread" ostracism—"I won't play" (87). Gilman observes children's behavior, and, seeing the "ethics" that children deploy, decides to use those same ethics to teach. The means involve "no ill-feeling" (88), just comprehensible, consequential response to a child's behavior. She describes children as more timid than adults and somewhat selfish (90). It is not "naughty" to be "inconsiderate of others," she contends, just childishly egotistic (91). The child can and should easily be taught "extension of sympathy" (91). The larger problem, instead, is that adult "ideas of right behaviour are so contradictory and uncertain, our execution of such ideas as we hold so partial and irregular" (96). More could not be at stake, for "ethics is the physics of social relation" (97). Adults actually "injure the baby brain" through their methods of teaching ethics (101). They do not treat children as fully human, after all, but as lower beings (104):

A woman who would not lie to a grown friend will lie freely to her own child. A man who would not be unjust to his brother or a stranger will be unjust to his little son. The common courtesy given any adult is not given to the child. . . . From the treatment they receive, children cannot learn any rational and consistent scheme of ethics. (101–102)

It is not human nature that is to blame, for the "child is temptingly open to instruction in ethics" (104); instead, the "good impulses" of the young "are checked, twisted, tangled, weighed down with many artificial restrictions" (103). The fact is that "the sense of justice develops very early" (105). Both "recognition of the rights of others" and "generosity which goes beyond justice" are "natural to the child" (109). What adults require, perhaps surprisingly, is a child's point of view (106), figuring out how to make such goals as self-control appear desirable and doable to children (107).

Repeatedly, Gilman rescues children from negative stereotypes about them, looking from children's natures instead to social causes to explain problematic behaviors held against young people. For example, she refutes the idea that children are "mischievous" (137) by pointing out that we "rear young creatures in a place where they must do mischief if they behave differently from grown people" (138), just as "a calf in a flower-garden would do considerable mischief, or kittens in a dairy" (137–138). She advocates creating environments that are truly made for children, from child gardens to daycare centers, places that would contribute to their social, intellectual, and moral development and education and bring out the best rather than the worst in them and their relations.

In *Concerning Children*, Gilman repeatedly urges a setup in which children learn unconsciously, via an "education which the child never knows of, but which surrounds him with helpful influences" (253). If Goldman emphasizes certain aspects of Rousseau's negative education, Gilman, we might say, emphasizes his adult construction of particular environments—"helpful influences"—for the young, bent not only on bringing out what is already latent in them, per Goldman, but also on presenting them with certain opportunities and teaching them specific lessons. She urges that school start in the very earliest years of life and that we alter the methods used and the ends pursued. When we prefer "submission to intelligence" (55) in our children, adults fail in a fundamental regard to fulfill their duties to the young: we keep young people credulous and dependent, when "what we "should do is to help the child to question and find out,—teach him to learn, not to believe" (56). But, as is beginning to be apparent in these quotes,

Gilman advocates for social engineering in her preferred arrangements for the young—it's just that the engineering never uses force; is built around the needs, abilities, and interests of the young; and considers the needs, abilities, and interests of the adults they will become, living in community. It is essential work, however, because "Human Nature is *the result of Social Conditions* far more than the conditions are the result of the nature!" ([1890] 1991, 44). Goldman would beg to differ.

Comparisons

While I have not emphasized it very much, Gilman and Goldman attempt to be inclusive when they talk about the nature of the child. Both consider how differently boys and girls are often socialized and treated, for example, and they absolutely urge equal treatment. Both also address children at multiple stages of life, looking at the earliest forms of socialization through things like adolescent sex education and employment. Often, in their critiques of current practices, the terrible differences in children's treatment and opportunities by class are also visible. Still, both also offer general assessments of what children are like and how they are wronged.

There is significant common ground in Gilman's and Goldman's views on the nature of the child. Both contest the negative stereotypes of children and argue for seeing children as full and able human beings in particular stages of life, with a broad range of intellectual and moral capacities, a stark contrast with the ways in which youth are usually underestimated. Such stereotypes have led to their miseducation and have been used to justify illegitimate authority and force over them and to demand their obedience (Goldman, like some of our earlier theorists, looks at children's acts of resistance "as very refreshing and encouraging," not as indictments against them [1972, 115]). Both are pained by the ways in which children have been misunderstood and mistreated, by the loss this treatment entails for them as young people and as future adults. Both figures argue against the most common ways of educating young people, even using similar language when, for example, they condemn force-feeding as a method in education, reject the mere passing on of an earlier generation's beliefs as knowledge, and urge elimination of obedience as the primary virtue for the young. They attribute to children a trustworthy curiosity and the eagerness and ability to learn. Both suggest that adults should work harder to better understand childhood and each individual child with whom we interact. Each talks about children's "souls," not in a religious way at all but in a manner that makes children have depth and individuates them.

Yet differences are just beginning to emerge despite the common ground. Goldman is pretty adamant that the child is a given: "Environment can only bring out what is inherent in human beings. It can never put anything in sterile ground" (cited in Wexler 1984, 3). The environment can do terrible things—oppress, constrain, and stifle the individual, for example, as Goldman stresses—but the most it can seem to do positively is allow or invite the individual to emerge, to fulfill its potential. What is needed, then, is opportunity for "free unfoldment and growth" (1907). Adults have a more instrumental role, and less of a role than we often give them, or than Gilman would prefer.

For Gilman, the interaction between the nature of the child and the environment is more dynamic, as we see even more in the next section. Certainly, she wants to individualize things like education and discipline, so that there does seem to be something akin to an individual's "nature" that she, like Goldman, works with. But Gilman's child is also shaped by and through society and social interactions, and not only in negative ways, which leads to her greater attention on those interactions, from child-child relations and adult-child relations in group settings, to more interpersonal adult-child interactions.

Gilman's work is grounded in a variety of observations of children and adult-child relations, including in families and schools; her focus is often on interpersonal relations first and then on the ideologies and structures that have wrongly directed them. Goldman observes schools and also shares some observations about the fates of children she has encountered, especially in impoverished families. For her, theory often seems to come first, which observed children then test and are informed by; one does not encounter in her work as many examples of everyday dynamics so much as examples of how social institutions and practices wrong children. The two rely disproportionately on information from different settings, which affects their different emphases. As we will see, this reliance leads Gilman to talk about justice in relations with children, and Goldman to focus on heavily on oppressive social dynamics.

Still, both look at how challenges to the dominant way of treating young people must be informed by theory, since those dominant ways are directed by ideas about everything from what a child is to what modes of social relations are most desirable. We cannot immunize children from social theory any more than we can imagine their treatment severed from social forces.

Goldman and Gilman want young people to interact with a less oppositional world. Both see children as having voice and agency that demands respect and space.

"Politicizing" Children

When our central figures "politicize" children, they understand them (1) to be affected deeply by politics, (2) to have social awareness, (3) to be gauges of the legitimacy of social practices, (4) to have (what are usually understood to be political) claims to liberty, and (5) to be individuals whose needs and abilities should influence and shape their environments. Their understandings of the nature of the child support their ideas about children's place in the social and political world. Gilman and Goldman provide models for the kinds of questions that political theorists should be asking about children. For political thinkers to ask such questions requires that their children be deemed relevant to politics and that they be deemed relevant not only because they will one day become adults but because, even as children, they are fully human and members of communities.

Both figures, I want to start by saying, believe that children have been powerfully and negatively affected by destructive social forces, factors that affect them directly and through their influence on the adults in their lives. Both believe that the environment in which we are raised and educated can prepare us either for freedom or for servitude, although they understand those things somewhat differently. They are both social and political theorists, and thus they look at how such forces as capitalism and individualism negatively influence the young, directly and indirectly, and at how other forces, such as anarchism or socialism, could dramatically improve young lives.

Emma Goldman

Goldman's children are far from politically oblivious. Reflecting on her own childhood, Goldman says, "Since my earliest recollection of my youth in Russia I have rebelled against orthodoxy in every form." And look at how many forms of orthodoxy the young Goldman recognized and resisted:

> I could never bear to witness harshness whether on the part of our parents to us or in their dealings with the servants. I was outraged over the official brutality practiced on the peasants in our neighborhood. I wept bitter tears when the young men were conscripted into the army and torn from homes and hearths. . . . I was indignant when I discovered that love between young people of Jewish and Gentile origin was considered the crime of crimes, and the birth of an illegitimate child the most depraved immorality. (1972, 386–387)

This politically aware image of the young Goldman is supported by other stories, such as that which tells how, at age twelve, when Czar Alexander II was assassinated and ideas of the Russian Populists and Nihilists were circulating, Goldman read Nikolay Chernyshevsky's *What Is to Be Done?* (1863) and made his Vera, a political organizer, her new heroine.[5]

Speaking again to children's social consciousness, Goldman declares that prostitution is "an institution, known almost to every child" (1972, 143). As a critical, thinking being, as we saw in the previous section, a child can see when "the lives of their parents are in contradiction to the ideas they represent" (114). Goldman's children are aware of and sensitive to injustice. They are not so unthinking as to be oblivious to hypocrisy, so self-centered as to be blind to inequality, or so impressionable as to accept proffered explanations for abuses heaped on others or themselves without question. Perhaps surprisingly, it is possible to see in Goldman's children what she hopes to encourage and support—to reclaim—in adults.

Like adults, Goldman's children are dramatically affected by their environments; although they are not internally shaped by them, they are thwarted or stimulated by them. Economically, because parents are overworked and underpaid, "the home has been left to the care of the little ones" (1969, 89). Economic forces also thrust "middle-class girls . . . into life's jungle at an early age" (1972, 129). Politically, patriotism requires parents "to sacrific[e] their own children" (1969, 133). Moral codes "condemn[] woman to the position of a celibate, a prostitute, or a reckless, incessant breeder of hapless children" (1972, 129). Because laws do not solve problems but are still our go-to solution, child exploitation flourishes in states where child labor laws prevail (1969, 64). Familial norms mean that parents "make their children pay for the outrage perpetrated upon them by their parents . . . by traditions and habits" (1972, 124). On her trip to Russia, Goldman notes how "the cruelty and infamy of the blockade was nowhere more apparent and crying than in its effect upon the sick and the children" (2003, 107). As these examples show, children's lives are deeply affected by economic, governmental, educational, familial, and cultural forces, both directly and through their effects on adults, and the impacts are always class- and gender-specific.

Because the lives of young people are so important and revealing to Goldman, she criticizes certain institutions in part because of their consequences for children. For example, her condemnation of marriage is based partly on its effects upon children, and on this subject her writing becomes quite passionate: "The sham, the hypocrisy of it! Marriage protecting the child, yet thousands of children destitute and homeless. Marriage protecting the child, yet orphan asylums and reformatories overcrowded, the SPCC[6] keeping busy in rescuing the little victims from 'loving' parents. . . . Oh, the mockery of it!" (1972, 164). The state, too, should be condemned not only for the terrible way militarism demands the lives of the young through forced conscription but also, in an everyday vein, for "the way the spirit of youth is emasculated [and] deadened" through patriotic training (110). And these various institutions do not operate in isolation but conspire against the development of the free individual: "The majority for centuries [have been] drilled in State worship, trained in discipline and obedience and subdued by the awe of authority in the home, the school, the church and the press" (93).

Most political theorists, despite their dramatically different political and philosophical perspectives, easily justify exercising authority over children and demanding obedience from them. Yet when Goldman talks about the pain and loss from "everlasting external interference" (108) in one's life, she looks hard at children, who are most obviously subject to widely accepted constraints. It is in writing on education, on children, that she says, "Discipline and restraint—are they not back of all the evils in the world? Slavery, submission, poverty, all misery, all social iniquities result from discipline and restraint" (1969, 165). Children, like adults, have claims to liberty, and the same institutions that oppose the liberty of the adult oppose that of the child, sometimes in the same way, sometimes differently. Failure to respect children's claims is attributed by Goldman to additional factors as well, including a misunderstanding of the abilities and nature of the child and a lack of liberty in the lives of the adults who control the conditions of children's lives. Goldman's analysis of the effects of obedience and discipline on children lead her to question such things as the structure of the family and the school and the demands of political and economic systems. This is a tremendously important point: Goldman understands children to be affected by politics in a broad sense, but she also, and consequently, views them as a critical gauge by which to measure the legitimacy of various institutions. Their needs ultimately help her envision inspiring anarchist alternatives.

Goldman's starting and ending points are the individual and individuality, which she says are the "enemy" of "every institution of our day, the family, the State, our moral codes" (1972, 107–108). In taking such a stance, Goldman sets the individual against most social and socializing institutions, which are making illegitimate or undesirable demands. She rues the "obstacles placed in the way of growth and development of character" (108) by these forces. It is such goods as "independence and freedom," "independent mental development," and "individual growth" that she applauds as goals for education, and she believes that we must "battle" and "struggle" for these things, starting in childhood. Community seems less prominent or even desirable in Goldman's dream that we "grow up into independent, self-reliant spirits" (112), as she puts it in "The Child and Its Enemies," or into "self-reliant, liberty-loving men and women" (1969, 150) as she puts it in her essay on Ferrer.

But the effects of such overwhelming social forces as statism, religiosity, capitalism, and patriarchy are not just evident on the isolated individual, Goldman asserts, for there is also a "crippling effect thereof upon [the individual's] social well-being" (1972, 109). Goldman clearly has an idea of constructive social relations, as we saw earlier in her very definition of anarchism. What does this social element look like, especially for children? The miserable situation we find ourselves in, and what we want to avoid as we revision and restructure, is being "individuals foreign to one another, and in everlasting antagonism with each other" (109). The alternative is to be somehow known by, familiar to, or aligned with others in cooperative relationships. There are limits to what Goldman can say about her imagined communities, however, for what should rightly reign under anarchy is "spontaneity of character" and, even socially, "eternal change, thousandfold variations, continual innovation" (109).

Goldman documents how several kinds of potential social bonds are broken or not nurtured in oppressive social relations involving the young, and we can search there for some visions of the positive as well. Included here would be transnational connections, which are hindered by the fact that what we are told as youth about our own political communities is that ours are "best," causing us to look down on other nations and their citizens. Also threatened or left untended are what should be the "tender and delicate chords" uniting parents and children; instead, "parents are the first to destroy the inner riches of their children" (111). The better alternative Goldman romantically describes thusly: children could find in parents "certainty of love and understanding, the feeling that whatever happens in his or her life they can find the strongest support and deepest understanding from their parents" (1975, 175). Even the sexual desire for others that Goldman sees emerging in adolescence, "cravings of love and sex," which could positively direct us to relationships, are thwarted by adults, "suppressed and fought like some terrible disease" (1972, 112). Goldman explains how the absence or moralistic content of sex education "still adhere to the antiquated notion that man and woman belong to two different species, moving in opposite directions, and hence, must be kept apart." Love could and "should be the impetus for the harmonious blending of two beings" (125), but even that is corrupted. A similar problem and alternative vision appear between teacher and young student: "the teacher, instead of opposing, or presenting as authoritative his own opinions, predilections, or beliefs should be a sensitive instrument responding to the needs of the child as they are at any time manifested" (120). Goldman speaks of the possibility of "mutual confidence and love between teacher and pupil" (2003, 182). This requires, among other things, that the teacher not present ideas in a way that "precludes the right to criticize or disbelieve" (1972, 120). Ideally, "the teacher may well evoke, through his own enthusiasm and nobility of character, the latent enthusiasm and nobility of his pupils" (120–121).

Prominent in Goldman's work is a negative version of community, one linked in important ways to childhood. Schools treat children "like a pack of sheep" (118) and thus teach us to be members of a herd: "Our present system of economic and political dependence is maintained not so much by wealth and courts as it is by an inert mass of humanity, drilled and pounded into absolute uniformity, and . . . the school today represents the most efficient medium to accomplish that end" (119). Even in its daily structure, schools assume, as Goldman quotes the educator Dr. Hailman, "that all should be interested in the same things, in the same sequence, and at the same time" (119). Not only what we learn but how we learn is implicated. So deeply dismayed by this destructive model of community is Goldman that she emphasizes its polar opposite throughout—the free individual—more than she does a different model of community, even among children. Her different education would aim to create "a well-rounded individuality" (108). In contrast with "compulsory feeding" (117), a child—fit to use their own judgment and initiative (121)—can and should be "directing his own efforts and choosing the branches of knowledge which he desires to study" (120). Authority over children exercised in schools, then, is criticized on exactly the same grounds as adult obedience to government and religion; more, they are necessary to each other. In Goldman's anarchist schools, there would be "no coercion" (120) of children, just as there would be none of adults where anarchism prevails. Ideal relationships are imagined as loving, harmonious, voluntary, and respectful, and they demand of each party a certain investment to know the other.

It is, of course, not enough to change schooling—in fact, one could not truly change schools to align them with an anarchist spirit and not change the world outside the school with which it is connected. In a more ideal childhood, the various environments in which children live would work together, differently: "Only when the material needs, the hygiene of the home, and intellectual environment are harmonious, can the child grow into a healthy, free being" (1969, 151). The familial environment, for example, would change: "A child born in freedom needs the love and devotion of each human being about him, man as well as woman" (1972, 138). Like teachers, parents would nurture the individuality of the child. Sex would be a topic of "intelligent discussion" (125). We would learn about and tend to a child's soul as we do sometimes now the child's physical well-being (112).

The fate of "love and human relation" in our childhoods, then, is not a pretty one, although Goldman stresses that these factors "alone make life worth living" and can be otherwise. Throughout "The Child and Its Enemies," Goldman mostly holds up as the goal "the free growth and development of the innate forces and tendencies of the child"; in the final sentence, however, she mentions community: "We hope for the free individual and eventually also for a free community, which shall make interference and coercion of human growth impossible" (115). Her "eventual" desired community has the descriptor "free," and part of what makes community free is that it eschews coercive practices of childrearing and those that impose external goals on the child. She offers similar thoughts in "Modern School," where, in the heart of the essay, the idea emerges that:

> the social purpose of the Modern School is to develop the individual through knowledge and the free play of characteristic traits, *so that he may become a social being*, because he has learned to know himself, to know his relation to his fellow-men, and to realize himself in a harmonious blending with society. (1972, 121; my emphasis)

"Becom[ing] a social being" is the goal, for then one can fully "realize [one's] self in a harmonious blending with society," a voluntary blending that has as prerequisites self-knowledge and an understanding of social relations capable of resisting class- and gender-based divisions. The anarchism to which Goldman devoted her life is built on the belief that humans are inherently capable of social life, of cooperation; these are not relations we have to be forced, persuaded, or manipulated into. Goldman's very definition of anarchism is as "the philosophy of a new social order based on the released energies of the individual and the *free association* of liberated individuals" (100; my emphasis). Those energies are released beginning in childhood, and the free individual in society will rightly demand that they be respected and developed among adults as well. She speaks of anarchist Peter Kropotkin favorably:

> Peter Kropotkin has shown what wonderful results this unique force of man's individuality has achieved when strengthened by *co-operation* with other individualities. . . . In his profound work, *Mutual Aid*, Kropotkin shows that in the animal kingdom, as well as in human society, co-operation—as opposed to internecine strife and struggle—has worked for the survival and evolution of the species.

He demonstrated that only mutual aid and voluntary co-operation—
not the omnipotent, all-devastating State—can create the basis for a
free individual and associational life. (95)

Even here, however, community partly takes on an instrumental role—it
strengthens individuality, although the relation appears reciprocal. Still,
"individuality remains the most fundamental fact of all human association,"
Goldman adamantly insists, "suppressed and persecuted yet never defeated,
and in the long run the victor" (94–95).

Charlotte Perkins Gilman

Like Goldman's, Gilman's children have a sense of social (in)justice. For
example, in the first years of her own life, Gilman realizes that being
"whipped just as severely for less offenses . . . was unjust" ([1935] 1963, 13).
She recalls at fourteen getting an unjust grade, "for which I carried a grudge
for twenty years or more" (27); so impactful are slights to the sense of right
of young people. And "even in those baby years," she recalls, she feels "an
enormous sense of social responsibility with power to handle it" (13), "deeply
impressed," for example, "with civic crime and the difficulty of stopping it"
(21). Gilman declares, "From sixteen I had not wavered from that desire to
help humanity which underlay all my studies. Here was the world, visibly
unhappy and as visibly unnecessarily so" (70). As a teenager, she is struck
by the "strange disproportion in the order of virtues, the peculiar way in
which they vary in the order of their importance by race, class, age, sex" (38).
Again, from Gilman's examples, we see that the young wrestle with questions
of justice and the reality of things like gendered and class-based injustices
in their own lives and the lives of those around them. According to her, the
wrongs they notice are to individuals and groups, and they almost always
reveal power inequalities that she, like Goldman, addresses in her proposed
good society. We need to take this aspect of young people's lives more seriously, to converse with them about justice, and to see anew and address the
inequalities that are obvious to them. Neither Gilman nor Goldman would
be surprised by the political activity of youth today cited earlier (such as the
movements to end gun violence and to address environmental challenges).

Interestingly, Gilman also suggests that children need *justice* in their
childrearing environment and practices, language not prominent in Goldman: "Kindness, politeness, constant love, and all due consideration the child
should have; but justice is as important to him as affection" ([1900] 2003,
196). This is a perspective that I believe we are still too unfamiliar with.

Being treated justly is important *to the child*. To further the point, Gilman asserts that, in a family, all parties "should be treated with justice" and that the way we come up with just solutions should be "always open to a child's understanding" (187). We need to be treated with justice as young people and taught through collective practice how to treat others justly. She is adamant about this need, repeating the idea in a number of different ways and contexts: "A child is a human creature, and entitled to be treated as such. A human body three feet long is deserving of as much respect as a human body six feet long" (180). And she clearly states that the bodies and the souls of the young demand such respect and justice. Our practices too often are discourteous to children (181), even expressive of contempt for them and their ways of being in the world (177). We fall into these patterns not because we are consciously choosing to be unjust or contemptuous, as was also claimed in the previous chapter, but because we are not so well trained in how to deal with young people as people (a theme to which I return in later chapters); because the environments in which we rear children tend not to bring out the best in us, in them, or in our relationships with them; and because we carry with us the baggage from too many unhappy childhoods. Such matters are fixable, and, if fixed, will contribute positively to the child's thriving, to positive adult-child relations, and to adults' well-being. Like Goldman, Gilman sees as one challenge to changing such patterns that we tend to impose on the next generation the injustices that were imposed on us: "In his subordinate position in youth he has no chance to escape from this injustice or to retaliate; and he [as an adult] strikes a balance with fate by assuming the same superiority over the new-comer" (159). Matters will not be taken care of on their own—we need to discuss and question and together rethink the principles that guide our childrearing practices and the social environments that support increased justice. We need to not leave so much in the hands of adults who are not well prepared to nurture and respect the young.

And Gilman's children rebel. As thinking beings, children early become "aware that they are 'minding' for the convenience of 'the grown-ups' the greater part of the time" (43). She herself "cherished an Ishmaelitish resentment against 'grown-ups'" (15), for example, and mentions the "inward rebellion" that accompanies outward submission to such things as stories being cut off at bedtime when interest in them is so keen (20). She feels more generally a "boundless sympathy for children, feeling them to be suppressed, misunderstood" (23). This feeling, of course, she would carry into her adult work. A "major event" in her young life is her refusal to apologize for something she hadn't done, despite her mother's demand that she do so, for doing so would be "flatly dishonest, a lie, it would be wrong" (34). Her takeaway? "I was realizing with an immense illumination that neither she, nor any one, could *make* me do anything. One could suffer, one could die if it came to that, but one could not be coerced. I was born," she dramatically concludes (34). It turns out that a version of freedom for children is as crucial to Gilman as it is to Goldman, connected for both to illegitimate yet pervasive adult authority over the young.

Faced with her own child's "disinclinations to 'mind,'" Gilman looks to options for relating with her other than commanding, which "would have meant a contest of wills, punishments, bitter unhappiness" ([1935] 1963, 154). Instead of resorting to adult "superiority to enforce the behavior" (155), Gilman lands on the power of suggestion, since "'Let's' is the magic word with them" (154). She also consciously works to establish herself as a credible authority in her daughter's eyes, carefully not, for example, overstating ills that might befall her. Too often, Gilman intimates, we fail to do the work that would rightly give children confidence in our judgments. Do we think that we do not need to earn their trust? Goldman agrees that we do, parents and teachers alike. Given that "children are preternaturally quick to recognize pretense in any form," Gilman offers her daughter "absolute honesty" (157).

Community looms large in Gilman's childhood, something much less visible or lauded in Goldman's. Even when very young, Gilman recalls in her autobiography, she finds special pleasure in "find[ing] a girl who played as I did" (18), and she remarks on a "splendid memory" and "soul-expanding experience" of a "visit with the aunts" and "the Stowe girls" that involves dramatic, imaginative political play (16–17). By contrast, she mourns the fact that as a quite young girl, she mostly "lived entirely alone," portraying it quite tragically, as having lacked "sympathetic listeners" (23). Her mother refused Gilman "intimate friends" (30). She marks the moment she meets extended family as a teenager and discovers "how lovely family life could be" (31). She names as her "first deep personal happiness" the establishment, in her teenage years, of what would be a life-long friendship built on the basis of a vow "to be always utterly frank with each other in word and deed, never to pretend anything we did not fully feel" (48). "More formative and valuable" yet is "friendship with the Channing family," where she finds "broad free-thinking, scientific talk, earnest promotion of great causes—life" (49). Impoverished, constantly moving, often alone, and "inured to denial" (51), the young Gilman is nonetheless moved especially by connection, even if she has "to work to acquire this virtue" of being "thoughtful of others" (57).

A dual devotion to community and individuality—unthinkable in many canonical political theorists—is found throughout Gilman's writing on children. Even when it comes to moral and intellectual training, those cornerstones of her much-cherished community, Gilman asserts that "the main purpose is that the child's conduct shall be his own,—his own chosen course of action, adopted by him through the use of his own faculties, not forced upon him by immediate external pressure" ([1900] 2003, 68). And along similar lines, she asserts that "a steady insistence on the rights of the individual is essential to the integrity of the social structure" (194). But this coming into one's own always takes place in a social context, and it does so from the earliest years. Gilman advocates for communal childcare from the start, because "we cannot have separately what we can have collectively" (129) in terms of affordable, quality care, and, even more so, because it is critical that we challenge the way in private families that "we grow up unnecessarily selfish, aborted in the social faculties . . . because each child is so in the focus of family attention all the time" (132), as it is in some of Goldman's more romantic moments. She "attack[s] the single-family home as economically wasteful, isolated from the community, and necessarily restricting in its view of the world" (Nies 2002, 141). Joint childcare, "a number of little ones together for part of every day, having their advantages in common, learning from infancy to say 'we' instead of 'I,' would grow up far better able to fill their places as helpful and happy members of society" (Gilman [1900] 2003, 132). It is clear that "she want[s] children's schooling to promote unity by teaching them to direct and adjust their own actions to those of others" (De Simone 1995). Among other connections, this is tied to Gilman's view of progress, which she believes in and sees attained through conscious social construction: "Humanity evolves through social relations" (Seigfried 2001, 78).

For Gilman, a social consciousness is easily learned but does require institutional attention and social resources. An easier childhood (for adults and children) and a democratic adulthood are at stake. Sounding very much like her contemporary Jane Addams, Gilman writes, "The human soul has grown to such a stage of development that we are capable of loving and serving great numbers of people" ([1900] 2003, 197). Such a sentence has no place in Goldman's writing, but Gilman repeatedly emphasizes that "the child should be trained . . . [in] service to humanity" (165). While she believes that children do and should have rights that adults respect, she finds the harder challenge for adults, one that deserves more attention, to be in "the deeper and larger sense of social duty . . . the devotion to the service of all [which] must be shown by personal example" (112–113).

Gilman asserts, then, that "the human being is not only an individual animal" but also "a social constituent" (19). And on the other hand, "a society is composed of the people who compose it . . . all of them, and, as they are, it is" (21). It is noteworthy how often her work on children appeals to the democratic future that she hopes they can create, sustain, and thrive in. For example, she talks of moving children out of private homes where they are surrounded by domestic work and domestic workers, for such an environment does not nurture "those civic virtues so pitifully lacking in us now" (254), while communal childcare centers would foster an "atmosphere of equality" (137). Gilman believes "civic responsibility (rather than subjective desire) to be indispensable to identity formation" (Davis 2001, 102). And this belief requires that parenthood be accommodated socially and that children be treated as and trained to be social actors.

Keeping with this political emphasis, Gilman's disdain for corporal punishment, and advocacy of natural consequences for "bad" behavior, are based on "the kind of discipline which makes wise, strong, self-governing citizens" ([1900] 2003, 95). Discipline based on the inconstant whim of the parent trains children in "primitive despotism" and make it difficult to adjust "to a free democracy" (89). Reminiscent of Mary Wollstonecraft's affection for the "romp," Gilman notes that under current, erroneous childrearing practices, "the rebellious and unruly boy often makes the best citizen. . . . [T]he most submissive and obedient—do not make the best men" (43). Referencing the American and French Revolutions, as well as the Protestant Reformation, Gilman longs for the extension of "triumphant disobedience" (35) over "hoary tradition" (36) in the home and school in the name of "what a full democracy will ultimately bring to us" (35). This, she hopes, will be the next, crucial, revolution.

Comparisons

Goldman's children, we have seen, are relatively self-contained and driven from within. Mostly, they need to be freed from oppressive adults, who bring the worst of capitalism, statism, religion, and patriarchy to bear on their relations with the young, treating them as gendered and classed commodities to be ruled and shaped from without by fear and force, among other tools. With honest, affectionate teachers to stimulate and expose them to the world, with free parents who respect and love them, and with their own judgment, their developing critical skills, and the natural consequences of their actions, they develop their potential fairly spontaneously. Raised in freedom, they are prepared for freedom, their love for learning and experimenting intact.

While Gilman's children should also be freed from oppressive adults who demand their obedience above all else, other adults, true "experts," are needed to rear and guide the young, to supplement and inspire their internal judgment, sociability, and learning from natural consequences. Gilman has a more specific vision of what children's intellectual and moral development should look like, and that requires not only an environment conducive to joyful learning, which Goldman, too, desires, but also expert assistance and carefully, consciously constructed learning and living environments mostly invisible to the child.

Goldman is relatively silent on the ethics of the young—the ethics they actually abide by or in which they should be educated—while this concern is of primary importance to Gilman; she only argues that children are not "bad" or "dangerous," and that there should be a commitment to honesty on the part of adults. Goldman's writing on morality is mostly negative, revealing the crimes that are committed in its name, from forced mother-hood (based on making birth control illegal and sex education a joke) to economic inequality (justified by a supposed meritocracy and a "right" to property). But ethics are about social relations, and it is this persistent con-cern of Gilman's that spurs her to investigate and talk about ethics among the young and between children and adults. Gilman is preparing the young for a certain kind of adult social life—one for which they will need to be encouraged by adults, but also one for which the seeds already exist, in as much need of being understood as nurtured. For Goldman, anarchism also requires certain kinds of relations among the adults, but as those social relations will be chosen and can vary (as long as they do not involve, for example, state power or force over individuals), children cannot be educated for them in quite the same way as in Gilman's work, nor does one pattern of social life emerge among the young or those older. For Goldman, adults would benefit from and continue the process of artistic self-creation, alone and together, that should define and guide our young lives. Gilman has more of a blueprint, although one that every society should continue to improve on; citizens are more likely to successfully erect a well-functioning society if the building blocks for it are well prepared and fit for it—if the pipe is laid, as she would say.

The threat to individual freedom obviously comes, for the anarchist Goldman, from the state, as from capitalism and patriarchy, but it also emerges from the "harmful constraint" of other individuals (Most and Goldman, 1896). She was reluctant in her own life to align herself with almost any group, operating as a political freelancer rather than associating for long with any organization (other than affiliating with *Mother Earth*). This opposition between self and all but the fewest others is a constant in her life and writings. Relations might be compromising; others might not urge us toward conformity and might even admire our individuality, but it is not clear, in the end, how much they really enhance it or even contribute to our sense of self. The opposite is true for Gilman, who believes that we come to ourselves through community. Social institutions can be a threat, but they also hold out the greatest hope for amelioration of injustice and achievement of progress.

Both figures challenge the idea that individuality and sociality are mutually exclusive, but in their depictions of childhood, Goldman's scale, despite her being a fairly communal anarchist, is weighted toward the first of these, individuality, and Gilman's is weighted toward the second, sociality. In her numerous comparisons of the "uniform and average" to the spontaneous and original person (1907) and elsewhere, it can seem that Goldman is talking about the most exceptional, most self-motivated children, the ones who will be, like her, the strongest individuals in least need of guidance and support. Gilman might be speaking to a greater range of characters and considering a greater range of relationships as potentially constructive, judged on more criteria than self-fulfillment. The contrasts between them are also partly the result of methodological differences, as noted earlier. Gilman begins by observing and learning from the behavior of children, then moves to social relationships, and then to social systems. Goldman, on the other hand, begins with observations of the social systems in which children reside and their mostly negative effects on the young. She is less the social scientist than Gilman aspires to be and more the social theorist and provocateur. That, too, can explain some of their different emphases.

Concluding Thoughts

Turning children into neither angels nor devils, Emma Goldman and Charlotte Perkins Gilman reveal to us two distinct feminist perspectives on childhood—one somewhat more individualistic, but where positive social relations are valued, voluntary, and aimed at self-fulfillment; and one more communitarian, but where individuality is still prized. Their political philosophies apply with equal force to adults and youngsters: they make crimes against children visible in their essays; one might even say that their political ideas are as shaped by the injustices done to children as they are informed by those visited upon adults. Their positive ideas about freedom and individuality have concrete consequences for the lives of children, just as they do for adults, and they demand the reshaping of educational, political, and economic practices in the interest of children. Both thinkers truly integrate children into their political theories—no small or common accomplishment.

As a consequence, both figures have much to teach us about how to incorporate children's lives into political thought. They use the same principles to reveal and to judge what children do and what is done to children as they use with adults. They examine the environments in which children spend their time with the same critical eye that they cast upon those that influence the lives of adults, but without losing the child's-eye view of them and without losing sight of the vulnerabilities or gifts of childhood. Their studies of children give them a deeper understanding of adults—of what they have endured and might regain. It gives them a more complete picture of the social environment, including interaction among its multiple parts.

The two agree on much about the fundamental nature of children and the negative impact of such things as sex roles and force-feeding in education. They equally disdain much of the dominant approach to rearing and educating the young. Both are repelled by the incessant authority exerted over youth. But because they are driven by different political visions and somewhat different views of human nature, the two also sometimes part ways in their theories. Individual freedom shapes Goldman's free communities; it is their essential prerequisite and end, while freedom in and through community is Gilman's vision. The distinction is as subtle as it is substantial. After all, Goldman's anarchism is "the philosophy of the sovereignty of the individual" (1969, 67), and this view applies not only to women as well as to men but to children as well as adults; still, Goldman thinks that this free individual will be "a force for real love, for peace, for harmony" (211). But "Goldman understands the individual as making up society, and not vice versa" (Brown 2003, 120), while individuals are more socially created in the communitarian Gilman's work and need community for self-fulfillment at every age. Nonetheless, both start with a condemnation of the dominant models of childrearing and education that persist today, and both reject the adult relations of domination and subordination that also persist, and that we are educated for and into. Their feminism informs the ways in which they question the bases and effects of power and illegitimate authority and in their commitment to the revival of dignity and voice for the oppressed.

It is her feminist anarchism that gives Goldman her particular perspective on children. Even the most benign non-anarchists are more attentive to what society and the state need children to be shaped into than they are to what individual children are and can become, and most nonfeminists are less attuned than she is to the effects of power in supposedly nonpolitical arenas, such as families and schools. Gilman shares that feminist attention to power and even justice in "private" relations. But it is Gilman's socialist feminism that informs her perspective on children. As such, she is driven to reveal and nurture the social potential even of very young people and to link their fullest development to the possibility of a collective and democratic society.

Those of us who have spent a good deal of time in the company of children may view childhood as anarchic in the negative sense of the word, for children certainly bring in their wake all kinds of disorder, as well as in the positive sense, for children have an endless capacity for experimentation and creativity. But we also know that neither set of anarchic possibilities is looked upon kindly enough, and much adult interaction with children seems bent on stamping them out, often using the most questionable means. I think it is precisely that aspect of childhood that brings both figures back to the subject in so much of what they write—not just trying to create better adults through better childhoods but trying to liberate children. In this broad sense, the two fit into the liberatory feminist history of reflections on childhood explored in the previous chapter.

Those of us who have had the opportunity to spend time in the company of *groups* of children cannot miss the social relations among them, either, which differ as they age, but to which they almost always seem drawn. The social impulse gets them in trouble, too often, because educational and recreational settings alike often strive to mold those relations in ways that limit either the number or the kinds of interactions the young have, as discussed in the earlier chapter on everyday silencing. In Gilman's autobiography, the craving for companionship almost defines her younger years, just as enabling such relationships constructively defines her social reforms and, as we see in a later chapter, her utopia. In Goldman's writing, however, the words "individual" and "individuality" outnumber positive uses of such words as "social" and "community" eight to three in "The Child and Its Enemies," probably overrepresenting the relative attention the latter gets overall in her writing on the young and representing her deep skepticism of the many social forces that Gilman sees as capable of being reformed. Gilman, unlike Goldman, thinks those young relationships (with adults and other children) need a good deal of nurturing and guidance to keep them respectful and democratic and suggests that we need to be actively educated about proper social relations and social goods; Goldman is fairly quiet on child-child relations and seems perhaps to trust more that the free, respected, self-developed child will enter free relationships and will be able to resist impingements from others, learning by natural consequences with minimal adult interference. It follows that Gilman's adults are more thoroughly social than are Goldman's, and even more motivated to act for the good of the whole—although for both figures, solitude (for study, artistic creation, etc.) is visible and valued. Gilman especially recognizes and challenges "the reluctance of parents to view their children as members of society and as members of families," a perspective that "narrow[s] the scope of a child's education" (De Simone 1999, 130).

Both endorse discipline through natural consequences, which include social consequences, as we teach one another what we desire in relationships, what we will not tolerate, and so forth. Neither imagines a tyrannical child except as damaged by such things as training in morally bankrupt forces such as patriotism, sexual inequality, and economic inequality.

We live in a world that thinks both figures are wrong about children. Many abuses of children easily get understood as problematic: for example, we are saddened when young children are put to work, made to bear arms, sexually exploited, or denied an education. But if Goldman is right, then our mistreatment of children includes not only child labor but also the ways in which we train children for deadening labor in a capitalist economy. If Goldman is right, our problems include not only sexual abuse but also denial of sex education, sexual freedom, and sexual choice. If Goldman is right, we need to address not only lack of access to education but also accessible education that takes from children much of what makes life worth living—creativity, individuality, spontaneity, and experimentation. If Goldman is right, we are wrong not only for sending children to war but also for training them in the nationalism and patriotism that will justify and garner their support for future wars.

If Gilman is right, our young people are already capable and desirous of participating in various communities, from small and extended families to school and community groups, including with adults, and we are wrong to exclude them based merely on age. If Gilman is right, adults need to enter relationships with children with renewed respect for them as partners and must (as for Goldman) eschew the use of force and forceful manipulations. If Gilman is right, we err if we fail to nurture young people as both distinct individuals and deeply social beings. Directed by her, we would not only do more justice to children but be in just relations with them, an even deeper commitment. Our obligations to young people are heavy, demanding not only that we do no harm but that we consciously construct environments in which they can flourish, in which they, too, can even learn about civic responsibilities. And for Gilman alone, the state should be one of the benevolent forces able to "favorably respond to children's needs" (Davis 2001, 112). It is Gilman who might be the fiercer critic of the family, for Goldman still sometimes looks for it to fill its traditional care functions for children (once it has been reformed by divorce from the capitalist, patriarchal state that depraves it). And because of that, while both advocate for changes in childrearing in the school and beyond, Gilman advocates for more changes in childrearing in the home and socializes more of what Goldman keeps private.

If both of our figures are right, we are committing great injustices against our youth. For the world to treat children with the dignity they deserve will require some modest and some revolutionary changes. Reforming and restructuring children's lives are crucial to progressive social reform, whether in anarchist or socialist directions. Informed by these two (sometimes converging, sometimes divergent) thinkers, we can make moves in a better direction with a deeper sense of youth as actors—young, but fully human, emotionally, socially, and intellectually, rather than only potentially so. Perhaps surprisingly, one of the opportunities adults have, to become freer and more dignified beings, in their own eyes and in the eyes of others, is in their relationships with children.

The biggest difference may come down to how much guidance one thinks we need from the get-go about how to treat one another well and justly and about what kind of society to build together. Is the elimination of oppressive social forces enough, or do we also need the conscious and active presence of certain positive ones (and which will those be)? How does this presence affect support for multiple models of a good life? Can we freely decide as adults what kind of society to create or enter, in a world that invites experimentation and celebrates variety, or do societies require more sustained support from members and more socialization into them, including for such tasks as childrearing? Can we learn to use a social blueprint as an ever-evolving guide without it becoming something inflexibly imposed from without, compromising freedom? The goals of voice, dignity, and freedom for children say something substantial about desirable social settings and relations, something beyond individuality as a good. Goldman often admits this but stops short of accepting being directed by social goods—no less being shaped by them—while Gilman steadily builds upon this idea.

Goldman and Gilman tug at me, relentlessly, and only sometimes in the same direction.

NOTES

1. Others categorize Charlotte Perkins Gilman differently. Josephine Donovan (1985), for example, considers her a cultural feminist, while Charlene Haddock Seigfried (2001) calls her a radical pragmatist feminist. The emphasis I document on her strongly communitarian and statist views justifies my categorization, in agreement with her major biographer, Ann J. Lane.

2. The exception is Joy Denman's brief "Emma Goldman: Crusader for Children." In some books on Emma Goldman, such as John Chalberg's *Emma Goldman: American Individualist* (1991) and Vivian Gornick's *Emma Goldman: Revolution as a Way of Life*

(2011), you will not even find in the index any entries such as child(hood), Ferrer, or education.

3. A helpful website I use here is the Jewish Women's Archive, "Women of Valor," available at https://jwa.org/womenofvalor/goldman. Accessed August 12, 2019.

4. There's an interesting parallel to Goldman's own life, where she compares the supposed danger she presents to the "far more egregious violence against labor by state and corporatist forces" that is somehow rendered less visible (Ferguson 2008, 735–736).

5. The Emma Goldman Papers, available at https://www.lib.berkeley.edu/goldman /MeetEmmaGoldman/earlylife-portraitofananarchistasayoungwoman.html. Accessed June 2019.

6. Society for the Prevention of Cruelty to Children, founded in 1874.

REFERENCES

Brown, L. Susan. 2003. The Politics of Individualism: Liberalism, Liberal Feminism and Anarchism. Montreal: Black Rose Books.

Davis, Cynthia J. 2001. "Concerning Children: Charlotte Perkins Gilman, Mothering, and Biography." *Victorian Review* 27, no. 1 (Winter): 102–115.

Denman, Joy. 1977. "Emma Goldman: Crusader for Children." *Educational Perspectives* 16, no. 1 (March): 27–32.

De Simone, Deborah. 1995. "Charlotte Perkins Gilman and the Feminization of Education." *WILLA* 4 (Fall). https://scholar.lib.vt.edu/ejournals/old-WILLA/fall95 /DeSimone.html.

———. 1999. "Charlotte Perkins Gilman and Educational Reform." In *Charlotte Perkins Gilman: Optimist Reformer*, edited by Jill Rudd and Val Gough, 127–147. Iowa City: University of Iowa Press.

Donovan, Josephine. 1985. *Feminist Theory: The Intellectual Traditions of American Feminism*. New York: Ungar.

Falk, Candace. 1990. *Love, Anarchy, and Emma Goldman: A Biography*. New Brunswick: Rutgers University Press.

Ferguson, Kathy. 2008. "Discourses of Danger: Locating Emma Goldman." *Political Theory* 36, no. 5 (October): 735–761.

———. 2011. *Emma Goldman: Political Thinking in the Streets*. Lanham, MD: Rowman and Littlefield.

Gale, Zona. 1963. Foreword to *The Living of Charlotte Perkins Gilman: An Autobiography*, xiii–xxxviii. New York: Harper and Row.

Gilman, Charlotte Perkins. (1890) 1991. "Human Nature." In *Charlotte Perkins Gilman: A Nonfiction Reader*, edited by Larry Ceplair, 44–53. New York: Columbia University Press.

———. (1900) 2003. *Concerning Children*. Walnut Creek, CA: AltaMira Press.

———. (1903) 1972. *The Home: Its Work and Influence*. Urbana: University of Illinois Press.

———. (1935) 1963. *The Living of Charlotte Perkins Gilman: An Autobiography*. New York: Harper and Row.

Goldman, Emma. 1907. "La Ruche." http://wiki.libertarian-labyrinth.org/index.php ?title=La_Ruche.

———. 1969. *Anarchism and Other Essays.* Mineola, NY: Dover Publications.

———. 1970. *Living My Life.* Vol. 1. Mineola, NY: Dover Publications.

———. 1972. *Red Emma Speaks.* New York: Random House.

———. 1975. *Nowhere at Home.* New York: Schocken Books.

———. 2003. *My Disillusionment in Russia.* Mineola, NY: Dover Publications.

Grimm, Robert Thornton, Jr. 1997. "Forerunners for a Domestic Revolution: Jane Addams, Charlotte Perkins Gilman, and the Ideology of Childhood, 1900–1916." *Illinois Historical Journal* 90, no. 1 (Spring): 47–64.

Lane, Ann J. 1990. *To Herland and Beyond: The Life and Work of Charlotte Perkins Gilman.* New York: Pantheon Books.

Most, Johann, and Emma Goldman. 1896. "Anarchy Defended by Anarchists." *Metropolitan Magazine* 4, no. 3 (October). http://www.revoltlib.com/anarchism/anarchy -defended-by-anarchists/view.php.

Nies, Judith. 2002. *Nine Women: Portraits from the American Radical Tradition.* Berkeley: University of California Press.

Robertson, Michael. 2018. "The Maternal, Feminist Utopias of Charlotte Perkins Gilman." Literary Hub, June 4, 2018. https://lithub.com/the-maternal-feminist -utopias-of-charlotte-perkins-gilman/.

Rosenberg, Rosalind. 2010. "Review of *The Feminism of Charlotte Perkins Gilman.*" *American Historical Review* 115, no. 4 (October): 1165–1166.

Seigfried, Charlene Haddock. 2001. "Can a 'Man-Hating' Feminist Also Be a Pragmatist? On Charlotte Perkins Gilman." *Journal of Speculative Philosophy* 15 (2): 74–85.

Van Wienen, Mark. 2003. "A Rose by Any Other Name: Charlotte Perkins Stetson (Gilman) and the Case for American Reform Socialism." *American Quarterly* 55, no. 4 (December): 603–634.

Wexler, Alice. 1984. *Emma Goldman: An Intimate Life.* New York: Pantheon Books.

6

———

Feminist Manifestos

Childhood on Feminist Agendas

W here else, in addition to the history of feminist theory, can we look to get a sense of the ways in which feminists have addressed childhood over time and to see the emptiness of the tired canard that feminists are somehow "against" children? In this chapter, I appeal to another, even less familiar or heralded set of sources than the treatises written by feminist theorists: feminist manifestos. An extremely accessible genre of writing, manifestos serve an agenda-setting function for feminists and therefore allow us to see what issues related to childhood make it onto the lists of problems that feminists have seen themselves as confronting and striving to overcome. Closing out the historical section of the book, this chapter also serves as a bridge to the contemporary, as the documents cover more than three centuries (the final chapter of the book does the same bridging with utopian literature).

Feminist manifestos are phenomenal, mostly untapped sources of information,[1] and they have arisen from virtually every region, written by people from every religious group, race, class, sexual identity, and caste imaginable. Those I use here are collectively authored statements, meaning they are the *result* of a political process as well as intended to *inspire* political action, and the ideas in them are not just those of isolated individuals, but of feminists working things out and committing themselves together. Most that I cite (and the page references in this chapter) are from the more than 150 I collect in my hefty tome *Feminist Manifestos: A Global Documentary Reader* (2018). As I noted earlier in the Introduction, I was struck as I amassed those documents by where and how, for centuries, children kept showing up on feminist agendas. Here is my chance to put those repeated mentions together into something of an argument.

The manifestos emerged from one-time gatherings as well as ongoing organizations. They tend to contain the following elements: a critique of the unjust status quo; a vision of a more egalitarian, sustainable, inclusive alternative; and some strategies for effecting change. They declare, variously, to themselves, the public, the state, other organizations, other feminists, and anti-feminists what they are working for and why. They are feminists' own statements of their projects. Given less consideration by political scientists (who usually examine original political texts) and feminists (who work to recover their own history) than they deserve, these group-authored and -ratified documents surprisingly and skillfully weave theory and practice together as they speak to multiple and diverse audiences. The documents come in a variety of forms: from prose arguments to lists of demands to oaths. But however written, and whether the focus is global or local, on one broad issue or a whole range of them, a condemnation of inequality and oppression is central, as is advocacy of ever-greater democratic practices in multiple arenas.

Where, then, do children appear on feminist agendas? What particular issues in the lives of young people show up repeatedly in these critiques of patriarchy (and racism, ableism, classism, and colonialism)? How does age intersect with gender and other identities in the manifestos? What goals do feminists have for better childhoods as they envision more feminist futures in these impressive documents? In this chapter, I quote widely from the documents, as I did the feminist theorists' writings, and organize them into seven broad themes after a bit of framing. I usually follow a chronological timeline within each complex set of issues. I allow the issues to overlap and gently have one lead to the next, from economic issues, to childrearing, to education, to sexual and reproductive issues, to forms of violence that affect the young. We see age treated with gender, race, and class from the very early manifestos on, often joined by issues of ability, religion, and caste.

Framing

Children often appear in feminist manifestos among the very reasons for participating in feminist movements. In many of the documents, for example, women speak from their experiences and standpoints as mothers in addition to their other identities (wage earner, activist, etc.), with their eyes on their own and others' children, and they reach out to other women on that basis in common struggle. In 1954, for example, delegates at the founding meeting of the Federation of South African Women established the following goals in their "Women's Charter":[2] to bring "the women of South Africa together to secure full equality of opportunity for all women, regardless of race, colour or creed; to remove social and legal and economic disabilities; [and] to work for the protection of the women *and children*" (4; my emphasis). Writing during a time of intensifying apartheid, they declare:

> It is we who feel the cries of our children when they are hungry and sick. . . . We know the burden of looking after children and land when our husbands are away. . . . We know the bitterness of children taken to lawless ways, of daughters becoming unmarried mothers whilst still at school, of boys and girls growing up without education, training or jobs at a living wage. (206)

It is from such experiences with their children that the participants come together, as feminists.

Striking a remarkably similar tone a half century later and an ocean away, members of the Housewives' Trade Union, Argentina's largest working-class women's organization, show in their 2002 "Women's Manifesto"[3] that they, too, come together as mothers and potential mothers thinking about themselves and their offspring:

> We are the women who have to send our daughters and sons to the soup kitchens because we have nothing to give them to eat, and those who still have something but don't know for how long. We are the mothers whose children have had to leave school, and those whose children stayed in school but now are leaving the country because the education they got doesn't help them get a job. . . . We are the teenagers who don't want to be mothers so young but are deprived of that choice. (393–394)

Very often in these remarkable documents, women want to change the world for the sake of young people.

This idea that pregnancy is an issue for more than the individual pregnant person is put forth in the 2004 "Manukan Declaration,"[4] issued in Malaysia by the Indigenous Women's Biodiversity Network at a gathering held to prepare for the Seventh Ordinary Meeting of the Conference of the Parties to the Convention on Biological Diversity (COP 7). They write, "Indigenous women recognize that the womb is the first environment of every person. The state of health in this sacred environment is intrinsically linked to, and

depends on, the health of the water, the air, the land, the plants and animals"
(408). Pregnancy and children can make us outward-looking citizens, with a
distinct stake in and perspective on the world.

The complaints about the conditions of children's lives that we encounter
in feminist manifestos tend to ring true through the decades, even centuries,
and around the globe: that too many children live in economic conditions
that compromise their possibilities that too many of them are poorly educated, that girls are given fewer resources and opportunities than boys that
war takes particular tolls on the young, and more. And the work to amelio-
rate or change these conditions is established in the documents as part of
feminism. Gabriela Women's Party, a group "dedicated to promoting the
rights and welfare of marginalized and under-represented Filipino women
through participation in the country's electoral system and organs of governance,"[5] puts it as follows in its 2007 "Declaration of Principles":[6] "Women
have the right to fight for children's basic needs like proper care, nutrition,
health, safety and play, protection from abuse and exploitation; [and] access
to a national, scientific and mass education which is non-sexist as well" (475).
For, as stated in "We, the Women of the World, Declaration to Stop Sex Trafficking," issued in Bulgaria in 2010 by the Ways Women Lead Collaborative,
as feminists we must and do commit ourselves to "our common values: to the
value of each woman, each girl and boy child, each human being, that each
of us may live safely, freely, creatively, with equal opportunity, and with equal
responsibility to our whole human family" (532).

Childhood is most definitely on feminist agendas. And, as we will see, it
has been on them for a very long time, everywhere.

Economic Issues

The 1789 "Petition of Women of the Third Estate"[7] provides the earliest
explicit mention of youth and economic issues. Written to King Louis XVI
in response to a call to groups of French subjects to create for their repre-
sentatives "*cahiers de doleance*," or "notebooks of complaints," the document
describes the daily lives of young working-class women. The petition makes
several complaints related to the economic status of the young: (1) that "The
women of the Third Estate are almost all born without wealth" (41); (2) that
they are sent to work while still youths; and (3) that "many, solely because
they are girls, are disdained by their parents, who refuse to set them up, pre-
ferring to concentrate their fortune in the hands of a son" (42). Summarizing
their training, the young women write, "Having fulfilled the first duties of
religion, [we] are taught to work. Having reached the age of fifteen or sixteen,

[we] can earn five or six *sous* a day" (42). The authors complain about what an early entry into paid labor, and the consequent early end to education, deprives them of, especially since their deficient education only leads to poor employment prospects, such as being servants (private household laborers, a job that children today still are employed in globally). Mostly, they mourn their unfulfilled "desire to learn" (42). Impressively, these issues, laid out more than two centuries ago, foreshadow many of the economic problems that feminist manifestos continue to raise today with regard to the young.

Some themes similar to the French "Petition" are seen in the 1836 "Constitution"[8] written by young mill workers who joined the Lowell Factory Girls Association in Lowell, Massachusetts, almost a half century later, during the Industrial Revolution. Like the authors of the 1789 "Petition," they want "fair and liberal recompense" (54). Like them, they declare a "love of moral and intellectual culture" (54) that terrible working conditions put beyond their grasp. They complain about the "ungenerous, illiberal and avaricious capitalists" who are to blame for their dire youthful situation (55), signaling a critique of capitalism that would become common in later manifestos. And the "seduc[tion]" of relatively powerless female workers, the "danger" they face (55, 54), is a workplace issue they name then, long before sexual harassment would be seen as a civil rights violation or the #MeToo movement would respond to it.

Child labor, alluded to in these two early documents, is a long-standing feminist issue, addressed a bit differently according to time and place. Hours worked by the young—how many and during what times of the day—are a major economic concern, as the authors of feminist manifestos attempt to limit child labor, ensure that child workers also get an education, and open other opportunities for young people.

An early salvo in demands not only that the workplace be made safe in general but that additional regulations be enacted based on age comes from the Second International Conference of Socialist Women, held in 1910 in Copenhagen, Denmark. One motion proposed "the six hours' day for girls above 16 and under 18 years of age; the four hours' day for children above 14 and under 16 years; [and] the prohibition of all wage-earning labor children under the age of 14" (124). The attendees in Copenhagen understood "that the tendency to make use of boy and girl labor in monotonous and uneducational work is destructive in its results upon the health, character and subsequent industrial efficiency of the boys and girls themselves and upon the rates of wages and chance of continued employment of men and women" (125). They pointed, then, to the immediate and the long-term effects of laboring youth, on them and on the economic system. The "Conclusions" written at the very large First International Feminist Congress of Argentina, also held in 1910, recommend "six hours for children until they reach sixteen years of age," with "thirty-six continuous hours to rest" as well as "obligatory instruction, in the form of daily classes . . . along with the enjoyment of their complete daily wages" (141). The delegates' approach was comprehensive, looking to the length of the work week as well as the work day, with the child's health in mind, with consideration of their economic contribution and reward, and with determination to bring education into the lives of working youth. They were trying to prevent those "children who work in factories and workshops" from having their education come to an early end (141).

The situation of young people too early entering a heartless workplace receives attention in numerous other documents. Women labor leaders from around the world passed a series of "Resolutions" at the First International Congress of Working Women held in Washington, D.C., in 1919 in hopes of influencing the newly formed International Labour Organization. They declare (we see the demands get stricter over time) that "no child shall be employed or permitted to work in any gainful occupation unless he is 16 years of age, has completed the elementary school and has been found by a school physician or other medical officer especially appointed for that purpose to be of normal development for a child of his age and physically fit for the work at which he is to be employed" (161–162). Here, educational minimums are attached to minimum age requirements. Further, the conditions of work are addressed not only in the above requirement that the youth be "fit for the work at which he is to be employed," but in further resolutions stating that "no young person under 18 years of age shall be employed in or about a mine or quarry" and that "no minor shall be employed between the hours of 6 P.M. and 7 A.M." or "in dangerous or hazardous occupations or at any work which will retard their proper physical development" (162). There is an acknowledgment that not all labor has the same impact on youth.

It is clear that much feminist activism, within and beyond the borders of labor activism, existed long before and influenced contemporary positions on universal education (about which more in a moment) and child labor. Young laborers and their advocates have tried to put restrictions on when and where youth could work, with attention given to the meaning of paid labor for children themselves, including as learners and as economic actors. In the end, as the Women's International League for Peace and Freedom puts it in the "Resolutions,"[9] from its 1919 Congress in Switzerland, nations should simply support the "abolition of child labour." Thankfully, since these early documents were written, more scholarship has been done about the existence of children as a reserve labor force, deromanticizing the labor of children and revealing the conditions that give rise to child labor in the first place.

Even more economic issues appear in the documents. The 2012 "Manifesto"[10] of the European Women's Lobby, issued in Budapest, Hungary, affirms "that gender relations strongly impact the entire life cycle from birth to old age, influencing *access to resources* and opportunities and shaping life strategies at every stage" (557; my emphasis). Sometimes, economic resources are unequally divided among children, for example, with the disadvantage usually to girls. So, such documents as the 2005 "Widows Charter,"[11] written by Widows for Peace through Democracy, advocate for "daughters . . . inherit[ing] equally with sons" (430). When economic resources are limited or scarce, girls tend to suffer disproportionately. The 1989 "Abuja Declaration on Participatory Development," put forth by the Regional Conference on the Integration of Women in Development, states, "It has been reported in some cases that males (sons) are still preferred over females (daughters) when purse strings are tight."[12]

In even more economically dire situations, according to the 2000 "Declaration of the Essential Rights of Afghan Women,"[13] written in response to restrictions enacted by the Taliban, "poverty and the lack of freedom of movement pushes women into prostitution, involuntary exile, forced marriages, and the selling and trafficking of their daughters." The commitment to girls' education is more tenuous, and the tendency to view them as economic burdens and as economic resources comes through in the demand that they marry very young or engage in the sex trade. This terrible economic situation is fully documented in the 2015 "Statement and Action Agenda" by the Girls in Emergencies Collaborative:

> In the severest moments of an emergency, adolescent girls function as a default safety net or virtual credit card. A girl's assets—labor, time, integrity, and safety—can be deployed to underwrite the risks and to "smooth" others' material needs. She is the last to access survival resources, but the first expected to provide; she actively seeks out food, fuel, and water for her family. She may be encouraged or driven by circumstances to trade sex for goods or money; she may be forced into child marriages or short-term sexual liaisons for which her family (and intermediaries) receives money. Her lack of education undermines her own ability to obtain accurate information, discern dangers, or define realistic choices. (653)

One document that testifies to a rich understanding of the intersections of capitalism, militarism, and patriarchy is the 1909 "Resolutions,"[14] from the Second Biennial Convention of the National Women's Trade Union League held in Chicago. It raises another economic justice issue for youth: "The interests of working women as women, as workers and as mothers are peculiarly bound up in the maintenance of peace and in the avoidance of armaments," since "industrial and social conditions are in time of peace disastrously influenced by the enormous expenditure of civilized nations upon battleships and other preparations for war, and in time of war by the depredations, cruelties, and horrors of war" (131). Where else, they wonder, could the enormous sums of money that go to the military be spent, especially in the interests of children rather than against them? In "Statement of Conscience: A Feminist Vision for Peace," the Feminist Peace Network boldly asserts, nearly a century later, "We repudiate payment for a war machine that compromises our capability to feed and educate our children" (404).

Neoliberal trends are exacerbating the already-precarious situation. India's 2012 "Womanifesto"[15] documents how "the singular pursuit of high economic growth has been accompanied with chronic food deficiency and hunger, . . . [and that] malnutrition is especially pronounced for children and women" (611). It says, too, that "the privatization of public services like health, education, transport, etc. is also increasing family burdens" (611); for example, "public expenditure for the provision of universal, affordable or free services like . . . child care . . . has sharply declined" (612). As the 2014 "Election Platform" of the Feminist Initiative makes clear, even in liberal Sweden, "we are seeing how the government is unable to prioritize for the good of the whole society and for future generations. We are seeing a welfare system being exploited by private profit motives" (600). We need to be moving in the other direction, it asserts, such as "grant[ing] state subsidies to the development of environmentally friendly, cheap public housing of several varieties to benefit different types of families and constellations" (603), ensuring that all children, in every type of family, are housed. Other provisions are needed too, such as "access to affordable healthy food for our neighborhoods" (644), according to the 2015 U.S. document "State of the Black Union."

Childcare, as just mentioned, is another economic issue on feminist agendas as one of the ways in which we provide for the young. It is part of and distinct from attention to education, which generally addresses older children. A few more examples of the breadth of such demands show what is at stake and what is envisioned. At the First National Conference of *Raza* Women, held in Texas in 1971, the following resolution was passed: "That the National Chicana Conference go on record as recommending that every

Chicano community promote and set up 24-hour day-care facilities, and that it be further resolved that these facilities will reflect the concept of La Raza as the united family, and on the basis of brotherhood (La Raza), so that men, women, young and old assume the responsibility for the love, care, education, and orientation of all the children of Aztlan" (248). Also accomplishing much in a single sentence, the Women's Network of Croatia, in its 2006 "Political Platform," asks for "accessible creche and kindergartens for all, during two work-shifts and, for the children of self-sustained mothers and those from poor families, services free of charge" (443). The 2015 "Manifesto for Rural Women" by the Northern Ireland Rural Women's Network states that "childcare is very difficult to find in rural areas" (656) and often needs to start earlier and end later than urban childcare, given the distance from work that rural parents often have to travel. It asks for "a Rural-proofed Childcare Strategy that delivers flexible, affordable, accessible childcare options for rural families" (656). The needs of all children, in diverse economic situations and from varying cultural backgrounds, are sensitively attended to in these manifestos.

There is even more specific economic attention given in feminist manifestos to provisions for the very young. The first time the needs of new mothers and babies are addressed is in the "Resolutions" and "Motions"[16] from the First International Conference of Socialist Women, held in Stuttgart, Germany, in 1907. The final motion urged "the adoption of a system whereby . . . mothers shall receive monetary assistance at the time of the birth of children, and whereby mothers with children dependent upon them shall receive continued adequate support to enable them to attend to their children without having to work for wages" (124). It is unsurprising that a socialist group was the first to raise this issue of economic support for mothers and very young children. The Second International Conference of Socialist Women developed this idea in even greater detail. One resolution "affirms, that it is the duty of the community to maintain the child-bearing women, infants, and children attending school" (124). Other resolutions for the earliest years speak to "nursing-rooms in factories" (125) and advocate for all sorts of provisions at schools, from "halls for swimming and gymnastic exercises and school gardens" to "school physicians and school dentists" (125). Where most children are, most services should be. For those children not in school for a variety of reasons, the document also mentions "school homes where unprovided children are looked after . . . in leisure times, including holiday," and supports "obligatory, gratuitous feeding of all school children, in school times, [and] of unprovided ones even in holidays and vacancies" (125).[17] How thorough and thoughtful!

A century later, the 2002 "Women's Manifesto" by the Argentinian Housewives' Trade Union largely agrees with the views of these early socialist women. It argues that "women must be prioritized for benefits distributed through employment plans without doing community work as a condition for receiving them, so that mothers in the greatest poverty with five, six or more children, are not prevented from taking care of them" (394). It even advocates for "a wage . . . paid for caring work since the care of people by women and girls is a priority activity which must be recognized and paid for," and, further, for "a benefit . . . paid for each child" (394). Children will be cared for, and their mothers will be financially able to provide care. The 1943 "Australian Woman's Charter" also advocates for a "Child Endowment" (192), and the 2006 "Political Platform" issued by the Women's Network of Croatia agrees, advocating for a "children's allowance that follows their life expenses, paid regularly" (443). The lack of provision for expectant and new mothers can have dire consequences. The 2015 "State of the Black Union" documents, for example, that "the infant mortality rate for Black mothers is more than double that of White mothers, due to factors like poverty, lack of access to health care, and the physiological effects of stress caused by living under structural oppression" (643). That situation leaves surviving newborns without mothers.

Feminist manifestos recognize that providing so much for the young would entail changes in social priorities and structures. The National Organization for Women's 1966 statement of purpose says, "We believe that proper recognition should be given to the economic and social value of homemaking and child-care" (217).[18] As expressed in the 1991 "Declaration of Intent" by Hungary's Feminist Network, "The concept of work must be redefined so that the work required to care for family and children and the tasks needed to sustain everyday life should be included within the sphere of important activities deserving social and material recognition. . . . A high-quality system of childcare institutes and family services must be created out of public funds" (335). As the 2012 European Women's Lobby "Manifesto" puts it, we need

> alternative economic models which are sustainable for the people and the planet. Such models should introduce new ways of valuing the "care economy," the contributions of which have so far been disregarded in economic decision making. Care work, paid or unpaid, formal or informal must be reassessed and re-prioritised politically so that investments in the sector reflect the fundamental economic and social contributions this sector brings to society. . . . [W]omen and men can contribute equally to society while raising future generations only when proper care infrastructures are in place. (559)

Finally, Estonia's 2014 "Manifesto" makes clear that "the social and political inequality and poverty of women are passed on to our children, diminishing their well-being and development possibilities" (619). Economic gender (in)equality among adults affects children. The European Women's Lobby "Manifesto" summarizes the point: "Gender inequalities are costly; equality between women and men must be considered as an investment" (558).

Custody

It is important to talk about guardianship, since we have been discussing the provisions for and care of the very young. It is another contested gender-based issue on which manifestos have been taking a stand for quite a long time. While not unrelated to economic issues, this topic carves out some different terrain.

The 1848 "Declaration of Sentiments,"[19] from Seneca Falls, New York, lists but one grievance that concerns children: it names as one "wrong" of patriarchal cultures that "he has so framed the laws of divorce, as to what shall be the proper causes and, in case of separation, to whom the guardianship of the children shall be given, as to be wholly regardless of the happiness of the women—the law, in all cases, going upon a false suppositions of the supremacy of man and giving all power into his hands" (78). Children "belonged" to fathers. The "Resolutions"[20] of the 1850 Ohio Woman's Rights Convention concur in describing the problem, but in even stronger terms, stating that "in those laws which confer on man the power to control the property and person of woman, and to remove from her at will the children of her affection, we recognize only the modified code of the slave plantation" (88). Twenty-six years later, on the one-hundredth anniversary of the U.S. Declaration of Independence, women issued a document to show that they were still second-class citizens. Their 1876 "Declaration of Rights of the Women of the United States"[21] announces that it continued to be the case that "in case of divorce, on account of the adultery in the husband, the innocent wife is held to possess no right to children . . . unless by special decree of the court" (103). Her rights were not secure but up to the discretion of judges (and women at the time did not participate in proceedings as jurors or lawyers, no less judges). Further, bringing about change was proving to be difficult: "Laws passed after years of untiring effort, guaranteeing . . . mothers the custody of their children, have been repealed in States where we supposed all was safe" (103). The writers of these early feminist documents, then, understood that women's general lack of rights and respect had broad repercussions, including an impact on their access to and influence on their own children, which, of course, affects children.

Guardianship comes up again in the next century. In the 1910 "Conclusions" of the First International Feminist Congress of Argentina, there is, for the first time, a recommendation that "if there is no objectionable cause of legal exception regarding the mother," in cases of divorce, "the children should stay under her care," but both parents "should cooperate to pay the costs of care, clothing, education, etc." (142). The document recognizes the need to establish that "a woman, being of age, whether single, widowed, or married, can be a legal guardian" (142). Women's own status as minors in many regions made giving her the custody of minor children problematic. In 1954, the Federation of South African Women mentions this problem: "Large numbers of women today are in fact the sole breadwinners and heads of their families. . . . Many of them are responsible not only for their own livelihood but also that of their children. . . . Yet the law seeks to enforce upon them the status of a minor" (207).

Custody continues to be fraught for specific groups of women later in the twentieth century and into the twenty-first. Thus, for example, in the 1989 "World Charter for Prostitutes' Rights,"[22] the authors, all current or past sex workers, demand that the law "guarantee prostitutes all human rights and civil liberties, including . . . motherhood" (303). The work one does to survive and to support one's children should not, in a cruel twist of fate, be the cause of losing one's children. In 2005, it is still necessary for the "Widows Charter" to say of another vulnerable group that "anyone who forcibly deprives the widow of custody of her children shall be guilty of a serious offence" (431). The 2006 "Action Plan," from Finland's Women's Network of Disability Organisations, demands that "taking children into foster care must not be caused by lack of necessary support services" for the person with disabilities and her family (447). The 2007 "Dalit Women's Charter," issued by the Feminist Dalit Organization in Kathmandu, Nepal, a group involved with fighting caste and gender discrimination, still has to say that "there should be provisions for Dalit women to receive guardianship of their children" (462). And in 2008, the Pan-Canadian young feminists recognize in their "Manifesto"[23] that "our government [still] steals children from poor and Aboriginal women" (495), and they declare, "DOWN WITH racist child welfare policies" (496).

Broad gains in guardianship for mothers have occurred, but not evenly, or for all women. They also acknowledge the sobering tenuousness of whatever rights are won. It is clear that something dear is at stake not only to the women protesting the unjust state of affairs but to power holders in the states working against them.

Fathers

While the previous section dealt with women's right to have guardianship over their children, the need and demand for fathers to play an equal role in childrearing is another long-standing theme in manifestos. It is mentioned in numerous declarations as something that would benefit fathers, mothers, children, and communities.

The 1982 "Anarchafeminist Manifesto,"[24] written at the Third Congress of the Anarchist Federation of Norway, realizes that feminist change must happen "for all levels of social life," where we often think of political change occurring, and "also [in] the private sphere" (297). It advocates for what it calls "radical sharing of work by the sexes in . . . domestic life," saying, "Nursing and taking care of the children must concern men just as much as women" (298).

The 2007 document "What Mormon Women Know" declares that "*fathers as well as mothers, men as well as women, are called to nurture*. Nurturing . . . communicates patience, peacefulness, and care" (567). The authors assert that "*effective parenting is a learned behavior, and, as parents, we learn and grow with each child*" (567), opening the task to everyone and making it a learning, growthful, powerful experience. They recognize that, "unfortunately, women and girls still perform the bulk of the world's low-paid and unpaid labor, . . . often at the expense of their own education, leadership, creativity, health, and well-being. Men and boys who share care-work and household responsibilities make it possible for all family members to live happier, more fulfilling lives" (567). Much is at stake. These ideas are echoed by the authors of the 2009 "Rio Declaration," written in Brazil at the Global Symposium on Engaging Men and Boys in Achieving Gender Equality. These authors, too, want to "transform the imbalance of power between men and women in . . . families" (511). They emphasize the costs of assuming that "women and girls have to take responsibility for care work, including domestic tasks, raising children and taking care of the sick and the elderly" (513). They "encourage men to share the joys and burdens of caring for others with women, including in their capacity as fathers and providers of child care" (513). "We know and affirm," they proclaim, "that men are capable of caring for their partners, themselves and their children" (510).

The 2004 "Women's Global Charter for Humanity," issued at the Fifth International Meeting of the World March of Women in Rwanda, gets a little more structural and declares it necessary that "measures [be] adopted enabling women and men to balance their paid work with family, social, political and cultural responsibilities" (427). Men and women, to be full citizens of the world, need equal opportunity in multiple spheres, and that again would require revamping social priorities and redirecting social resources. The 2009 "Framework for Action," emanating from the Global Meeting of Musawah: For Equality in the Muslim Family, in Kuala Lumpur, Malaysia, continues this social emphasis. These authors, who are engaged in a dramatic feminist rethinking of male authority within the Muslim legal tradition, write that "equality between men and women requires equality in the family" (508). Going a bit further, they link this equality in the "private" sphere to justice within and beyond the family, not just to individual choices: "Women and men alike are entitled to equality and justice within the family, as well as respect and recognition for their contribution. The acknowledgement of joint responsibilities within the family must be accompanied by equal rights, equal decision-making practices, equal access to justice, equal property ownership, and equal division of assets upon divorce or death" (508). That attention to public *and* private not only must persist but must persist because progress in one cannot happen without progress in the other.

The 2014 "Manifesto" of Estonia's Sixth Women's Congress states, "We are of the opinion that both parents should participate equally in raising children," and it speaks of the need to value fatherhood more, including by making "parental leave, and parental benefits . . . supportive of fatherhood" (619). Looked at from the other direction, the 2014 "Political Manifesto for the Emancipation of Our Bodies,"[25] written in Peru at the thirteenth *encuentro feminista* (feminist meeting), calls for the state to stop "seeing the carework of women as a resource to be tapped freely in order for the state to cover its obligations to protect and care for life" (637).

I end this section on fathers with Yugoslavia's 1990 "Charter of Intentions," written by the Serbian Women's Party. It asks for the "establishment of equality in relations among [family] members; [and] equal participation in housework and the upbringing of children and social recognition of household labour" (328). "Equality in relations among . . . members" of the family is a beautiful feminist vision—the language does not just say "equality between the parents," although it includes that, but "among [all] its members," including children. This sentiment serves as an umbrella over the demand that parents participate equally in housework and childrearing, and it connects intrafamilial equality with peace. I turn next to educating these children.

Education

The goal of equal education seems clear. In 1954, the Federation of South African Women expressed their support "for the development of every child through free compulsory education for all" (208). And, as seen in the 1997 "Kigali Declaration on Peace, Gender and Development," emanating from a Pan-African Conference, feminists ask that we "promote education which develops the full potential of girls and boys and ensures that they play active and constructive role[s] in their societies."[26] But, unfortunately, it is not so simple. How do we accomplish this equality, and what sort of social priority is it? The 1837 Anti-Slavery Convention of American Women resulted in a resolution that states that "it is the duty of abolitionists to do all they can to establish and sustain day, evening, and Sabbath schools irrespective of color" (62), and it celebrated the first integrated colleges. Education has long been tied to emancipation; feminists, however, ask many questions about who is being educated, how, and for what ends.

Another early document, the 1848 "Statutes"[27] by the Viennese Democratic Women's Association, an organization established to spread democracy, asserts that we should "strive for the equality of women by establishing public primary schools and higher educational institutions, to reform the curriculum for women, and to improve the state of the poorer girls through loving advancement" (82). In this brief statement, we see attention given to class, to accessible education, to curriculum reform, and to the end of women's in equality.

Directed toward older youth, the "Official Statement" of the First International Council of Women, written in 1888 in Washington, D.C., directs "that all institutions of learning and of professional instruction, including schools of theology, law, and medicine, should, in the interests of humanity, be as freely opened to women as to men; that opportunities for industrial training should be as generally and liberally provided for one sex as for the other," too (109). Here, we see emphasis on granting females access even to instruction most associated with males, industrial training, "in the interests of humanity." Nonetheless, the 1904 International Woman Suffrage Alliance's "Declaration of Principles," issued in Berlin, speaks of how "laws, creeds and customs . . . discourage [girls'] education," and "impede the development of their natural gifts and . . . subordinate their individuality" (120). The impact on children of gender-based discrimination is front and center here, limiting girls' very individuality. The emphasis on nurturing children's individuality and talents is new. The alternative being sought is education that encourages the education of all young people and develops their specific talents, for themselves and for the communities of which they are a part.

Old themes are reinforced and new ones are introduced in the 1910 "Conclusions" of the First International Feminist Congress of Argentina, the first such gathering held in South America. The delegates demanded that governments "use all means necessary to serve elementary education, . . .

[which] should be secular as well as mixed, and equal for both sexes" (134). The "Conclusions" are attentive to the ends of education—that the purpose "may not be just to instruct the child, but also to give attention to the formation of the child's character, and to prepare the child for the struggles of life" (134). The means to the ends are also elaborated upon; for example, they advocate for nurturing a child's imagination with stories to "contribute to the development of children's ideas" (135), emphasizing children's intellectual capacities. As youth grow, their needs change, and the document advocates for "vocational and trade schools [to] be created for women" as well as "gardening and horticulture schools," all "as a means of making women skillful in a productive occupation that also is of general benefit" (137). Linking the education of females to the well-being of the national community, it asks "that women's education be given a scientific orientation, permitting women to carry out her part in society's progress" (140). This document looks at the intellectual life of young people in some new ways, although the insistence on secular and scientific education appears in many other documents. The National Organization for Women's 1966 Statement of Purpose continues the emphasis on educating girls: "We believe that it is as essential for every girl to be educated to her full potential of human ability as it is for every boy . . . and that, for a girl as for a boy, education can only be serious where there is expectation that it will be used in society" (217).

The sheer question of access to education is still not resolved in the contemporary era everywhere. The 1989 "Abuja Declaration on Participatory Development" links the economic, which we have explored, and the educational. It reports, "In some cases . . . males (sons) are still preferred over females (daughters) when . . . there is a choice to make between sending girls or boys to school, particularly beyond the first level." The 1997 "Kigali Declaration on Peace, Gender and Development" suggests that there is a need for "affirmative action measures to keep girls in school, accompanied by information campaigns for parents and supplementary measures to facilitate girls' entry to schools." South Sudan's 2009 "Juba Declaration" speaks to ongoing "stereotypical traditions that prevent the girl child from going to school" (520), something which it notes contributes to higher illiteracy among women compared to men and thus to unequal civic participation. The document still finds it necessary to advocate for "free education for girls and construction of at least one girls' only secondary boarding school in each state in Southern Sudan" (522). Even more recently, India's 2014 "Womanifesto" commits to creating "action plans to accelerate quality education for girls" (608), which is still lacking.

Once everyone is granted access to free, compulsory, secular education,[28] other questions will arise, including who is teaching what. The 1896 "Resolutions" of the Colored Women's Congress pay special attention to who is doing the teaching, especially in racially segregated schools. It states, "Realizing the gravity of our social and economic condition, and the wide influences of our teachers in assisting in the formation of the character of our children, . . . [W]e urge upon those in authority to exercise the greatest diligence in selecting trained, competent teachers, who are imbued with the love and true spirit of their work" (115). All children deserve quality teachers, ones who are well-paid (per the "Resolutions" of the 1927 All India Women's Conference on Education, 174) and attentive to the needs of their students and their students' communities. This also means what we sometimes call "culturally competent teachers." As stated at the First National Conference of *Raza* Women in Texas in 1971, "In order that women may leave their children in the hands of someone they trust and know will understand the cultural ways of their children, be it resolved that *Raza* child-care programs be established in *nuestros barrios* [our neighborhoods]. . . . In order that she will not be deceived by these programs, be it further resolved that these programs should be run and controlled by *nuesta raza*" (246). Parents want their children's cultures to be known and respected by their teachers.

This important point is repeated in manifestos across time and place. To cite one more example, in the "Manukan Declaration," issued in 2004 by the Indigenous Women's Biodiversity Network, the authors point out that "non-Indigenous systems of education have had a negative impact on Indigenous knowledge and ways of life. Indigenous Peoples have had the right to protect, develop and perpetuate their own systems of education which are consistent with their cultural and spiritual values. This is an integral aspect of self-determination" (407). The authors worry that Indigenous knowledge is endangered, and they strive to pass it on to the next generation, their declaration emphasizes, as do those of other groups.

The fates of children who are members of minority groups and cultures receive repeated attention from a number of additional angles. The "Declaration," from the Second International Conference of Roma Women in 2010, protests the facts that educational segregation of Romani children is the norm in several European countries and that they are systematically placed "in schools for the mentally disabled throughout Europe" (529). Not surprisingly, they have high drop-out rates in a system that fails to "address this and to promote a diverse school environment" (529). Educational systems must take it upon themselves, these authors continue, to "combat discrimination in education," and they think that governments have a role, too, but that educators should learn *from* and encourage the participation of the Romani community in trying to better educate Romani children by using, for example, their "model of Roma teaching assistants and school mediators" (530). With regard to another minority group, the 2015 "State of the Black Union" deplores the fact that "our schools are designed to funnel our children into prisons," and it demands, instead, "quality education for all" (644). And Diverse Voices and Action for Equality issued a "Declaration: LBT [lesbian, bisexual, transgender] Women in Fiji, for Gender Equality, Human Rights, and Democracy" in 2014. It acknowledges that "educational institutions in Fiji are powerful social and cultural institutions in constructing gender identity," and it, too, calls for "affirmative action programs," this time "directed at the enhancement of young LBT women's formal and informal education" (628).

The materials and curricula used in education also receive sustained attention in feminist manifestos. To start with what might be the most obvious feminist concern, the Feminist Network of Hungary suggests, in its 1991 "Declaration of Intent," that "the books and activities of nurseries and schools must be examined critically in order to prevent the continued propagation of obsolete and destructive prejudices regarding gender roles" (335). Yet there is still worry, as expressed in the 2006 "Political Platform" of the Women's Network of Croatia, that "society, particularly in its educational system, supports traditional gender roles and stereotypes" (444). The "Manifesto" of the 2008 Pan-Canadian Young Feminist Gathering agrees that "we are taught, from the time we are children, and through television and magazines, that how we should look, dress, and act is determined by our sex." It advocates for "freeing our children and ourselves from the gender binary" (497).

The concern with actively combating unequal and differential treatment based on gender stereotypes, starting in childhood, crosses astonishing boundaries of time, class, and race. Work remains even on this seemingly simple task. The manifestos want us to reach further, to dream bigger, as they turn to other aspects of the curriculum.

First, we have to bring children in on these efforts. The 2004 "Women's Global Charter for Humanity" demands that "measures [be] adopted to eliminate gender inequality among children and adults" (426), even when we do not often think of the need to work on and with gendered relations among children. The 2009 "Rio Declaration" advocates for "early and active involvement in programs that promote gender equitable behaviour" to "systematically create an environment where girls and boys are viewed as equals" (514). Clearly, "gender justice issues must be included in the school curricula from the earliest ages with a focus on promoting a critical reflection about gender norms" (515).

The concern with what children are being taught is an old one. An early American set of feminist manifestos emerged from female anti-slavery associations. Three national conventions were held between 1837 and 1839, and numerous local and state organizations were active around the country. They politicized motherhood by appealing to women *as mothers* to oppose slavery and discrimination, "by the blessings of their own and their children's freedom, and by all the contrasted bitterness of the slave-mother's condition" (60). This politicization changes the task of mothering—now they are, it was said in 1837, "to guard with jealous care the minds of their children from the ruining influences of the spirit of pro-slavery and prejudice" (60). Put more positively, "we recommend to mothers to educate their children in the principles of peace, and special abhorrence of that warfare, which gives aid to the oppressor against the oppressed" (61). It was expressed at the 1838 anti-slavery gathering "that every mother is bound by imperative obligations, to instruct her children in the principles of genuine abolition, by teaching them the nature and sanctity of human rights, and the claims of the great law of love, as binding alike on every member of the human family."[29]

Children should be politically educated, against racial discrimination, and for universal human rights. Variations on this theme occur for almost the next two centuries.

The very first demand of the 1848 "Manifesto," written by the Society for the Emancipation of Women, addresses education: "What do we mean by the fulfillment of our rights? First, independence of our persons, assured through the largest equal, obligatory, and free primary education system for both sexes" (71). The document advocates for a curriculum "showing the misfortunes of people, . . . [the] ways [they have] found themselves exploited" (73). Do not just teach the victor's stories. Later during that very revolutionary year in Europe, the First Viennese Democratic Women's Association said its political goal was "to inspire the love of freedom in a child's heart from the very beginning of a child's upbringing" (82). Such a strong vision is also captured beautifully in the "Resolutions" of the 1851 Women's Rights Convention held in Akron, Ohio:

> Resolved, That as the main hope of beneficial change and effectual reform of public evils depends upon the direction given to the mind of the rising generation, we urge upon all teachers, upon all parents, and especially upon mothers, the duty of training the mind of every child to a complete *comprehension of those principles of natural justice* which should govern the whole subject of Human Rights, and, of course, Woman's rights, and to an accurate perception of those

departures from them in human institutions and laws, which necessarily oppress woman primarily, and thereby injure man as well as woman ultimately. (96; my emphasis)

Change needs to happen in households and schools, through education about justice and injustice, and in social structures and practices. We cannot be silent about oppression with our children: as the feminist theorists of previous chapters made clear, children see and care about injustice.

It is important to teach about power broadly, including at the grass roots. The "Conclusions" of the 1910 International Feminist Congress of Argentina suggest "that the children in our schools be taught patriotism," but with the interesting caveat that teachers "simultaneously avoid[] disrespect for others' patriotism or an exclusivist feeling" (134). Also, they recommend that "special preference be given to those things that reveal the various progressive aspects of communities and societies, more than to the narration of wars and battles" (135). They call on "the women of the world to unite in order to work for universal peace, as well as so that the principle of arbitration might be applied both to international issues and to all challenging issues." What follows from this call is attention to the means: "We desire that this principle be the main orientation for the education of children" (137). How amazing and inspiring to make "the main orientation" one of arbitration, of dispute resolution.[30] At the 1915 International Congress of Women at the Hague, held during and responding to World War I, the attendees similarly "urge[d] the necessity of so directing the education of children that their thoughts and desires may be directed towards the ideal of constructive peace" (148).[31] They knew what happens otherwise.

The International Association of Radio Women organized in 1951 to promote international relationships and to represent women's points of view in media. One of its resolutions is especially noteworthy, as it respectfully treats children as knowing subjects capable of understanding global dangers, such as pollution, and implicitly calls on adults to help educate children accordingly. In 1972, its members called for stations to "redouble their efforts to expose the danger of pollution throughout the world," in part "by emphasizing the urgent need that children should understand the dangers of pollution" (203).

Political concern with education, with a progressive curriculum, continues as one century ends and another begins. The authors of the "Zanzibar Declaration," passed in 1999 at the First Pan-African Women's Conference on a Culture for Peace and Non-Violence, "commit ourselves to work with governments to revisit all education systems in order to: Establish a culture of peace as the pillar of education and socialization; Include counseling and special programs and training modules in conflict resolution and peace negotiations in curricula at all levels of formal and non-formal education."[32] This theme is obviously dominant and perhaps not as often associated with feminism or even childhood as it should be.

There is also concern with teaching "herstory." Croatia's 2006 "Political Platform" not only calls for "abatement of gender stereotypes in manuals and education" but adds "adequate valorisation of women's roles in history and present" as well as "introducing the principles of non-violent communication and non-violent conflict resolution in primary school education" (444). The 2009 Pan-Canadian Young Feminist's "Manifesto" encourages "learning and teaching true herstory and histories of our victories and struggles, especially those of women of colour and Aboriginal women" (497). The 2015 "State of the Black Union" "demand[s] a public education system that teaches the rich history of Black people" as well "and [that] celebrates the contributions we have made to this country and the world" (644). Again, so much work remains.

Finally, Sweden's Feminist Initiative, in its 2012 "Election Platform," reminds us of the broad feminist framework for thinking about educational means and ends: "The democratic mission of the education system needs to be strengthened through a long term strategy centering on critical thinking and a deepened knowledge of human rights and non-discrimination" (602). We might tie this relatively recent iteration to a very early one, found in the "Resolutions" passed at the 1850 Ohio Woman's Rights Convention, that emphasizes how women have been educated for second-class citizenship: "The prevalent ideas of female education are in perfect harmony with the position allotted her by the laws and usages of society" (89). What we should mandate is "that the education of woman should be in accordance with her responsibility in life, that she may acquire that self-reliance and true dignity so essential to the proper fulfillment of the important duties devolving on her" (89) in her new, larger role. Education has a role, either in oppression or liberation. It cannot be neutral.

Children and War

So much attention was given to teaching for peace in the previous section on education that it warrants more illumination of the effects of war on young people as discussed in feminist manifestos.

A general concern with the effects of war on the young is one of the oldest matters evident in the manifestos. Way back in 1642, in the "Petition of the Gentlewomen and Tradesmen's Wives" (a document affirming these women's very right to speak in public), women mourn that they might "see their children dashed against the stones" (31) or rendered fatherless by conflict. Leveller women, too, in the English Civil War, remark in their 1649 "Humble Petition of Divers Well-Affected Women"[33] that the effects on men from war reach "their wives, children, and families" and, in fact, that the latter are as "liable to the like unjust cruelties [of war] as they" (35). The 1849 "Appeal of the Married Women and Maidens of Württemberg to the Soldiers of Germany"[34] challenges male soldiers to end the counterrevolutionary movement. Its authors swear never to marry such men and mourn those "whom you, in blind madness have made into widows and orphans!" (85). Children, they recognize, easily become casualties of war. These early documents are powerful first salvos in the fight against war with an eye to the costs for young people.

The effects of conflict on the young are so numerous and diverse as to be almost mind-boggling, making clear why there is so much attention paid to peace in education. The Women's Peace Network speaks to some of the distinct impacts of war on children's psyches in its 2002 "Statement of Conscience": "We resent and resist the gratuitous encouragement of fear. We become more cynical toward the source and motives of each new rumor of imminent terrorist attack. But our children do not have our insight, and their childhoods are being destroyed by nightmares about powerlessness and destruction" (404). The "Chiang Mai Declaration on Religion and Women,"[35] issued in Thailand in 2004 by the International Committee of the Peace Council, notes that "women and children disproportionately populate the camps of refugees and displaced persons" (413), often due to armed conflict.

War renders parents unable to care for their families, as indicated in the 2004 "Manukan Declaration" by the Indigenous Women's Biodiversity Network: "In regions where conflicts exist, we as Indigenous women are the first victims of the destruction of biodiversity. Dependent and linked to the lands, but displaced as a result of war, [we] are unable to provide for the needs of our families" (410). The 2005 "Widows Charter" recognizes "the extreme vulnerability of widows and daughters of widows in the instability of societies in the aftermath of war." In the 2008 "Women's Declaration: Rights, Empowerment, and Liberation," issued at the First Asian Rural Women's Conference, the participants warn that "within the context of [the] War on Terror the top nuclear powers continue nuclear explosion testing." And radiation, they note, "affects primarily women of fertile age and their children" (482). They again call for "the prioritisation of budget allocations for food production, education and health, social services and empowerment of women over military budgets" (483).

Other concerns related to youth and war are elaborated upon in the 2009 "Rio Declaration," which emerged in Rio de Janeiro, Brazil, from the Global Symposium on Engaging Men and Boys in Achieving Gender Equality. It rues the fact that "girls and boys are increasingly drawn into armed conflict, both as victims and perpetrators" (513). More, we socialize them for these terrible roles, as Emma Goldman earlier argued. Thus, the "Rio Declaration" criticizes the ways in which we have "raised boys to be men" (emphasizing such things as dangerous risk taking, fighting, and dominance) and then, relatedly, "sacrificed [them] in wars" (510). It urges us "to embrace healthier and non-violent models of manhood" (511), starting with youth. In complete agreement with this view, Sisters Against Violent Extremism (SAVE) vows, in its 2008 "Declaration against Violent Extremism," "I will support the young generation with non-violent alternatives in their search for a better life" (499).

Children often become perpetrators in war, too, a problem addressed in the 1999 "Zanzibar Declaration: Women of Africa for a Culture of Peace"[36] (although many also see children being drafted as their being victimized by war). The document "condemn[s] the use of African children as soldiers," and the authors "commit ourselves to help release, demobilize, re-socialise, protect and actively integrate these children into constructive development processes." Children who go through rehabilitation programs have the opportunity to heal and to become members of a society committed to and knowledgeable about achieving peace.[37]

The multiple forms of violence directly perpetrated on the young in war, and the demand that they be understood as an absolutely inevitable part of war, is a dominant concern in the documents. The Feminist Peace Network, in its 2002 "Statement of Conscience: A Feminist Vision for Peace," emphasizes the "detention, rape and torture of women and children *as a strategy of warfare*" (403; my emphasis), not something incidental to it. It notes, too, how war often "forces upon women and children the obscene choice between prostitution and starvation" (403). Another consequence of the chaos of war is the "opportunities for abduction and trafficking," which hit the young especially hard.

Along similar lines, the "Letter to Women Legislators of the Coalition of the Willing: Neither Blood nor Rape for Oil" was penned in 2004 by London's Black Women's Rape Action Project and Women Against Rape. The authors are concerned that "the rape and other torture of women and girls has been largely hidden in the 'war on terror.' While the rape of men (and increasingly boys) is beginning to be acknowledged, the rape of women and girls was initially dismissed as 'a soldier had sex with a woman prisoner'" (417). They confront the fact that "rape survivors may be unmarriageable, ostracized and even killed" (418). They note sarcastically, "How convenient for the troops that the women and girls they rape should be too vulnerable to tell the truth" (418). Officially, "there has been no statement and no apology regarding the rape and other torture of women and girls" (418), and, in fact, the military may be complicit in the cover-up of atrocities. Since "everyone acknowledges that in war rape is inevitable" (419), the rape of women and children should be no surprise. The authors wonder, "Why were no questions asked about rape during the debate about whether or not to go to war?" (419). Would that have changed the calculations of governors?

The 2007 "Nairobi Declaration on Women's and Girls' Right to a Remedy and Reparation"[38] also emphasizes that acts of sexual violence against women and girls "are weapons of war" (469). These authors, from the Coalition for Women's Human Rights in Conflict Situations, understand that "gender-based violence committed during conflict situations is the result of inequalities between women and men, girls and boys, that predated the conflict" (470) and that dealing with such "unimaginable brutality" (470) through restorative processes must be done carefully, allowing girls (and those acting on their behalf) "to determine for themselves what forms of reparation are best suited to their situation," thus maximizing their "autonomy and participation" (471). Restorative processes must actively work to "overcome those aspects of customary and religious laws and practices that prevent women and girls from being in a position to make, and act on, decisions about their own lives" (471). Like restorative efforts with child soldiers, this work with girls is delicate and crucial.

Sexual and Other Violence against Children

Violence against children does not, of course, only happen in war.

Sexual harassment of young people was briefly mentioned in the "Economic Issues" section, as it is a problem that overlaps the economic and sexual arenas. In one of the earliest international feminist gatherings, the 1878 First International Congress of Women's Rights, held in Paris, the authors of the "Series of Resolutions" urge, in the language of their day, that all nations enact "a law establishing as a misdemeanor the act of seduction of an underage girl, accomplished with the help of lies and a false promise of marriage" (107). Among the "Resolutions" put forth by the General Union of Syrian Women at its 1930 Oriental (Eastern) Women's Congress is one that advocates for "the minimum age of marriage be[ing] fixed at 16 for girls and 18 for boys, and that child marriage should be abolished by legislation" (178).

We see this early concern again in recent documents condemning the marriages of young girls. For example, in the 2010 "Declaration of Romani Women Networks," written at the Second International Conference of Roma Women held in Athens, Greece—by the first group to bring together Roma women's groups from Eastern and Western Europe—the participants condemn "the failure of state and non-state actors to seriously discuss and address the practice of early marriages in the context of patriarchal dominance and poverty, with a view towards prioritizing the rights of Romani children" (529).

Child marriage, which has formally been considered a violation of human rights since the 1948 Universal Declaration of Human Rights, continues to have severe consequences for girls. It truncates girls' childhood, stops their education, limits their development of a peer group, increases the odds of domestic violence, and is the source of sexual and pregnancy-related risks. Child marriage has far-reaching health, social, economic, and political implications for the girl and her community. "Child brides" do not pick their own mates but are forced into marriage through family poverty and consideration of girl children as financial burdens. Ending child marriage requires the consent of all those involved, from fathers to religious leaders (Nour 2006). As the Women's International League for Peace and Freedom puts it, "All customs, whether social, religious or domestic, which entail the sale, barter, or disposal of women or girls in marriage or otherwise, should be decreed to be contrary to international law, and the law against slavery should be applied in such cases."[39]

The issue of sexual violence in the lives of the young is mentioned as a problem in many of the communities whose members author the manifestos. Hungary's Feminist Network says, in its 1991 "Declaration of Intent," "We protest against violence within families against women and children, which is widely known about but not discussed. Now is the time for it to be given the public attention it deserves" (335). The 2005 "Nunavik Inuit Women's Manifesto: Stop the Violence," written by the Canadian Saturviit Inuit Women's Association, is built on stunning data showing that one adult in three in their communities experiences sexual abuse during childhood, and about one woman out of two reports having been forced or having faced attempts to force them to perform a sexual act while a minor. They write, "The future of Nunavik lies with our children. We wish to assert the right for our children to grow in peace and security, and only in this way will the cycle of violence be put to an end. . . . Child sexual abuse is absolutely intolerable and must end" (435). Calling themselves out, they state that "if we continue to not act against this violence, we and our children will continue to bear the scars, for inaction perpetuates the cycle of violence" (436).

Speaking to another form of sexual violence among youth, the 2005 "Survivors of Prostitution and Trafficking Manifesto,"[40] written by the Coalition Against Trafficking in Women—the first organization to fight human trafficking internationally—declares that "women in prostitution do not wake up one day and 'choose' to be prostitutes. . . . Most women are drawn into prostitution at a young age" (440). As we have seen, war is one cause of this, poverty is another, and the low status of girls is yet another. And there is more.

The 2010 "We, the Women of the World, Declaration to Stop Sex Trafficking," issued in Bulgaria by the Ways Women Lead Collaborative, declares that "violence against women and their children is a gross breach of human rights. It prevents women and the children they raise from exercising their basic freedoms. Sex trafficking and slavery, still widely spread, are the most repulsive forms of violence, threatening women and children's inherent integrity of being" (532). It asserts that "sex trafficking of women and children is not a private or family or religious matter, but rather a crime and its prevention and judgment is the responsibility of all public institutions" (532). The 2014 "Manifesto" by Canada's Indigenous Women Against the Sex Industry makes clear as well that, because of colonialism and racism, prostitution and pornography "disproportionately harm Indigenous women and girls and our sisters of colour" (621). The authors say these issues are "opposed to our traditional ways of life where women and girls were valued, loved, and treated with the respect we deserve" (622). They question "the unchallenged male demand for sexual access to the bodies of women and girls" (622) and a "sex industry [that] treats all women and girls as hated objects . . . [with] Indigenous women and girls and our sisters of color . . . subjected to the worst and most degrading forms of male violence" (622). We are living in a world, however, according to the "Chiang Mai Declaration on Religion and Women," in which "globalized capitalism has reduced everything to a commodity," including, in sex trafficking, "women's and children's bodies" (413).

Children need to be informed and empowered. And, as emphasized throughout this book, adults need to listen. India's 2014 "Womanifesto" advocates for the creating and funding of "a comprehensive scheme to prevent sexual abuse of children, including safe childcare for children in villages and urban jhuggis, and awareness campaigns among children and parents" (607).

Not all violence against children is sexual, of course. Violence against children, including gender-based violence, begins early, as one "example of femicide is the killing of infant girls simply because they are females"

(632), according to the "Position Statement: Femicide"[41] issued in 2014 by the Canadian Council of Muslim Women. It views such acts as being at "the extreme end of the same continuum of violence against women and girls" (632). As put forth in the 2013 "Public Statement"[42] by the Third International Intersex Forum, very young intersex children have been subjected "to mutilating and 'normalising' practices such as genital surgeries," and it recommends, instead, that "intersex people must be empowered to make their own decisions affecting [their] own bodily integrity, physical autonomy and self-determination" (596). The 1989 "Abuja Declaration on Participatory Development" is one of several documents to bring attention to other "hazardous traditional practices" that affect young girls, including "female circumcision," and it notes that "such practices often inflict permanent physical, psychological and emotional damages, even death." The 1997 "Declaration of Women's Rights in Islamic Societies" simply asserts that girls "should not be subject to gruesome ritual mutilations of her person," and the 1994 "Women's Declaration on Population Policies"[43] agrees that "harmful practices such as genital mutilation or unnecessary medical procedures, violate basic human rights" (359).

The 2009 "Rio Declaration" importantly reveals that "girls and boys suffer from large-scale abuse and violence (including corporal and other forms of humiliating and degrading punishment) in the home, community, school and institutions that are charged with protecting them" (512). It happens everywhere, even in "institutions that are charged with protecting" young people. And, unsurprisingly, such "violence often follows gendered patterns" (512). The challenge of ending such widespread and normalized violence is complex and must be addressed by a multiplicity of parties, ranging from national governments to schools to local communities. For example, the authors of the 2010 "Declaration of Romani Women Networks" suggest that, among other efforts, "Roma activists should work with Romani communities to raise awareness of their children's rights and their parental responsibilities" (530).

As always, distinct groups of children are particularly vulnerable, often to distinct forms of violence. As INCITE! notes in its 2001 "Manifesto: Gender Violence and the Prison Industrial Complex," "LGBTI [lesbian, gay, bisexual, transgender, and intersex] street youth and trans people are particularly vulnerable to police brutality and criminalization," and it urges correcting the fact that "the anti-prison movement has failed to sufficiently organize around the forms of state violence faced by LGBTI communities" (386). And the 2005 "Widows Charter" urges giving particular attention to the "sexual exploitation, prostitution and trafficking" of the children of widows (432).

Reproductive and Sexual Justice

Sexual and reproductive issues raised in the declarations continue beyond matters of abuse. Positive recommendations usually support the sexual integrity and autonomy of young people.

One of the earliest issues to arise is sexual morality, especially the sexual double standard that establishes different guidelines (and punishments) for the sexual behaviors of boys and girls. An early iteration of this, the "Resolutions" of the National Colored Women's Congress, passed in 1896 by the oldest secular African American women's organization still in existence, points to the issue of equal moral standards, starting in youth. The congress frames this matter in educational terms: "That we require the same standard of morality for men as for women, and that the mothers teach their sons social purity as well as their daughters" (115).

The double sexual standard has long been contested from a variety of perspectives, with some challenging and restricting male behavior and some expanding behavioral options for females. The *La Raza*'s 1971 "Workshop Resolutions" state, "Mothers should teach their sons to respect women as human beings who are equal in every respect. No double standard," for "it is the responsibility of Chicanas with families to educate their sons and thus change the attitudes of future generations." As expressed in the "Women's Declaration on Population Policies" in 1994, "Men also have a personal and social responsibility for their own sexual behavior and fertility and for the effects of that behavior on their partners and their children's health and well-being" (358). And it is repeated in the 2012 Mormon document "All Are Alike unto God," which asks us to "recognize that girls and boys, women and men are equally responsible for appropriate sexual behavior, and avoid reducing morality to sexuality, and modesty to a preoccupation with women's and girls' clothing" (569). Sweden's Feminist Initiative said it well in 2012: "We believe that men are capable of taking responsibility for their actions and respect[ing] their fellow human beings" (603). The "Rio Declaration" adds, "Men's and boys' accountability and engagement for social transformation is essential to ensure violence-free lives for women and girls" (512).

The dominant angle on sexuality is definitely educational. In the "Workshop Resolutions" that emerged from the National Alliance of Black Feminists at the 1977 Black Women's Conference, the participants passed a resolution urging that the group "develop female sexuality awareness programs for adolescents" (282). The 1994 "Women's Declaration on Population Policies," too, says, "All women, regardless of age . . . have a right to information and services necessary to exercise their reproductive rights and responsibilities."

It emphasizes that "women require information and services not just in the reproductive ages but before and after" (119).

Young feminists have taken on these issues themselves. Realizing Sexual and Reproductive Justice (RESURJ) is an alliance of younger feminists from the global South. In its 2014 online "10-Point Action Agenda,"[44] it advocates for

> comprehensive sexuality education programs [that] promote sexual
> and reproductive rights, gender equality, self-empowerment, knowl-
> edge of the body, bodily integrity and autonomy, and relationship
> skills development; are free of gender stereotypes, discrimination,
> and stigma; and are respectful of children's and adolescents' evolv-
> ing capacities to make choices about their sexual and reproductive
> lives. (537)

The content and impact of sex education is understood quite broadly here. Some statements, as in Croatia's 2006 "Political Platform," advocate for very early and continuing sex education, including "liberal sexual education in kindergartens, primary and secondary schools" (444). They worry that "stereotyping of male-female relationships is growing, and liberal sexual education has vanished from the curriculum" (444). Similarly, in the 2011 "Manifesto of Young Feminists of Europe,"[45] written by about seventy participants in a weeklong camp in Paris, we see support for the "provision of sex education (in schools, through popular education, the media, etc.)" (555). But these young authors know that such programs can be hijacked, and so they demand, radically, that "feminist points of view on sexuality . . . break with the patriarchal, heterosexist system that creates sex- and gender-based inequalities" (555). The answer to age-old concerns about sexual vulnerability must include feminist-informed, racially-sensitive programs that address sexuality and inequality. The European Young Feminists' agenda is wide-ranging and inclusive. It proposes, for example, "freedom to choose our sexual identity (lesbian, transsexual, queer, intersex, etc.)" (555).

Sex education must be inclusive and tailored to the special needs of diverse populations. For example, the 2006 "Action Plan," put forth by the Women's Network of Disability Organisations in Finland, asserts that "disabled women and girls have a right to information about growing up into womanhood, as well as information about female sexuality and reproductive health" (446). RESURJ is in complete agreement, as it demands that we

> protect women's and young people's human rights in sexual and repro-
> ductive health programs by guaranteeing that services are designed

to respond to individuals' health needs and overcome barriers faced by marginalized groups, including through service provision that is free from stigma, coercion, discrimination and violence, based on full and informed consent, and that affirms the right to pleasure. (537)

"Feminist Principles of the Internet,"[46] produced in 2014 in Malaysia at the Gender, Sexuality, and the Internet Meeting of the Association for Progressive Communications, puts a very contemporary addition into the educational conversation:

> We recognize our role as feminists and internet rights advocates in securing a safe, healthy, and informative internet for *children* and young people. This includes promoting digital and social safety practices. At the same time, we acknowledge children's rights to healthy development, which includes access to positive information about sexuality at critical times in their development. We believe in including the voices and experiences of young people in the decisions made about harmful content. (625, my emphasis)

Children Are Affected by Politics

There is one final, overarching issue to touch on, hinted at throughout. Feminist manifestos understand that children are deeply affected by a wide variety of social, economic, and political events, as our feminist theorists earlier claimed. This means that, in working to establish environments in which children can thrive, we need to be attentive to the larger world in which children live—they are in no way isolated from it. It also means, as noted in the chapter on Goldman and Gilman, that we should use its effects on children as an important way to judge politics. So, look at some of the social, political, and economic trends that feminists have pointed to as deeply touching the lives of young people (all the italics are mine):

- "Increasing *poverty* . . . is affecting the lives of the majority of the world's people, in particular women and children" ("Beijing Declaration,"[47] Fourth World Conference on Women, Beijing, 1995).
- "The majority of the world's women and girls are adversely affected by the unequal power relations created at the national, regional and international levels by the *new trade regime*" ("Women's Caucus Declaration,"[48] Third Ministerial Meeting of the World Trade Organisation, Seattle, Washington, 1999).

- "Pressures of the *globalized economy* have led to even greater violence against women and children" ("Chiang Mai Declaration on Religion and Women: An Agenda for Change," International Committee of the Peace Council, Thailand, 2004, 413).
- "*Imperialist globalization* is causing ethnocide among indigenous women, their children and their communities. . . . *[F]undamentalist* and communal forces . . . are unleashing violence on society, particularly women and children" ("Rural Women's Declaration: Rights, Empowerment, and Liberation," First Asian Rural Women's Conference, India, 2008, 481, 483).
- "Under conditions *devoid of their rights*, women find themselves and their children in a situation of permanent danger" ("Declaration of the Essential Rights of Afghan Women," Dushanbe Conference on Afghan Women, Tajikistan, 2000, 382).
- "The impact of the *food crisis* is likely to be much more severe among women and children" ("A Women's Declaration to the G8: Support Real Solutions to the Global Food Crisis,"[49] MADRE, New York, 2008, 485).
- "With *food scarcity*, the health and wellbeing of the new generation are at risk" ("Mandaluyong Declaration," Global Conference on Indigenous Women, Climate Change and REDD Plus,[50] Philippines, 2010, 541).
- "*Imperialism* in our region has resulted in an increasing number of victims of its policies and ever more risk to the lives of people, especially women and children" ("International Women's Day Statement,"[51] Union of Palestinian Women's Committees, Palestine, 2015, 647).

This is a pretty good cross section.

Given how affected young people are by politics, in its 2010 "Vision Statement," RESURJ argues that "every woman, adolescent and young person must have full citizenship and access to an enabling environment in order to realize their sexual and reproductive rights" (535–536) and more. In its 2014 "10-Point Action Agenda," RESURJ calls "on all decision-makers" to "expand decision-making opportunities for women and young people by ensuring," for example, "their meaningful participation in all stages of design, monitoring and implementation of sexual and reproductive rights policies and programs at national, regional and international levels" (536). Sweden's Feminist Initiative agrees in its 2012 "Election Platform," declaring that "the right of the child to care and participation should be the guiding principle for all political decisions concerning children" (601). Further, it adds, "Every child and young person should be aware of their rights and to have somewhere to turn to, should these rights be violated" (602). Hence, feminists demand certain kinds of education, as we have already explored.

Concluding Thoughts

There is more. There is always more. The declarations talk about additional issues, from education for special-needs children, to the need for nongendered socialization, to the rights of "illegitimate" children. The documents show that the forces compromising children's lives are not only familial, where we focus so much, but also social, economic, and political. Too, these forces are gendered and racialized. We fail to meet the needs of children through our everyday practices in schools, homes, and workplaces as well as in more extraordinary moments (becoming more commonplace) of war and displacement.

What this study also shows is that feminists around the world have long had children on their agendas—children, in all of their diversity—and have been working for a more just and egalitarian world where all of them have their basic needs met and, more, a supportive environment in which they can flourish. As was the case with the historical feminist theorists, we see another history that we can be proud of, that we should know about and remember, and that we can continue to build and improve upon.

Behind all the work of the groups that wrote these documents is the commitment, as expressed in the 2008 Pan-Canadian Young Feminist "Manifesto," that "*we will:* Believe that a better world is possible and work to achieve it" (497). The "Women's Global Charter for Humanity" reminds us that "our feminist struggles and those of our foremothers on every continent have forged new freedoms for us, our daughters and sons, and all the young girls and boys who will walk the earth after us" (422). Feminism has already contributed to children's increased well-being and has the potential and the drive, the politics, to contribute even more.

The visions in these documents as well as the experiences of the activists/ theorists who wrote them can guide and inspire us. The 1896 "Objectives" of the National Association of Colored Women's Clubs link the state of women and children in three of their seven items: "To promote the education of women and children," the first reads; "To work for the moral, economic, social, and religious welfare of women and children," reads another; and "To protect the rights of women and children," states yet another (112).

There is an idea here that what contributes to welfare of one group contributes to the other's welfare, an idea that both demand attention, and the notion that feminism's commitment is to both. Also central in nearly all the documents is the understanding that solving problems related to children is not just a burden that should fall to individual women, and especially not just to individual mothers. As the National Organization for Women's 1966 "Statement of Purpose" puts it: "Above all, we reject the assumption that these problems are the unique responsibility of each individual woman, rather than a basic social dilemma which society must solve" (216).

We must continue, along with RESURJ, to "envision a world where every person's human rights are affirmed and upheld. A world guided by equality and equity, where . . . young people in all their diversity are empowered . . . [and] have the ability to live with dignity and autonomy through the different stages of their lives" (535). When it comes to working for better childhoods, we might recall the work of the 2008 "Guatemalan Feminist Declaration": we "will not favor one group or struggle over another because [we] recognize that all individuals and all struggles for freedom are interdependent in this process of building another world" (492). We must understand, along with the European Women's Lobby, as expressed in its 2012 "Manifesto," "that a sustainable future . . . is possible only if all women, men, girls and boys are free to contribute equally to society regardless of where they are situated in the 'circle of life'" (557).

NOTES

1. I say "mostly untapped" because a very few have been published a number of times in feminist anthologies. The most popular include the 1848 "Declaration of Sentiments" from Seneca Falls and the 1977 Combahee River Collective's "A Black Feminist Statement." We miss a great deal of global feminist theory and activism by not reading more broadly than this.

2. Available at https://www.sahistory.org.za/article/womens-charter. Accessed on October 18, 2019.

3. Available at https://caringlabor.wordpress.com/2010/07/29/housewives-trade -union-santa-fe-argentina-womens-manifesto/. Accessed on October 18, 2019.

4. Available at http://www.ipcb.org/resolutions/htmls/manukan.html. Accessed on October 18, 2019.

5. Available at https://gabrielanews.wordpress.com/about/. Accessed on July 11, 2019.

6. Available at https://wunrn.com/2012/04/the-philippines-gabriela-womens-party/. Accessed on October 18, 2019.

7. Available at http://chnm.gmu.edu/revolution/d/472/. Accessed on October 18, 2019.

8. Available at http://americanantiquarian.org/millgirls/items/show/54. Accessed on October 18, 2019.

9. Available at https://wilpf.org/wp-content/uploads/2012/08/WILPF_triennial _congress_1919.pdf. Accessed on October 18, 2019.

10. Available at https://www.womenlobby.org/Manifesto-Women-s-Socio-Economic -Rights-and-Gender-Equality-from-a-life-cycle. Accessed on October 18, 2019.

11. Available at https://projects.iq.harvard.edu/files/violenceagainstwomen/files /wpdwidowscharter.doc.pdf. Accessed on October 18, 2019.

12. Studies in wealthy countries show that parents today continue to spend money on children in very gendered ways. The *Mirror* reports, for example, on a relatively minor example: "The gender divide starts young as boys have more spent on their rooms than girls for their gear is worth almost £1,000 more at £3,279.45 compared with £2,315.60." Ruki Sayid, "Parents Spend £1,000 More Spoiling Boys Than Girls," the *Mirror*, March 21, 2016, available at https://www.mirror.co.uk/money/parents -spend-1000-more-spoiling-7601756. Accessed on October 12, 2018.

13. Available at https://kabultec.org/the-roqia-center/declaration/. Accessed on October 18, 2019.

14. Available at https://iiif.lib.harvard.edu/manifests/view/drs:2577309$2i. Accessed on October 18, 2019.

15. Available at https://secure.avaaz.org/campaign/en/womanifesto_redirect/. Accessed on October 18, 2019.

16. Available at https://www.marxists.org/archive/kollonta/1907/is-conferences .htm. Accessed on October 18, 2019.

17. Recent attention to providing meals to young people from low-income families during times when school is not in session builds on this long tradition.

18. Available at https://now.org/about/history/statement-of-purpose/. Accessed on October 18, 2019.

19. Available at https://www.historyisaweapon.com/defcon1/stantonsent.html. Accessed on October 18, 2019.

20. Available at http://www.salem.lib.oh.us/wp-content/uploads/2015/11/WellDone Sister.pdf. Accessed on October 18, 2019.

21. Available at https://awpc.cattcenter.iastate.edu/2017/03/21/declaration-of -rights-of-the-women-of-the-united-states-july-4-1876/. Accessed on October 18, 2019.

22. Available at https://www.walnet.org/csis/groups/icpr_charter.html. Accessed on October 18, 2019.

23. Available at http://www.socialistvoice.ca/?p=342. Accessed on October 18, 2019.

24. Available at https://theanarchistlibrary.org/library/anonymous-anarchafeminist -manifesto. Accessed on October 18, 2019.

25. Available at http://www.sacw.net/article11532.html. Accessed on October 18, 2019.

26. Available at http://repository.uneca.org. Accessed on July 10, 2019.

27. Available at https://ghdi.ghi-dc.org/sub_document.cfm?document_id=452. Accessed on October 19, 2019.

28. There was much demand for secular education. The "Declaration against Sexual Apartheid," issued in 2008 by "Equal Rights Now: Organisations Against Women's Discrimination in Iran," is but one manifesto calling for the "absolute separation of religion from the state and educational system" (478). Some also call for change in

religious education. One early demand from the First Feminist Congress held in Mexico in 1916 urges no "religious teaching to minors under the age of 18" because they "accept everything" and also come to fear "a vengeful and irate God" (150).

29. Available at https://www.loc.gov/item/33001926/. Accessed on October 18, 2019.

30. My students tell me, in 2020, that they believe that they lack the tools of civic discourse and that such resources have not been taught or provided as part of their education.

31. Available at https://wilpf.org.uk/wp-content/uploads/2015/03/20-Resolutions.pdf. Accessed on October 18, 2019.

32. Available at https://www.africa.upenn.edu/Urgent_Action/apic_6799.html. Accessed on July 9, 2019.

33. Available at https://quod.lib.umich.edu/e/eebo/A94690.0001.001?rgn=main;view=fulltext. Accessed on October 18, 2019.

34. Available at http://germanhistorydocs.ghi-dc.org/sub_document.cfm?document_id=451. Accessed on October 18, 2019.

35. Available at https://www.peacecouncil.org/ChiangMai.html. Accessed on October 19, 2019.

36. Available at https://www.culture-of-peace.info/annexes/declarations/Zanzibar.pdf. Accessed on October 19, 2019.

37. This is reminiscent of the Feminist Dalit Charter, although the concern there is not with war per se but with bringing children back more generally from destructive experiences: "All Dalit children below the age of 18, who were forced to engage in risky jobs, inside and outside of the country, should be rescued and proper arrangements should be made to improve their lives" (458).

38. Available at https://www.fidh.org/IMG/pdf/NAIROBI_DECLARATIONeng.pdf. Accessed on October 19, 2019.

39. Available at https://www.wilpf.org/wp-content/uploads/2019/08/WILPF_1919-Congress.pdf. Accessed on March 5, 2020.

40. Available at http://nomas.org/survivors-of-prostitution-and-trafficking-manifesto/. Accessed on October 19, 2019.

41. Available at http://ccmw.com/wp-content/uploads/2014/08/CCMW-Position-Statement-on-Femicide_FINAL-Version-1.pdf. Accessed on October 19, 2019.

42. Available at https://oiieurope.org/public-statement-by-the-third-international-intersex-forum/. Accessed on October 19, 2019.

43. Available at https://iwhc.org/womens-declaration-population-policies/. Accessed on October 19, 2019.

44. Available at http://resurj.org/10-point-action-agenda. Accessed on October 19, 2019.

45. Available at http://caravanafeminista.net/who-we-are/the-network-of-young-feminists-of-europe/. Accessed on October 19, 2019.

46. Available at https://feministinternet.org/. Accessed on October 19, 2019.

47. Available at https://www.un.org/womenwatch/daw/beijing/platform/declar.htm. Accessed on July 10, 2019.

48. Available at https://ratical.org/co-globalize/WCdec.html. Accessed on October 19, 2019.

49. Available at https://www.commondreams.org/views/2008/07/08/womens -declaration-g8-support-real-solutions-global-food-crisis. Accessed on October 19, 2019.

50. Available at https://asianindigenouswomen.org/. Accessed on October 19, 2019.

51. Available at https://english.pflp.ps/2015/03/11/international-womens-day -statement-from-the-union-of-palestinian-womens-committees/. Accessed on October 19, 2019.

REFERENCES

Nour, Nawal. 2006. "Health Consequences of Child Marriage in Africa." *Emerging Infectious Diseases* 12 (11): 1644–1649.

Weiss, Penny. 2018. *Feminist Manifestos: A Global Documentary Reader.* New York: New York University Press.

IV

Contemporary Threads

Interlude: The Stories
(Shared Hopes, Dreams, and Fears)

While the other interludes are composed of my own stories, collected over time, I solicited this set via short conversations, in person and on FaceTime.

In many areas of our lives, we are guided, I think, by our positive wishes—the things we aim for—and by what we are trying to avoid. So, in line with the chapter in this section on childhood in feminist utopias and dystopias, I asked people, "As you rear(ed) your children or work(ed) with young people, what are/were some of your fondest hopes for them, and what are/were some of your fears and worries?" Here are the answers from a few of the people in my life.

#1: Thirty Years Old, a Clinical Social Worker

"In the here and now, I hope to show the kids I work with—to bring out in them, introduce them to—play and joy, and the sense that the world invites and wants these things. I see my work as offering slight changes. Often, I see it as seed planting, not as creating major change—little things that hopefully will be built on. No—not seed planting, but fertilizing. Good things are already there in most kids (most humans), but not getting the nourishment they need. I want them to get some affirmation that they can carry with them. When, later, someone else affirms that, it can come to fuller fruition. Institutions more reinforce a false self—one that falls in line, who meets the needs of others, who adapts to the outside world, and follows the rules. That's necessary, but there's also spontaneity, a real self. When someone catches that self, there will be some recognition, a sense of being known. That real self is valid, wanted, something the world needs.

"I worry that the kids won't know themselves or won't have a language for themselves. That prohibitions in their world will be so restrictive that it will cause them to act out too much, or to hate, and to be unbalanced.

"But behind every kid who's acting out is a kid who's aware that something isn't right. That shows they want something healthier: more stability, more love, more support. Underlying every call I get about a problematic kid is a kid who's trying to communicate they want something better for themselves."

#2: Retired Father of Three Young Adults

"I was walking down the hallway of the elementary school to pick up my child for an appointment. He was in first grade. As I passed each classroom, I saw the rows of desks filling each room—third-grade classrooms, second grade, first grade. I thought, 'I can't put my kid in years of this.' It looked so regimented: lockstep, uncreative.

"I didn't hate school myself, but was often bored and wanted to move at a different pace. Walking down that hall, I decided to invest in the alternative school that was being talked about. I put my hopes for my kids in a school that was kid-centered: that was fun, that developed curiosity, where they could make good friends. In the end, I felt that the alternative school gave them a good foundation to manage standard public schooling and college—they did well (though the public high school was a little tough—they weren't the problem, the school was, even when they got in trouble). As they got older, I had some gender-based fears: I worried my son would be twenty at a time of war and would be drafted, and I worried my daughters would get sexually assaulted."

#3: Self-Described Dog Mom and Archetypal Queer Aunt

"When I walk my dog around, he barks at kids—it's fear-based aggression. I use that as an opportunity to explain to the kids that it's about the dog, that they haven't done anything wrong. I make it a lesson on bodily autonomy and consent. I say, 'If you want to say hello kind of quietly, he might say hi back.' I crouch down on their level and translate the dog's body language. If the dog doesn't cooperate, I thank them for trying. I try to invite the kid into it and make it okay for the dog not to say hi, just like they don't have to 'go hug grandma.'

"There were two rambunctious kids who would drop their scooters and start to run over, but then they'd come over real slow and hold their hands out and say, 'He's going to figure out that we're nice kids who aren't going to hurt him.' I hoped the dog would read positivity from the kids and the kids would feel proud.

"When I hear parents telling their kids to sit down and be quiet, I worry they don't understand how kids work—the kids *need* to be doing something. But I try to give parents grace and leniency. The parent might be busy, and the kids are maybe supposed to be doing something. I try not to ascribe more. There's so much gray.

"I want my niece and nephew to like me and think I'm cool. I think they're the coolest people. I want to help bring that about. I do thoughtful, themed gift-giving, and send them postcards from everywhere I go, to build a relationship. I love to get to play with them, to vibe on the same level. But I'm not that used to kids and am a little nervous getting to know them. I worry we won't connect, and I want them to be able to have me as a resource, someone who is always there at a second's notice. I want them to know I love them more than anything."

#4: Mother of Two Young Adults

"I think I was worried [about ensuring] that my son not develop stereotypical, domineering kinds of habits more than I was about my daughter being meek and falling into a stereotypical female role. I think I assumed my daughter would see me working and see that her dad and I shared chores—that she'd see me in a certain way and not assume her dad was the household authority. It didn't work that way. My children still accepted their dad as the more authoritative parent, because he's more insistent and gave orders, while I had a different approach. If they didn't jump, I didn't pay too much attention. 'A' [her partner] and I had different manners, more than different philosophies about rearing our children. The way 'A' grew up, gender roles were very clear, and children were given orders. My parents were the opposite. Both parents worked full time. My father talked to me about children being independent—making their own decisions. He would talk things through with me but wouldn't suggest anything, even when I asked for advice. From where I sat, 'A's' manners were more stereotypically masculine. And I reacted in an overly contentious way, in front of the children. They thought we were arguing over minor things, but to me these were serious points about patriarchal ways of doing things. I wanted them to see that. I should have explained more why it bothered me. I didn't do that.

"They pick up so many habits outside the house. I thought when my daughter saw me, she would learn from that. But when she saw a female pediatrician, she was stunned, because she thought the doctor should be a man. Once, we were reading old fairy tales. My daughter said, 'So Daddy's the king of the house,' and 'A' said, 'And Mommy is the queen?' She said, 'No, Mommy is the housemaid.' She still thought that was my job, my responsibility, despite the fact that my partner and I both worked and shared childcare and household responsibilities. She answered the phone one time when she was maybe eight, and the caller asked for 'Dr. C.' She replied that he wasn't home. She said to me, 'But Daddy's not a doctor.' I was teaching at the time. I'm a Ph.D. I said, 'Daddy's not a doctor. I am.' I had never explained before that my students call me 'Dr. C.'

"My son never thought he had to be primary or that his ways had to come first. He picked up some things that I hoped he would. I wanted my children to be honest and kind, and I think that they are. I wanted them to have personal initiative and to be confident without being self-centered. He got it really early. There's a smaller house across the street that some neighbors wanted to buy up collectively and remove in order to bolster the value of their own property. We said no. My very young son said, 'What do they want them to do, live on the street?' I loved that. My daughter got it, too, but at a broader policy or societal level. Their brains work different ways. She's more theoretical, while he's a blend of theory and practice.

"I thought yelling at your child is violence. And yet I was contentious with 'A' at times—but in order to establish equality. But why would the kids get that? I never explained the reason, except to 'A,' and not in front of them. But they saw the contention. There are ways to talk to children about that. I needed to make more time.

"Now that they're young adults, my concerns are more practical: will they keep their jobs, for example? I appreciate the partners both of them have chosen, who are good people, good for them, good for their kids. They have partners who might gently mitigate tendencies that they might have in the wrong direction. And there's a real extended family they've joined. My kids have always seen our commitment to that, and now have picked up on it. They've seen 'A' take care of his aged parents and flown in for family parties for their grandparents. You have to be able to afford that, and we've supported them to do that. We made it possible. But now they are keeping a pattern of behavior they observed. I hope they'll take care of us when we're decrepit."

#5: Father of Two Very Young Children

"Fears . . . there's not much specificity. It's that despite what I do to prepare my kids to be creative, empathetic, critical-thinking, conscientious people, that the world may be too out of whack for them to come through unscathed. There's no way to prepare them for everything they'll face, and if what I do isn't enough—if I can't influence or protect them . . . I can't think of anything more helpless than that. There's some pretty messed-up, negative societal values, weird crazy things the world puts people through.

"They're not improbable things I'm thinking about. I think the big one is some version of 'power comes from aggression and violence. You must listen to me because I'm more aggressive.' That comes out even with kids—the loudest kid gets their way. I try really hard to raise gentle kids, so that one's really problematic. I think with you and I, if someone tried to be violent, we would have so many strategies to outthink or outmaneuver them, but that takes sophistication that not every kid has, especially when they need it the most. And then what will happen? I worry that if they lose that confrontation, if they're overpowered by someone hurtful, that they won't try again, they'll be scarred, they won't forget that. And I won't be there when that happens. It's too easy to be mean and violent, and it's hard, with limited life experiences, to be ready to respond in the moment. I can give them so many examples and stories, but the thing I don't think of will happen.

"Our neighbors have a puppy that's bigger than the kids. We've introduced them multiple times. My two-year-old was playing ball with the dog for the first time. The neighbors were trying so hard—their concern was that this highly energetic puppy would jump on the kid in a way that would traumatize him. The neighbors wanted so much for them to coexist peacefully. That's good people. The more I surround my kids with people that do that, the better I'll feel.

"Parenting is the thing I've been waiting to do. The only thing that comes close to the effort I feel driven to put in is watching my partner teach. I want her to be free to do that. You can't be in a utopia by yourself. It's a social vision. We worry about whether kids have heat in their homes, no less social power in their lives. How can we move forward as a society—how do we give kids what they need in their classrooms, not only in their families?

"People tell me, 'Just wait until they're teenagers, or terrible twos.' Of course they'll have phases, that's how personality develops, and they have to push boundaries and learn what boundaries to respect. I took 'Z' for a walk this morning, and we found a little footbridge. He went running to the side of the path to look underneath the bridge. I grabbed him, to make sure he didn't fall. He pushed me away. I realized he already knew to kneel down carefully, and I was stopping that. He was trying to do it safely! He knows near water, you kneel down to keep your balance and look. I don't want him to fall or walk in and get in trouble. I actually made him feel unbalanced by trying to protect him, and he did it just right by himself. I smiled and didn't touch him. He wasn't being a 'terrible two' for not needing my help and pushing my hand away. He wanted to watch the creek flow under the bridge. I didn't want to get in the way of that.

"I ran into someone who's expecting their first kid. He wanted someone else to be as excited as he was. It is too rare, especially for two men, to love the idea of parenting, to want to be 100 percent all in. I knew he wasn't hearing that enough from others, so I stopped to have a longer talk and let him know that other people just love being a parent. To be reassuring. To tell him that it's awesome and amazing—even when they are throwing up on you—and that I was excited for him to experience it.

"A few years ago, I left the food co-op and was walking behind a four-year-old and her grandmother. The girl asked, 'Why are peaches fuzzy?' The grandma immediately asked, 'Why do *you* think they are?' and the girl straightaway made up a story in response. It was so clear they were enjoying each other, exploring the world around them together. That's what I want.

"I noticed in the grocery store that I'm always talking to 'Z' and 'A.' It's mostly one-sided, a lot of pointing out things and asking questions and handing them things to put in the cart. I didn't realize how other people listen to me. There's no doubt that in the quiet store, I'm really unusual. They're just not having fun. I am. It's just a way of being, and not everyone is comfortable with it. I try to put ripples out there, maybe have an effect. If our silly grocery-store conversations make someone else smile, maybe they'll do it, too, next time.

"The dominant narrative is that kids are a burden. I feel like (a) I don't ascribe to that and (b) the only thing I can do is not dip my toes into that way of thinking. I'm trying to change the narrative. It doesn't take a lot of effort. There's not enough people doing that.

"I see all these parenting feeds, like how to juggle work and family during the pandemic. They sometimes seem to have the wrong priorities. The idea is that it's a burden to have the kids there because you need to work. The presumption is never that kids' needs are equal to yours or that you can take care of both together. But instead of just worrying about setting boundaries—about 'don't come in the room when I'm on a conference call'—go for the win-win. I can take calls outside while I walk with the kids sometimes, and my coworkers don't mind when I accommodate the kids or they interrupt.

"I feel like it's easy to dwell on what the negatives could be. I think about that, but I'm optimistic. I can envision what's better. *Will* it be better? I'm not sure. I'm cautiously, pragmatically optimistic. You have to nurture hope. The harder the battle, the more you have to be able to imagine the possibilities. Optimism gets a bad rap."

7

Learning from
Feminist Epistemology

I move now from *past* feminist reflections on childhood to explore different threads in *contemporary* theory. I have chosen three diverse, feminist-friendly theories with broad contemporary appeal to see what they might contribute to liberatory feminist thinking about childhood. The theories may address children incidentally or centrally and more or less imperfectly, but that does not necessarily affect their ultimate ability to promote more respectful adult-child relations. In the end, I want contemporary theories to be accountable to young people—to say that they cannot really be liberatory, as they intend to be, without advocating for more justice, autonomy, and participation in the lives of youth. But I also want to mine these theories, to learn from them, to see how their support for various forms of voice, diversity, and equality can help us frame ever-more-effective arguments that promote the interests of youth.

I start, then, with an important trend in epistemology, laid out in Miranda Fricker's highly esteemed *Epistemic Injustice: Ethics and the Power of Knowing* (2009). Focusing on epistemic injustice brings us back, interestingly, to concerns discussed earlier in the book regarding the everyday silencing of children. Then, in Chapters 8 and 9, I see what can be learned from disability theory and from queer theory.

On Back Talk

Dictionary definitions of "sassing off" frequently reference a teacher or parent who is the unlucky and undeserving recipient of a youngster's "back talk." A

Google search of "talking back" reveals an entire first page of pieces offering advice to parents on what to do with "smart-alecky" kids. Examples of back talk on those popular sites include a child saying, "This isn't fair, you don't understand, you don't love me," a "child who wants you to understand their point after you've already said 'no'" (Lehman, n.d.), and nonverbal acts "such as eye-rolls and lip smacks" (Reece 2013). All the articles end with advice on something like: how to "nip your child's bold and brash behavior in the bud" (ibid.). Why is there such an overriding concern to halt these acts? All such "bold and brash" behaviors supposedly involve disrespect—in particular, disrespect of the legitimate authority of parents and teachers over children.

We do not have words equivalent to "cheeky" and "mouthing off" to describe the disrespectful tone or content of speech by adults to children. In a way, this absence is curious, because adults have more social power than children, and those with more power have more opportunities to dole out or withhold respect and can show disrespect more frequently with fewer consequences. Possibly, it's *more* likely that adults are disrespectful to children than vice versa. But, of course, the absence of words to negatively describe such behavior when engaged in by adults is completely predictable because, as authority figures, adults make, impose, and enforce the rules. Those rules mandate children's submission and obedience, justify it as reasonable and for children's own good, and mark children's nondocility as disrespect (if not a behavior disorder). Adults' own disrespect simply gets called "proper authoritativeness" or "necessary discipline," and we "understand" it more than we question it. We do not really have a robust enough notion of the legitimate autonomy and dignity of young people to be able to capture their violation by adults in everyday speech acts. Further, we do not generally even see the power of adults over children as problematic, only capturing its misuse in extreme cases of neglect and abuse, not in ordinary acts of conversation. Yet in everyday conversations, children being children are regularly dismissed, disrespected, and silenced.

Widely accepted views on the nature of children support this silencing. Even in those instances when someone is explicitly condemning the practice of judging what someone says by who they are, it is common to make an exception for young people. As Linda Alcoff writes, for example, "Except perhaps for one's status as an adult, what can social identity have to do with perceptual ability, judgement, trustworthiness" (1999, 78)? But *is* childhood so strongly linked (or even synonymous) with erroneous perception, poor judgment, and lack of trustworthiness? Is adulthood so strongly correlated (or synonymous) with perceptual accuracy, sound judgment, and reliability? Do not children sometimes know more or better or enough to be treated as members of epistemic communities, genuine and competent participants in conversation, rather than as vocal irritants to adults, or as people who have nothing to offer adults in the way of additional knowledge or alternative perspectives?

Why do we so regularly make an exception for young people in our ethics? Why should age be an automatic proxy for "perceptual ability, judgement, [and] trustworthiness"? Let us remember what we are talking about, after all, when we mark children as inherently lacking credibility. Systematically—automatically, regularly, in multiple locations—challenging the credibility of young people because of who they are means deploying "coherent prejudgments" (prejudices) "that are sanctioned and maintained by dominant social narratives" about their cognitive ability and reliability (Code 2008, 298). As described by Lorraine Code, "large parts of most people's everyday lives depend" on testimonial exchanges (294), and receiving the words of a group of individuals with systematic incredulity "undermines not just the 'truth' of the[ir] experiences, but their sense of self, of credibility, of trustworthiness" (291). The effects are disempowering—both the story and the storyteller suffer. This constitutes a case, I argue, of what Fricker calls epistemic injustice: "normal" discourteous treatment toward young people that has its foundation in prejudicial stereotypes about them and in notions of about "proper," "respectful," noncheeky adult-child relations.

In Chapter 3, I argued that the silencing of children should be recognized as part of everyday, "normal" practices of rearing, educating, and interacting with young people, and I used as my primary examples, first, the omnipresent classroom rules that dictate when students may speak, to whom, about what, where, and in what tone; and second, the ways in which adults *regularly* interrupt children's speech and quietude, but balk at children interrupting theirs. The idea of everyday silencing I offered is certainly broad enough to also cover problematically labeling as "disrespectful sass" a child's simple desire to be understood, even after they have been told "no." I make the case here that things like "back talk" are not simply a matter of vexation for and offense to adults, but involve fundamental questions of *justice* toward children. To do so, I expand Fricker's notions of epistemic injustice and justice to show that our characterizations of and limits on children's speech feed off (usually unthinking but nonetheless) morally objectionable prejudices that result, like all social prejudices, in individual injury and social loss. However, to use Fricker's work, I need to rectify the ageism that she herself is guilty of perpetuating. I make this correction while extending her concepts of testimonial and hermeneutical injustice to apply to children.

Sara Ahmed explores "how willfulness is used as an explanation of disobedience" in children (2017, 67), and, of course, how such disobedience is perceived as a fault. The adult who is imposing their will on the child is *not* seen as problematically willful, while judging a child as willful "is a crucial part of the disciplinary apparatus" (67). Children are supposed to be willing to obey, willing to not have a will of their own. Ahmed finds that this idea is likely imposed more on girls than on boys, noting that "perhaps boys are more likely to be described as strong willed and girls as willful because boys are encouraged to acquire a will of their own" (68). Girls, on the other hand, are to learn "to will what is willed by others" (69). This is surely a lesson they are to take into adulthood, as Mary Astell explains in "Some Reflections upon Marriage," wherein she rues the fact that woman "puts her Fortune and Person entirely in his Powers; nay even *the very desires of her Heart* . . . so as that it is not lawful to Will or Desire any thing but what he approves and allows" ([1704] 1996, 48; my emphasis). The child who protests the injustice of an adult's will is "sassing off" because "speaking out against injustice becomes yet another symptom of willfulness" (Ahmed 2017, 70). Children, especially girls, are not supposed to have wills or voices of their own. Is this really a scenario that we should be prepared to support?

The popular literature on classroom rules and household back talk generally reference not just questions of what respect we should all show to one another, but also questions of power. Power comes up in two ways. First, the situations described in definitions and popular literature as evoking back talk generally involve an adult making demands or imposing rules on the young—exercising power. Second, the child's response is often explained as resulting from a sense of powerlessness (Lehman, n.d.) or the need to have "some control over the course of [their] day" (Miles, n.d.). This common framing of varieties of "giving lip" is a recognition that parents and teachers have power over children and that children often resist its exercise in the name of autonomy—a form of resistance that we have seen talked about (positively) in the history of feminist theory. Nothing is especially unique to adult-child relations about this power dynamic—one party believes that they have authority to exert control and attempts to exercise it, and another party resists being controlled and exercises a will of their own; what is unusual, however, is the general refusal to problematize adult power over children in any situations short of abuse—our reluctance to consider the ethics and politics of this adult-child power relationship according to the standards by which we dissect, evaluate, and check other power relationships, between ruler and subject, men and women, employer and employee, and so forth. At least in the case of epistemic injustice, I suggest, our reasons for such exceptionalism are unsatisfactory.

Fricker's Text

Fricker's *Epistemic Injustice* is an excellent contemporary source for exploring the adult-child relationship with an eye to greater justice. She does not confine "epistemology" to relative inaccessible philosophical debates about "knowledge that" versus "knowledge how," internalism versus externalism, or *a priori* versus *a posteriori* knowledge. Instead, she explores how we come to see and treat ourselves and other people as likely or improbable sources of knowledge in the broad array of ordinary conversations (testimonial exchanges) that constitute our daily social lives. Further, she connects being seen as a giver and receiver of knowledge with what it means to be fully human; having "epistemic authority" is essential to being a participant in those everyday testimonial exchanges that are a critical aspect of a full life.

Fricker's framework is attractive for three reasons. First, she says at the outset that her interest "is in injustice specifically in the sphere of epistemic activity, and certainly in this sphere I believe that there are areas where *injustice is normal*" (2009, vii; my emphasis). Her focus on ordinary, common injustices matches my concern with how the everyday, normalized speech and conversational practices involving children contribute to and reflect their unequal social status. This common ground excites me and leads me to wonder what her epistemic framework can add to more liberatory models of childhood. Second, Fricker asserts that "wherever power is at work, we should be ready to ask who or what is controlling whom, and why" (14). This mandate validates further inquiry into those epistemic practices involving children that we seem loath to pursue. Legitimately or not, the power of adults over children's lives clearly defines the norms regulating those practices—from classroom rules to norms of interruption—and it deserves or even demands scrutiny. Finally, because Fricker emphasizes how prejudices often determine who has what degree of epistemic credibility in what contexts, she invites us to reflect on how prejudices regarding the young might be behind unjust, disrespectful treatment of them, prejudices that are not nearly as often discussed, challenged, or forbidden as are, say, stereotypes based on sex or race.

Fricker makes the case for two distinctively epistemic forms of injustice, which she calls "testimonial" and "hermeneutical" (which I define shortly). In both cases, she sheds light on discursive practices essential to the maintenance of identity-based oppressions, such as oppressions based on sex, class, sexuality, and race. Unfortunately, Fricker's notion of epistemic injustice develops largely without the perspectives and experiences of children, and contains no sustained treatment of age-based prejudices or the epistemic fate of minors. Her work falls into the pattern of "literature [that] is still remarkably silent on [the] child and how ageism influences what 'we' (adults) regard as 'real' knowledge," largely, in this case, because "children are still invisible in mainstream academic philosophy" (Murris 2013, 247–248). The absence of reflection on children, in a book devoted largely to what it means not to be taken seriously as a giver and a receiver of knowledge, is no accident— it's indicative of the very prejudices about children that we need to examine.

Further, when children do show up in Fricker's work, it is not, so it seems, to provide examples that help define the very problems to be tackled, nor is it to explore or understand how conversational practices between adults and youth do or do not fit into her framework. Instead, they show up either in familiar stereotyped ways, as we will see, or as examples of something not centrally about them—a common fate for oppressed groups in the history of philosophy. Despite the ripeness of Fricker's framework for reconsideration of epistemic practices involving the young, then, her actual attention to minors is unsatisfactory, the result of familiar prejudices about them that she does not critically explore at all, contrary to the requirements that she herself establishes for epistemic justice. Hence my questions: Were those prejudices challenged, would the notion of epistemic injustice be a way to capture and critique the everyday silencing of young people? Should we understand the silencing of young people as a case of identity-based prejudice? Does Fricker's portrait of epistemic *justice*—inclusive, attentive, respectful conversation— provide a useful model for needed changes in epistemic practices between those older and younger? And, overall, what are the strengths, limits, and adaptability of a theory of injustice built only around the experiences of adults? In the end, my initial attraction to Fricker is vindicated but significantly moderated, and I modify and extend her theory in the name of greater epistemic justice; this focus on epistemic injustice toward young people also clarifies certain aspects of her framework.

Children and Testimonial Injustice

The essence of testimonial injustice is when, due to prejudice based on someone's identity, "the hearer makes an unduly deflated judgment of the speaker's credibility, perhaps missing out on knowledge as a result; and the hearer does something ethically bad—the speaker is wrongfully undermined in her capacity as a knower" (Fricker 2009, 17). Being repeatedly treated by hearers as lacking credibility has numerous and deeply damaging consequences. Incredulity is a wrong by which we "undermine, insult, or otherwise withhold a proper respect for the speaker qua subject of knowledge" (20), and, when this incredulity is based on prejudice, it constitutes an "ethical poison in the judgement of the hearer" (22). Its presence may be revealed by such behaviors as inattentiveness to someone's words, polite disregard, active skepticism, and silencing; in the case of kids, its presence might even be seen in such sentimental but sometimes condescending acts of endearment as "smiling, laughing, or expressions such as 'oh, how sweet'" (Murris 2013, 248).

Curiously, even fascinatingly, Fricker barely addresses children as victims of testimonial injustice, despite the frequency with which we fail to take them and their words seriously as sources of knowledge, even about themselves. Her numerous examples of victims of testimonial injustice, some fictional, include a professional woman whose ideas are only heard when voiced by men (2009, 46–47); a woman whose statements are ridiculed as "intuitions" and therefore unworthy of consideration or reasoned response (14–15); a junior Chicana professor undermined by a student's complaints about her that are not believed to have been made "until a senior white professor suffer[s] the same sort of complaints from the student" (48); a Black man, convicted of rape by a White jury, who has no "chance of being heard as truthful" (24); and a nineteenth-century woman with an "interest in political affairs" who "expresses her beliefs and . . . receives a blank wall of incredulity from her hoped-for conversational partners" (54–55). But not a single child appears whose opinion is not sought, or whose voice is "endured," or whose perspective is too quickly discounted.

Identity-based testimonial injustice—dismissal of someone's words based on who they are—relies on myths and overgeneralizations that are present in multiple arenas, each reinforcing the others. Regarding women's epistemic incredulity, for example, Fricker notes intersecting notions, such as "women's innocence of the truths of men, and their need to be protected from such truths; ideas of feminine intuitiveness being an obstacle to rational judgement; and even ideas of a female susceptibility to hysterics" (90). Regarding race, ideas relevant to testimonial injustice include, from *To Kill a Mockingbird*, "that *all* Negroes lie, that *all* Negroes are basically immoral beings" (90). The Chicana professor referenced above may have been burdened with prejudices against her, including that her English is less than proficient and that her politics are predictably liberal (Desmadre 2008). All these myths and overgeneralizations have more than epistemic consequences—they affect opportunities and actions in the workplace, in classrooms, on the streets, in homes, and in organizations—but epistemic undermining is crucial to all of them.

Fricker never addresses the possibility that an analogous list of prejudices affects the epistemic status of young children and teenagers. Yet, for example, there is a "discourse of children as lacking competence and requiring protection and nurturance, and in the process of becoming persons rather than persons now, [that] has often been used to deny them agency and limit their citizenship rights" (Taylor and Smith 2009, 18). Too, generally "adults believe, tacitly or explicitly, that children cannot tell the difference between fact and fiction, or readily make things up" (Carel and Gyorffy 2014, 1256). Legal practitioners concerned with the reliability of courtroom testimony, and psychologists who often hear the stories of abuse that bring children to courtrooms, emphasize "the childish disposition to weave romances and to treat imagination for verity" and view the young as "dangerously suggestible," especially with regard to sexual abuse (Myers 1995). In medicine, despite the fact that practitioners are "treating the child's own body," children's testimony often is dismissed on the basis of "potentially harmful [adult] biases," for, to them, "children may seem irrational, with reduced powers of reasoning, flawed or non-existent memories, and be easily swayed." (Carel and Gyorffy 2014, 1256) This list is comparable to and even lengthier than the ones Fricker condemns as the bases of testimonial injustice toward various groups of adults and surely constitutes "a grim catalogue of clichés more or less likely to insinuate themselves into judgements of credibility" (Fricker 2009, 23; also see 36).

As a result of the ubiquity of such notions about the young, "prejudice is built into the very way children are imagined" (Young-Bruehl 2012, 5). Replacing sex- or race-based groups in Fricker's work with "children," her own conclusion should be that deployment of such myths "not only . . . undermine[s] [the child] in a capacity (the capacity for knowledge) that is essential to his value as a human being, it does so on grounds that discriminate against [the child] in respect of some essential feature of him as a social being" (Fricker 2009, 54). We know some of the unjust epistemic consequences of these stereotypes. In the recent sex abuse scandal in Australia, for example, Cardinal George Pell "said children were not often believed" and that, despite the fact that "he was aware of rumours and complaints against paedophile clergy when he was a young priest in the 1970s, . . . church superiors tended to give priests the benefit of the doubt" (Gayle 2016) rather than believing the children. Or, in certain schools in South Africa, racist and ageist assumptions regarding the Black child combine, leading to views of them as "sneaky," "lazy," and undisciplined. Despite the fact that they often carry great responsibilities in their families and communities, to their teachers, "their talk is mere disruption, not worth listening to" (Murris 2013, 256). Examples are, unfortunately, unlimited.

In general, instances of testimonial injustice take on a vastly different degree of importance and destructiveness when the denial of credibility is based on one's membership in an oppressed group that endures dehumanizing insults, bans, limitations, and injuries in multiple aspects of life. While most people might respond, "Prejudice against children?" because "Who even acknowledges its existence?" (Young-Bruehl 2012, 2), we have seen that children suffer deeply and disproportionately from many social ills, such as poverty, war, and hunger, and that prejudices about them are behind their dismissal as potential and actual knowers. Too, they experience these wrongs in multiple locations—in schools, families, and organizations—perhaps even during most of their waking hours. Epistemic injustice toward youth meets the requirements of Fricker's paradigmatic case of identity-based prejudice.

The effects of testimonial injustice on children may be more devastating than on adults. First, Fricker tells us, "keeping one's dignity" in the presence of persistent testimonial injustice "can take great courage" (2009, 54). One aid to maintaining one's dignity, to finding courage, is a "community in which to find resources for resistance" (54). Yet this resource may not be available to children if, for example, they are too young to develop it, are isolated in the home, or generally lack sufficient opportunities to create and sustain such a community (especially when schools and even organized extracurricular activities so regulate children's interactions). Fewer resources for children that support their resistance mean more unchecked adult power, with all of its consequences: from lower self-esteem and diminished self-confidence in children, to compromised democratic processes, and reduced opportunities to learn. And for children, low self-esteem is especially consequential, for it relates to their willingness to try new things and their ability to cope with failures, qualities essential to exploring oneself and the world, qualities so important in young lives and to resisting oppression.[1]

The effects of testimonial injustice may be especially devastating for children for a second reason. Fricker's example of the nineteenth-century woman is used to show "just how debilitating testimonial injustice might be in circumstances where psychological resistance would be a social achievement that is more or less out of the subject's reach. Persistent testimonial injustice can indeed inhibit the very formation of self" (55). My concern is that not only are the resources for resistance more difficult to obtain for children than for adults, especially before the more independent teenaged years; any harm that has the potential to "inhibit the very formation of self" (55) will inflict the greatest damage on those whose sense of self is very much still emerging. Children are being *shaped by prejudices* against them (56).

Fricker talks about two aspects of testimonial injustice—not just the effects on the ones whose words are dismissed, ignored, or ridiculed, as just explored, but also the epistemic effects on the listener, who is "missing out on knowledge as a result" of such dismissals, which are fed by stereotypes about children in this case. Adults "miss out" when they fail to listen to young people. This idea is critical. As educational researcher Karin Murris explains: in most child-adult interactions, meaning is supposed to be offered by the adult and received by the child in a one-way rather than an interactive process (2013, 246). But such a process not only fails to "develop the democratic habit of mind and skills that are characteristic of a 'thick' or participatory notion of democracy"; it also buys into the assumption that adults cannot learn *with* or *from* children, a loss of knowledge for adults, of content emerging, for example, from "the trust, honesty, enthusiasm, openness and playfulness children can bring to their intellectual explorations" (247). I explore this co-creation of knowledge more in the next chapter. For now, it is important to hold the idea that testimonial injustice hurts both participants in the conversation epistemically, in different ways. As Murris concludes, "Learning *with* children could possibly be a life changing transformation for the adults involved" (247). It will require some alteration in adults' conception of themselves as the *only* epistemic authorities in virtually all encounters with children.

Children and Hermeneutical Injustice

Hermeneutical injustice gets less attention (one chapter) from Fricker than testimonial injustice does, but its consequences, she notes, are at least as dire. Hermeneutical injustice occurs when "someone has a significant area of their social experience obscured from understanding owing to prejudicial flaws in shared resources for social interpretation" (Fricker 2009, 155). Our interpretive resources—the language and ideas we have to help us make sense of our experiences—are collective, or social, and when there are systematic gaps in those resources, it becomes more difficult to understand one's own experiences or to be understood, which is especially problematic when it is very much in one's interest to render one's self intelligible.

The most common explanations for any hermeneutical injustice experienced by children—any inability they might have to find or use concepts to understand or to be understood—revert to their limited epistemic capacities. First, children may lack the more precise and extended vocabulary of adults, so the problem would seem to be less one of inadequate social resources than individual or group incapacity. That relative lack, however, to the extent that it exists, need not cause hermeneutical injustice. Many groups of people have less precise or smaller vocabularies than other groups, whether based on degree of education, more limited facility with a second language, less expertise in a specialized subject, or communication disorders, among numerous other examples. The question remains open regarding what others do in response. Are they patient hearers? Do they assume that there is sense to be had in the speech even when it is not immediately apparent to them? Do they do some of the work involved in facilitating better communication? Do they develop adaptive communication devices? Do they develop language that is accessible, as Charlotte Perkins Gilman recommends in *Herland*, for the sake of children?

The question of children's rational (as opposed to speech) capacities might be seen as another source of children's difficulty in understanding and having their experiences understood by others. If they are insufficiently rational, that is, we might expect them simply to be incapable of understanding the world or expressing themselves comprehensibly. We have already encountered some of the myriad myths dismissing children as fabulists, liars, and so forth. But, interestingly, hermeneutical injustice is fundamentally a question of *social* resources or capacities rather than *individual* ones. The issue, then, is whether young people have adequate concepts to capture their experiences (some perhaps developed with adult help), and whether adults help them grasp and convey their experiences, making use of children's words.

Here is the hermeneutical danger (there are variations on it): children's "interpretative frameworks are at risk of rejection by adults, who, with few exceptions, cease to readily understand the child's world. When the two interpretative frameworks clash, the adult interpretation usually trumps the child's" (Carel and Gyorffy 2014, 1256). What Havi Carel and Gita Gyorffy describe is not so much an insurmountable obstacle erected by children's limited faculties of speech or reason, but an adult inadequacy (they "cease to readily understand") and exertion of power ("the adult interpretation usually trumps the child's"). We are back to unjust use of, or illegitimate, power. In a medical setting, for example,

> children will always be at a hermeneutical disadvantage within an adult-governed health-care system, because their interpretative frameworks are foreign to such an adult system. The adults who wish to understand them need to make the effort to enter their interpretative frameworks, or world, and to understand their testimonies from within it. It is, therefore, up to health professionals and paediatricians, in particular, to spot the clues in children's stories. Of course, this is true in many other contexts as well, such as education. (1256–1257)

Adults "need to make the effort" to understand young people on their own terms; it is "up to" them to do so, in many contexts. With great power, we might say, comes great responsibility.

What Fricker allows us to grasp as injustice, although she herself does not grapple with it, is that most of our collective resources for understanding are developed by and for adults. When those resources are developed by and for men, the result is, according to Fricker, the long absence of a concept such as sexual harassment (and many others, including domestic violence, the glass ceiling, and date rape). In that case, the more powerful harassers have structured workplaces and streets and classrooms, on the one hand, and the legal system, on the other, so as to make sexual harassment common but not taken seriously as a harm; consequently, women have had difficulty expressing to themselves and others exactly what happens to them when they are harassed, although it is very much in their interest to understand and stop it. Instead, women who contest harassing behaviors are characterized as overly emotional, overly sensitive, and so forth, rather than as violated, objectified, and discriminated against, and the injustice continues largely with impunity. If, as is surely the case, young people have less influence on collective social understandings than do adults, and if most social institutions and practices are built for adults with little attention to how children, can be heard and accommodated—from our teacher-centered classrooms to our theories of epistemic injustice—then children's questions will be called "back talk," and their descriptions of events will be "reinterpreted" for them. They will lose faith in their own intellectual abilities. We can, indeed, use Fricker's work to better understand how young people are subjected to systematic hermeneutical injustice.

Consider two-year-olds, who are generally at a stage during which they "begin to struggle between their reliance on adults and their desire for independence," and frequently say "No!"[2] They are described as oppositional and prone to temper tantrums. Adults call this period the "terrible twos." Doing so, however, surely causes us to listen less well to children of that age: to discount what they say and to attribute every resistance only to their age; thus, it is a source of testimonial injustice. But there is more. Naming it "terrible" (and "naming" is a hermeneutical resource) does not capture the joys and limitations, the risks and the rewards of the period from the *child's* point of view, only the frustration of the adult. How, then, can adults be helpful to children experiencing what I might call this "first adolescence"? What might we call this period if we named it from the child's point of view? What would we call it if the emerging independence of children was something we educated for and celebrated rather than faced ambivalently and unsystematically? Children and young adults do not have social power, and social power influences collective forms of social understanding. Would we have paid earlier, more serious attention to schoolyard bullies and pedophile priests if we had listened better to children about what was happening in their lives (testimonial justice) and worked with them to understand, from their perspective the very phenomena of schoolyard bullies and pedophile priests (hermeneutical justice)?

Testimonial injustice also causes hermeneutical injustice. "Growing up without opportunities for play and for dialogue poses the gravest danger for the growing child. . . . Without playing, conversing, listening to others, and drawing out their own voice, people fail to develop a sense that they can talk and think things through" (Belenky et al. 1997, 32–33). When a sense that one can think things through is at stake, hermeneutical justice looms ominously. Yet "most schools continue to provide meager opportunities for the give-and-take of dialogue. Verbal interchanges tend to be unilateral and highly constrained as they are predominantly teacher-initiated and -dominated" (34). Children's ability to come to an understanding of their own experiences and to convey that understanding to others is clearly at risk not because of something inherent in childhood but because of adult social structures and practices.

Something like a consensus exists in the theory of young people's talk, although practice varies from it. The theory is that children have stories to tell, that "learning to tell our stories helps us find our own authentic voices and . . . having our own voice builds confidence . . . [and] increas[es] cognitive skills" (Parnass 2013), as Fricker posits with adults. It matters that "kids become their own content creators, not just content consumers," and "find and understand their place in the world" (Chutter and Bains 2012). Children *can* "find and understand their place in the world," but "teachers on the whole like to be in control of how educational texts are interpreted" (Murris 2013, 251). This is the main hermeneutical issue for young people—and a distinctive one based on their age. Children don't get to determine meaning, either in relations with each other or with adults, for lack of opportunity to talk or lack of listeners with whom to talk.

The one example involving children that Fricker presents in her discussion of hermeneutical injustice is of a fictional teenage boy who is coming to terms with his homosexuality in a 1950s world filled with prejudices about homosexuality as an abnormality and psychiatric illness. Unfortunately, this case does not involve distinctive age-based prejudices, as the damaging epistemic resources affect all homosexuals (everyone, really). Fricker has not yet confronted the adult nature of our collective resources. On the other hand, what is wonderful about the example is that it allows her to grapple for just a moment with the particular impact of hermeneutical injustice on a "younger self being formed through the lens of all these constructions" (2009, 164).

She asks, "Is hermeneutical injustice sometimes so damaging that it cramps the very development of self?" (163). Unfortunately, again, this is the same question she asks of adults, and so, again, she misses an opportunity to confront the particular impact on children. And there is a distinct impact.

This topic demands more attention, as we are addressing practices that *"cramp[] the very development of self."* The discursive practices of adults interacting with children might be thought of as quite regularly falling into this horrid category of restricting or deforming the development of the selves of youngsters. Youth hear that they are terrible, smart-alecky, and just imagining things; that they cannot understand, should be seen and not heard, and are just too young; and that they are "deficient in reason, emotion control, responsibility and maturity" (Murris 2013, 253). All of this should give us pause. Parents, schools, and adults in general tend not to invite youngsters to speak up, and, when youth do speak, adults tend not to hear or heed their words. How are young people to learn, grow, and contribute under such circumstances? One scholar notes, for example, that one "source . . . is rarely heard in the discussion of school reform for marginalized students: the students themselves" (Howard 2001, 131). We never seem to expect that children's perspectives—their ways of understanding—might lead to constructive "re-examination of [adults'] own beliefs and assumptions" through collaborative conversation (Murris 2013, 252).

We adults need to confront the fact that when we silence the voices and stories of those younger, we are, in fact, engaging in familiar practices of the privileged: paying inadequate attention to the needs of others, assuming that our stories and perspectives are more important and valid, and ignoring others' feelings and experiences from our entitled position of thinking that we possess the truth, or at least more of it. Like adults, in situations of testimonial and hermeneutical injustice children will eventually self-censor, choosing not to speak up when they believe that they or their stories are unsafe or unsupported. And what it takes to make a child feel safe and supported is sometimes the same and sometimes different from what it takes for an adult, as we recognize in courtrooms and truth commissions (UNICEF, n.d.).

Children and Epistemic Justice

Fricker's main solution to epistemic injustice is, of course, epistemic justice. Rather than unethically and systematically deflating someone's credibility, or a group's credibility, and thus undermining their very humanity, epistemic justice calls on us, spontaneously or with conscious effort, to be "virtuous hearers." The process by which we make credibility assessments, based on prejudice or more fairly, has cognitive and emotional aspects that we need to be aware of as we strive to become better listeners.

Fricker pays some attention to children as virtuous hearers. Unfortunately, even here, they appear in ways that can contribute to their being received as untrustworthy givers and receivers of knowledge—an outcome that seems quite contrary to Fricker's overall aim of making the moral wrong of epistemic injustice more visible and resisted.

In a book that makes central use of literary figures, one child makes two appearances in Fricker's work: Huckleberry Finn. He exists as an example of how someone can experience "conflict between . . . beliefs [that Jim, as an escaped slave, should be turned in] and his perceptual faculty" (2009, 40), which shows Jim to be a good person. Fricker concludes that "this possibility of a subject's unprejudiced perception of another human being winning out against his prejudiced beliefs is crucially important for our understanding of how social change is possible" (41). Beliefs can correct perceptions, and perceptions can also reform beliefs. In Huck's case, he is knowledgeable about racist law, but his unprejudiced perception of Jim as a good human being leads him to act contrary to the law. He experiences a conflict and makes a praiseworthy decision. Later in Fricker's book, however, Huck reappears, along with Harper Lee's character Scout from *To Kill a Mockingbird*, as an example of someone who possesses testimonial justice *not* by "neutraliz[ing] the impact of prejudice in her credibility judgements" (92) but by possessing a "native capacity for unprejudiced social perception" that remains "sufficiently untouched" by the prejudiced society in which they live. Huck's perception, like Scout's, is now portrayed as having "somehow escaped the prejudicial corruptions of the day" (93), even though Fricker also says that "their beliefs had *not* escaped prejudice" (93–94; my emphasis) and that they experienced "dissonance" (94). The consequences of this failure to reckon with children's acquaintance with prejudice will be clear in a moment.

Scout, too, comes onto the stage as a person who might display the virtue of testimonial justice "spontaneously" (92) or "naively" (93). In opposition to those of us who have to work consciously against the prejudices of our society that we have imbibed and that structure our world, this freedom from prejudice as an uncorrupted "native capacity" by definition involves *no* "reflexive critical awareness," no "conscious, deliberative reflection" (92):

> Perhaps a child—someone in the fast-moving initial phases of ethical and epistemic socialization—growing up in a relevantly prejudiced society might present an example of a person who (partially at least) displays the virtue of testimonial justice more or less naively. . . . As she

gets older, the possibility of possessing the virtue naively will diminish, reinforcing the need to possess it in its corrective form. (94–95)

But why is Scout only "*en route* to acquiring the virtue of testimonial justice" (94), "on her way to possessing the anti-prejudicial virtue of testimonial justice" (94)? Fricker's assessment falls into a pattern of treating the adult as the norm—a static, nondeveloping norm—and the child as "different," developing, and only on the way to becoming a citizen, a reflective person, and so forth. But other frames are possible, including ones that are less tied to developmental psychology, that essentialize children, distance them from adults, and see them "as 'becomings,' not 'beings,' as 'persons in the making,' not 'persons'" (Murris 2013, 254).

Fricker asserts that "testimonial responsibility requires a distinctly *reflexive* critical social awareness" (2009, 91). She adds that "such reflexive critical awareness of the likely presence of prejudice, then, is a prerequisite in the business of correcting for prejudice in one's credibility judgement. . . . When the hearer suspects prejudice in her credibility judgement—whether through sensing cognitive dissonance between her perception, beliefs, and emotional responses, or whether through self-conscious reflection—she should shift intellectual gear out of spontaneous, unreflective mode and into active critical reflection" (91).

Huck and Scout are aware of the social beliefs of their times, especially as embodied in law, but also in their daily experiences in societies built on slavery and Jim Crow, respectively. They have to make a choice, as the various forces leading to action are discordant, and so they experience dissonance. That seems enough to meet Fricker's necessary conditions for reflexive critical awareness—but a problem arises: Scout simply "is too young to be reflectively aware of the force of the prejudice all around her, and so too young for corrective deliberation as such" (94–95). She is just too young for it to be so, even though, Fricker says, there "is also a corrective aspect to her judgement." Fricker ends up with a mushy "in-between" category, concluding that Scout's testimonial justice "has a corrective aspect but is none the less broadly naïve" (95). The distinction between being just "more or less naively" (94) is, perhaps unsurprisingly at this point, not explored with Fricker's customary analytic rigor.

Associating the young with such words as "native" and "naïve" is as potentially reinforcing of their epistemic second-class status as is their distancing from "conscious, deliberative reflection." It is evocative of John Stuart Mill's shocking claim that young people are incapable of being engaged in and improved through discussion. Granted, adults can also be in this naïve category, when, for example, they are unexposed to prejudices that might exist in another culture, but Fricker's fictional children cannot *but* be in this category, despite the fact that they are decidedly *not* unaware of relevant prejudices and of evidence that conflicts with them.

It is worth noting that the fictional Huck Finn is about thirteen years old, and Scout is six to eight. Fricker, like most people, believes that humans are born unprejudiced. But she neglects important facts: children become aware of gender differences beginning at about two years old and of racial differences by four—and what they are aware of is different *treatment*. By preschool, "children have already learned stereotypes or acquired negative attitudes toward 'others'" (Anti-Defamation League 2001). "A considerable body of research demonstrates that children in the U.S. are aware, at a very early age, of physical and cultural differences among people, and they learn the prevailing social attitudes toward these differences whether or not they are in direct contact with people different from themselves" (Derman-Sparks, Higa, and Sparks, n.d.). "Scholars who study racial and ethnic development in young children from a socialization perspective believe that the ethnic identity process for children of color begins at birth—at the earliest interactions between the child, family and community" (Southern Poverty Law Center 1997). Children actively try to make sense of their experiences. Like Fricker's fictional children, most youngsters have conflicting information from multiple sources. A process of learning about one's own and each other's identities is needed, and unlearning prejudice is required, although most parents and teachers shy away from teaching about such things as institutional racism and sexist social systems.[3]

When it comes to testimonial justice, then, Fricker should consider children to be people aware of and capable of reflecting critically on and resisting social prejudices. Even more, as the fictional examples show, young people are as capable as those older of embodying spontaneous and reflexive epistemic justice: they might be rich sources of knowledge as well as receivers of knowledge in conversations on overcoming bias. Such a state of affairs, learning from young people, requires first resisting stereotypes about children— acting epistemically justly toward them, as defined by Fricker, a topic to which I return in the next chapter. As evidenced by the stereotypes of youth in Fricker's work, we definitely need to reflect critically on prejudices toward young people.

Concluding Thoughts

I have shown that Fricker's notions of testimonial and hermeneutical injustice are profoundly useful for understanding the character and consequences of the everyday silencing of children. Certain aspects of her theory even become clearer when looked at from this vantage point, such as the limited relevance of the intellectual tools of the speaker to epistemic injustice; in turn, aspects of the everyday silencing of young people, such as the impactful role played by ageist prejudices in discursive practices, become clearer when placed in Fricker's frame. However, Fricker shortchanges children as potentially virtuous hearers, does not attend to the more devastating impact of epistemic injustice on children, and misses an opportunity to show just how common and pervasive silencing can be in young people's lives. We should not think of or treat childhood as a stage in which people are simply deemed too young to be listened to as conveyers of knowledge, nor should we consider childhood to be a stage lacking in the capacity for making sense of experience. (In fact, it might be best to think less often of childhood as a stage rather than as a state of being, and as one with much in common with adulthood, including being *en route* to other things.)

Alongside the prejudices and practices that Fricker acknowledges as supporting *testimonial* injustice, we should add stereotypes of youth (at various ages, of different races and sexes, etc.) and social practices from informal norms of interruption to formal institutional rules (with real consequences for disobedience) regarding who may speak and under what conditions. The notion of *hermeneutical* injustice is tremendously important for showing how particularly harmful the silencing of children is, because they spend proportionately more time than do adults trying to make sense of the world and explaining themselves to adults, and because their silencing has profound, life-long consequences.

We know enough to condemn epistemic injustice based on the consequences common to adults and children alike. But one additional distinctive impact on the young mandates that we pay even more attention to its everyday presence in the lives of children. Dauntingly, epistemic injustice toward young people practically guarantees epistemic injustice toward adults. "The experiences we have in childhood of growing up in systems of power and control creates a world-view that persists into adulthood. We learn to believe that domination is just the way the world works" (Brett 2016). The everyday epistemic injustices experienced by children function like a trauma that brings us into adulthood somewhat damaged and mostly acquiescent to and complicit in continued oppression. While we might like to think that experiencing (epistemic) oppression makes us more likely to resist it, it is, in fact, unreasonable to expect that being treated unjustly automatically makes people more sensitive and insightful; instead, we often use the same power exerted over us to oppress those weaker, to experience feelings of strength and control that we were previously denied, and because it seems the norm to do so.

It does not matter that adults do not see themselves as silencing children, or even that they do not intend to silence, for the effects are basically the same either way; in fact, in cases of "silenced dialogue" where the silenced are members of marginalized groups, silencers "are seldom aware that the dialogue has been silenced," especially when the silenced eventually stop disagreeing (Delpit 1988, 281). But where the adult lack of awareness *is* relevant is as an indication of problematic inequality and of unacknowledged privilege that needs to be checked. "Those with power are frequently least aware of—or least willing to acknowledge—its existence" (282) and most willing to exert their "authority to establish what [is] to be considered 'truth' regardless of the opinions" of the more marginalized (284). Too, "when childism pervades a society . . . even people who want to make the world better for children may find it hard to realize that it exists" (Young-Bruehl 2012, 4).

Feminists, including Fricker, have learned many hard-won lessons about power, including its multiple varieties, locations, and consequences. These should be extended to adult-children relationships, for, to return to Fricker, "wherever power is at work, we should be ready to ask who or what is controlling whom, and why" (2009, 14). We must admit, for example, that "the *power* that an adult has is not inherently good." Further, adults can and "should use their power in such a way that the *power over* children is eliminated. As children become empowered, they can become equalized with adults, such that there is no longer a *power over* anyone" (Stollar 2015). Epistemic justice can be one means to eliminating power over the young. Treating children as "knowledge bearers" has "far reaching implications" (Murris 2013, 253). As Lisa Delpit notes, "To act as if power does not exist is to ensure that the power status quo remains the same" (1988, 292). We have the ability to bring about change—can consideration of our complicity in injustice help create the political will?

NOTES

1. "Your Child's Self-Esteem," KidsHealth, July 2018, available at http://kidshealth .org/en/parents/self-esteem.html.

2. Jay L. Hoecker, "I've Heard a Lot about the Terrible Twos. Why Are 2-Year-Olds So Difficult?," Mayo Clinic, March 9, 2019, available at https://www.mayoclinic .org/healthy-lifestyle/infant-and-toddler-health/expert-answers/terrible-twos/faq -20058314.

3. Louise Derman-Sparks, Carol Tanaka Higa, and Bill Sparks claim that "the vast majority of texts on child development and early childhood education," texts "used to train teachers, psychologists, [and] social workers, reinforce the myths that children are color-blind and unaware of prejudice" (n.d.).

REFERENCES

Ahmed, Sara. 2017. *Living a Feminist Life*. Durham, NC: Duke University Press.

Alcoff, Linda. 1999. "On Judging Epistemic Credibility: Is Social Identity Relevant?" *Engendering Rationalities*, edited by Nancy Tuana and Sandra Morgen, 53–80. Albany: State University of New York Press.

Anti-Defamation League. 2001. "Talking to Your Child about Hatred and Prejudice." Cited in "Hate Is Learned and Can Be Unlearned." Social Science LibreTexts. https://socialsci.libretexts.org.

Astell, Mary. (1704) 1996. "Some Reflections upon Marriage." In *Astell: Political Writings*, edited by Patricia Springborg, 1–80. Cambridge: Cambridge University Press.

Belenky, Mary, Blythe Clinchy, Nancy Goldberger, and Jill Tarule. 1997. *Women's Ways of Knowing: The Development of Self, Voice, and Mind*. New York: Basic Books.

Brett, Teresa Graham. 2016. "Power over or Power with Children?" Parenting for Social Change. https://www.parentingforsocialchange.com/power-over-children-html/.

Carel, Havi, and Gita Gyorffy. 2014. "Seen but Not Heard: Children and Epistemic Injustice." *The Lancet* 384 (October 4): 1256–1257. http://www.thelancet.com/pdfs /journals/lancet/PIIS0140-6736(14)61759-1.pdf.

Chutter, James, and Pavel Bains. 2012. "To Raise a Generation of Creative Kids, Let Them Make Their Own Stories." Fast Company, September 4, 2012. http://www .fastcoexist.com/1680486/to-raise-a-generation-of-creative-kids-let-them-make -their-own-stories.

Code, Lorraine. 2008. "Incredulity, Experientialism, and the Politics of Knowledge." In *Just Methods: An Interdisciplinary Feminist Reader*, edited by Alison Jaggar, 290– 302. Boulder, CO: Paradigm Publishers.

Delpit, Lisa. 1988. "The Silenced Dialogue: Power and Pedagogy in Educating Other People's Children." *Harvard Educational Review* 58, no. 3 (August): 280–298.

Derman-Sparks, Louise, Carol Tanaka Higa, and Bill Sparks. n.d. "Children, Race and Racism: How Race Awareness Develops." http://www.teachingforchange.org /wp-content/uploads/2012/08/ec_childrenraceracism_english.pdf.

Desmadre, Al. 2008. "13 Common Myths, Misconceptions and Stereotypes about Mexican-Americans." LA Eastside, September 19, 2008. http://laeastside.com/2008 /09/13-common-myths-misconceptions-stereotypes-about-mexican-americans/

Fricker, Miranda. 2009. *Epistemic Injustice: Power and the Ethics of Knowing*. Oxford: Oxford University Press.

Gayle, Everton. 2016. "Children Were Not Believed, Cardinal Tells Australia Abuse Commission." *Euronews*, February 29, 2016. http://www.euronews.com/2016/02 /29/children-were-not-believed-cardinal-tells-australia-abuse-commission/.

Howard, Tyrone C. 2001. "Telling Their Side of the Story: African-American Students' Perceptions of Culturally Relevant Teaching." *Urban Review* 22 (2): 131–149.

Lehman, James. n.d. "Sick of Your Kid's Backtalk? Here's How to Stop It." Empowering Parents. https://www.empoweringparents.com/article/sick-of-your-kids -backtalk-heres-how-to-stop-it/.

Miles, Karen. n.d. "Talking Back: Why It Happens and What to Do about It (Ages 6 to 8)." *BabyCenter*. http://www.babycenter.com/0_talking-back-why-it-happens -and-what-to-do-about-it-ages-6-t_67686.bc.

Murris, Karin. 2013. "The Epistemic Challenge of Hearing Child's Voice." *Studies in Philosophy and Education* 32 (January): 245–259.

Myers, John E. B. 1995. "New Era of Skepticism Regarding Children's Credibility." *Psychology, Public Policy, and Law 1* (2): 387–398.

Parnass, Ava. 2013. "Emotional Benefits for Children Making Up Their Own Stories or Songs." MommyPerks, April 14, 2013. http://www.mommyperks.com/parenting-articles-2/emotional-benefits-for-children-making-up-their-own-stories/.

Reece, Tamekla. 2013. "What to Do When Kids Talk Back." *Parents*, October 13, 2013. http://www.parents.com/kids/problems/rebel/kids-talk-back/.

Southern Poverty Law Center. 1997. *Starting Small: Teaching Tolerance in Preschool and the Early Grades.* Teaching Tolerance. http://www.tolerance.org/sites/default/files/kits/Teachers_Study_Guide.pdf.

Stollar, R. L. 2015. "Child Liberation Theology: The Power of Adults over Children: Oppressive or Liberative?" Overturning Tables, July 25, 2015. https://rlstollar.wordpress.com/2015/07/25/the-power-of-adults-over-children-oppressive-or-liberative/.

Taylor, Nicola, and Anne Smith. 2009. *Children as Citizens? International Voices.* Dunedin, New Zealand: Otaga University Press.

UNICEF. n.d. "Sierra Leonean Children Tell Their Side of the Story." http://www.unicef.org/sowc05/english/conflictfeat_sierra.html.

Young-Bruehl, Elisabeth. 2012. *Childism: Confronting Prejudice against Children.* New Haven, CT: Yale University Press.

8

Learning from Feminist
Disability Theory

"Professionals often implicitly associate impairments with childlike features or childhood, inadvertently infantilizing patients
with impairments and reinforcing the credibility hierarchy"
between patients and their health care providers.

—**Ho**, 2011, 113–114

Disability theorists, and those living with disabilities, rightly object to
and contest being infantilized by medical practitioners. In "Trusting
Experts and Epistemic Humility in Disability," quoted above, Anita
Ho challenges the credibility hierarchy between patients with impairments
and their healthcare providers (HCPs) that leads to and reinforces infantiliza-
tion; in its stead, she asks for a therapeutic relationship in which knowledge
about the needs and interests of patients is not determined by HCPs alone,
based on their medical expertise, but co-created by patients and their HCPs
in consultation. Because Ho reminds us that the traditional model of medical care risks establishing a relationship between providers and patients with
impairments that has been (in some unfortunate regards) like that between
adult and child, I am led to wonder about the extent to which her reframing
of the provider-patient relationship may also, as an unintended consequence,
help us revision the adult-child relat2ionship. What is especially intriguing
is that Ho's reframing of the therapeutic relationship is not dependent on
seeing provider and patient as contributing the same or equal things to their
new collaborative relationship, yet she is still able to challenge the epistemic
hierarchy between them and demand that greater weight and respect be
given to the views of the previously discounted party. Because the relationship between adult and child is also in many ways an unequal one, Ho's
work should be explored, as should feminist disability theory more generally,
for the unexpected insights it can offer into more collaborative adult-child

relationships: ones in which the views of those younger are understood and treated as important.[1] Disability theory built upon the provider-patient relationship has repercussions extending to numerous other relations between people who differ but all still want a voice in a relatively democratic scheme.

The Status Quo Being Critiqued

The prevailing myth of provider-patient relationships is that they are unproblematic relationships of trust: patients should trust the goodwill and expertise of HCPs to act in the patients' best interests. The HCP-patient relationship is so constituted, in fact, that *not* trusting and following the HCP, acting "noncompliantly," against doctor's orders, is seen as inherently unreasonable, even stupid (Ho 2011, 106).[2] After all, HCPs have the training, credentials, and social responsibility to work for their patients' good; their biomedical knowledge is based on information that is well-tested and objective and hence trustworthy.

Ho invites us to be curious about and critical toward the taken-for-granted aspects of this widely accepted trusting relationship. She proposes that the bond so constituted can work in ways precisely opposed to its desired ends, *negatively* affecting the therapeutic relationship and missing the mark of working for the best interests of patients with impairments. The relationship is compromised because the knowledge the patient brings to it is discounted as subjective and thus unreliable. This discounting means that potentially relevant information is not given its due weight or is simply ignored in decision making (regarding diagnosis, treatment, resource allocation, etc.), leading to inferior or flawed judgments and recommendations. Further, the patient's status as a knower is diminished when their input is cast aside, contributing to their continued marginalization and silencing as a person with impairments and also increasing their dissatisfaction with their healthcare. No one desires these outcomes, of course—quite the contrary, in fact; nonetheless, the predominant setup inadvertently promotes them.

The mythologized relationship between adult and child, the way it is assumed to work—unproblematically—is similarly based on the child's trusting the adult to govern in the child's best interest. Based on life experience, training about, social responsibility toward, and/or care for the child, the adult is assumed to know more and to be motivated to guide well. A child disagreeing with their parents or teachers, like the disabled patient disagreeing with their HCP, is seen as inherently unreasonable (perhaps even punishable, in this case) and rightly overruled. Parents and teachers, after all, are presumed to have the practical wisdom, education, and concern to best understand and attend to the child's needs and interests. An adult who follows a child is generally ridiculed, seen as working against what is best for the child and perhaps even irresponsibly contributing to the creation of an unreasonable, overly demanding youth, a "spoiled" character who is almost demonized in popular literature about children.[3]

The insights of feminist disability theory raise many questions about adult-child relations. Is it possible that, just as a doctor-patient relationship based on one-way trust in the HCP's knowledge is liable to be destructive of its desired goal of making decisions in the patient's best interests, the adult-child relationship based on one-way trust in the adult's knowledge is similarly inadvertently destructive of the child's best interest? Might this recommended one-way trust, which Ho says leads to patients' dissatisfaction with their healthcare, also be a cause of children's discontent with their relationships with many important adults in their lives? Does the child, like the patient, have a rightful role in the co-creation of knowledge regarding their needs and interests? Do children have knowledge about themselves and their lives to contribute to decision making about them and even their communities? If so, what is the nature of that knowledge, and what changes to the predominant model of adult-child relationships does recognition of it require? What are the resistances to seeing and treating young people as knowledgeable about their own needs and interests, and able to participate in decision making, and how might we overcome those obstacles? Feminist disability theory not only helps us pose these questions but also can help us address them.

The Analogy

The analogy I am working with—the traditional notion that HCP-patient = adult-child—requires a little more development. In what ways are Ho's patients with impairments thought to be like children? How are HCPs thought to be the "adults," like parents and teachers? And, finally, how are the relationships analogous, and what particular aspects of those relationships form the basis of this comparison?

What Ho stresses about patients with impairments is the ways in which they are deemed unfit, by HCPs and more generally, to decide for themselves about their treatment, on two grounds: by virtue of their impairments, which somehow automatically mark them as less competent, and due to their lack of medical expertise. Along similar lines, in "Epistemic Injustice and Mental Illness," theologian Anastasia Scrutton discusses how patients with mental illnesses enter treatment with already deflated credibility, with their epistemic authority diminished, simply due to their mental illnesses (2017, 348). In making the analogy, I am using the fact that children, too, as discussed in earlier chapters, are also viewed with suspicion epistemically. They are seen as unable to govern themselves and are not characterized as knowers, simply by virtue of their age; age of minority is readily linked in the public imaginary[4] with immature judgment and ignorance about the ways of the world.

Renowned feminist disability theorist Eva Kittay adds a related but distinct aspect to the analogous position of patients and children. We "stigmatise those who cannot be independent . . . the ill, those with many sorts of disabilities and frail elderly persons. Even children are not given their full due, a regard for their agency and due consideration of their judgment because of the low esteem in which we hold being in a state of dependence" (2007, 50). Once recognized as dependent, even one's independence of judgment is challenged. Kittay emphasizes the unnecessary cost to the agency of the young and the disabled and the lack of weight given to their ideas even by those with whom they are in important, intimate relationships, because of the dependence that almost comes to define them. She suggests a profound rethinking of the character and consequences of various "dependencies."

People with physical, cognitive, or emotional impairments, on the one hand, and children, on the other, enter relationships with HCPs and adults, respectively, with what Miranda Fricker calls "credibility deficits"—a "prejudice [about them that] will tend surreptitiously to . . . deflate the credibility afforded the[m]" (2009, 17). Fricker rightly assumes that in conversations we are always making credibility assessments about the speaker and that negative identity-based stereotypes about various groups like children and the mentally ill can inadvertently but decisively tip those assessments to incredulity. The relationship between people with emotional impairments and their HCPs often involves the patients being ignored, disbelieved, or misinterpreted, in large part due to the prior diagnoses they have received. Prejudice about the mentally ill can potentially color the entire exchange between them and their HCPs, determining, for example, whose interpretation of the "lesser" party's experience is correct; similarly, stereotypes about children at various ages can shape the discursive exchanges between them and adults, regarding tone and content. In ongoing relationships, this credibility deficit can have cumulative effects, such as decreased confidence in one's own story among those who are repeatedly doubted or ignored.

In all of these cases, the parties just described are in relationship with people who have greater epistemic authority, who possess socially superior claims to knowledge. These claims are so superior that HCPs/parents/teachers frequently ignore, disbelieve, or overrule them and can expect to be backed up by peers and even society more generally for doing so. In these relationships, the knowledge of the "lesser" parties is discounted, on a wide variety of grounds, ranging from its subjectivity to its immaturity to its insanity. This dismissal reinforces their diminished status as knowers, a significant loss that has consequences beyond the particular relationship (Fricker 2009). We do not usually think of them this way, but the "greater" parties in these relationships, including adults in adult-child relations, possess what Fricker calls "credibility excess" (17), meaning that as speakers, based on their identity, they are granted more credibility than they objectively merit. Ho knows that merely raising their voice in disagreement with an HCP can even become a justification for the HCP further dismissing the voice of a person with an impairment: "The reasoning of those who disagree with the expert's opinion is often automatically considered inferior, to the extent that the patient's [or child's] capacity to make medical [or other] decisions may be questioned" (2011, 115). Such is the effect of a credibility hierarchy. The simple act of speaking up or "talking back" works against you, marking you as one whose views should not be taken seriously in other contexts or on other matters, regardless of the accuracy or importance of your speech.

In my scenario, the analogies are epistemically based: the feature of them I am emphasizing relates to questions about who is deemed a knower, about what, on what basis, and with what consequences. All are relationships between parties considered to have greater, more important, or more respected (forms of) knowledge, and others supposed to have less, less important, or more devalued (forms of) knowledge. Both the content of and the basis for the knowledge are contrasted. In all cases, the contrast becomes a justification for dismissing, or not even asking for, the input of the "lesser," more "inexpert" party.

Breaking down some of what these credibility hierarchies entail brings us to the question of whether they are necessary or desirable—whether they rightly characterize the various parties or set up relationships conducive to the ends they seek. Just as Ho and Scrutton challenge the dichotomy between expert doctor and inexpert patient, so does Kittay tackle the sharp line drawn between the competent and the incompetent (2007, 39). In fact, she says, even in the most severe cases of compromised competence, "there are some pockets of agency . . . that still require consideration, voice and respect" (39). Further, judgments of who has contributions to make often ignore the ways in which social, political, and institutional settings (including medical) rather than abstract individual competence, per se, influence those assessments. Educational and familial settings, too, rather than a child's abstract (in)competence, most certainly affect how much input into decision making they are allowed or invited to offer. Like Ho and Scrutton, Kittay argues that medical relationships of one-way trust, which she terms "paternalistic," are destructive of their desired goals:

> Those who argue for the need for paternalistic interference rarely weigh the dodgy question of whether the harm that will occur from paternalistic interference itself will be *greater* than the harm resulting from refraining from paternalistic interference. . . . [For example,] in addition to failing to give due respect to the individual's autonomy, paternalism in medicine also undermines a relationship between medical practitioner and patient (and often the patient's family) based on trust. (37)

We so easily characterize the young/impaired as incompetent, unable to represent themselves or ideas in meaningful ways, and those older/healthier as always more knowledgeable and able to represent not only themselves but also others—dependents—accurately and in their interest. We are trained, it seems, to overlook the persistent and glaring exceptions and qualifications to this and to not see how social structures and settings (rather than abstract individual [in]competence) shape abilities, perceptions of abilities, and possibilities of participation. We often avoid thinking about how self-defeating the relationships are that are built on these supposedly stark and unavoidable contrasts in competence, and about how unnecessarily unhappy so many are with medical/familial/educational relationships.

Alternative Models

Scrutton urges that we treat the mentally ill as participants in any diagnostic process, inviting them to offer information and perspectives that "supplement" medical ones (2017, 350). She thinks that people with mental illnesses should negotiate the meaning and the value of their experiences in a "dialogical process" (352) in therapy with their HCPs. Even when their interpretation "loses" in negotiation, the very fact that the HCP has "listened closely" (353) means that patients have not experienced "the silencing that is a structural facet of psychiatric diagnosis and treatment [that] is, in and of itself, deflating" (350).

One obstacle to this collaboration that Scrutton wrestles with is that the kind of knowledge that mental health providers may privilege is third-person medical perspectives; consequently, they invalidate the knowledge that the mentally ill bring, which is primarily first-person. But first-person knowledge, Scrutton claims, should be viewed as a hermeneutical resource, something that should be neither silenced nor marginalized. Those who experience mental illness have subtle knowledge of what their experience is like, including its difficulties and advantages, and have ideas about what is good and workable for them in terms of treatment options. Scrutton says that by virtue of their experience with mental illness, they are epistemically privileged—they have "distinctive and/or unique forms of knowledge" (347) about their condition. This knowledge should be considered when coming to decisions about treatment. Focusing on epistemic contributions, Scrutton shows how patients can "sharpen," "deepen," and "clarify" an exclusively medical understanding (351) and can offer "insight" (352). What is distinctive and important to the patient should matter, be heard, and be counted. This consideration is more likely to lead to a constructive relationship—not one in which the parties are contributing the same things to the relationship, but one in which each contributes something real and distinctive that together lead to better healthcare outcomes and greater epistemic justice.

Ho, too, argues for a more collaborative relationship between HCPs and patients with impairments. It is HCPs who most need to change, in her preferred scenario, given the described hierarchy we begin with. The change they need to make is an epistemic one: they need to commit to epistemic humility, to a recognition of the boundaries and the fallibility of their expert knowledge, and their need for "the potential contributions of patients with impairments in knowledge creation" (Ho 2011, 103). As Elizabeth Barnes insists, "We ought to take disabled people as very good sources of evidence about what it's like to be disabled. Or at least we ought to take them as *better* sources of evidence than the beliefs of the non-disabled" (2016, 142). What then replaces exclusive knowing and all-knowing is an interdependent and collaborative model between patient and HCP that, in fact, beautifully *builds* trust through the co-creation of knowledge, rather than assuming that it should exist automatically and in one direction only. Multiple forms of inquiry and knowledge, including the local and the subjective, are granted credence and importance in this collaboration—again, the distinct knowledge of both parties is acknowledged, and no one is wronged in their capacity as a knower.

What is so radical in feminist disability studies is the way that previously dismissed views and voices are now deemed credible and important, even when in disagreement. In the new relationships, everyone is assumed to possess some expertise and to have the potential to work together, to negotiate. At that point, the patient and the HCP can come to an enhanced understanding of the patient's healthcare situation and can look at the personal costs and benefits of various treatment options. In some ways, this process can seem fairly ordinary, but it involves a truly extraordinary reevaluation of what counts as knowledge, who counts as a knower, and how collaborative a relationship can be even between unequal participants.

What does this analysis of provider-patient relations entail for the adult-child relationship? For the analogy to hold as we move to alternative models, we have to make the case, as we have in medical contexts, that young people have knowledge to contribute in adult-child relations and that consideration of that knowledge leads to better decisions more fully in the interests of the child and to an enhanced relationship between them and adults. I think that it is important to show as well that having this collaborative adult-child conversation is practicable.

How might children's ways or kinds of knowledge be characterized? Are they similar to the forms of knowledge that Ho and Scrutton so ably resuscitate—those which, for some examples, are local, intuitive, first-person, subjective, and narrative-based? To be sure, feminist disability thinkers argue for openness to multiple forms of knowledge, for recognition that people in relationships can know different things in diverse ways, and for consideration of all of these in relationships.[5] Again, it is the fact that an "asymmetry of knowledge and skill between patient and medical caregiver" (Kittay 2007, 26) is compatible with an interdependent relationship between them that makes this whole analogy with adults and children so enticing.

What do adults not necessarily know or understand about the lives of young people? What might adults learn from them, especially (although not exclusively) as they make decisions that influence children's lives? What kinds of knowledge are children able to contribute? Interestingly, we readily advantage children with certain mental faculties, such as imagination, creativity, and curiosity, although we also too often unfortunately and needlessly downplay the value of those capacities in hierarchies of knowing. There is a vicious circle at play. "We might begin to pay careful attention to what *we* can learn from *their* knowledge, [instead of] just trying to fill them with our own" (Minkel 2017). What might adults learn if they were more open to what children knew, perhaps through faculties such as imagination and curiosity?

In addition to having, and sometimes even exemplifying, certain mental capacities, young people also share many epistemic features with those older. We know that "from birth, children are active participants in building their own understanding" (Vanderbilt Child and Family Center, n.d.). They are active learners from infancy. They construct knowledge of things familiar to adults—how to express oneself, how to build relationships, how to understand the ways various things work—and do so using familiar tools, such as observation, experimentation, and participation. And, of course, as these infants grow into teens, still minors and still too often discounted, these capacities expand. Adults and children, even the very young, are not speaking totally different epistemic languages. This common ground, were we to acknowledge and build upon it, would potentially facilitate conversation and negotiation.

Just as HCPs need knowledge of the individuals with whom they are working to come up with the best individualized treatment plans, so do educators and parents need knowledge of and from individual children to best educate or rear them. As Kittay says, an HCP "must elicit the patient's own understanding of what the patient really needs, in light of what the patient, as *this* concrete individual, really cares about" (2007, 25). Since children, too, are individuals, and a one-size-fits-all approach doesn't work any better for them than it does for patients seeing their HCPs, then the case is made that adults need knowledge of specific children. How do they obtain that? Certainly, there are standard external assessment measures available that give some information, and teachers and parents also learn from making their own observations. But firsthand reports from children contain readily available and essential information about their likes and dislikes, strengths and difficulties, needs and interests, ideas and questions.

What the feminist disability theorists discussed here emphasize is the experiential knowledge that patients bring to their relationships with HCPs; they have firsthand knowledge of what it is like to be in their situations or to have particular conditions and have reflected upon their experiences. And this individual knowledge, to be sure, is something that young people can bring to their relationships with adults. One child knows, from experience and reflection on that experience, what it is like to be poor when their friends have more access to financial resources and want to go out. What could we learn from them about poverty and about feeling left out and less than? And might what we learn direct adults to do such things as make free or affordable social opportunities for young people more available or to ensure that kids have a "home base" where they do not always feel different? Another child knows, from experience and wrestling with that experience, what it is like to be asked to sit still for hours in a classroom when their energy makes this a nearly impossible task, and when their inability to abide by the dictates of the classroom frequently lands them in trouble. What could we learn from them, about everything from what this individual's energy feels like, to the labeling of certain kids as "problems"? Might we think better, because of this conversation, about how this child feels, the help they might benefit from, and the importance of more flexible and inclusive classroom structures and mandates? Another young person knows, from experience and rumination on that experience, what it means to be overwhelmed with worry and fear about the violence in their household or neighborhood. What could we learn from them about the costs of violence and the varied coping strategies that individuals develop? Might we make our schools more trauma-informed after learning from such children?

The opportunities for insight and action are potentially endless. Adults, parents and teachers especially, can learn from the young more about the individuality of the child and about general social phenomena, from intimate partner violence to the classroom-to-prison pipeline. Often, the experiences that children share with us or confront us with will send us out seeking more information or opportunities to act, as it turns out that there are limits to our "expertise," after all, and even limits to what our care for them can tell us about what is good or best for the young people in our lives. But some of the gaps can be filled simply by listening better to children. Adults, like HCPs, need epistemic humility. It will make us smarter and more able to accomplish the positive goals we have in relation to the youth with whom we interact.

Obstacles

Ho writes that HCPs "are not trained to understand the perspectives of people with impairments" (2011, 118). And they have to contend with the fact that those perspectives have already been deemed "irrelevant or unreliable" (111) in their professional training. The additional information that patients bring may be annoying, to boot, as these new perspectives may "critique or challenge [HCP's] determinations" (110). Scrutton further points out that being able to hear the perspectives of the mentally ill may require of HCPs the ability to "facilitat[e] linguistic and non-linguistic ways of expressing the experience" (2017, 351). Kittay adds that "medical personnel have time pressures and unrealistic work schedules" (2007, 46). She acknowledges that such time constraints tug against what the more disabled require: "Although an identity and individuality is still realizable by those who are deeply dependent and cognitively limited, determining this requires caring persons who are willing and capable of being attentive to that identity and individuality" (41). And even in less complicated circumstances, time constraints on medical practitioners are not conducive to conversation. All of this is to say that the obstacles to two-way negotiation in the HCP-patient relationship are significant. Nonetheless, we are right to expect, even demand, that HCPs hear the perspectives of their patients in order to enhance their own understanding of the situation and to avoid "subjecting patients to a form of epistemic injustice" (Ho 2011, 120). Securing the patient's best interest, the very goal of the therapeutic relationship, is at stake.

It can take time and energy for an adult to listen to a child, too, and to negotiate with them. Dealing with the demands of the rest of the class or the rest of the family can present obstacles. And just as "professionals often understand and experience the world differently from patients with impairments" (120), so may adults no longer effortlessly understand the perspectives of those much younger, in terms of what is being conveyed, how, or why. The world that children inhabit is different from the world adults grew up in, as is, often, the language they speak. The obstacles to co-created knowledge that can productively be used to make decisions about children's lives are not inconsiderable. But we are right here, too, to expect, even demand, that adults hear the perspectives of young people in order to enhance adults' own understanding and to avoid "subjecting [youth] to a form of epistemic injustice" (120). We need ultimately to think about what kinds of adult-child interactions and environments are most conducive to respect for the child, collaboratively built knowledge, and sustainable relationships.

Some norms governing adult decision making and adult-child conversation—and medical decision making and interaction—are being challenged here, to be sure, and even our thinking about the nature of conversation itself requires some tweaking to facilitate this reconsideration. In "What Does It Mean to 'Speak as a Woman'?" philosopher Agnes Callard writes, "When we converse, we have the goal of thinking with our interlocutor, and you only invite someone into your mind to the extent that you are willing to lay it open before them; and because you expect them to do the same" (2018). Callard is presenting another challenge to all interlocutors: to be open with and to the other in conversation. People on the tops of hierarchies may be unfamiliar or uncomfortable with this practice and even be loath to pursue it, viewing it as antithetical to their position and the authority that comes with it. They are, perhaps, more comfortable with the idea of the less privileged parties opening themselves up; indeed, some hierarchies are noticeable as such by the requirement of speech or revelation from one party only. Introducing a sort of vulnerability to the practices of such people as teachers, parents, and doctors may feel—well, even a little threatening, to the individual and the order they strive to create. That might give them some insight into how the other party *regularly* feels. But it might also be liberating. For there is an incredibly positive definition of vulnerability explored by the feminist philosopher Erinn Gilson in "Vulnerability, Ignorance, and Oppression." Gilson's intriguing argument goes as far as to associate the refusal to be and to be recognized as vulnerable with practices that are "ethically and politically dangerous" (2011, 308). While the pursuit of invulnerability is commonplace, it is undesirable, she argues, and what she recommends especially is epistemic vulnerability—an openness "to being affected and shaped by others" (319). Such newfound "relationality" (321) includes, among her examples, openness to those differently abled and, among my examples, openness to the young. Rather than openness to harm, we might reconsider vulnerability as openness to learning: "cultivating the attitude of one who is epistemically vulnerable rather than that of the masterful, invulnerable knower who has nothing to learn from others" (324).

Paying attention to the words and experiences of youth is desirable, then, on multiple grounds. I wonder whether it is also more feasible than we might imagine, whether the obstacles to it can be overcome or recognized as exaggerated. One way that I think we make open conversation, negotiation, and the co-creation of knowledge seem unrealistic is by overestimating the difference between what is needed in ordinary adult-adult interactions and what is being asked for in everyday, respectful adult-child interactions. I challenge this supposed difference by comparing what the literature says about active listening in adult-adult relationships with that describing what it takes to listen well to children. This comparison enables me to claim that the demand to listen to young people is not only an ethical imperative but also something practical, reasonable, and doable.

The literature on listening to children emphasizes that it is an active process of receiving, then interpreting, and then responding to them, verbally and nonverbally. It means tuning in to the individual in the context of their everyday lives as well as in cases of specific issues or events (Clark 2004). It takes time and even patience and imagination, more so if the child has communication difficulties, lacks confidence, or lacks experience in speaking. Listening well on the part of the adult involves observation and an openness to receiving input in a variety of forms, including nonverbal. It requires letting the other play an active role. It may entail respect for their privacy and their silence rather than demanding speech or thoughtlessly sharing what is learned from them. It requires withholding judgment and evaluation while the child speaks and not interrupting or prematurely solving their problem. An attentive adult listener cannot be distracted by something more important on their own agenda.

The sophistication and complexity of listening openly should not be underestimated. Listening well is a learned skill and requires practice. The literature seems to assume that most of us were not well listened to as children and are therefore not particularly good at it as adults. As a result, our abilities as adult listeners are compromised, and this limitation should worry us as we make decisions for and about children based on the compromised knowledge that results.

How does this advice for listening to children compare with that regarding good listening in adult-adult conversation? An article in the *Harvard Business Review* emphasizes that good listeners are not silent; rather, they "periodically ask questions that promote discovery and insight" (Zenger and Folkman 2016); they make "the conversation a positive experience for the other party," conveying confidence, support, and cooperation; and they provide feedback, which is not the same as prematurely offering solutions. The authors offer the image of a trampoline rather than a sponge, seeing listening as part of a two-way conversation, not just absorption. Lindsay Holmes, another analyst of good listening among adults, emphasizes that it requires being mindful, empathetic, humble, open-minded, emotionally intelligent, nondefensive, and responsive and includes asking questions (2017).

The conclusion, perhaps, is obvious. The skills and effort required and expected of adults in listening to other adults in professional and personal relationships alike do not differ much from those needed and expected in listening to children. In co-creating knowledge with young people, adults are not being asked to do some unfamiliar, impossible task. We are just being asked to treat children as fully human interlocutors. Listening to young people, then, is ethically desirable and practical.

What's at Stake

We have opportunities, even in everyday interactions, to make our interlocutors feel either valued or dismissed—to bring about greater epistemic justice or contribute to the devaluation of people based on stereotypes of what they cannot be or know. Alison Clark writes (although I turn her words into a list): "We listen to children (1) because it acknowledges their right to be listened to and for their views and experiences to be taken seriously about matters that affect them; (2) [because] of the difference listening can make to our understanding of children's priorities, interests and concerns; (3) [because] of the difference it can make to our understanding of how children feel about themselves; (4) [and because] listening is a vital part of establishing respectful relationships" (2004). Clark reiterates, then, that listening is necessary for the child and the adult, much as Ho, Kittay, and Scrutton argue that listening to patients is important for the patient and the HCP. Children, like patients with impairments, have the right to be heard and to be taken seriously, especially in decision making that affects their lives. They have their own "priorities, interests and concerns" (ibid.) with which adults must learn to be comfortable and competent negotiating.

Listening to children establishes relationships between them and their adults that are more likely to be appreciated and to lead to decisions and practices in the children's best interests. The young experience what it means to be treated as a knower, as a valued participant in conversation. "By listening to them, you are communicating that they are worthy of your attention. . . [and] you are demonstrating that their view of the world has merit" (The Center for Parenting Education, n.d.). One-way trust and exclusive claims to knowledge in Ho's analysis lead to a destructive therapeutic relationship that results in unsatisfying outcomes for the patient (and more dissatisfaction with the medical establishment) and compromised knowledge on the part of the HCP; so, too, do one-way trust and exclusive claims to knowledge on the part of adults lead to destructive adult-child relations. By listening to children, we have it in our power to increase their satisfaction with and trust in their relationships with adults. For example, "Active Listening can help empower your child by aiding her in getting clear about what her feelings are and even in coming to some decisions on her own about how she wants to handle a situation. Ultimately it brings . . . parent and child closer together" (ibid.). Too, listening to children gives adults more knowledge, affecting adult understanding—it "can provide unexpected insights" (Clark 2004).[6]

Callard tells us something else that informs why we should challenge and reshape our practice of hierarchical adult-child conversation: "The ideas of respect and equality have many applications in civic life, especially in a democracy, but one of the most basic is conversational: mutual recognition as having equal standing to contribute to the discussion of some question" (2018). She is emphasizing "equal standing to contribute," not necessarily "equality of contribution," it is worth noting, just as feminist disability scholars do. That is what democratic respect for others requires of us. But, somehow, we do not usually think about respecting children, in conversation or otherwise. The first dictionary definition of "respect" that appears in a Google search, from *Merriam-Webster*, explains why: it defines respect as "a feeling of deep admiration for someone or something elicited by their abilities, qualities, or achievements." We do not readily think about "admiring" young people, especially not based on their "abilities" or "achievements," and especially not in the course of everyday conversation. Along similar lines, Vocabulary.com emphasizes showing respect to those "who are impressive . . . such as being in authority" and gives the familiar example of respecting one's teacher. These definitions are not wrong or wholly inapplicable. But the emphasis too easily leads to disrespect for the voices of those *not* in authority and *not* socially elevated, such as children, which this whole chapter problematizes. Nonetheless, we can reclaim a definition farther down on Merriam-Webster's list that will help us understand that respect for youth is essential and appropriate in conversation, for this definition associates respect with "an act of giving particular attention: CONSIDERATION." Showing respect to children need not involve, to cite other definitions, "deference" to someone one "esteems"—just consideration. Children need no longer be excluded by definition from those parties deemed worthy of the respect that conversation requires. Let us make primary, then, as a contribution toward dismantling another obstacle to co-creating knowledge between adults and children, that definition of respect that is secondary in the dictionary—simply being worthy of attention by virtue of being human and having the potential to contribute to knowledge.

Listening to those younger or more dependent is mandated by a commitment to democracy. Democracy works most easily when everyone is relatively equal: adult, able-bodied, educated, able to express themselves well, and so forth. It is more challenging in the face of inequalities. Yet we spend much of our lives in unequal relations—as parents and children, teachers and students, employers and employees—and the democratic impulse need not and cannot be utterly irrelevant in such situations. This chapter urges us to recognize that even in the face of significant differences between parties, the views of those who have been so easily and regularly written off, in fact, merit full consideration, even when that consideration puts demands of time and translation upon the listener. Committing to this work and this type of relationship involves a steadfast democratic faithfulness to participatory processes, with democratic outcomes of shared, jointly built knowledge.

Concluding Thoughts

Harlan Hahn writes:

> Paternalism enables the dominant elements of a society to express profound and sincere sympathy for the members of a minority group while, at the same time, keeping them in a position of social and economic subordination. It has allowed the nondisabled to act as the protectors, guides, leaders, role models, and intermediaries for disabled individuals who, *like children*, are often assumed to be helpless, dependent, asexual, economically unproductive, physically limited, emotionally immature, and acceptable only when they are unobtrusive. . . . Politically, disabled people usually have been neither seen nor heard. (1986, 130; my emphasis)

As feminist disability theorist Amber Knight has said, "While many disability rights activists insist that people 'stop treating me like a child,' they rarely question whether it's appropriate to treat children in such a controlling or dismissive way either."[7] I argue that we should take Knight's liberating argument that patients "should not be denied the ability to speak for themselves or play a role in directing their own lives" and extend it to young people rather than having the disabled (and other groups) claim rights based on their differences from the young. No one, not the disabled or the young, should be treated only as "helpless, dependent, asexual, economically unproductive, physically limited, emotionally immature, and acceptable only when they are unobtrusive" (Hahn 1986, 130). While disability rights activists rightly cringe at the analogy that seems to equate the patient and the child, I use the analogy to extend their insights about unequal relationships to another dyad. Because these activists and theorists challenge and reframe the traditionally unequal relationship between HCPs and patients, we can learn from their work and lives about challenging and reframing other unequal relationships, including those between adults and children.

Disability rights activists and theorists have contested the notion that those with impairments have suffered some personal tragedy and consequently require the services of (especially medical) professionals. They look at disability in cultural and political contexts, instead, where things like access are either impeded, allowed, or enabled. And they do not limit the whole person to whatever their impairment may be or entail. So, too, is being young not some inferior condition—just something to be endured until it is outgrown—but a stage and state of life with great integrity and possibility. Here, too, we can ask not just about the limits of childhood, as if, like disability, it exists in a vacuum, but about whether environments are youth-friendly, whether procedures include or negatively segregate those younger, and whether the young's input is actively welcomed, merely tolerated, or even aggressively discouraged. The young are dependent in many ways, but so are we all, in many unrecognized and unheralded ways, and that isn't all that any of us are.

A mantra of the disability rights movement is "nothing about us without us." This democratic idea conveys that those who are affected by a policy or decision should have a role in its making. Despite the fact that they have long been labeled and treated as "mere" dependents, "politically active people with disabilities are beginning to proclaim that they know what is best for themselves and their community. This is a militant, revelational claim" (Charlton 1998, 4). It is indeed a revelation, and a revolution, a new seeing and a turnabout in relationships among individuals and between the individual and the community. Those arguing for a liberatory childhood can learn from this oft-repeated lesson: those who have been deemed necessarily (if unfortunately) outside the participatory circle in fact have a rightful role within it. There are multiple roles to play in participatory decision making, and children are perfectly suited for many of them; too, they learn from early inclusion how to participate ever more fully and effectively. As we will see in the chapter on utopias and dystopias, children can easily be imagined as participants in diverse decision-making processes or can continue to suffer from being treated as irrelevant to them. Respect for them as individual human beings and as members of various communities demands that their participation be considered, encouraged, and enabled.

NOTES

1. I cannot stress enough that I am *not* saying that patients with impairments are (like) children; I am aware that I run the risk of such a misreading by using the analogy at all. The charge by those with disabilities, especially cognitive disabilities, is that they're wrongly *treated* like children. I'm looking at whether rejecting being "treated like children" is a rejection of a certain kind of treatment that should also be rejected for those who actually *are* children. Ultimately, I'm trying to learn from disability theory about relationships between "unequals."

2. Interestingly, Anastasia Scrutton, discussed below, notes that patients experiencing mental illness may find their HCP "stupid" for not fully understanding them due to the limits of the dominant medical perspective they employ (2017, 350). Clearly, if both parties can feel this way, something is amiss.

3. This character seems to me to be analogous to the female "shrew" who is disobedient and must be brought back under male control.

4. The term "imaginary" is used across academic disciplines, which Brigitte Nerlich explains thusly: "When you type 'imaginary' into a certain search engine, you get the following definition: 'The **imaginary**, or social **imaginary** is the set of values, institutions, laws, and symbols common to a particular social group and the corresponding society through which people imagine their social whole.' But . . . imaginaries are more than that. Social imaginaries 'are ways of understanding the social that become social entities themselves, mediating collective life' and shaping the way we live now and into the future." Brigitte Nerlich, "Imagining Imaginaries," Making Science Public (blog), University of Nottingham, April 23, 2015, available at http://blogs.nottingham.ac.uk /makingsciencepublic/2015/04/23/imagining-imaginaries/.

5. This is an important claim in diverse fields, from feminist epistemology (see, for example, Stone-Mediatore 2007) to feminist legal theory (see, for example, M. Barnes 2006).

6. We need to ask why the insights are "unexpected," which takes us back to assumptions of children's incompetence. Scrutton also uses the word "surprising" (2017, 351) to

describe the input of patients—surprising because it is unexpected and not covered by the dominant interpretive framework. Our default is epistemically biased.

7. Personal correspondence, February 26, 2019. I am indebted to this conversation especially for ideas and references in this last section.

REFERENCES

Barnes, Elizabeth. 2016. *The Minority Body: A Theory of Disability*. Oxford: Oxford University Press.

Barnes, Mario. 2006. "Black Women's Stories and the Criminal Law: Restating the Power of Narrative." *U.C. Davis Law Review* 39:941–990.

Callard, Agnes. 2018. "What Does It Mean to 'Speak as a Woman'?" *New York Times*, December 3, 2018.

The Center for Parenting Education. n.d. "The Skill of Listening." https://center forparentingeducation.org/library-of-articles/healthy-communication/the-skill-of -listening/.

Charlton, James I. 1998. *Nothing about Us without Us: Disability Oppression and Empowerment*. Berkeley: University of California Press.

Clark, Alison. 2004. "Listening as a Way of Life." National Children's Bureau (London). https://exeter.anglican.org/wp-content/uploads/2014/11/Listening-to-children -leaflet_NCB.pdf.

Fricker, Miranda. 2007. *Epistemic Injustice: Power and the Ethics of Knowing*. Oxford: Oxford University Press.

Gilson, Erinn. 2011. "Vulnerability, Ignorance, and Oppression." *Hypatia: A Journal of Feminist Philosophy* 26 (Spring): 308–332.

Hahn, Harlan. 1986. "Public Support for Rehabilitation Programmes: The Analysis of U.S. Disability Policy." *Disability, Handicap and Society* 1 (2): 121–137.

Ho, Anita. 2011. "Trusting Experts and Epistemic Humility in Disability." *International Journal of Feminist Approaches to Bioethics* 4 (2): 102–123.

Holmes, Lindsay. 2017. "9 Things Good Listeners Do Differently." *HuffPost*, updated on December 6, 2017. https://www.huffpost.com/entry/habits-of-good-listeners_n _5668590.

Kittay, Eva Fedder. 2007. "Beyond Autonomy and Paternalism: The Caring Transparent Self." In *Autonomy and Paternalism: Reflections on the Theory and Practice of Health Care*, edited by Thomas Nys, Yvonne Denier, and Toone Vandevelde, 23–70. Durham, NC: Duke University Press.

Minkel, Justin. 2017. "What Children Know That Adults Don't: Celebrating the Magic of Childhood." *Education Week*, January 10, 2017. https://www.edweek .org/tm/articles/2017/01/10/what-children-know-that-adults-dont-celebrating .html.

Scrutton, Anastasia. 2017. "Epistemic Injustice and Mental Illness." In *Routledge Handbook on Epistemic Injustice*, edited by Ian Kidd, Jose Medina, and Gaile Polhaus Jr., 347–355. New York: Routledge.

Stone-Mediatore, Shari. 2007. "Challenging Academic Norms: An Epistemology for Feminist and Multicultural Classrooms." *NWSA Journal* 19 (Fall): 55–78.

Vanderbilt Family and Child Center. n.d. "Children Gain Powerful Knowledge through Play." https://www.vanderbilt.edu/child-family-center/child-care-center /knowledge-through-play.php.

Zenger, Jack, and Joseph Folkman. "What Great Listeners Actually Do." *Harvard Business Review*, July 14, 2016. https://hbr.org/2016/07/what-great-listeners-actually-do.

9

Learning from Queer Theory

Queer theory is a term that emerged in the late 1980s for a body of criticism on issues of gender, sexuality, and subjectivity that came out of gay and lesbian scholarship in such fields as literary criticism, politics, sociology, and history. Queer theory rejects essentialism in favor of social construction; it breaks down binary oppositions such as "gay" or "straight"; while it follows those postmodernists who declared the death of the self, it simultaneously attempts to rehabilitate a subjectivity that allows for sexual and political agency.

—ROBERT TOBIN, "Queer Theory"

According to Anna Sparrman, queer theory offers "new ways of thinking critically about children, childhood, adulthood, and sexuality" (2013, 79). "The fact that queer studies brings children into research signals something new" (79), she continues, making a "contribution to understanding children as a figure and children's everyday lives" (80). While not necessarily known for its attention to the young, queer theory looks at the child from a number of distinct yet intersecting angles: "'child' as: descendant, offspring, imitation, or disciple, and an idea, creation, or product of the imagination" (80). As with other characters and characteristics, it overturns the image of the child "as the most stable, the most fixed, the unquestioned and unquestionable" figure (Lesnik-Oberstein and Thomson 2002, 35); it thus unsettles aspects of everyday praxis as well as challenging much theorizing about childhood. I am interested in how queer theory might be building on the history recovered earlier in this book (knowingly and explicitly or not), where it treads on new territory, and what we can learn from it about liberatory childhood.

In line with queer theory's receptivity to experimentation with form, and given my own somewhat unsettled relationship with queer theory, my writing in this chapter returns to the collagelike character of Chapter 1 rather than being in pursuit of a single argument. I unsystematically follow a variety of intriguing threads in queer theory that pertain to childhood. I also intersperse personal reflections with reflections on the literature. Always I wonder, from the overall perspective of this book, how is liberatory thinking about and interaction with the child potentially aided by a theory that explodes familiar images of childhood and replaces them with pictures of an unfixed agential being who shares much with adults? How does this theory add to the conversations about silence and voice and about oppression and resistance? How does it help us envision and reach toward a world that is friendlier to and more respectful of young people, in their lives with one another and with adults?

Queer theory is broadly associated with the idea that sexuality, like gender, is broadly socially constructed. It asserts that:

> whether and how people act on their desires, what kinds of acts they engage in and with whom, what kinds of meanings they attribute to those desires and acts, whether they think love can be sexual, whether they think of sexuality as having meaning for identities, whether they form communities with people with like desires—all of this is shaped by the societies in which people live. (Rupp 2006, 8)

The questions that queer theory asks about children include "Why do we turn away from the child-as-a-sexual-subject? Who are we protecting, and from what? How are adult and child sexualities intertwined?" (Sparrman 2013, 79). Also explored is "where to find and how to talk about the queer child" (Šepetavc 2015, 61). Related, Angel Matos asks, "Why is there such a hesitancy to label a child as queer?" Intriguingly, Matos takes this question a step further: "Is it possible that all children are queer (at least in some sense of the word)? How does a child grow, when said growth is being heavily monitored, delayed, and controlled?" (2013). I pursue these issues in the rest of this chapter, after introducing an important theme from queer theory—disdain for "the Child."

Disdain for "the Child"

> Edelman happily dispenses with the child, or rather the Child, remarking in a much cited paragraph: "Fuck the social order and the Child in whose name we're collectively terrorized." . . . The Child, he proposes, is vital to compulsory heterosexuality and normative sociality, the linchpin not merely of family values but of "reproductive futurism." (Kidd 2011, 183)

I wrestled uncomfortably with Lee Edelman's book *No Future: Queer Theory and the Death Drive* (2004), which I found nearly unreadable,[1] if vital, but

I grasped and sort of love his idea that Kidd restates here. Sometimes we reverence anything that can possibly be said to be "for the children," and we become more conservative supposedly "for their sake." They need stability, or a two-parent family, or heterosexual parents, or the best school . . . and whatever someone authoritative confidently says they need, someone else is obligated to try their best to provide (lest they be labeled "bad parents" or even lose said children), although ideally at minimal social cost. Usually that someone else who must do this providing is female, and she should—for the sake of the children—provide all this loving mothering not only for free but also for her own fulfillment and thus happily, almost gratefully (and there are few figures as potent as the "bad mother" or as troubling as the unhappy mother). We all know the prescriptions, although certainly they vary across time, place, class, and caste, among other factors. Most of the time, what children are said to need tends conveniently to support critical aspects of the status quo, especially to be in line with what those most vested in it propose and posit as necessary or best for the next generation, which coincides with their own self-interest. For example, as Sara Ahmed discusses, "understandably," we "redirect children [such as the feminine boy] out of fear that they would be unhappy . . . to avoid the costs of not being in line" (2017, 51), even though we are directing them into inequality. Or, for another example, even if you can send your children to college, as intense childrearing mostly ends, you should responsibly make sure that they study subjects vested interests say they and the marketplace require of them and will reward them for. Children, thus, can make adults conservative. And then those conservative adults create conservative children. Queer theory (and Edelman) is right to say that this is not a scenario that we should support.

I sometimes think that the best thing I did for my children was working with others to open the New Community School, originally a small, family-run, alternative school (which recently closed after some twenty-five years). Its mixed-age classes led the students to build a larger variety of child-child relations than most encounter in traditional schools. The steady presence of a host of parents gave them a range of adults to choose from to meet their needs, whether for trustworthy conversation or help with writing. The fact that they got to see their own parents investing so much time and energy into the school gave them the ideas that community work is important and that education is worth all this effort. The school was experimental and child-centered, especially as compared to many other settings. I did, at least in this regard (and I hope many others), not let being a parent make me more conservative; in fact, mothering nearly *forced* me to stray from the traditional, "for their sakes." I could not bear some of the racism and sexism that we were encountering in preschools and elementary schools, formally (in the curriculum) and informally (in teacher-student and student-student interactions), not to mention the structures of the classrooms, which were oppressive. Yet prospective parents so often asked us about our students' later success in traditional school settings, on standardized tests, and so forth, as if "the costs of not being in line" had to be avoided rather than handled well.

I urge us not to be taken in. Everything from warmongering politics to neoliberal economics has been explicitly, slyly defended as meaning a better future for our children, and we *must* see through the persuasive, even compelling rhetoric that is so familiar to us as to seem "natural" and right. Such things hurt children. Even the prods to send them to "the best schools" and to try to live, for them, in "the best neighborhoods" beg questions about who then gets far less than the best, what systems better serve everyone's needs, and whether by the "best" we mean the most privileged, reinforcing injurious inequality in the next generation—all supposedly "for their sakes."

The Adult-Child Distinction

Feminists are familiar with the overuse of readily available distinctions between the sexes and the ways in which people have been left out of and stigmatized by facile overgeneralizations about properly masculine men and exquisitely feminine women as well as by the binary itself. We know how policies and practices in every imaginable realm of life (from who can do what work in what way to who can wear what items in what colors) have been shaped, unfortunately but deeply, by often-insidious and usually irrelevant categorizations. Feminists, thus, have learned to be suspicious of easy divides between "us" and "them," to question the basis of such distinctions, and to be wary of what are said to be the necessary consequences of any actual differences between various groups of people.

What happens if we rigorously apply such hard-learned lessons to our conceptualization and categorization of children, as queer theory urges us to do?[2] Are the ways in which adults and children are normally and casually placed in separate categories always valid, or do the bases for the distinctions deserve reconsideration? For example: are children really asexual, to be contrasted with sexual adults? Are adults also always developing, like, rather than differentiated from, growing children? Is it the case that these categories are overlapping and fluid, so that we often encounter "childish" adults and "adultlike" children? These questions are encouraged and explored well by queer theory. More queries follow along these lines that are not so much queer theory's concern: When the two groups are different, what consequences flow from those differences? Sometimes the consequences of real differences are negligible: children, despite less experience and education, are not always less credible, for example. But do some differences deserve recognition?

Our often-thoughtless characterizations of children, at various stages, can pose problems for them and for adult-child relations. For feminists, seeing additional sites where questions about contrasting, mutually exclusive categories can be asked is critically important and should be welcome. Pursuing such work contributes to more deeply appreciating the character of the child and the diversity among children.

I tried never to "talk down" to my children, and I tried to be as honest with them as I could be (which wasn't always perfectly so). I think in our conversations, we were all just "people," not an authoritative adult with submissive, subordinated, or less substantial young people very "different" from me. I feel best about that. I listened pretty well, genuinely curious about their takes on the world. However, having grown up myself in a very conflictual family, and one in which I too often had to fill "adult" roles, I felt pulled to keep my kids out of certain contested terrain, such as problems between me and their dad, about our finances, or about my health. In retrospect, it's not as if they didn't know; I mostly just denied them a place to talk about such things. The idea of "protecting" kids is hard to resist, even if it is based on a problematic, overdrawn distinction between "us" and "them," and even when the tactic is self-defeating.

The Innocent Child

What exactly are we "protecting" in such instances, and more generally? Queer theory answers: children's supposed "innocence." Feminists seem especially well prepared to ask certain questions of the "innocent" child, from experience probing the "innocent" and "pure" woman imagined in and demanded by patriarchy. In the case of childhood, we should know to inquire about several issues: From what threats are children supposedly being "protected"? How does this protection measure up against the real threats to their well-being? What other possible ways of characterizing or remedying the threatening situation exist? Is it *really* threatening? To what, exactly? For what purpose is protection offered? At whose request? Who is left unprotected, because they cannot or will not conform to innocence, and with what consequences? Whom does innocence actually endanger? Queer theory, determined to destroy the image of the innocent child, welcomes this set of questions, even its links with questions about innocent womanhood (although its emphasis is, perhaps, somewhat more obliquely political than is feminism's).

Queer theory is adamant, first, that we have not "gifted" all children the odd present of innocence. As Kathryn Stockton explains, since innocence presumes weakness, "the black boy quite simply, is not weak enough to come across as innocent. He is a paragon of strength and experience" (2009, 31). Streetwise children, too, Stockton says, are somehow beyond innocence, beyond childhood. We have recently seen child asylum seekers, who have acquired "more awareness of life, giving them a maturity supposedly beyond their years," become suspect at the U.S. border and excluded for lacking the requisite "vulnerability" associated with the sexually innocent and white child (Humphreys, n.d.). The desirably innocent child, idealized, leaves out or marginalizes so many actual children, with consequences for how they are treated (the classroom-to-prison pipeline, for example) and what resources they gain access to or are denied.

Queer theory goes further with the idea of childhood innocence. Through innocence, it suggests, we adults have actually made children and childhood queer. Innocence is not just a description (which would be less problematic, for its accuracy might easily be tested and possibly even remedied) but, more potently, a prescription. Innocence *requires* that children be different from, distant from, adults, especially the adult realities of things like "labor, sex, and painful understanding," making the child "stranger, more fundamentally foreign, to adults" (Stockton 2009, 5). Innocence queers children, both from adults, who are not innocent, and "from what they approach: the adulthood against which they must be defined" (31). I find this contribution of queer theory to be most intriguing.

What follows from the revelation of this problematic idealization and categorization? One implication would seem to be that adults can do things to bridge the self-imposed gap between themselves and those younger—the chasm is not, according to queer theory, "natural" or inevitable. We can stop demanding that youth conform to adult ideas about what a child either "is" or "should be" like, especially (but not only) with regard to innocence. Such labeling blinds us to children's other ways of being, rendering us less able to know them and to act in accord with more accurate knowledge of them. We must accept that "the figure of the child does not fit children" (6).

The labeling of children as innocent puts them in a bind too. They can try to conform despite the ways in which they know or sense themselves to differ from the idealized norm, leading to everything from resentment of adults to problematic self-censorship to self-hatred; or, they can go ahead and be more explicitly queer, which will leave them feeling "different, odd, out-of-sync . . . with no established forms to hold" themselves (6). Such double-binds are red flags of oppressive, undesirable circumstances.

We can change the rules of this lose-lose game. We can become more accepting of children in all their amazing diversity.

Two of my biological children were drawn early to death and darkness, one through poetry about death, to which she added her own contributions, sometimes written in a graveyard she favored, and the other through news stories and TV shows about deaths, especially if they involved a child. Their interest in death far surpassed my own, and I remember wishing for it to go away, to end, as I was grilled, for example, for the latest news about JonBenét Ramsey's murder. What might have happened if I had joined them a little more willingly on their journeys, or at least been unbothered by their travels? What would the effects have been on their thinking and action, and on my own? Their interest did not, as I remember, just fail to coincide with mine; it perplexed and even troubled me a bit. I was, without consciously knowing it, assuming that "the Child" (i.e., my children) should be innocent of and disinterested in certain difficult, "adult" realities. I was wrong.

The Queer Child

Edelman points out that the queer child is an impossibility in a way, because queerness "is understood as bringing children and childhood to an end" (2004, 19). Queer theory often focuses on "the non-normative child that usually stays hidden in the formulation of the child as an innocent but presumably heterosexual human being" (Šepetavc 2015, 61). The queer child becomes a means to raising questions about all children (and about the distinction between adults and children), since the very notion of a "gay child" implies that all children potentially have agency and sexuality (Matos 2013). Queer children are made even queerer by the fact that "scholars of childhood . . . didn't see, or never said they saw, the ghostly gay child" (Stockton 2009, 10), and so they remain "underrecognized, oddly conceptualized, or not even seen" (17).[3]

Queer theorists are rightly fascinated by the "synchronous assumptions of the child's a-sexuality and proto-heterosexuality" (Dyer 2014). Most cultures fail to adequately confront how actively heteronormativity is impressed upon children. Eve Sedgwick was among the earliest queer theorists documenting adult "desire for a non-gay outcome" (1991, 24) in their childrearing and the pervasive efforts to "fix" and "straighten out" any potentially queer child's future, "withholding support for non-normative sexual development" (Dyer 2014). How conditional adult love and support can be.

The answer, some warn, is not simply liberal "acceptance." Jessy Parker Humphreys, for example, warns that "the acceptance of queer kids into heterosexual culture can actually involve them being pushed to exist within heteronormative expectations of queerness, rather than allowing them to create their own cultural forms and traditions" (n.d.).[4] We potentially co-opt them rather than encouraging them to be agents of change. As a consequence, Humphreys does not necessarily see the queer child as automatically disruptive, as queer theory perhaps suggests, or as inherently "represent[ing] some kind of alterity" (ibid.) to the generalized idea of the child. Although, if, as Dyer notes, "queer childhood [is] that which exceeds the confines of normalcy" (2014), being a queer kid doesn't leave everything intact in a heteronormative world, either. Still, we shouldn't reconceive "the child as a blank space on which to write uncomplicated resistance to homophobia" (ibid.). Adults need to actively "support[] a child's potential queer future" (ibid.).

I love Dyer's phrase encouraging us "to release children's potentials without guarantees" (2014, 163). Such wording not only (somewhat negatively) makes our conditional love more visible but (more positively) inspires and emboldens adults to be led by who individual children are and what they need rather than being directed by predetermined ends or what we "need" them to become (as Emma Goldman earlier suggested).

In talking about "the queer child," queer theory is not suggesting that such a child necessarily adopt or be bestowed a fixed gay identity. Queer theory's notion of sexuality is more fluid than that. For many people, sexual "attraction may shift depending on factors like time, intimacy with certain partners, changes in hormone levels, and so forth," and one may not only be attracted to one sex or the other but also "to non-binary or genderqueer people" (Uwujaren 2012). Does the idea of such mobile, shifting sexual selves make it even harder for adults to accept, accommodate, nurture, and love children? What are we to hold on to? How is our acceptance, accommodation, nurturing, and loving possibly supposed to adapt to a child's potentially shifting, fluid sense of self?

This enterprise might sound harder than it is. Adults already know how to do this! We adapt to fluid children all the time. We don't speak with, show affection to, or entertain our two-year-old the same way we do our eight-year-old or our fifteen-year old. Our love can still be constant through such evolution, as can our respect for the child. Queer theory is asking us to expand the ways in which we think of the child as fluid, the ways we adapt to their always-emerging sense of self.

One of my children came out as bisexual as a young teenager. Her failure to conform to heteronormativity was pretty obvious to me, too, by then. Later, she identified as "queer." She also says that she is asexual. I feel incredibly honored that she has talked with me about all of this. Her evolving sense of herself, and even of our evolving social categories, is simply something that I have to keep up with, as someone who loves her. She helps me keep my own sense of myself more open, too, a gift for which I am most appreciative.

The Sexual Child

The queer child raises questions about the sexual child more generally, a figure of much interest to queer theorists. I sense some tension between queer and feminist approaches to childhood sexuality. As one essay by Steven Angelides puts it: feminism was responsible for reshaping thinking about childhood sexual abuse—feminists "were particularly influential [in the 1970s and 1980s] in challenging the notion that children subjected to sexual abuse were somehow complicit in the crime (by seducing adults, 'asking for it,' or fabricating charges) or that child prostitutes and children involved in pornography or intergenerational sex could knowingly consent to such activities" (2004, 142). He believes that this feminist accomplishment pulls in opposite directions from queer recognition of childhood sexuality, which he calls "a normal and natural reality" (143), including even intergenerational sex; feminists do, indeed, have trouble with the latter. I am nonetheless curious about possible common ground and desire as well to understand possible partings of the ways, and I want to trace the status of liberatory childhood through those shared and divergent views.

Angelides defines our current era as being embroiled "in the climate of pedophilia panic" (146). He rejects the idea that adults are relatively powerful and children relatively powerless, in general and in sexual relations. Belief in such an "inherent power differential" was used, he argues, "to counter the widespread belief that children were willing, desiring, culpable participants in sexual encounters with adults" (149). (This "willing" child, like others described above, was not counted among the innocent.) He thinks that the "pedophilia panic" (and feminists in particular) wrongly imagines children as powerless and asexual. But can one not come down against child sexual abuse and still acknowledge the sexuality of young people at various ages?

Instead of asking, as our historical feminists did, that we check and reduce the power of adults over children, Angelides simply asks that we stop making relatively egalitarian adult-adult sexual relations normative for adult-child relations (150) and instead just accept that unequal power is a reality in human relations, among adults and between adults and children. Such unequal power is not problematized and should not seen as an obstacle to adult-child sexual relations any more than it is an obstacle to nonsexual adult-child relations. Importantly, though, feminists do see it as an obstacle not only to supposedly consensual, desirable, sexual relations between adults and children but to constructive, respectful, nonsexual relations as well. We needn't merely throw our hands up at unequal relations, as the chapter on disability theory makes clear, and feminists shouldn't be urged to "get over" our "obsession" with inequality either. Too, it is plausible that sexual relations among unequals pose different problems or challenges than do nonsexual ones, a concern that Angelides seems to dismiss. And this does not mean, Angelides notwithstanding, that feminists are so simplistic as to reduce power relations to all-or-nothing terms or are wrong to think that "a society of egalitarian social relations is possible" (152) and desirable (as we will see in the next chapter). As Humphreys puts it, "exposing the hypocrisy surrounding narratives of childhood sexual abuse"—we sexualize children and then forbid attraction to them, for example—"does not require denying its existence. . . . By suggesting that all stories of childhood sexual abuse are sensationalized, [we] prioriti[ze] an attack on the generalized child above the needs of specific children" (n.d.). The real, injurious experiences of actual children matter more than abstract ideas even of a reconceptualized child.[5]

The root of the problem, to Angelides, is the feminist intersection between talk about sexuality and talk about power. But when we educate about sexuality (which we should do, beginning with preschoolers), can and must we not also educate about the many forms of power and about how to, variously, exercise them responsibly, check them, and challenge them? It is an overstatement to claim that "the feminist use of power has functioned to evade, silence, erase, and repress a signifier of child sexuality" (Angelides 2004, 154). Why does so much seem to be at stake for queer theorists in reclaiming adult-child sexual relations, especially releasing them from the supposed grip of these now demonized "child sexual abuse feminists" (157)? We can recognize sexuality and sexual relations as complicated and diverse but still guided by an ethics of respect and messily intertwined with unequal power that must be reckoned with, not ignored. Angelides does claim "not [to] deny that there are important differences between child and adult forms of sexual expression, or that adults must be accountable for their behavior toward children" (158). There is even more common ground: most of us would agree that "we must provide children with discursive spaces and subject positions that enable them to negotiate their own emerging sexualities and to empower them to act on their own behalf" (161). Still, I argue that feminism is among the least of our obstacles to doing so; historically, it has been an ally, if not a prime mover, in multiple campaigns for sexual liberation, including some documented in the earlier chapter on manifestos.

I applaud queer theory for wrestling with the sexuality of young people (and those older) in terms that have the potential to be quite liberatory. Angelides is right in saying that "notions of child powerlessness and child sexual ignorance stand as unsubstantiated assumptions [in need of] . . . a systematic and exhaustive deconstruction" (152). He is also right in asserting that "sex education . . . is routinely a question of adult attempts to control children's access to knowledge about sex and sexuality—that is, attempts to ensure power *over* knowledge" (152). I just don't see the feminists I have been recovering in this book as being in cahoots with those who resist theorizing either the "age stratification" or "normative assumptions about sexuality" (167). They do bring a politics to such inquiry, one that is committed to ending oppression.

Children's Sexuality Goes to Court

There are definitely many problematic ways to reckon with the sexual lives of young people. One of those ways has occurred in law cases dealing with student-on-student sexual harassment. To give just a bit of background, Title IX of the Education Amendments Act of 1972 states that "no person in the United States shall, on the basis of sex, be excluded from participation in, be denied the benefits of, or be subjected to discrimination under any education program or activity receiving Federal financial assistance." This is generally considered to be parallel to Title VII of the Civil Rights Act of 1964, which prohibits severe or pervasive sex discrimination in the workplace. In both locations, sexual harassment has been declared to be an instance of sex discrimination and understood as a bar to equal opportunities, either in employment or in education. In Title IX and Title VII, harassment covers not only the more easily grasped behavior between one with more power (a boss or a teacher) and one with less (an employee or a student) but also behavior among those who are in some ways (but not every way) peers—behavior among co-workers or among classmates. In these instances, too, harassment can take place, but rather than being about, say, getting an "A" or a promotion for engaging in sexual behavior, peer harassment creates what courts call a "hostile environment" that degrades and excludes. Title IX protects students from the discriminatory conduct of their peers. Thus, sexual harassment of students by other students can, in fact, constitute discrimination "on the basis of sex" because it can be so severe and pervasive as to deny them educational opportunities.

In decisions about peer sexual harassment, some judges have talked about the general (nonharassing) sexual behavior of young people in troublesome terms. I take just one case as an example, the 1999 U.S. Supreme Court case of *Davis vs. Monroe County Board of Education* (526 US 629). A fifth grader, LaShonda, "was allegedly the victim of a prolonged pattern of sexual harassment by one of her fifth-grade classmates." Over a period of months, her classmate touched her breasts and genital area, made repeated vulgar statements, acted in a sexually suggestive way toward her with an item stuffed in his pants, and rubbed his body against hers. No disciplinary action against the offending student was taken, despite repeated complaints to teachers and the principal. The question before the court in *Davis* primarily concerned "whether, and under what circumstances, a recipient of federal educational funds can be liable in a private damages action arising from student-on-student sexual harassment." That doesn't necessarily sound like the most exciting or relevant of cases, although the question of when school districts or boards might be financially liable for indifference to or complacency about peer harassment *is* quite significant. But for our purposes here, what is interesting is the way that the sexual behavior of young people is characterized and discussed by the highest court in the United States, especially in the four-person dissent, after the majority held that a "deliberately indifferent" board *could* be liable if it failed to reasonably use its authority over the harasser and the environment to take remedial action in response to severe, pervasive, and objectively offensive harassment about which it had knowledge.

The majority make clear that all sorts of "insults, banter, teasing, shoving, pushing, and gender-specific conduct" would persist after the *Davis* decision without any available legal remedy, including "taunting" and even "bullying." They speak (in somewhat defeatist terms) to "the inevitability of student misconduct." They set a very high bar for when school districts would be liable in peer-harassment cases. But they do at least set a bar by envisioning and demanding effective response from teachers, principals, and school boards to known severe and pervasive sexual misconduct.

The dissenters—four justices of the Supreme Court—go further, not only disagreeing about the appropriateness of liability in these relatively extreme cases and worrying about federal regulation of "one of the most sensitive areas of human affairs" but wondering how peer harassment could be distinguished from "the *normal* teasing and jostling of adolescence." When these justices start to describe what counts as "normal," problems arise. They first raise the possibility that harassing behavior could be attributed to "serious emotional disturbance" on the part of the harasser, behavior that might then be covered by the Individuals with Disabilities in Education Act, which would constrain disciplinary actions and thus release the school from financial liability. (I'm torn by this possibility. On the one hand, if harassment was confined only to such a group, how much rarer it would be! But on the other hand, what if we actually called harassers "severely emotionally disturbed"?) It is a disconcerting turn by the minority—a way to not question the much more common harassing behavior by kids without documented emotional disabilities, and to not acknowledge that kids with emotional disabilities can generally also be schooled on sexually appropriate behavior. This early foray foreshadows and is not even as disturbing as what follows.

Justice Anthony Kennedy reminds us how, in general, young people "are not fully accountable for their actions because they lack the capacity to exercise mature judgment." Thus, we should expect schools to be "rife with inappropriate behavior." That seems like a pretty big jump, from lacking fully mature judgment (and thus acknowledging "some" judgment?) to rampantly exhibiting inappropriate behavior for which there is not full (but "some"?) accountability. Schools (like "dog-eat-dog" workplaces of old that were deemed inappropriate for women) then are described in a cited amicus brief as "rough-and-tumble" places filled with a "dizzying array of immature or uncontrollable behaviors by students." The justices return again and again to how rampant teasing and taunting are, calling it "ubiquitous" and, somehow, "innocuous." The dissent continues, "It is doubtless the case, moreover, that much of this inappropriate behavior is directed toward members of the opposite sex, as children in the throes of adolescence struggle to express their emerging sexual identities." The justices caution that we should not "label this immature, childish behavior gender discrimination" nor put on these childish misbehavers the "stigma" of "harasser." We have only recently even called it "misconduct," they admit.

Despite their gender-neutral language, the upshot of the opinion seems to be saying that girls, especially, should expect such "childish" behavior by "uncontrollable" boys. There's nothing to be done, by definition, about what is deemed "uncontrollable." Are girls alone supposed to be "mature" enough to understand and even tolerate this behavior, perhaps to remain somehow unaffected by it, while "immature" boys have no comparable "judgment" directing them to refuse to harass? Are girls not as "childish" as boys? Have boys usurped the definition of that too?

We have no comparable saying to "boys will be boys" for girls, nothing like that for boys which tolerates and even encourages gender-stereotypical behavior among them, even when it is at the expense of girls. Yet the court dissenters cite an amicus to the effect that there is no power relation between male and female students. Academic literature and popular culture support the view that "adolescent boys are believed to possess an active, independent, and virtually irrepressible sex drive, whereas adolescent girls are seen as passive recipients of male sexual interest, with little or no indigenous sexual desire" (Bay-Cheng and Lewis 2006, 72).

The dissenting justices think it impossible for schools even to identify peer harassment. They seem to find that Title IX is no guideline at all when it says that we would label harassing behavior discriminatory once it becomes "systemic" or "so serious, pervasive, and objectively offensive that it denies its victims the equal access to education." Yet something comparable is exactly what is used to determine workplace harassment: whether it is sufficiently severe or pervasive (here it is "or," while in Title IX it is "and") so as to alter the environment. We think ourselves perfectly well-guided in that instance to decide when behavior becomes discriminatory—so why not when children are involved? They also think that the comparable Title VII standard for determining whether behavior is harassment—whether a "reasonable" person in the victim's situation would find it as such—is unworkable in the case of children, because of the mysteriousness, I think, of the "reasonable child," as I have discussed in other chapters. Who, they ask, can possibly "gauge the sensitivities of, for instance, the average seven year old"? But don't adults claim to know what those same youngsters need, what's best for them, what they think, and so forth *all the time*? Why now can we not read them at all, especially when, in this case, one student made repeated complaints about another student's behavior and was not even the only student making such complaints? Is this not abstract nonsense? No effect on the victim seems sufficient to the dissenters to count as evidence of having been harassed, either, simply because such effects can have other causes in other situations. Where is the logic in that?

The barely losing minority on the court warns, finally, that there will "be no shortage of plaintiffs to bring" harassment complaints after *Davis*, citing the 1993 American Association of University study finding that "fully 4 out of 5 students (81%) report that they have been the target of some form of sexual harassment during their school lives." Of course, a comparable percentage of women report harassment at the workplace at some point in their working lives, and that has not stopped us from saying that such behavior constitutes a violation of their civil rights and is sex discrimination. Does its frequency make it *not* an offense? Or does its frequency mean, instead, that we should be tackling it with greater energy and more resources? If we dealt with peer harassment assertively among fifth graders like LaShonda, would there be less of it among tenth graders?

The dissenters are right that school districts have sometimes called kids out for minor offenses, things that were not severe, pervasive, and systematic. That doesn't mean that the sexual acts don't constitute misconduct that we should be addressing. And that's less a problem with the standard than with people getting used to calling kids on what's sexually problematic and talking with them about sexuality in the first place (this is written in a country where only thirteen states mandate factually accurate sex-education programs).

I think this issue goes back to queer theory's wrestling with what it means to acknowledge kids as sexual beings. If we adults are so uncomfortable with that in the first place, then how do we suddenly become competent to say to LaShonda's harasser, "There is a line, and you have crossed it. Here, for example, is what consent requires that you are obligated to abide by. Here is what you *can* do with your sexual desires (and what you cannot do), with whom, and under what circumstances"? Queer theory might well disagree with others about what constitutes problematic sexual behavior, for it doesn't like categorizing almost any sex as inherently "bad" sex, but it does draw a line at consent, and harassment draws a similar line at "unwelcome."

It seems to me that if troubling sexual behavior is pervasive, it might be especially important during the period of sexual "emergence"—to use the court's word—to help kids draw some distinctions. To cite Rebecca Traister on the topic of workplace harassment: maybe it only seems like we're over-reacting now because we've been underreacting for so long (2017). We need to stop thinking about sex education as being dramatically different from education in every other subject, stop thinking of it, as the minority of the court does, as so overwhelmingly "complex and sensitive" and having such "delicacy and immense significance" that we become ever more fearful of even talking about it.

The details of this case, especially the dissent, captured my attention. In its own odd way, the case might confirm queer theory's idea that children have sexual selves. It also confirms queer theory's sense of adult ignorance of those young sexual selves and of adults' discomfort talking with young people about sexual behavior. That leads to problems for all parties. But the case is further interesting because it makes *problematic* sexual behavior seem pervasive and uncontrollable, even labeling it *normal*, and I'd like to see more of queer theory's take on that.[6] My own take is that if we were to see analogous problematic racial harassment among kids, we would think it right for parents and teachers to step in and stop it, because we understand that it reduces educational opportunities for the racial groups involved and has destructive effects on a classroom learning community, and because as a society we're trying to commit ourselves to ending white supremacy. We don't any longer just throw up our hands and say, "(White) kids will be (White) kids." We know that if we let their racist behavior go unchecked, it will, in fact, continue unabated, not only in the classroom over the course of the K–12 years but later in life, too, when we will have to deal with racial harassment in the workplace, in voting rights, and so forth.[7]

The dissent in *Davis* makes clear that many think that the sexual mistreatment of youth by other youth is (1) pervasive, (2) normal, and (3) uncontrollable. Perhaps we do not have enough of a sense of, or do not make enough room for, perfectly acceptable sexual behavior of youth toward other youth with which to contrast this misconduct. Perhaps, too, we have mistaken sexual mistreatment for something "normal" and unavoidable only because, like past racial mistreatment, we have allowed and even encouraged it and are used to it, not because it somehow inherently and inevitably springs from something internal to children. Queer theory is clear that sexuality is largely socially constituted, influencing such things as to whom we are attracted and in what acts we find fulfillment. Harassing behavior is socially constructed, too, and we should both discourage it proactively and encourage adequate response to it retroactively. Young people should be in conversations about what it looks like, what the effects are, how sexual desire can be channeled, and so forth.

The idea that we cannot or should not intervene is an adult problem that raises at least as many questions about adults' sense of right and wrong, consensual and unwelcome, as it does of children's. Perhaps if we were more comfortable acknowledging the sexual selves of young people, we would be more comfortable walking with them as they are "beginning to explore their own sexuality and learning how to express it," as the dissenting justices say, rather than turning our backs, walking away, and hoping no one gets too seriously hurt. For the dissenters also state that "parents and schools have a moral and ethical responsibility to help students learn to interact with their peers in an appropriate manner."

The Gendered Child

"Queer theory is often mistaken as a theory about and for lesbians and gays," Mindy Blaise and Affrica Taylor rightly assert (2012, 91). Instead, however, they suggest that it "is a framework that offers insights into how seemingly 'natural' and 'normal' gender, as constructed by dominant gender discourses, is regulated by being linked to seemingly 'natural' and 'normal' discourse of *sexuality*" (91). Gender norms are inseparable from "the dominant discourse of sexuality" (91) in queer theory. Speaking especially to teachers of young children, Blaise and Taylor demonstrate how children comply with yet also actively contest sexualized gender norms (and gendered sexual norms). They show how boys and girls struggle over power in their relationships (90), and they urge us to see how young people use multiple discourses available to them to challenge gender and sexual norms (even though the discourses can conflict with one another, and even though they may also be limiting). Even in the preschool or early elementary setting, "heterosexual assumptions are an everyday yet unacknowledged routine occurrence" (91). But children negotiate with heterosexual discourses, for better and worse. The authors believe that "simultaneously consider[ing] gender and sexuality, as queer theory invites us to do," helps us "see children's gender behaviors in a new way" (91). Seeing how "gender and heterosexuality discourses work together to produce and reinforce gender stereotypes" ultimately offers some ways to interrupt and challenge those stereotypes (92).

It is a step forward in recognizing the agency of children to see that they "make sense of and actively work toward determining what it means to be 'girl' and/or 'boy'" (92) and do not just conform to settled and concretized options. Queer theory problematizes heteronormativity, which children absolutely feel in their lives and often imitate and impose on one another. The bottom line in this confluence of systems of oppression still seems to be female subordination to males, and in this sense, "romantic heterosexual play is anything but cute or innocent" (93; this is contra the *Davis* dissent). However, even while they might not be completely overturning old ones, through "gender-bending performances . . . [children] actually create new gender identities" (94). The authors offer advice for adults on better challenging gender roles in light of queer theory, which includes proactively supporting "children's curiosity about gender and sexuality" (95) and thus making them more reflective, in the name of "a more equitable world" (96).

Despite this hopefulness about "gender-bending performances" and "new gender identities," we live now with the 2013 *Diagnostic and Statistical Manual (DSM)* category of "gender dysphoria," which replaced the 1980 category of "gender identity disorder in childhood" (itself still linked to the removed disorder category of homosexuality):

> It describes gender dysphoria as a marked incongruence between one's experienced/expressed gender and one's assigned gender, the latter of which is based on, and conflated with, natal sex. The diagnostic criteria include a child's strong preference for the clothing of the other gender; a strong preference for cross-gender roles in make-believe or fantasy play and for the toys, games, and pastimes more typical for the other gender; and the attendant stress that accompanies such incongruence. (Spurlin 2018)

What Blaise and Taylor see as progress challenging heteronormativity and gender roles in the preschool classroom, mental health workers and others still potentially see as "illness" among the gender nonconforming. What is a child to do or to think? Their gender is still policed by adults as well as other children, with tactics from shaming to bullying to pathologizing.

Zanne Nilsson writes:

> When I was young, the only word I really knew for not totally "fitting in" as a girl was "tomboy." To be a tomboy meant a very rigid and specific set of things at the time, and I didn't fit with all of them—especially the assumptions that being a tomboy meant being violent and athletic. Later on I learned the word "transgender," but the experiences of the people I knew who identified that way— their dysphoria, their certainty about their true gender, their need to transition—didn't fit me either. . . . When I finally came across the term "genderfluid" and heard the concept explained in personal terms, everything clicked. "That's me," I thought, "and it isn't just me!" (2018)

These are tricky times for children who don't abide by prescribed gender roles in their dress, their play, or even their sense of self. Are they trans, desirous of having their sex, gender identity, and gender performance made congruent through various gender-affirming strategies? Or are they gender-benders untroubled by incongruence—budding feminists, perhaps, who agree that "biology is not destiny"? Or are they genderfluid or genderqueer, tossing out the categories of "male" and "female" altogether or interacting with them playfully and experimentally? Have the options for resisting heteronormativity expanded for young people? Have the pressures on them abated even as the categories to capture their "transgressions" have proliferated? Are they being offered (or taking) enough opportunities to reflect on all of this?

Does gender matter more or less than it used to, in the lives of children as well as those of adults? Do we want to "affirm" it, announcing our pronouns, as it were, or reduce its significance, moving perhaps to gender-neutral pronouns for all? Is there "tension between believing that it is possible to feel, act or look so much 'like a woman' that you should be acknowledged as one, and believing . . . that a woman can act in any way she wishes without casting doubt on her womanhood"?[8] These are not easy questions. Does being trans "disrupt dichotomous categories of sexuality and gender" or (also?) reinforce them (Connell 2012, 862)?

How much of the general social discourse about these matters is based on the lives of children, in a world that knows how to and values listening to their voices and conversing with them? I worry that the same adults who claim to be unable to identify harassing sexual behavior among the young, and who respond to it reluctantly and ineffectively, will be unable to name well their varieties of gender-bending behavior and to accept and respect their expression.

Concluding Thoughts

There are many important and exciting contributions that queer theory makes to feminist reflections on childhood. I love how Stockton challenges the child-adult distinction in her brilliant idea of "growing sideways" (rather than "up"), seeing growth as an ongoing process, ultimately not restricted by age. She argues that "'growing up' may be a short-sighted, limited rendering of human growth, one that oddly would imply an end to growth when full stature (or reproduction) is achieved" (2009, 11). Stockton's notion of "growing sideways" not only captures much about childhood but potentially makes the child and the adult more similar, less queer to one another.

Studies seem to show that more young people than ever see gender as a spectrum rather than as a binary, and more identify as trans. Queer theory has clearly had an impact, and perhaps a greater impact on youth than on adults, which may be unusual for theory. Options for self-definition have expanded beyond what an earlier generation may have imagined as possible—Facebook now has seventy-one gender options to choose from, for example.[9]

If we move away from rigid, inaccurate, and injurious (if often romantic) conceptions of the child, we might think about moving toward the children we discussed in the last two chapters: knowing children whose views matter in dialogic processes. We can draw from and build on "the tremendous resources that can be learned from those experiencing childhood: children themselves. . . . positioning children as subjects—or experts on their own lives" (Lo 2018), even regarding their (current) location on the spectrums of genders and sexualities. Adults, again, must give up the idea of always knowing more and better than children, especially about children themselves. We have the power and assume the right "to make meaning of children's experiences on behalf of the children" (ibid.) but can and should do better. We know from our historical feminists that children see where there is good cause to resist and do so. We could be working together more. We can recognize and evolve with children's own agency, the agency that queer theory, like earlier feminist theory, celebrates. It might be true that "letting go of adult power can be an emotional and threatening experience" (Davies 2003, 152, cited in Lo 2018), but it can also be a liberating one.

NOTES

1. I take my own guidance from Mary Astell's late-seventeenth-century *A Serious Proposal to the Ladies, Part II.* She considers obscurity to be "one of the greatest faults in Writing," and says that "if therefore we desire to be intelligible to every body, our Expressions must be more plain and explicit than they needed to be if we writ only for our selves, or for those to whom frequent Discourse has made our Ideas familiar." She considers "they Write best perhaps who d't with the gentile and easy air of Conversation." Gutenberg version online, 178 and 192. Available at http://www.gutenberg.org /files/54984/54984-h/54984-h.htm.

2. We have seen in earlier chapters that it is not only queer theory urging us in this direction. Many figures in feminist theory and activism have raised this possibility, although queer theory does so quite centrally.

3. It seems that the feminist theorists of earlier chapters did see such children.

4. Many contend that gay marriage is the adult equivalent here.

5. Others, too, have worried about queer theory's prioritization of the abstract child, and not only with regard to sexual abuse. Julian Gill-Peterson, for example, discusses how seeing "the child only as symbolic or as a proto-memory of an adult subject" often misses "the child as a living body and a contested national resource bound to histories of eugenic medicine, policing and incarceration, and the struggle between the state and the family over children as unfinished persons" (2015).

6. The majority opinion was supported by an amicus brief from the feminist NOW Legal Defense and Education Fund, the dissent by one from the conservative Independent Women's Forum. There were no identifiably "queer" voices in the conversation.

7. "Starting Small" suggests, "Their day is full of little injustices. . . . I want to help them develop skills and discernments that will enable them to address larger injustices later in their lives. I want them to know that injustice is not overcome by magic or wishes. People make it happen. You can make it happen." Southern Poverty Law Center, "Starting Small: Teaching Tolerance in Preschool and the Early Grades," 1997, available at www.tolerance.org/sites/default/files/kits/Teachers_Study _Guide.pdf.

8. "Making Sense of the Gender War over Transgender Identity," *The Economist*, November 16, 2017, available at https://www.economist.com/international/2017/11/16 /making-sense-of-the-culture-war-over-transgender-identity.

9. See, for example, Rhiannon Williams, "Facebook's 71 Gender Options Come to UK Users," the *Telegraph*, June 27, 2014, available at https://www.telegraph.co.uk /technology/facebook/10930654/Facebooks-71-gender-options-come-to-UK-users .html.

REFERENCES

Ahmed, Sara. 2017. *Living a Feminist Life*. Durham, NC: Duke University Press.

Angelides, Steven. 2004. "Feminism, Child Sexual Abuse, and the Erasure of Child Sexuality." *GLQ: A Journal of Lesbian and Gay Studies* 10 (2): 141–177.

Bay-Cheng, Laina, and Amanda Lewis. 2006. "Our 'Ideal Girl': Prescriptions of Female Adolescent Sexuality in a Feminist Mentorship Program." *Affilia: Journal of Women and Social Work* 21, no. 1 (Spring): 71–83.

Blaise, Mindy, and Affrica Taylor. 2012. "Using Queer Theory to Rethink Gender Equity in Early Childhood Education." *Young Children* 67, no. 1 (January): 88–96.

Connell, Raewyn. 2012. "Transsexual Women and Feminist Thought: Toward New Understanding and New Politics." *Signs: Journal of Women in Culture and Society* 37, no. 4 (Summer): 857–881.

Dyer, Hannah. 2014. "Becoming Otherwise: The Queer Aesthetics of Childhood." Ph.D. diss., University of Toronto. https://tspace.library.utoronto.ca/bitstream/1807/68298/1/Dyer_Hannah_M_201411_PhD_thesis.pdf.

Edelman, Lee. 2004. *No Future: Queer Theory and the Death Drive*. Durham, NC: Duke University Press.

Gill-Peterson, Julian. 2015. "Queer Theory Is Kid Stuff: A Genealogy of the Gay and Transgender Child." Ph.D. diss., Rutgers University. https://rucore.libraries.rutgers.edu/rutgers-lib/47661/PDF/1/play/.

Humphreys, Jessy Parker. n.d. "What Is at Stake in a Critical Analysis of Childhood and Sexuality?" https://lse.academia.edu/JessyParkerHumphreys.

Kidd, Kenneth. 2011. "Queer Theory's Child and Children's Literature Studies." *PMLA* 126, no. 1 (January): 182–188.

Lesnik-Oberstein, Karín, and Stephen Thomson. 2002. "What Is Queer Theory Doing with the Child?" *Parallax* 8 (1): 35–46.

Lo, Rachel Skrlac. 2018. "Changing Childhoods: Using Queer Theory and Intersectional Methods to Reconsider the Epistemic Resources of Children with Gay and Lesbian Parents." *Global Studies of Childhood* 8 (1): 91–104. https://doi.org/10.1177/2043610618758404.

Matos, Angel. 2013. "An Overview of Kathryn Bond Stockton's [The Queer Child]." Angel Daniel Matos, September 2, 2013. https://angelmatos.net/2013/09/02/the-queer-child/.

Nilsson, Zanne. 2018. "What the Heck Is Genderfluid? Part 1." Medium, May 12, 2018. https://medium.com/th-ink/what-the-heck-is-genderfluid-part-1-dd0f8b120ea9.

Rupp, Leila. 2006. "Everyone's Queer." *OAH Magazine of History* 20 (2): 8–11.

Sedgwick, Eve. 1991. "How to Bring Your Kids Up Gay." *Social Text* 29: 18–27.

Šepetavc, Jasmina. 2015. "Queer Child Wanted: Queering the Child and Childhood." *Družboslovne razprave* 31 (79): 45–62.

Sparrman, Anna. 2013. "Queering the Sexual Child?" (book review). *NORA: Nordic Journal of Women's Studies* 21 (1): 79–83.

Spurlin, William J. 2018. "Queer Theory and Biomedical Practice: The Biomedicalization of Sexuality/The Cultural Politics of Biomedicine." *Journal of Medical Humanities* 40 (1): 7–20. https://link.springer.com/article/10.1007/s10912-018-9526-0.

Stockton, Kathryn. 2009. *The Queer Child, or Growing Sideways in the Twentieth Century.* Durham, NC: Duke University Press.

Tobin, Robert. 2001. "Queer Theory." In *Encyclopedia of Postmodernism*, edited by Victor E. Taylor and Charles E. Winquist. London: Routledge.

Traister, Rebecca. 2017. "Your Reckoning and Mine." The Cut, November 2017. https://www.thecut.com/2017/11/rebecca-traister-on-the-post-weinstein-reckoning.html.

U.S. Supreme Court. 1999. *Davis vs. Monroe County Board of Education* (526 US 629).

Uwujaren, Jarune. 2012. "How Fluid Sexuality Fits into the LGBTQIA+ Spectrum." Everyday Feminism, October 19, 2012. https://everydayfeminism.com/2012/10/fluid-sexuality-lgbtq-spectrum/.

10

Childhood in Feminist Dystopias
and Utopias

> As women, we need to examine the ways in which our world can be
> truly different.
> —AUDRE LORDE, "Uses of the Erotic"

> Utopia . . . entails refusal, the refusal to accept that what is given
> is enough . . . the refusal to accept that living beyond the present is
> delusional, the refusal to take at face value current judgements of the
> good, or claims that there is no alternative.
> —RUTH LEVITAS,
> "Looking for the Blue: The Necessity of Utopia"

> The complexity of feminism is reflected through the diversity of voices
> heard through feminist fabulation.
> —DEBORAH HALBERT, "Feminist Fabulation:
> Challenging the Boundaries between Fact and Fiction"

In this final chapter, I turn to feminist science fiction for created and creative visions of worlds that enable the flourishing or limit the prospects of the young. Much literature has explored the practice of mothering in feminist utopias,[1] but precious little has focused on childhood in that same genre. Yet historical and contemporary feminist science-fiction writers have spent more creative energy thinking about childhood than the secondary literature suggests. I aim to reclaim that intellectual treasure trove and perhaps inspire or challenge others to do the same. In several of the texts, the main characters include a youth. Centering children as protagonists or narrators can give readers an important youthful perspective on the utopian and dystopian communities portrayed as well as on the experiences of children. Even when the portrayal of youth is not central, these books offer intriguing bits of knowledge about how and why children might prosper or fail to thrive.

I start with a list of questions: How do the insights from authors using this genre compare to those in the feminist theories and feminist manifestos already explored? What about childhood in patriarchal cultures do these authors of speculative fiction most subject to critique; that is, what social structures are seen as most damaging to the young in either the present or in an even more dystopian possibility? What constitutes a more ideal, a more feminist, childhood, and why? What variety of adult-child and child-child relationships are socially supported by (in)egalitarian societies?

To answer these questions I explore ten novels and one anthology, all written between 1915 and 2017, which provide a wonderful historical range enhanced by the varied ideological allegiances of the authors. I look first at what proves to be dystopian for children (as judged by the authors, not me), and then what they consider to be utopian.

Like the authors I treat here, I believe that imagining is essential to acting for change. In the words of Ursula Le Guin: "Only the imagination can get us out of the bind of the eternal present, inventing or hypothesizing or pretending or discovering a way that reason can then follow into the infinity of options" ([1980] 1997, 45).

Dystopian Childhoods, Childhood Dystopias

Claire Owens's The Unpredictable Adventure

Claire Owens's *The Unpredictable Adventure: A Comedy of Woman's Independence* (1935) is likely the least familiar of the books selected.[2] It was banned from the New York Public Library for its "risqué" content and was out of print for decades despite its initial popularity. The philosophical journey of self-discovery recorded in this quest allegory was recognized for "its unabashed exploration of female sexuality, its subversive examination of Christianity, and its fierce intelligence" (VH 1995). The author (who loves wordplay) begins with a critique of childhood in relatively dystopian Smug Harbor, which is nestled in the land of Err. The main character, Tellectina Femina Christian, or Tina, is an inquisitive, determined, irrepressible, and adventurous soul, a far cry from what a good, respectable, Christian girl should be like. The book asks what a young girl ought to know.

Young Tina, socialized by her Puritan parents to live on the straight and narrow path (Owens [1935] 1993, 35), lives in fear of "the terror of hell which her ancestors had felt for nineteen hundred years" (141). Children in her society are taught to "repeat by rote the sentences of tutors, and, as they grow older, of the men of talents" (232). Tina is a "good" student, who believes blindly—although she occasionally recognizes and rankles at her confinement. Like most children, Tina does not always get answered when she speaks to adults, despite the fact that, as she says, "You always tell *me* it's impolite not to answer when I'm spoken to" (2). Owens's dystopia contains the familiar demand that children be seen and not heard (15)—what we have seen is now called "epistemic injustice."

As queer theory leads us to expect, Tina is characterized by multiple adults as "innocent." She is said to need protection from potentially corrupting people, such as her mischievous, adventurous, sexual, cursing, blasphemous Aunt Sophistica (2), protection that even limits where Tina can go on the grounds of her family's estate (3). Tina is prevented from being more knowledgeable by the general fog in which the Errorians choose to live (3), the rituals, sophistry, and superstitions that keep them "sleeping confidently" (3) and "happily oblivious" (14). Aunt Sophie, however, reveals other possibilities—of intellectual, political, and sexual adventure and knowledge.

Tina struggles with crippling "conscience pains" (9) that prevent her from doing what she wants to do, due to Sunday schools that "make you feel so wicked, even after you've tried so hard to be good" (8) and a culture that doesn't "want any child . . . to be too different from other people" (15). Aunt Sophie, however, finds that such "pains are unnatural in a healthy child," deems Smug Harbor "no place to bring up children" (10; also 14), and regrets that children are "defenseless" (11) against the forces of gendered socialization and patriotic (13) and religious indoctrination. For girls in Err, "all interesting things are . . . forbidden and unladylike" (17).[3] Tina, persuaded and enticed by her aunt, opts to leave the "safety" of Err to tackle the dangers awaiting her in the land of Nithking (an anagram of Thinking), where "excitement is the breath of life" and she can use her wits to survive (19).

Aunt Sophistica is right when she says to Tina's father, "There is someone here who leads a double life. Another life goes on behind [Tina's] sweet little smile which is all she shows to an unsuspecting world" (21). Tina is incredulous that her aunt knows about her questions and longings when she thinks she has led her "double life" invisibly (although she is also somewhat surprised that her father has no clue about it [21–22]). It turns out that she is not so "innocent," after all; the youngster already understands that she is to "lock[] her secret joy fast in her young heart" (24), already knows that "her parents d[o] not wish to hear the truth" (41).

Owens is a critic of normal, everyday, respectable, patriarchal childrearing practices, practices not confined to the era in which she writes. Her dystopian targets—like those of the historical feminist thinkers and activists we've explored—include force-feeding in education and fear-based socialization. She wishes to upend many traditions (268), although she does not venture into consideration of childhood in a utopian setting in this long book. Patriarchal

Christianity, the moral of her story goes, smothers children with images of an omnipotent and punitive God and makes them feel abnormal for being passionate and curious (245). Owens also reveals what children know but are not recognized as knowing—how they understand that secrecy and artificiality are required of them, for example, to maintain "good" social relations and to please their parents. Uniquely, Owens especially cries out against disbelief or disinterest in the intellectual lives of the young.

Owens critiques Puritan childhood and womanhood alike, showing that they have much in common. Both women and children are supposed to be without the desire or ability to explore; both are to accept the status quo passively rather than embody a spirit of inquiry; in neither is individuality (202), inner strength, sexuality, or autonomy thought to be possible or desirable; and neither should expect to be taken seriously by adult men (161). Over the harsher realities of the lives of women and children are thrown veils of innocence, protection, and adoration, when all that is really preserved and celebrated is conformity to the norms that sacrifice their well-being and individuality.

Joanna Russ's The Female Man

Joanna Russ's postmodernist *The Female Man* (1975) is "one of the most famous novels of feminist science fiction, written by a giant of the field" (Allbery 2013). It contains multiple worlds that confront inequality differently, inhabited by four J-named characters. The characters are somehow related but don't exist in the same time (or are they "the same woman in four very different incarnations" [Clare 2014]?), and as they interact they bring things to light in one another's world. The scenarios include Joanna's United States of the 1960s; Jeanine's more exaggerated version of the same, from a never-ended Depression era, without the liberatory movements that followed it; Jael's even more dystopian alternative, where the "battle of the sexes" structures society; and Janet's Whileaway, a utopian, all-female alternative nine hundred years in the future, where a plague has eliminated all the men. Children's lives are briefly portrayed in all the non-utopian settings.

In Joanna's United States of the 1960s, there is a potent, cringe-worthy critique of the gender-based socialization girls receive: "the vanity training, the obedience training, the self-effacement training, the deference training, the dependency training, the passivity training, the rivalry training, the stupidity training, the placation training" (Russ 1975, 151). What a list! In Jeanine's world, which is definitely more sexist than Joanna's, children are shown as vulnerable to everyday sexual harassment and assault, and their stories of such events are discounted. As the character Laura puts it (sounding somewhat like Octavia Butler's later character Lauren), "Being young, too, that's a drag. You have to take all kinds of crap" (67). In Jael's even worse, even more dystopian parallel universe, the sexes live separately, and "Manlanders buy infants from the Womanlanders and bring them up in batches . . . keep them in city nurseries until they're five, then out into the country training ground . . . [where] little boys are made into Men—though some don't quite make it; sex-change surgery begins at sixteen" (167). Children are not only commodified but altered to re-create traditional sex roles in an all-male world.

Russ understands the political nature of children's fate and the diverse fates that await them in worlds organized differently, socially and economically. While girls are shown as the subjects of gendered socialization and gender-based violence, commodified boys in the all-male world are subjected to horrors of their own, through militarization and imposed physical alteration. Their fates are differently awful and yet still linked to sex.

Marge Piercy's Woman on the Edge of Time

Childhood is more deeply investigated in Marge Piercy's *Woman on the Edge of Time* (1976), "a contemporary classic" (Booker 1994, 337) that continues to speak to readers more than forty years after its initial publication. In the dystopian present, Connie (aka Consuelo) Ramos, a poor Chicana, has already lost her young daughter to child protective services. After an act of violence against her niece's brutal pimp, Connie finds herself in a madhouse, for the second time. Here, she becomes a "receiver," getting messages from alternative futures. Her actions may help determine which future is realized: one that addresses the problems of her time or one that amplifies the injustices and inequalities.

Involuntarily committed to "the strange twilit childhood of the asylum," Connie has landed in a structure with its own system of "advancements and demotions, its privileges and punishments, its dreary air of grade school" (Piercy 1976, 83). In the analogy of the asylum to childhood, readers come to see both as confining patriarchal constructions in desperate need of grand reconception. In the madhouse, as in childhood, others have power over you that is exercised arbitrarily; permission must be granted even for the most mundane tasks (165); it is exceedingly difficult to get heard and even more so to be believed (124), no matter how valid the complaint (142); the running assumption is that you—child or patient—lack epistemic credibility and thus can rightly be spoken to in terms that range from patronizing and condescending to impatient and authoritative; and resistance is unacceptable—speaking up "too much" is a fraught, dangerous act, rage is never acceptable or productive (45), and rebellion must be punished (112). Both children and inmates are likely to end up with more severe diagnoses and more medications when they resist (92). Being silent and obedient is equated with being a good child and a good patient, being at the mercy of more powerful others an always-present reality that must be considered when weighing one's actions (89). Speaking truthfully is simultaneously mandated and unwelcome (90, 112).

The fact that childhood is made analogous with a situation of involuntary commitment, irrationality, and unfreedom speaks powerfully to our norms of childhood and the poverty of adult-child relations. The surveillance involved in both situations, the absence of real choices (351, 356), the enforced immaturity, and the lack of privacy are surely at the center of the parallel, alongside the fact that men in power seem to believe, in Piercy's words, that "feeling itself [is] a disease, something to be cut out like a rotten appendix. Cold, calculating, ambitious, believing themselves rational and superior," they turn against the young, the female, and the weak (282).

Piercy's alignment of childhood with coercion, vulnerability, and despair is further developed in her portrayal of multiple characters as parents and children in the also dystopian, patriarchal present—especially Connie's experiences with her now-lost and constantly mourned daughter, Angelina. Angelina, like most children in the foster care system today, is non-White.[4] Piercy does not shy away from the fact that Connie neglected and abused her child during a period of deep despair over her the death of her imprisoned partner caused by a medical experiment performed on inmates (again, speaking to the racism and brutality of the carceral state). But we also learn from Connie's sorrowful experience about the lack of decent childcare available to the poor, the surveillance of poor parents of children of color, and the lack of community support for single parents. Piercy notes that when Connie worked long hours, "it had taken her so long to come and go on public transportation she had had no time to spend with her own child" (394).

Yet more problematic adult-child relations are portrayed. Connie's sister-in-law Adele, ensconced in a recognizably "desirable" but familiarly unhappy marriage, is shown "patting the baby's face with a napkin and cooing, while she floated in a sky-high hammock behind her eyes" (390), a different form of drug-linked neglect more protected by class than Connie's is. Connie's Americanized brother coercively gathers his dispersed offspring for a Thanksgiving ordeal meant to display his masculinity and wealth as well as his ownership and power over his children. Their obvious discomfort is either unnoticed or irrelevant, as the feelings of those younger so often are. Connie's beloved niece Dolly, a prostitute, is unable to keep her daughter Nita with her much, although like most children not living primarily with their biological parents, she is with a relative, her grandmother, despite the fact that "without her, you don't love yourself" (329).

These dreary situations, in all their variety, seem intended to reveal how the precarious positions of many parents unacceptably lead to the vulnerability of their children, despite adults' often-obsessive focus on their (and exclusively their own) children. All this, Piercy wants to imagine differently—and for the sake of the young, not just to shift the burdens of childbearing and childrearing from falling so heavily on women. She mourns children's lack of safety; their isolation; their exaggerated dependence; their inability to be heard, believed, and heeded; and the inequality that trickles down to them.

Joan Slonczewski's A Door into Ocean

In Joan Slonczewski's intriguing, anarchist, ecofeminist *A Door into Ocean* (1986), a youthful "commoner" travels from the relatively dystopian Stone Moon of Valedon to the egalitarian Ocean Moon of Shora. Shora is a planet covered by water and inhabited by naked, peace-loving, purple, female Sharers. The visitor is invited there as part of a quest to understand whether the Valans are humans, humans with mental defects, or another, more primitive, species (79–80). Can the two worlds and peoples cooperate, Shorans wonder?

Among Slonczewski's main characters are the Valan teenager Spinel and another teen from Shora, Lystra. The story begins in Chrysoport, on Valan, a place where "many people led parched lives, thirsting for the faintest drop of empathy . . . crav[ing] someone to listen" (223) and where the "police . . . keep order in street and market" (225). The contrast is clear: "Valedon would be in chaos without someone to lay down the law. Yet on Shora, things worked just the opposite: no one person could set a law for anyone else, and even if they tried, it would only create chaos, not curb it" (225).

Stone Moon is ruled by an off-planet, all-powerful, manipulative, artificial intelligence, the Patriarch, who supposedly tends to his "children" (93) on some ninety planets in a decidedly nonmaternal version of parenting (there are always uprisings, quelled with varying degrees of force, including obliteration). Spinel is a poor, older teen who hated and failed in eight years of school (61, 136, 359), as he still cannot write a sentence well (127) or think fast (136). The implication is that Valan schools mostly indoctrinate the young into the conflict-based, capitalist, inegalitarian beliefs of the Patriarch (50, 72); consequently, "teaching someone a lesson" has primarily a negative connotation (72, 107), children prefer to daydream through (61) or skip school

(5, 14), and the powerful alone decide what knowledge is open or forbidden and to whom (82). Spinel sees himself as lacking intellectually (162) and as an apprentice to his stonecutter father. He is portrayed as a disappointment to and burden on his parents (23, 34), and "failing" them looms large on his horizon, pressuring him to find some way, almost any way, to prove himself (12, 16, 18).

Children defer to their parents, who simply have "the last word on everything" (12, 83). Spinel's multigenerational, biological family is packed into a small house, with some of the crammed space given over to the family business of stonecutting. The father is portrayed as overworked and underpaid, the accountant mother as wrought with anxiety over finances and her children, and the grandchildren as demanding and whiny (35). The household as a whole is pictured as chaotic but still taking care of basic business.

The ways in which the world of politics intrudes on the household are numerous: when the town is invaded, room and board for soldiers must somehow be provided; reproduction outside marriage is punished by the state (21), and the number of children one can bear is limited according to the desirability of a person's "gene quotient" (17); taxes and high prices in the marketplace keep the family near poverty; and the son-in-law dies in an act of resistance to the supreme ruler's invasion (177). Thus, there is and is not a public-private divide, depending upon whether the state decides to respect or violate it. Private struggles do not seem to be of concern to the state, and Spinel's family gets no help with anything like daycare (a concern emphasized in multiple manifestos). General Realgar, who is in love with someone who lives among the Sharers but who will nonetheless help orchestrate the invasion of their world, has two children who add more layers to the variety of dystopian childhoods. They are raised "strictly" and ordered about constantly (190). More obviously than in other families, his offspring are trained for warfare, as when his daughter becomes a proficient shooter and both children are given military toys with which to entertain themselves (189).

In all the Valan families, children are not taken seriously, and what counts as caring for and protecting women and children is determined from a patriarchal point of view (201, 394, 399). Children are always "excused" from serious, adult conversations. The youth on Stone Moon are often deemed a nuisance by adults (11)—later, Spinel returns the favor to the youth on Shora (55, 83).

We learn more about dystopia when Spinel travels to the Ocean Moon of Shora. Shora is challenged first by Valan traders who have "done as they wished there for forty years" (10), including overfishing and "dump[ing] noxious waste chemicals" (26) into the precious ocean, and then, more militarily, by the Patriarch itself. The Patriarch believes that the Sharers "have powers that interest him. Forbidden sciences" (32), and thus they need to be controlled (131, 216). Yet the web-footed Shorans lack a concept like obedience. The Patriarch is ultimately revealed as being manipulative, but for most of the story, Valan citizens—on Valendon and on Shora—seem impervious to how their patriotism is used to justify one useless military expedition after another. They are trained in blind loyalty from youth, when they learn that "all power must stem from one lord" (21). When the Valans invade Shora, they employ brutal tactics that include "mind-bending" and burning at the stake as well as, importantly, imprisoning and killing the young.

The general leading the charge on Shora is unable, even in the end, to understand the "other" who is so much like himself yet who is characterized as "vermin" (323). On Shora, as on Valan, during an occupation, children become "victims and soldiers both" (186). As too many Indigenous peoples have learned, the drive for colonization is without limits, and the young are fair targets.

Octavia Butler's The Parable of the Sower *and* The Parable of the Talents

Octavia Butler's *The Parable of the Sower* (1993) and *The Parable of the Talents* (1998) helped establish her as "an early pillar of the subgenre and aesthetic known as Afrofuturism" (Aguirre 2017). They are mostly told from the viewpoint of a female, Black character, Lauren Oya Olamina. Lauren is a young prophet who dreams big from within her walled neighborhood—walled against the poorer and even more desperate. She is intent not only on survival but also on something more, based on a new and better faith that she calls Earthseed, that she "had been thinking about since [she] was 12" (Butler 1998, 126).

The story begins in 2024, with the once-powerful United States collapsing from "coinciding climatic, economic, and sociological crises" (Butler 1993, 8). Oppressive company towns that create indentured servants are back, and there is an abrupt end to the separation between church and state. Crimes, ranging from theft and assault to sexual abuse and murder, are commonplace.

Among the first things we learn about young Lauren is that she lets herself be baptized only to please her father (importantly, she has her own religion) and that when she offers her own ideas about how to perform that ritual, "no one paid attention to me" (8). Like Owens's young protagonist Tina in yet another aspect, for Lauren, "there's a world of things I don't feel free to talk to anyone about" (52). Kids in the neighborhood don't get much of a childhood, as they are set to work putting out fires (32), learning to shoot for self-preservation (39), or, like Lauren, teaching those even younger than themselves (33). Girls have children when they are too young to care for them (32), and too many children are unloved (33).

The relations between adults and children seem fraught in ways large and small. On more than one occasion, the younger folks in the story are impatient with those older telling them "how great it's going to be when the country gets back on its feet" (8, 14–15, 56), feeling either condescended to (62) or that adults themselves are deceived (25). Lauren seems to disapprove of the way "family business" is hidden (11–12), as if knowledge seeping beyond household borders could only be damaging. This secrecy is an especially dangerous mentality in a world where, for some, "the only power she has in the world is her authority over her children and her money" (88), "and the only way to prove to yourself that you have power is to use it" (143). Lauren is resigned to having to engage in endless activities she doesn't care about, although many of them make her father proud (24). During the best moments between Lauren and her father, she wants him to know her and he listens to her (64–66), but, due to everything from the conditions of the world to the norms of the family, these moments are rare.

Adults often misunderstand or underestimate the importance of children's pleasures, Butler suggests, such as how wonderful it feels to walk in a rare rain (48). Lauren is hungry for knowledge and willing to learn from every person and source, from a wayward brother (104) to eavesdropped nuggets of information (69). She longs for the day "when people are able to pay more attention to what I say than to how old I am" (78), a yearning that makes her sometimes hate being a kid (83). Luckily, Lauren studies survivalist training, and so she is relatively well prepared for the life on the road that ensues when her neighborhood is destroyed and she loses or loses touch with her entire family.

In Butler's dystopia, no one is safe, but some suffer more than others, mostly due to age, class, and race. An even worse world threatens outside the small, armed community near Los Angeles in which Lauren was raised. As we will see with Starhawk, too, much of the squalor beyond the walls is portrayed via the lives of children. The poverty that children endure, the rapes that they experience, and even the slavery that they are sold into are the new norm for most.

We learn about the "filthy, gaunt, half-naked children" who make even Lauren nervous, for "they might try to pull us down and steal our bikes, our clothes, our shoes, whatever. Then what? Rape? Murder?" (Butler 1993, 9).

Youth are not just innocent victims, then, for these youngsters—often left to raise themselves—are also responsible for many of the dangers on the street. Youth, addicted to a new drug (Butler 1998, 115), wantonly set fires for sexual pleasure and commit a dreadful range of crimes, up through cannibalism. "There's nothing new about thieving or murderous children" (282), the story reminds us. Lauren's new world is full of terrible things, as when she sees "a little girl, naked, maybe seven years old with blood running down her bare thighs" (Butler 1993, 13) and learns that "out here in the world, they kill kids every day" (170).

Lauren and the friends she collects on the road establish Acorn, the first Earthseed community. It lasts for six years, until the forces of Christian America—backed by an evangelist President Jarret—deem it a "devil-worshipping" heathen cult (Butler 1998, 20), take over the facilities, enslave the adults, and put the children up for adoption in "good, Christian homes" (207). Lauren's infant, Larkin, is among the stolen children, and the loss haunts mother and child for decades, much like Connie's loss of Angelina in Piercy's *Woman on the Edge of Time*. Lauren's child is brought up in yet another dystopian family, one reminiscent of Tina's in that religion is force-fed (263). The kidnapped Larkin's new family is worse than that imagined in Owens's *The Unpredictable Adventure*, as here, the strictness of the religion forbids most childhood pleasures (277, 328), the mother resents and doesn't love Larkin (221), and the father molests her (224, 330), a recurring event in children's lives in the story. At best, "there was no love in the Alexander house. There was only the habit of being together" (349, also 378).

Larkin's is not a child-friendly world, even with regard to the basics: "Public schools had become rare in those days when ten-year-old children could be put to work. Education was no longer free, but it was still mandatory according to the law. The problem was," as Emma Goldman would understand, "no one was enforcing such laws, just as no one was protecting child laborers" (23, also 367–368). Larkin learns in her family, as in her Christian school, "to be quiet and keep out of their way . . . make myself invisible. . . . Thinking and questioning were bad" (264–265). Again, this is what a supposedly innocent child already knows.

A precarious world always poses distinct dangers for the young. Butler teaches that a flourishing childhood is dependent on a social world with a significant degree of safety, stability, and opportunity as well as supportive relationships (including, but extending beyond, the family). When those conditions are not met, children become targets—relatively easy prey. They cannot as readily obtain what they need to survive, defend what they have, or fight off attackers. "Little girls" are supremely endangered "because they can be used in so many ways, and they can be coerced into being quick, docile, disposable labor" (40). When the welfare of children becomes the subject of corrupted politics, "protecting" the young often becomes a façade for indoctrinating them into oppressive religions, using them as capitalism can make them profitable, and actively ignoring real, everyday threats to their well-being. Children again become the currency in betting games that are not really about them, even though the outcomes of the contests can dramatically affect their lives.

Butler shows young characters like Lauren nonetheless persisting, alone and in fragile communities where trust is next to nonexistent—but they have to be old enough, tough enough, or lucky enough to make it, and they do so at the cost of what is generally recognized as their childhood. Lauren, who has brought everything from seeds to a belief system to the new community called Acorn, will be a bridge to a utopia, but one who will continue to do battle with the forces on every side that are tearing communities apart, from late-stage capitalism with its indentured servitude to new technologies, such as "dream masks," that distract people from less desirable realities (220, 344).

Starhawk's The Fifth Sacred Thing

Finally, Starhawk's post-apocalyptic *The Fifth Sacred Thing* (1993), set in California in 2048, conveys the struggle between two communities: the first is a pacifist, pagan, collectivist, ecofeminist community, where the sacred elements (air, water, earth, and fire) belong to everyone and to no one; the other is an authoritarian, militaristic, capitalist, theocratic nation of scarcity established by the Millenialists and Stewards, and they want the resources of the utopian enclave. As the two are pitted against each other, each uses the "weapons" appropriate to it, so that guns and passive resistance—violence and nonviolence—come face to face. The main protagonists include the elderly Maya (elderly women compose the city's entire defense council), her nominal granddaughter Madrone, and her grandson Bird. The latter two directly confront the Millenialists, each in their own way, while Maya helps sustain the community they fight for.

Outside the utopian territory, "life for the majority of souls . . . is just a long round of starvation, misery, torture, and early death" (41). Even among the most privileged in this unequal world, the lives of women and children are limited and precarious; they are still ruled by patriarchs within the household and in society. Their culture is a successor to the age of endless wars, where

every time there was a glimpse of peace, we scurried to find a new
enemy so we could continue this mindless wasting. Blowing up our
wealth, burning it off, turning it into poisons and toxins, shooting
it in the belly, shipping it home in body bags, murdering our own
children and everybody else's. (239)

The harms that children suffer are not accidental or rare, but predictable,
common, and intentional. One of Starhawk's youths represents the ways in
which malevolent social forces can play out in the lives of the young: racism,
capitalism, and sexism intersect in her story. Five-year-old Angela is hidden
in a house of the relatively privileged, suffering from untreated leukemia
because her very existence cannot be made known: she is the offspring of a
denounced relationship, one that is interracial and extramarital. The White
aunt and Black grandmother—the "woman-of-the-house" and the maid,
respectively—conceal Angela, who lives in constant pain (268–269). Like the
adults in this world that is structured by systems of oppression, some children
are marked as lesser than and even as "illegitimate." Anyone who violated
the Moral Purity laws "officially lost your immortal soul, which made you
fair game for rape and enforced prostitution, if you were a woman, and your
children prey for all sorts of abuse" (298).

One clear, enduring message of *The Fifth Sacred Thing*—as in Butler's
books—is that social conflict always affects the young in distinct and dire
ways. There are many troubling stories among the Millenialists involving
youth, from schools becoming "indoctrination camps" (273), to a teenager
being imprisoned for "stealing water one too many times" (23), to a fourteen-
year-old holding a gun to a stranger (199). Avenging Angels—near-identical
pale youths deemed less than human by those who actively breed them for
sexual slavery (303)—use brutal tactics as they wage war against the Stewards. Soldiers, "bred for the army" (413) in what are called "the pens," "like[]
to brag about whippings they'd received and beatings they'd endured as children" (376). Whatever side young people take, whatever the conflict is really
or ostensibly about, every conflict affects children and, unfortunately, shapes
yet another generation. Sometimes children in particular are systematically
taken advantage of for sex and labor (like under the authoritarian Stewards,
backed by the fundamentalist Millenialists), due to connections that Starhawk invokes between patriarchy, militarism, capitalism, and the exploitation
of children. As the character Bird escapes his imprisonment and rediscovers
his utopian city, "he f[inds] himself shaking. He had wondered, sometimes,
if there would be any children left" (117).

Common Threads in Dystopias

A feminist understanding of power is clearly central to dystopian critiques of unjust and impoverished childhoods. As in Slonczewski's *A Door into Ocean*, feminists "get" that those on the bottom have to weigh their words (1986, 178); that "resentment" against those on the top "smolder[s] in hidden ways" (178); that those who dominate are "everywhere, watching" (181, 216); and that they impose their will by force and threats of force (186, 190, 222), even if they have to break their own rules to do so (191, 391). Those on top claim for themselves a higher level of civilization or humanity (188), debate how human or civilizable others are, and monitor the participation of the subordinate in whatever they deem to be important matters (190, 197). In important ways, the subordinated are not taken seriously (197), such as when they are called naïve, innocent (219), and, unfortunately, childish, although they are treated as potentially treacherous (216).

Feminist utopias always grasp this general understanding of power and effectively apply it to the relations between those older and younger to explain the often-underestimated frustrations and injustices of childhood. The best novels wrestle deeply with the power that adults have over the lives of children. After all, as the more recent utopian literature puts it,

> We, the larger ones, possess a degree of power over the lives of children that we would find inconceivable and unspeakably tyrannical in any other context. Yet, we mostly wear this power as some divine right not to be questioned, not to be wrestled with. . . . Or we try to minimize and trivialize this power . . . or we pretend we do not have this power. (Jordan 2016)

Most of the feminist dystopias are on Earth, although elements of others are otherworldly. The portrayals of barely livable lives are in times past, the present, and the future. The authors use real-world institutions and social tendencies to portray the undesirable, the threatening, and the truly intolerable. Ordinary, everyday events and the extraordinary ones are shown to have distinctive negative impacts on young people.

In these texts, children are damaged by militarist, patriarchal, and racist families, schools, religions, and states. These institutions sustain each other, and none has children's well-being high on its agenda; instead, their well-being is often sacrificed for "higher" ends, although the language of caring for the young is still spoken regularly, deceptively, even seductively. The practices these institutions engage in regarding children include threats and violence to obtain obedience; sexual abuse; and pitiful, erratic, and unequal education. The injustices perpetrated on children have parallels with those inflicted on other subordinated groups, whether they be a sex or a species. The acceptance and celebration of violence by political leaders or gods trickle down to children, who become its victims and even its perpetrators.

Some of what is most distinctively positive about the young—be it their energy or their curiosity—is targeted and deemed objectionable or even dangerous, even by those who care for and put energy into them. Parents transfer their own fears onto their children, and their weaknesses and limitations lead to limits and vulnerability among their offspring. Few competing forces can come to their aid. The societies are gendered, with expectations of conformity to heterosexist norms. A good child is deferential, obedient, and mostly quiet.

Children actively struggle with all of this. They are aware of double standards that injure them and of lauded goals that are not supported by actual practices. They come up with a variety of ways to cope and to resist—but they do so from a position of structured inequality. Always, they labor just to be heard, to be taken seriously; they suffer from overregulation; they are resourceful, and they fight back, but often, in dystopias, they use the same tools that were used against them.

Utopian Childhoods, Childhood Utopias

Charlotte Perkins Gilman's Moving the Mountain *and* Herland

Charlotte Perkins Gilman's nonfiction work on children was discussed in Chapter 5. She is also famous for her utopian literature, especially *Herland* (1915), and she also wrote *Moving the Mountain* (1911), which forms part of a trilogy together with *Herland* and *With Her in Ourland* (1916). It is "a baby Utopia . . . [that] involves no other change than a change of mind" (1911, 20). The text reminisces on the past: "We used to have a sort of race-myth about 'happy childhood,' but none of us seemed to study the faces of the children" (203). Now, by contrast, "we, as a community, provide suitably for our most important citizens," reaping the benefits of an "advance in human intelligence" (197) that results from youth being "observed intelligently . . . [by] child-lovers who had had hundreds of [children] to study" (220).

Moving the Mountain tell the story of John Robertson, who travels to Tibet at the age of twenty-five and suffers an accident that results in complete memory loss. Thirty years later, he is found by his sister Nellie, recovers his memory, and returns to the United States. Nellie introduces him to a world that has changed more "than an ordinary century or two" (16). His conservative views on women and children provide the contrast with the new world.

The United States has adopted an improved-upon scientific socialism. "Everything is better; there is far more comfort, pleasure, peace of mind; a richer swifter growth, a higher happier life in every way" (43–44). The progress is economic, social, and medical: "There is no such thing in the civilized world as poverty—no labor problem—no color problem—no sex problem—almost no disease . . . no one needs to work over two hours a day and most people work four" (48).

Gilman consciously creates a child-friendly world. Newborns rarely cry (209), and they explore and take "joy . . . in the use of their own little bodies in as many ways as possible" (212). The most special spaces are those created for children, including child gardens, which are cared for collectively by those with children (210). Children's care is left "to the best professionals in child culture" (88, also 219), just as writing "new story-books" is in the hands of first-class writers (149), and "the greatest artists work for children" (204). Speaking about children's spaces, Gilman reveals a refreshing approach to "bad" children:

> Strange that we always punished children for sliding down unsuitable things and never provided suitable ones. . . . What we used to call "naughtiness" was only the misfit. The poor little things were in the wrong place—and nobody knew how to make them happy. (212–213)

It is a society adapted to children, not the other way around.

As we might expect from the earlier discussion of Gilman's nonfiction, her fictional children are taught *processes* rather than *facts* (202): they are "trained to think . . . to question, discuss, decide; they could reason" (223). Further, "we wish to have the first impressions in our children's minds, above all things, true" (207). It is taken for granted that the young have an insatiable thirst for knowledge (220–221) and for activity (217). Answering the call for better-educated parents, too, Gilman acknowledges a distinction between childbearers and childrearers, asserting that "all women who wish to, have babies; but if they wish to take care of them they must show a diploma" (106). She continues, "It is the vision of all the great child-lovers; that children are people, and the most valuable people on earth. The most important thing to a child is its mother. We made new mothers for them" (195).

Relations between children and a whole variety of adults are normalized: "Children had not lost their mothers . . . but each child kept his own and gained others" (218). Also more celebrated are the relations among children, as Nellie explains: "They like to be with the others, you see. . . . [S]he's always running off to The Garden when she can" (154).

In stark contrast with the dystopias, children are raised without gender roles (107, 223), poverty (197), or fearful religious ideas (201), and they get a great deal of attention. "They all have proper nourishment, and clothing, and environment—from birth" (197). Even the young might contribute to the community, creating energy, for example, by riding a bike, which can then be stored. As children age, "they all ha[ve] a year of travel" (215), like the later children of Russ's Whileaway.

Gilman's later novel, *Herland*, portrays a two-thousand-year-old, all-female utopia that is hidden from outsiders, although it is ominously portrayed by them as a "strange and terrible Woman Land . . . dangerous [and] deadly" (1915, 2). The three American male explorers who come to this isolated land are "objective" sociologist, Van; fawning, tender-hearted Jeff; and sexist, aggressive Terry. None of the three is, "in the least, 'advanced' on the woman question" (10), as the understating Gilman puts it.

While motherhood is the central theme in this 1915 serialized novel, the lives of children *are* talked about. The virtues of mothers serve the lives of children well: they possess "subtle understanding, . . . instant recognition of our difficulties, and readiness to meet them" (30). Too, adults "ha[ve] the evenest tempers, the most perfect patience and good nature—one of the things most impressive about them all [i]s the absence of irritability" (50). What a blessing that would be to the young. By contrast, as in Owens's *Unpredictable Adventure,* we're told that a parent in the United States "doesn't really know [their child]" (152). For diversity among their relatively small population, the Herlanders depend on being able to recognize and accentuate even small differences among the young to maximize individuality. Gilman thus builds a bridge again between socialism and individuality. In Herland, there is no spoiling and no smothering, and a great deal of independence and community exists among children.

A distinctive version of childhood comes to the fore in the men's first impressions of the women in the place they name Herland. The women appear to the visitors to have "no more terror than a set of frolicsome children" (16) and to be "as free from suspicion as a child who has never been rebuked" (17). They're not wrong, but likely not for the reasons they ascribe: the adult residents, in fact, do *not* live in terror and were never punished as children, and the joyfulness and freedom associated with childhood are not necessarily things that have to be left behind by adults. Gilman positively describes the adults of Herland as possessing that childlike quality of "frequently jar[ring] one's self-esteem by innocent questions" (67), paying especially unusual honor to the ways of children; in fact, that youthful curiosity is considered a form of reasonableness, giving new stature to children's inquisitiveness.

The children of Herland are loved by all and, again, rarely utter a cry. They are provided with an interesting list of goods: "plenty of everything," which includes "room, air, solitude even" (77). Children's space and individuality are emphasized even within the strongly communitarian society: "From earliest childhood each ha[s] a separate bedroom with toilet conveniences, and one of the marks of coming of age [i]s the addition of an outer room in which to receive friends" (135).

Education seems to take place everywhere *except* in a classroom. Force-feeding of the brain, which Gilman's nonfiction work also detests, doesn't exist. The educators are again the best of the best—especially those who work with the very young. Youth are educated "continuously but unconsciously, . . . grow[ing] up as naturally as young trees; learning through every sense" (103). Children in Herland do not have surnames, because they are not the property of their mothers or only of concern primarily to them.

Gilman's texts clearly center the young: they have space, language, relevance, and community. Children as young as babies take part in communal rituals and, soon after, some forms of work. The child-centered mores are most striking. As visitor Van describes it, "No Herland child [has] ever met the overbearing rudeness we so commonly show to children. They [a]re People, too, from the first; the most precious part of the nation" (108–109). Most uniquely, the very language in Herland is "deliberately clarified, simplified, made easy and beautiful, for the sake of the children" (110). What an innovation to counter the testimonial injustice that youth usually face on a daily basis.

Dorothy Bryant's The Kin of Ata Are Waiting for You

Attention to a positive childhood is also significant in Dorothy Bryant's *The Kin of Ata Are Waiting for You* (1971). Her protagonist is not a very sympathetic character: an unnamed man mysteriously brought to an island after murdering his lover and crashing his car. The book involves the contrasts between his ruthless worldview and the spiritual, seemingly primitive ways of the islanders.

It turns out to be no accident that the first three members of Ata that the surprised visitor awakens to are young people who tend to his injuries and feed him as he recovers in a dark, sheltered space. The young people have roles in everything—sometimes identical to those of adults, sometimes different—and they are never out of the picture. They carry water to field workers (40), for example, and have parts in the most sacred rituals (42). The kin of Ata on this hidden island live to dream and value strong dreamers. Children, too, dream, share their dreams, and determine on their own what to take from those visions. Distinctive to Bryant's work, children of Ata as young as three participate in the care of those younger, especially infant care (63), and they also aid the elderly (87)—a bringing together of the ages that is common in utopias.

The new arrival—a successful author running from his demons—notes that babies on Ata are "inconspicuous because they [a]re quiet," a now-recurrent theme also seen in Gilman's work. "During the whole time I was there I never heard a baby cry" (20), he muses. Of the child he eventually sires in Ata, the visitor says, "The baby was held and played with by the older children. . . . She was truly, from the beginning, not our baby. She belonged to everyone" (155).

The visitor is surprised at the first ritual he attends, when "a child who couldn't have been more than three" is listened to by a teen "as attentively as if he were hearing the most important thing that had ever been told him" (16). While it is striking to him—and likely would be to many of us—perhaps it is not surprising for a culture in which citizens are exquisitely skilled at knowing their own and one another's needs (17). Accommodation is the rule: for example, snacks are always available for those—including children and nursing mothers (99)—who cannot wait until the next communal meal to eat (18). Similarly, it is important to note, there are always parts to be played by the elderly (58).

According to *The Kin of Ata*, the more important the role that games, dances, rituals, and stories play in a community, the easier it is for children to be part of that community. And the less important obedience is—and the more that balance and self-regulation are modeled and encouraged (98)—the easier the relations are between those younger and older (76). The virtues, so to speak, among the kin of Ata are a "harmonious disposition" (193) and "patience, stillness, and acceptance" (196); the vices are "anything that br[eaks] that rhythm—anger, impatience, sometimes just talking"—all things that can especially plague the lives of the young, as we have seen.

Sexual play among youth of all ages and in various couplings is relatively uneventful (51–52) and the site of neither intervention nor embarrassment. "Up to the age of sexual maturity the children [a]re naked and long-haired" (19), the visitor notices, a stance against enforced sex roles as well as for sexual liberation.

At one point in the book, a discussion arises concerning the nature of children. The idea of purity and innocence is outright rejected, and in its place is the idea of "desire." One character elaborates on this while explaining why they regulate the population, saying that children "are pure desire. And they must not be thwarted, for if they are they will never grow. They must give up gradually of their own free will. To force is donagdeao" (forbidden). "They must try everything, have everything—too many would destroy our way of life faster than any invasion from outside" (152). This view of children's "nature" is somehow refreshing, for it leads to making room for youthful energy rather than condemning and breaking it, and it does not overly divide youth and adults into two distinct camps.

Joanna Russ's The Female Man *(Again)*

Only Russ's 1975 *The Female Man*, among all the authors and works covered here, emphasizes and establishes multiple stages of childhood/adulthood rather than just one transition. On high-tech Whileaway, children are raised communally and in large kinship groups for the first five years, during which time mothers are freed from other obligations. This period of time for mothers is characterized as one of "indulgence, pleasure, and flowering" (52).

Then the youngsters enter regional schools, which are said to be one cause of the "characteristic independence" of the Whileawayans (52). "We have a saying: when the child goes to the school, both mother and child howl; the child because it is going to be separate from the mother and the mother because she has to go back to work" (39). The care that the children receive is still nurturing and individualized. In schools, "children are cared for in groups of five and taught in groups of differing sizes according to the subject under discussion. Their education at this point is heavily practical" (50).

After the big change at five years old, there are several more. At puberty, young people are endowed with something called "Middle-Dignity and turned loose; children have the right of food and lodging wherever they go, up to the power of the community to support them. They do not go back home" (50). They use this independence in a variety of ways: "Some, wild with the desire for exploration, travel all around the world—usually in the company of other children. . . . The more profound abandon all possessions and live off the land. . . . Some make a beeline for their callings" (50–51). All are "raised in a world where children and women regularly travel alone in the great wilds" (Clare 2014). A few years later, "at seventeen they achieve Three-Quarters Dignity and are assimilated into the labor force" (Russ 1975, 51). Full-Dignity comes at twenty-two, around our oldest age of majority. Then they enter families at about twenty-five, which gives them a geographical home base and a "family" group of about twenty to thirty others that shifts over time.

The setup on Whileaway makes worlds that would otherwise threaten children safe for them. It provides them with meaningful democratic peer groups from a young age, without succumbing to warehousing. It allows for multiple ways for them to explore the world and thoughtfully and gradually draws them into full adulthood, or "Full-Dignity," which is primarily associated with being grounded in a community. It allows for a variety of connections for people of all ages, although it prohibits cross-generational sexual relationships and weakens life-long parent-child bonds. While Russ is mostly silent regarding what children contribute to larger communities, the all-female society positively uses technology "to fully realize their potential; for instance, they have raised the population's overall intelligence through genetic engineering" (Martins 2005, 405).

Marge Piercy's Woman on the Edge of Time *(Again)*

On Connie's first visit to futuristic Mattapoisett in Piercy's *Woman on the Edge of Time* (1976), she is struck by the space that children take up: their art is on the walls of common rooms along with that of every level of adult artist, they easily command attention as they stand and tell stories (74), and they are present in every setting (128). Piercy seems to imply that the more comfortable a society is with freedom of expression (physical, verbal, artistic, and emotional) and with diverse levels of energy, the more seamlessly children fit in more situations (74–75, 118). Gender norms as we know them have vanished—indeed, for some time, Connie struggles with trying to figure out the sex of various characters in the future she visits, an obsession with gender not shared by those characters in anything from their dress to their couplings to their gender-neutral pronouns.

With regard to parenting and childrearing, some people in Mattapoisett are "kidbinders" (74), people who mother everyone's kids. And, from the other end, every child is everyone's—"they're all ours," Morningstar establishes (78). Chiseling away more at the patriarchal family, Piercy endows every child with three "coms," or co-mothers, who together make an explicit and socially endorsed decision to adopt a child from a mechanical "brooder." Each child also has numerous relationships with folks of every age in a complex and supportive web of communities based on interests, affections, work, and art (133): "We grow up closest to our mothers, but we swim close to all our mems" (113).

"Naming" is an important personal and social ritual that marks the "end-of-mothering" and the beginning of being a youth, or adolescent citizen. It endows the very young adult with greater confidence and entails a period of three months during which they do not speak with their coms, allowing preexisting ties of dependence to gently shift (114–115). Piercy's children themselves thus have the power to avoid enforced and prolonged dependence, although, as is the general pattern in Mattapoisett, children seem easily to talk through their decisions with the adults in their lives. In the book, we see young people take on what we might call responsible social and political roles as well, as when a teenager insightfully mediates a "worming" between two adults whose tensions are negatively affecting others.

In Piercy's utopia, youth is "a time for freedom and experimentation" (Rosenthal, n.d.), which is mirrored in the educational "system." Children "study with any person who can teach" them, first in their own village, but then anywhere after the naming process (Piercy 1976, 53). Picking the subject and the teacher, young apprentices again have decision-making power and are endowed with epistemic authority, recognized as and trained in self-knowing. Working in groups of four or five, they are not at the mercy of chance or subject to the required "discipline" of group classrooms; by virtue of learning in the field, their theory and practice always inform each other (131). Like adults, young people past babyhood have living spaces of their own, among but not with their family, and for the same reasons: to have the space to "meditate, think, compose songs, sleep, study" (72). This complex family arrangement also means that "the child will not get caught in love misunderstandings" (74) among their parents, again reducing that vulnerability of the young to their parents' well-being that is part of Piercy's dystopia.

Children are more like than unlike adults in *Woman on the Edge of Time*. When adults as well as children play games and create stories, a divide is breached (172, 240). Because everyone is always learning and developing, such features do not mark childhood alone. Children experience psychological problems, just as adults do, and the community takes them seriously (122). They are taught "inknowing and outknowing" (140)—the skills of understanding themselves and others—by perhaps the age of six (228). Mattapoisett is comfortable with freedom of expression—verbal, emotional, and artistic—and with diverse levels of energy on the part of adults as well as young people, so such features, too, cannot provide some firm divide. Because adults, coms, or just a friend who wants a youngster for company (135) often take youth with them as they work and play, distance from the adult world is also not a distinctive feature of childhood. As Connie's futuristic guide

Luciente puts it, "I think maybe growing up is less mysterious with us since the adult world isn't separate" (132).

The only times when something relatively negative is said about children—such as that they go through numerous, melodramatic names after their initial self-naming (121) or get restless during long rituals (173)—the issues are easily accommodated. Those difficulties are not thought to apply only to the young, even if they mostly occur with them, and they carry no overgeneralized, slighting connotations. Children do not have to learn to play at deference and conformity to be heard, developing no socially destructive patterns of artificiality and manipulation.

Children are indulged as they experiment sexually, although they are also schooled against roughness and bullying. Residents do not "find coupling" among the young to be "bad unless it involves pain or is not invited" (139). They are taught to fear the real enemies: not strangers kidnapping them, as it were, but "power and greed—taking from other people their food, their liberty, their health, their land, their customs, their pride" (103). And the goods the young are taught are true goods: "growing to care, to connect, to cooperate. Everything we learn aims to make us feel strong in ourselves, connected to all living. At home" (248).

All said, Piercy's utopia is made for *every* age, giving to people in each period of life the space, resources, opportunities, responsibilities, freedom, and community they need. The young are a part, they have voice, and they are respected and cherished. This cultural shift truly does not seem beyond the possible, and it does seem deeply nourishing for the young at every stage of childhood.

Joan Slonczewski's A Door into Ocean *(Again)*

In Slonczewski's *A Door into Ocean* (1986), the protagonist Spinel's views of himself and of inequality are challenged. On the egalitarian Ocean Moon of Shora, Sharers "envision a life force, a sort of living ether, that pervades every atom of their universe" (102). They understand that "every creature has its niche, its function" (350). Here, everything from information to sleeping rooms to food is readily shared. In this strongly communitarian world, Spinel finds a society where "every conception of a child [is] a decision of the Gathering" (158), and evenings are devoted to "sharing learning" by all ages and for a lifetime (87), for "all work and no learnsharing turn[s] minds into mud" (140). Importantly, they must all, young and old, use their individual and collective skills to survive threats—from large cephaglobinids that can destroy their raft-homes to an invading army from another planet. Shorans keep the individual in community alive by using such means as the isolating meditative state called "whitetrance" (366) and by operating by consensus, whereby an individual can feel so strongly as to block action (76). The author, a biologist, believes that "animals are equally capable of altruism as are humans, and that moral codes of behavior that aspire to altruism are entirely compatible with human biology" (Slonczewski 2001).

In this universe, "lovesharers" couple—or "twin"—and merge ova to reproduce (Slonczewski 1986, 89). Sexual relationships are portrayed positively, including those among adolescents (341). Like those who are older, adolescents are sexually comfortable and creative. Children are raised by their biological mothers but in a tightly woven raft community that is reinforced in such daily activities as the Gatherings and collecting food. Shora's small communities "minimiz[e] the need for grand political hierarchies" (Jesse 2016). Attending to the needs of the very young is so important that their cries alone can bring adults out of whitetrance. Adolescents maintain strong, loving ties with their mothers: "There [i]s no mistaking the emotion that stretche[s] between them" (Slonczewski 1986, 56). Although teenage impatience is also evident (112, 219, 324), it is dealt with relatively easily because young adults have great independence, especially after self-naming, and because parents are parts of communities beyond those made with their offspring.

Shoran children are regularly and actively seen participating in social activities with folks of all ages, whether helping their community survive life-threatening ocean storms, solving crucial community disputes (79), collecting food (94, 101), or participating in festivities. Invading General Realgar, in fact, notices with annoyance how "children ha[ve] found their way into everything" (209). Adolescents become fully equal members and "protectors" (28, 61) of a community, or a Sharer "raft Gathering," upon self-naming (26), although in this watery world, one names oneself by one's greatest vice, as did Merwen the Impatient, Lalor the Absentminded, and Nisi the Deceiver. "A selfnamer takes a name that fits . . . and spends the rest of her life disowning it" (74). In this aspect, as in others, the "utopia" is shown to possess and actively confront personal and political problems. Even prior to naming, youngsters casually and uneventfully question and advise their elders (56, 168). The young learn through apprenticeships (142) or hands-on training, seamlessly taking on more and more responsible roles as they grow.

Children play a crucial role in the Ocean Moon's ultimate nonviolent resistance against the invading soldiers of the Patriarch. Herded together by the Stone Moon invaders in an attempt to get their mothers to give in and follow orders (291), the youngsters (ages two to twelve, as the Patriarch thought best, to avoid "troublesome infants and adolescents" [292]) decide together, first, to scream (294) until the guards cannot stand it and thus eventually let them out to swim, and then to go on a hunger strike (298), which damages the soldiers' morale, makes them question their mission, and leads to the youngsters' release. Their cooperation with each other, bravery, and persistence show their understanding of Shora's values and inspires their mothers in other forms of direct, nonviolent resistance. It justifies them self-naming at a younger age than usual, which the other community protectors accept, although there is concern that circumstances have forced "the children [to] grow[] old before they [have] grow[n] up" (268).

Slonczewski shows mothers and daughters in particular, and adults and children more generally, in peaceful, respectful relations. Multigenerational relationships are relatively freed from the destructive hierarchical overtones they carry in the patriarchal alternative. The need for cooperation is apparent to all, as are the contributions of every age. Age-appropriate tasks are designed for daily life and for times of crisis. The oldest might lead the singing at a Gathering (141), while the youngest might feed the elderly (62), do the housekeeping, or keep watch.

Starhawk's The Fifth Sacred Thing *(Again)*

Starhawk's egalitarian community in *The Fifth Sacred Thing* (1993) is guided by the idea "that we are part of the earth, part of the air, the fire, and the water, as we are part of one another. . . . We believe we can continue to live and thrive only if we care for one another" (17). Coming out of a period of conflict and scarcity via a successful resistance called the Uprising, and despite being "surrounded by hostile enemies who might, at any moment, attack and destroy us" (152), the residents of the utopian enclave "pledge[] to feed one another's children first" (18). They structure their society so that "no child lacks a home," no one goes hungry, and no one lacks care (19). The well-being of children seems to be part of the city's very ideological and economic foundation, simultaneously providing a motivation, a standard for living, and criteria by which to hold the community accountable. The city is aesthetically pleasing and utilitarian:

> I admit the beauty of this city. It has a beautiful beating heart. It cares for its own, and for the stranger. Its streams run with clear water, and the trees that line its pathways bow under the weight of fruit anyone is free to pick. (111)

Rather than being the subject of sustained attention, children's images are scattered throughout the book, in perhaps the same way that children are meant to appear ordinarily in most scenes of life. One child is solemnly holding the Talking Stick during circle (19), another blesses the food and drink before a feast (20), several join the "liveliness" (214) and "fighting" (216) at the Passover Seder, and many rush out "with bowls and pots to catch the . . . [precious] rainwater" (125). While it is difficult to understand the motion picture of children's lives through these snapshots, Starhawk makes the young visible in every scenario. They are integrated into and integral to the community's life.

Much of what we learn about childhood in Starhawk's utopia is by way of characters' memories, "the lessons of childhood" that persist into adulthood, which, of course, are told from the adult's point of view and mostly when the lessons urgently need to be recalled. We find out, for instance, when an adult needs the skill, that every schoolchild learns things from basic electronic technologies (63) to "how to use her power" and invoke the Goddesses (79). We know, from the ways in which adults use the skills, that children learn to trust their intuition, "to notice if [they] see an aura or feel the energy move" (95, 136), to change states of consciousness (228), and to recognize the need to heal (132) and to talk something out (136). Girls are "trained to monitor [their] cycles pretty closely, from the time [they] first begin to bleed. And [they] know how to block conception" (319).

We grasp something of the community's general approach to education as well as seemingly random bits about it. One character, a gifted musician, recalls having "learned to drum before he learned to count, adding and subtracting and dividing by changing beats before he was ever introduced to numbers" (97). Youth learn rock-climbing at age fourteen, not so much to complete the task itself but to grasp that one "could face a fear and move on through" (248). They learn to shoot a pistol to understand history (253); in fact, everything in the curriculum seems to have multiple purposes, to be the product of considerable and holistic thinking, and to have a pragmatic side in a place whose continued existence is under threat. And the pedagogical approach is distinctive:

That was the way Johanna ran the schools; she believed children should be taught about things from beginning to end. So they learned to make fire from sticks, and how to put out fires, and then studied all the chemistry and physics involved as they built steam engines and solar panels and tracked the course of the sun. He supposed it was a good way to learn; certainly they had never been bored, and he was always coming across bits of useful knowledge. (71)

The utopian city is thoughtful about caring for children, who mostly seem to live with extended biological families. First, "every household gets credits for a certain number of working hours per person, for home maintenance and for child care, or care of anyone who might need it" (275). "Wages" for housework and care work are thus established. One can choose full-time care work too: "That's a personal arrangement between the people involved. . . . But it's no longer an economic arrangement. If a woman—or a man—wants to stay home and take care of the house and the kids, they'd collect all those work credits and they'd be valued just as much as for work done outside the home, because all work is valued the same" (275).

Children in every form of family are protected. Starhawk is explicit about this and worth quoting at length on the point. Asked about whether there is "incest and child molesting," the character Madrone replies,

> We don't have the kind of social isolation that breeds it. We have a lot of different kinds of families. Some of us grow up in big collectives. . . . Some are in extended families . . . some in small nuclear families. But we make sure that no family is isolated. The Neighborhood Councils form support groups of people from different kinds of households and backgrounds—to give different perspectives. So every kid has half a dozen aunties and uncles from the time they're tiny. They're encouraged to talk about things, to ask for help, to protect themselves. And we train all our children, early on, in self-defense. . . . [W]e don't have the climate of secrecy and shame that lets it go on for any length of time. I'm not saying it never happens, but nothing supports it. (276–277)

Unusually, the book notes that different generations have different relations to their locale: "The young ones. They're different from us. They don't see this city as some precarious achievement like attaining the summit of Kanchenjunga. To them, this is base camp. Just a starting point toward heights they have yet to reach. And it's home, all they know" (111). Yet when the city is invaded, the youth participate in multiple forms of noncooperation to defend it, along with the adults, as if it does have a shared meaning among them. As in Slonczewski's *A Door into Ocean*, Starhawk's youth show that they have deeply adopted nonviolence as the norm and are as capable as adults of understanding and participating in sustained political action. In another similarity between the two books, it is, in fact, action by youth that ultimately creates the first cracks in allegiance among soldiers on the other side (336–337): somehow, some among the opposition still see torturing and killing the young as different from and less justifiable than killing and torturing adults, leading them to question their side's leadership. In sacrificing themselves, the young villagers (like the adults) see less of an age-based distinction. But in making young deaths decisive in the battle for the life of the utopian city and planet, Starhawk and Slonczewski, respectively, reinscribe the distinction.[5] Both sets of children "refuse to be enemies" (154) and thus contribute to sustainable political change rather than mere military victory.

Octavia Butler's The Parable of the Sower *and* The Parable of the Talents *(Again)*

Butler develops her dystopian visions more than her utopian ones, as her life was cut short before she could complete the book series she had planned; nonetheless, we do get some insight into a better future in *The Parable of the Talents* (1998), where the village of Acorn grows.

When Lauren is forced to leave the community of her childhood and become a traveler, she is terrified (Butler 1993, 156) and in mourning for those in her family and community whose lives were lost. "Everything we'd known and treasured was gone" (197). She is determined to survive, connecting with two other refugees from her community. She learns to trust the variety of people her small group then collects over the miles.

Children play an interesting role in establishing trusting relationships among the adults: the presence of a baby leads to reaching out to new members in one case (203), the relationship between children opens the door for one between adults in another, and the presence of children in their growing group makes them less threatening to strangers (259) and thus less of a target. And kids often bring out the best in adults, even in the worst circumstances, from motivating them to survive (285) to evoking their loving sides (308). "Children [a]re the keys to most of the adults present," Lauren muses. She prepares the way for the future by declaring, like Starhawk's characters, that "a community's first responsibility is to protect its children" (321).

Acorn, the first Earthseed community, is utopian. Lauren imagines that all Earthseed communities should be small, for "in small communities, she believe[s], people are more accountable to one another" (170). Children take to it immediately (359):

> Here was real community. Here was at least a semblance of security. Here was the comfort of ritual and routine and the emotional satisfaction of belonging to a "team" that stood together to meet challenge

when challenge came. And for families, here was a place to raise children, to teach them basic skills that they might not learn elsewhere and to keep them as safe as possible from the harsh, ugly lessons of the world outside. (63)

Knowledge is perhaps the highest good in Acorn and the school the most beautiful building (Butler 1998, 261). "Anyone who join[s] the group, child or adult, ha[s] to begin at once to learn . . . two languages . . . and to acquire a trade. Anyone who ha[s] a trade [i]s always in the process of teaching it to someone else" (23, also 74). The practice of turning everyone into an instructor bridges one of the main divides between children and adults (who are usually characterized only as students and teachers, respectively) and makes learning a life-long activity, a common theme in the utopias. "We've survived as well as we have because we keep learning" (27), Lauren asserts. Children take care of other children (28, 72), and some adults are the equivalents of Piercy's kid-binders, people who "love[] kids, and [whom kids] seem to trust . . . as soon as they meet" (37, also 390).

The multiracial nature of the adult community trickles down to families in the most positive way: "We're you name it: Black, White, Latino, Asian, and any mixture at all. . . . The kids we've adopted and the ones who have been born to us think of all the mixing and matching as normal. Imagine that" (42). Kids thus play a role in normalizing progressive interracial and multicultural relations. The ties of biological families are not irrelevant but are no more intense, or even distinct, from adoptive relations born in collected communities in troubled times. "So many members of our community have come to us alone or with only little children that it seems best . . . to create family bonds that take in more than the usual godparent-godchild relationship" (65–66). These extended families are strong and are "taken seriously here . . . [It's] a real commitment. The family relationship is not only with the new child, but with its parents as well" (66). And having children, of whatever origin, "makes us more truly a community, somehow" (174).

Children work (73) in age-appropriate tasks "as part of their education" (148), integrating them further into the community. They take part in the Gatherings, those regular problem-solving and discussion times so essential to community sustenance (66). Too, "everyone over 15 vot[es]" (72). In special celebrations, the young have a place as well. Maybe, for example, they write or stage the play for all to see (72), or they do dramatic readings (143). "We all feed one another's hungers" (72). Likewise, the religious foundation of the community, Earthseed, is contained in proverbs accessible to folks across the age spectrum. And the dream it contains, of going to the stars, gives people of every age "a focus, a goal, something big enough, complex enough, difficult enough, and in the end, radical enough to make us become more than we ever have been" (357). All of this participation enables the "partnership" that "is giving, taking, learning, teaching, offering the greatest possible benefit while doing the least possible harm. Partnership is mutualistic symbiosis. Partnership is life" (136).

Children are treated as having some autonomy. For example, in a tree-planting ceremony that marks a death, two sisters remember their lost brother: "The little girls plant[]their seedlings under our guidance, but not with our help. The work [i]s done by their hands" (56). Butler acknowledges the importance of a process of grieving that has been created so that all ages can meaningfully participate; children's emotional lives are reckoned with. The young don't have to wait elsewhere while adults alone bury and mourn. It's a perfect example of their place in community.

Butler's utopia, while less developed than her dystopia, contains important lessons regarding childhood that respond to the darker prospects she lays out earlier. In Acorn, children are most fundamentally treated as fully human: emotionally, socially, and intellectually. Their dependence on others is not construed as being qualitatively different from that of adults—who also clearly need others to survive, learn, and grow.

When interdependence is maximized and even celebrated, the dependence of young people is less likely to be used as a weapon against them. Relationships among young people are given as much space and importance in Acorn as are their relationships with adults, and the latter are seen as two-way streets, even in areas like education, where expertise is usually not granted to minors. This recognition opens the door to more learning by adults, too, enriching the whole. A strong yet fluid sense of family binds people together within and across generations and beyond blood, making the family broader and safer for children, a real resource for them. Youth are understood to be the cement of the community and are valued as such, and they are recognized as contributing to it in myriad ways, including culturally and politically. Butler's contribution is creating a world where there is a childhood, but where having one does not relegate young people to second-class citizenship.

Concluding Thoughts

Common themes unite feminist speculative fiction with earlier feminist treatises and manifestos, similarities in what is seen as diminishing childhood and in what is understood as contributing to a full life for young people. There is, in fact, a tradition within feminist reflections on childhood. Most criticized are: the surveillance to which children are relentlessly subjected; the needless, artificial ways in which they are separated from adult worlds, often due to their prescribed "innocence"; the way that their need for protection is thought to justify all sorts of intrusion into and control over children's lives; and the ways in which general norms of participation nonetheless manage to exclude them. The language of smothering children recurs, sometimes referring to what happens in nuclear families and sometimes commenting on the pressures of socialization in general.

Multiple texts speak to the silencing of children, to epistemic injustice, especially the difficulty the young have being heard and believed. They also speak to force-feeding in education—which is a tool of oppression in many of the dystopias (showing, as did the manifestos, that not only access to education matters, but also what is taught and how)—and to fear-based religions imposed on children. The fates of women and children are often the same and linked in the dark portrayals, with girls usually especially vulnerable. Every single book tackles the gendered socialization of young people.

This body of literature recognizes with what enormous, nearly irresistible force the norms and events of a given society influence and shape children as well as the responsibility this places on adults to have more meaningful and open relations with youth. They urge that there be less fear and restriction and more opportunity, independence, and variety in the lives of the young. Respect for the young could reinforce more democratic and egalitarian relations elsewhere. Wouldn't it be amazing if our first experiences in life as young people were not experiences of being silenced and subordinated?

Shared and social responsibility for children is a nearly universal theme in feminist utopias. Such a change is thought to contribute to the happiness and safety of young people as well as to greater freedom for adults. It leads to alterations in housing, love relationships, and understandings of belonging and duty. Sometimes children are given their own space and sometimes they live together, but never do they live only with two biological parents isolated from community. Children have close ties with truly varied adults. This aspect of feminist utopias, too, is part of the general feminist project of "creating new relationships absent domination and control, abuse and inequality" (Halbert, n.d.). "Let's close our eyes and imagine what that might look like: a world where all children are welcome and communities take a collective responsibility for raising the young people in their midst. . . . It makes you wonder how different your childhood would have been" (Gumbs, Martens, and Williams 2016, 107, 113).

Feminist utopian literature reveals and challenges patriarchal assumptions and myths about children, which, like those about women, are shown to be unreasonable (if not outright nonsensical) and destructive to individuals and to communities. The ideas about children that are contested include their overwhelming and necessary dependence on adults, their essential vulnerability, their asexuality, their inherent lack of credibility, and their inability to participate in social institutions. Reckoning with them as complex beings, utopias often distinguish youth from adults in terms of their energy rather than their intellect. In questioning the degree and forms of dependence on adults, these novels make more room for children's diverse relationships with each other and openly reckon with adults' similar dependence on others.

In the utopias, children are everywhere. They have multiple sets of relationships, meaning that the intensity of the parent-child bond is moderated and that care relations are more diffuse. At very young ages, children are acquainted with the skills, virtues, and rituals of adults, even if in simplified form. Adults are not "other," and thus children and adults are both seen as members of various communities. Being seen and heard is no more difficult for a child than for an adult, and power over the young is looked at with the same critical eye that is cast upon other forms of power. Every child is a wanted, celebrated person, not only by their (sometimes biological) parents but also by many others and by the community. Equal educational opportunities and job training are central to individual and communal flourishing. Despite how children today are often condemned to second-class status on the basis of a supposedly less-developed rationality, these books often take adults to task for facilely thinking that they understand children or even know their own individual children. A great deal of emphasis is placed in these utopias on knowing oneself and others, and the skills by which we do this are thought to be learnable in childhood.

Philosophically, feminist utopian reflections on children bring additional and interesting content to debates that often exclude them. Included here would be consideration of how people of different ages can contribute to various communities, whether in the name of democracy, self-realization, or sound policy; how children can and do resist adult power, and with what consequences; how the range and nature of adult power over young people can contribute to definitions of legitimate and illegitimate power; how relationships between unequals can still be just; what it means to be fully human; what it means at various stages of life to know oneself and others; with what and whom one can communicate; and how all members can contribute to holding a constructive community together.

We learn quite a bit in these stories about the virtues that we should encourage in adults for the sake of children. Such qualities as patience, emotional intelligence, and epistemic humility, for example, are necessary for respectful relations with the young and also, conveniently, enhance those among adults. Similarly, we learn quite a bit about what social values are conducive to the flourishing of young people. These utopias minimize the practice of having "power over" others, for example, and teach democratic processes from the start of life and in all realms. They actively tear down those structures and practices that support the abuse of young people as well, from racism and sexism to isolation and defenselessness. The stories believe that there are standards of justice as well as of care that apply to adult relations with the young, and that we impoverish young lives and the lives of communities by our failures to uphold those standards. They teach us the importance of actively challenging stereotypes about the young that do not, in fact, protect them, but limit them.

It is not "utopian" in the sense of unattainable to think about making the lives of children better. In fact, the authors of these science-fiction books, like those of the feminist treatises and manifestos of earlier chapters, fully believe that justice, voice, and respect for young people are eminently achievable goals that should and could be among our highest social priorities. Further, they think that achieving them is in *everyone's* interest. We can commit ourselves to making the world more—from families and schools to organizations and states—more child-friendly, and should think of our communities as accountable to the young. In our personal relations with young people, we should trust them more, value our varied connections with them more (even when they are not "easy"), listen to them more often and more openly, and learn with and from them. It is possible to appreciate what is distinctive about the various stages of life and what unites them. In our relations with young people, we adults have opportunities, every day, to be more fully human.

These science-fiction authors were not "ahead of their time," as is so often said of feminist writers, for we have seen feminist writers in every era urging us to right these wrongs to children and to establish more humane and inclusive social values and structures. We have a long, diverse feminist tradition to build upon—one that emerges from all over the world and is expressed in a range of forums and genres. It deserves, even demands, our sustained attention.

NOTES

1. There are a variety of sources and angles I can only hint at here. See, for example, Maureen LaPerrière, "The Evolution of Mothering: Images and Impact of the Mother-Figure in Feminist Utopian Science-Fiction," 1994, available at https://escholarship .mcgill.ca/concern/file_sets/0v8381465, accessed on October 26, 2020; Lathrop 2006; Elaine Orr, "Mothering as Good Fiction: Instances from Marge Piercy's 'Woman on

the Edge of Time,'" *Journal of Narrative Technique* 23, no. 2 (Spring 1993): 61–79; Bryn Gravitt, "A Feminist Utopia? Revisions of Family in Mary Shelley's Falkner," *Parlour: A Journal of Literary Criticism and Analysis*, September 21, 2016. Also see several chapters that add some dystopian elements in Maki Motapanyane's *Motherhood and Single-Lone Parenting: A Twenty-First Century Perspective* (Bradford, Ontario, Canada: Demeter Press, 2016).

2. Claire Owens (1896–1993) was the author of short stories, novels, radio plays, and autobiographies as well as being a magazine columnist. She became a prominent figure in the human potential movement.

3. It appears that Owens herself "struggled to define herself against the expectations of her mother, Susan Allen Myers, and her maternal grandmother, Laura Smith Allen, fundamentalist Baptists who romanticized the ideals of antebellum South." "Owens, Claire Myers," *Encyclopedia.com*, updated October 8, 2020, available at https://www.encyclopedia.com/arts/news-wires-white-papers-and-books/owens-claire-myers, accessed on October 25, 2019.

4. Such children are more apt to be removed from their families than are those in White families with the same problems, who receive other forms of support and remain intact. For statistics, see https://www.statista.com/statistics/255404/number-of-children-in-foster-care-in-the-united-states-by-race-ethnicity/. "African American and Native American children represent double the percentage of the foster care population than they do in the general child population." Don Lash, "Race and Class in the US Foster Care System," *International Socialist Review* 91 (Winter 2013/2014), available at https://isreview.org/issue/91/race-and-class-us-foster-care-system, accessed on May 1, 2018.

5. Similarly, Bird is "rehabilitated" after prison in part through his relationship with the young Rosa (Starhawk 1993, 212), whose later mistreatment further affects him when he is reimprisoned (416).

REFERENCES

Aguirre, Abby. "Octavia Butler's Prescient Vision of a Zealot Elected to 'Make America Great Again.'" *New Yorker*, July 26, 2017. https://www.newyorker.com/books/second-read/octavia-butlers-prescient-vision-of-a-zealot-elected-to-make-america-great-again.

Allbery, Russ. 2013. "Review of *The Female Man*." The Eyrie, December 31, 2013. https://www.eyrie.org/~eagle/reviews/books/0-8070-6299-5.html.

Booker, Keith M. 1994. "Woman on the Edge of a Genre: The Feminist Dystopias of Marge Piercy." *Science Fiction Studies* 21, no. 3 (November): 337–350.

Bryant, Dorothy. (1971) 1976. *The Kin of Ata Are Waiting for You*. New York: Random House.

Butler, Octavia. 1993. *The Parable of the Sower*. New York: Open Road Media.

———. 1998. *The Parable of the Talents*. New York: Open Road Media.

Clare. 2014. "Review: The Female Man." The Literary Omnivore, March 17, 2014. https://theliteraryomnivore.wordpress.com/2014/03/17/review-the-female-man/.

Gilman, Charlotte Perkins. 1911. *Moving the Mountain*. New York: Charlton.

———. 1915. *Herland*. New York: Global Grey.

Gumbs, Alexis, China Martens, and Mai'a Williams, eds. 2016. *Revolutionary Mothering: Love on the Front Lines*. Oakland, CA: PM Press.Halbert, Debora. n.d. "Feminist Fabulation: Challenging the Boundaries between Fact and Fiction." http://www.futures.hawaii.edu/publications/half-fried-ideas/J2/halbert.pdf.

Jesse. 2016. "Review of *A Door into Ocean* by Joan Slonczewski." Speculiction, March 15, 2016. http://speculiction.blogspot.com/2016/03/review-of-door-into-ocean-by-joan.html.

Jordan, June. 2016. "The Creative Spirit: Children's Literature." In *Revolutionary Mothering: Love on the Front Lines*, edited by Alexis Pauline Gumbs, China Martens, and Mai'a Williams, 11–18. Oakland, CA: PM Press.

Lathrop, Anna. 2006. "Herland Revisited: Narratives of Motherhood, Domesticity and Physical Emancipation in Charlotte Perkins Gilman's Feminist Utopia." *Vitae Scholasticae* 23 (Annual): 4–17.

Le Guin, Ursula. (1980) 1997. "Some Thoughts on Narrative." In *Dancing at the Edge of the World: Thoughts on Words, Women, Places*. New York: Grove Press.

Martins, Susana S. 2005. "Revising the Future in 'The Female Man.'" *Science Fiction Studies* 32, no. 3 (November): 405–422.

Owens, Claire. (1935) 1993. *The Unpredictable Adventure: A Comedy of Woman's Independence*. Syracuse, NY: Syracuse University Press.

Piercy, Marge. 1976. *Woman on the Edge of Time*. New York: Alfred A. Knopf.

Rosenthal, Miriam. n.d. "Woman on the Edge of Time: Observations." Department of Political Science Futures Studies, University of Hawai'i.http://www.futures.hawaii.edu/publications/half-fried-ideas/J2/rosenthal.pdf.

Russ, Joanna. 1975. *The Female Man*. New York: Bantam Books.

Slonczewski, Joan. 1986. *A Door into Ocean*. New York: Arbor House.

———. 2001. "A Door into Ocean: Study Guide." Joan L. Slonczewski, Kenyon College. http://biology.kenyon.edu/slonc/books/adoor_art/adoor_study.htm.

Starhawk. 1993. *The Fifth Sacred Thing*. New York: Bantam Books.

VH. 1995. "Feminist Utopias." *Science Fiction Studies* 65, no. 22 (March). https://www.depauw.edu/sfs/birs/bir65.htm.

Afterword

As this book goes to press, much of the world is experiencing some version of "stay-at-home" orders, due to a novel coronavirus, or enduring other limitations on their activity. We will be wrestling with the toll taken by the pandemic for years to come.

One thing we learned early in this crisis is that COVID-19 is exacting the most from the people already suffering in various systems of inequality: people of color, refugees, the imprisoned, the poor, those employed in low-wage labor, and so forth. The disease brings to the fore preexisting *social* conditions that make people more vulnerable—such as dangerous working environments and inadequate health care systems—as much as preexisting *medical* conditions that elevate risk.

Children have also struggled due to the pandemic. Schools closed around the globe, and online education, which replaced classrooms, was impossible for the millions of kids who do not have internet access at home. Inevitably, some will never return to school. Even having enough to eat has been challenging for the more than three hundred million children who usually depend on school meals for their nutrition,[1] especially since, at the same time, household income has been reduced for so many. Too, with everyone "staying in place," children are left with fewer safeguards against family violence. And, like adults, they have lost social networks that sustain them.

The news has spent much more time detailing how youth are less *physically* vulnerable to the virus than it has covering the ways in which they are distinctly vulnerable to it *socially*. How do we miss that? It's further evidence that children's lives—their complex emotional, intellectual, social, political lives—are often not even on our radar.

I started writing this book with the assumption of positive intent, believing that we, as individuals and communities, care about children. And—even given the criticisms and observations of harm contained within this tome—I still mostly believe that. But I worry that defensiveness may color or cloud the response to this book. For many of us, our instinctive response to criticism (whether it be perceived or real, legitimate or unjustified) is to be defensive, especially when it comes to how we treat children. It hurts to think that we may have hurt children or that others may see us in that light. But the problem doesn't lie solely with individuals, as I said at the outset, and—if we can listen past our defensiveness—we can hear voices that could lead us to act more truly with children and in their interest, enriching adult lives too.

The problem is systemic, and the solution needs to be too. "Caring" is not enough. Care must be combined with—and is not a replacement for—sound information about children that guides childrearing and education, social services that meet their needs, institutions and processes that hear their voices, and social practices that treat them justly. It won't be easy. Everything—from our conversational norms to our family dynamics to our school structures to our public policies—directs us to think about and act toward children in unproductive (and, too often, harmful) ways.

The pandemic has led to much soul searching about what life after quarantine and "social distancing" should look like. In a feature article on inequality and COVID-19, the *New York Times* asserts that "one of the most important steps the United States can take to ensure all children have the opportunity to thrive is to bulldoze enduring patterns of racial and economic segregation."[2] All the feminists I have studied would agree with that, adding sexism and militarism to the list of systems that harm the young.

The feminist thinkers, writers, and activists discussed in this book name and make visible the harms that young people experience, including abuses of power in adult-child relations, force-feeding in education, and the silencing of children's perspectives in everyday life. Positive feminist values—from voice, individuality, and respect to democracy, community, and equality—can help us envision where we should be headed. We *can* do better, by and with children, and not only with regard to the coronavirus.

In this book, I have argued that we need to better understand the situations of various young people: the prejudices that legitimize the silencing of children's voices and the devaluing of their experiences and ideas; their relative invisibility in political discourse and policy debates; and the ways in which age-based discrimination intersects with systems of oppression based on ability, race, sexuality, and class. I have argued that one commitment we need to make to reach this understanding is to exhibit more epistemic humility in our interactions with children—to become more receptive listeners and more eager interlocutors in everyday conversation and in social decision making. I have argued that we need to be consistent in our demands that institutions and processes be, for example, participatory and just, even when the people involved in those institutions and processes are young. Whether with respect to mounting threats posed by climate change, income inequality, and political conflict, or with regard to opportunities presented by changing forms of the family and more fluid senses of identity, we need to be accountable to young people.

Feminists are committed to dismantling systems of domination, one of which is age-based oppression. Luckily, contemporary advocates don't have to start from scratch. Feminist thinkers across centuries and continents have left an invaluable, underappreciated legacy.

The voices of youth will continue to be essential to this work; their voices, feminists have long argued, can help adults see the wrongs from which young people suffer, express resistance to injustice, and positively brim with good ideas. Their contributions and perspectives are necessary to the co-creation of truly liberatory knowledge, institutions, and practices. My hope is that these feminists' reflections on childhood will help inform, influence, and inspire us to give young people the voice and respect they have so long deserved and been denied.

NOTES

1. See https://www.theguardian.com/world/2020/mar/21/coronavirus-300-million -children-to-miss-school-meals-amid-shutdowns.

2. See https://www.nytimes.com/2020/04/09/opinion/sunday/coronavirus -inequality-america.html.

Index

Penny A. Weiss is a Professor of Women's and Gender Studies at Saint Louis University. She is the editor of *Feminist Manifestos: A Global Documentary Reader* and coeditor of *Feminism and Community* (Temple), as well as the author of *Canon Fodder: Historical Women Political Thinkers* and *Conversations with Feminism: Political Theory and Practice*, among other books.

www.ingramcontent.com/pod-product-compliance
Lightning Source LLC
Chambersburg PA
CBHW020338270326
41926CB00007B/223